The Contemporary Law Enforcement Anthology

Challenges and Opportunities for Today's Officers

First Edition

Edited by Robert Michael Magee
University of Texas – Rio Grande Valley

cognella
SAN DIEGO

Bassim Hamadeh, CEO and Publisher
John Remington, Executive Editor
Gem Rabanera, Senior Project Editor
Abbey Hastings, Production Editor
Jess Estrella, Senior Graphic Designer
Kylie Bartolome, Licensing Associate
Natalie Piccotti, Director of Marketing
Kassie Graves, Senior Vice President of Editorial
Jamie Giganti, Director of Academic Publishing

3970 Sorrento Valley Blvd., Ste. 500, San Diego, CA 92121

Contents

Chapter 1

Progression of Diversity in the Law Enforcement Workforce

FIGURE 1.1   US Customs and Border Protection student trainees.

INTRODUCTION

This book begins with discussing the progression of diversity in the ranks of policing. A police force that reflects the population it serves is more likely to gain authoritative legitimacy with that community. This process necessarily begins with recruiting, selection, screening, training, and enculturation of new police officers. The law enforcement community is a distinguishable subculture within our nation. In order to have a viable, legitimate policing organization, it must truly live out our national motto, "E pluribus unum," which means, "Out of many, one." Diversity in law enforcement requires that men and women with various backgrounds, ethnicities, colors, and subcultures bring the richness of their heritage with them as they each become part of a unified policing subculture. Diversity in law enforcement has been a historical issue in law enforcement, and it will likely always be an issue in law enforcement.

The following readings address the professional workforce in the field of law enforcement, because it is the people in that workforce that implement the policies, practices, and laws in our communities. In the readings, we will examine the importance of developing a recruiting system for new practitioners in the field of criminal justice—one that attracts those that are both technically qualified and have a desire for this type of public service career. Although the United States has had a very diverse population, the law enforcement workforce was dominated by White men with a Western European ethnic heritage for over a century. That began to change with the passage of the Civil Rights Act of 1964, but substantive changes did not occur until years later. For example, Christina Davis became the first female US Border Patrol Agent in 1975, and Lee Roy Young became the first African American Texas Ranger in 1988. Today, we find a diverse group of senior law enforcement leaders around the country, and most agencies do have a diverse workforce. As the demographics of the country continue to change, the recruiting and development of a diverse workforce in law enforcement will continue to be an issue.

Figure Credit

Fig. 1.1: Source: https://www.cbp.gov/careers/students-and-recent-graduates/we-are-hiring.

Reading 1.1

Hispanics Stand Tall

Mitchel P. Roth and Tom Kennedy

I N THE YEAR 1950, THE HOUSTON Police Department leadership perceived a problem with the Hispanic community. A Hispanic suspect killed an Anglo, prompting police to believe they needed a "Latin American Squad" to deal with cases involving similar circumstances. A called meeting at the Civil Courts Building attracted 200 people, including a number of prospective police cadets. The League of United Latin American Citizens wanted Hispanic officers selected "according to the same standards as real policemen."

The police representative present asked that each Hispanic male interested in joining the force to please stand up. Then he outlined basic requirements of a prospective cadet one at a time: You must be between the ages of 21 and 35, have a high school diploma and no criminal record. Some portion of the prospects sat down when they failed to meet these qualifications.[1]

"And you must stand 5-feet-10 1/2 inches tall," the recruiter said. Most of the remaining young men sat down. HPD immediately fell short of the number needed for a Latin American Squad. Only five remained and just one, Raul Martinez, a share cropper's son, really wanted the job. He was twenty-seven years old and saw nothing but problems with his job as an orderly that paid fifty cents an hour. Martinez soon got a call from highly respected Mexican restaurant owner, Felix Tijerina, who said to him, "We need you. Why don't you go down there and apply?"[2]

Thirty-nine years later, Martinez said he felt he could make a difference and went down to City Hall, officially applied and found it hard to believe his acceptance until he saw it in writing. Meanwhile, he trained to become a barber and earned seventy-five cents a cut every Saturday at the Gallegos Barber Shop on Preston. The barbering and his orderly job put Martinez in a high income bracket. The police job actually meant a pay cut and required him to work six days a week for a $60 salary.

The entire community encouraged him to become an officer since Houston had no uniformed Hispanic police officer at the time. Martinez faced tough recruiting questions from Ray Floyd, the Civil Service director at City Hall. Floyd cited Martinez' heavy accent and asked him how he would handle insulting comments from Anglos he might have to arrest. Martinez responded by saying he would be trained and paid to be called names he was called already.[3]

Martinez passed the written examination and the physical before undergoing more interrogation. The questioners gave him spirit when they never brought up the fact he was Hispanic. He entered the academy in March 1950, becoming the first academy-trained Hispanic police officer in HPD history. He went on to earn a college degree from the University of Houston under the GI Bill and served twenty-three years on the force before Harris County Judge Bill Elliott appointed him constable of Precinct 6. He served five terms there. He died on August 23, 1990. On September 17, 2003, Precinct 2 County Commissioner Sylvia Garcia led a dedication ceremony of the Raul C. Martinez East End Courthouse Annex.

***

Victor Trevino grew up on Houston's eastside in the 1950s, becoming adept with a broom-stick from the time the broom stood taller than he was. Over the years as one of nine children parented by a Mexico-born day-laborer for Southern Pacific Railroad and his stay-at-home wife, Trevino worked in several mom-and-pop grocery stores, graduating from sweeper to stock boy, then sacker, and on to stocker, meat cutter and cashier.

As he became a teenager, Trevino loved helping people, a satisfaction that inspired a desire to become a police officer after he graduated from Austin High School. By 1970 the depart-ment lowered the police academy eligibility age to nineteen. Trevino was nineteen, biting at the bit to join up, but he faced a requirement he couldn't measure up to.[4]

The HPD height requirement was five-foot-ten; Trevino stood five-foot-seven. The height requirement ruled out all but the tallest Hispanics. So Trevino became a butcher at an east side Weingarten's during the Herman Short era in HPD when only Anglo officers patrolled Hispanic neighborhoods. There was only one Hispanic cop for the area and investigations were tough since Hispanics wouldn't talk to police.

Trevino thought that intelligence and policing ability had nothing to do with height. He wanted to enter HPD as early as 1975 but soon learned he faced yet another obstacle—he was not legally an American citizen. He had entered the country legally at age seven, and he assumed he was a citizen. But he wasn't. He took courses at San Jacinto College, enabling him to earn citizenship in January 1976, just as HPD lowered its height requirement to five-foot-seven.

Over the years business leaders such as Houston restaurant entrepreneur Felix Tijerina instructed Hispanic applicants to apply first thing in the morning when they were taller. Next time, Trevino applied in the morning and qualified for HPD Cadet Class No. 74 in 1976 at age twenty-four. He was one of seven Hispanics to qualify, a new record at that point in history. One class member, Jesse Garza, became a sergeant, while another, Joe Zamarron, died in the line of duty on April 18, 1981, when he was struck by a car while directing traffic on Market Street.

The height policy changed again. In March 1977, with Harry Caldwell at the helm, a management consulting company conducted a study that changed the department's hiring practices. The firm was Lifson, Wilson, Ferguson and Winick Inc. LWFW surveyed all officers and their job descriptions and developed criteria to measure effectiveness. Among its findings was that since August 14, 1968, HPD had used a height and weight chart developed by the U.S. Air Force. In hindsight, many in the department believed the chart requirements had a disparate impact on females, blacks and Hispanics. Coincidentally, LWFW had earlier validated the agility test that critics felt effectively eliminated many female applicants. HPD changed the height policy in 1977 to be height in proportionate to weight—a major turning point in the recruitment of women and Hispanics.

Trevino succeeded another former Houston police officer, Raul Martinez, as constable in the predominately Hispanic Precinct 6 on the east side. He was a founding member of the Organization of Spanish Speaking Officers in 1981 and served as OSSO's second president. He looked back on the day in July 1976 that he was sworn in to wear a badge and gun with the Houston blue with good humor. He and the largest-ever graduating class waited for that memorable moment when Police Chief Pappy Bond pinned on their badges. Taking his turn, Victor Trevino stepped up and stood tall—all five-feet-seven-inches of him.

As Bond did the honors, Houston's newest police officer was looking down at a chief obviously shorter than he was.

***

The visibility of the improving numbers of Hispanics in HPD blue captured the attention of a teen-aged girl who thought she could become a police officer and make a difference. The department recruited more actively with minorities to develop a more positive image through outreach programs at weekend events and at high schools during the week. Martha Morena sensed there were still problematic issues—but none she couldn't handle.

Morena was born in Ecuador and came to Houston with her family at age five to live in the East End, just outside of downtown near the original Ninfa's Restaurant on Navigation. Hearing the recruiting pitch, Morena thought the pay and benefits HPD offered were extremely high for a young Hispanic female with a high school diploma from Incarnate Word Academy. Encouraged by the recruiting booths at East Side community events, she was impressed that the department actually viewed Hispanics as people different from the bad guys on the beats or in the lead story on the evening news. Hispanic recruiters were there, as were African-American and Anglo officers.[5]

Morena joined HPD in 1979, stepping into Police Cadet Class No. 90 and graduating in May 1980. In earlier years, HPD regularly assigned new female officers to either the Juvenile Division or the jail. Morena was assigned to Central Patrol, as were the other two African-Americans and two Anglos in her cadet class. Her first sergeant, Robert Hill, fit the old-school image—paternal, decisive and always eager to give advice applicable to both professional and private lives.[6]

Morena married and became Martha Montalvo. That was not the only change. She earned bachelors and masters degrees in Criminal Justice Management from the University of Houston—Downtown and Sam Houston State University, respectively. Montalvo found that the vast majority of officers accepted a Hispanic female officer as long as she was productive on the job and remained strong and determined to achieve her professional goals.

She felt a major turning point in public perception of the department happened when Mayor Kathy Whitmire appointed Lee P. Brown to become the first African-American police chief in 1982. Brown was eager to answer the hardest possible questions from all minority communities and to convince leaders he needed their support through both dialogue and positive actions. It wasn't easy coming from people who felt they were overly policed and targets of suspicious arrests and traffic tickets. Chief Brown required officers to dialog with community leaders and convince them that police were there to serve everyone.

Like many of her police contemporaries, Montalvo was seldom pleased with Whitmire's attitude toward police officers. She participated in demonstrations against the mayor by members of the Houston Police Patrolman's Union that were common early in Whitmire's ten-year tenure. At one heavily attended HPPU meeting with Whitmire, members sat silently as the mayor entered the room, the clicking heels of her shoes echoing in the large meeting room. Montalvo sat on the end of a row and felt sorry for the trembling woman. She saw that the mayor feared police, definitely a bad omen for the city.[7]

FIGURE 1.1.1   Martha Montalvo became the first Hispanic female to serve as executive assistant chief. In 2012, Montalvo headed Investigative Operations. (HPD Archives)

Montalvo worked in Central Patrol after spending time at the academy as an instructor. She didn't let a stubborn mayor deter her from stepping up the management ladder. After being shifted back to Central, she became a sergeant in 1985 and promptly got assigned to the jail, where she worked with Lieutenant Robert Montalvo, the man she married. Montalvo went on to serve as one of four executive assistant police chiefs under Police Chief Harold Hurtt, the highest ranking Hispanic female in history.

***

Wilfred Navarro got out of the service in February 1948 and went from one job to another until 1950 when LULAC began its big push to get the police department to hire Hispanics. Navarro took notice of the articles in local newspapers and attended the same meeting in which Raul Martinez learned he was tall enough to qualify. B. W. Payne was police chief and an inspector, L. D. Morrison Sr., was Payne's spokesman at the meeting. Morrison said the reason that the department wasn't hiring Mexican Americans was that the majority weren't as tall as Martinez.[8]

Navarro met the requirement and told Morrison he would apply. Yet when he went to the ninth floor of City Hall, Civil Service Director Roy Floyd said he was five-eighths of an inch too short. Floyd suggested that Navarro become a firefighter and wound up getting the applicant a job as a junior police clerk because he could type. Navarro worked as a clerk under three lieutenants, R. J. Clark, Foy D. Melton and Sid Rowe. One day Rowe gave him the same advice as Tijerina: apply early in the day when you're taller.

When Navarro showed up, the man there to do the measurement was George Hogan, a clerk who later became the business manager for police chiefs from Jack Heard to Lee P. Brown. Hogan found him to be a half inch *above* the requirement.

Originally, Navarro was scheduled to start Police Cadet Class No. 4 in March 1950, the same as Martinez, but he was rescheduled for Class No. 5 in September because of a problem with his work as a police clerk. Police Chief L. D. Morrison Sr., the recruiter, pinned on Navarro's badge on December 28, 1950, and the new officer started his first duty on New Year's Eve.

Other Hispanics in Class 5 were Jesse Ontiveros, Roy Beltran and Pete Fuentes (all deceased). The four Hispanic cadets made a conscious decision not to hang around with each other in their effort to get to know all of their classmates and not seem standoffish. They all went to Patrol with the feeling they were disliked because of their race but believing only a small percentage of officers were actually prejudiced against them. They were encouraged that some higher-ranking officers such as A. C. Martindale, a leader in the Houston Police Officers Association, discouraged discrimination at every opportunity and accepted them as equals.

FIGURE 1.1.1 Ephirne Leija became the first Hispanic captain in HPD history in 1980, a time when Chief Harry Caldwell was working diligently to improve HPD's relationship with Houston Hispanics in the wake of the death-in-custody of Jose Campos Torres. (HPD Archives)

Navarro went on to work Dispatch, Evening Patrol and Day Patrol at the North Shepherd Substation until one day when Lieutenant Chester Massey called him to become his administrative officer to work the desk for Downtown Patrol. He worked there until 1970, when he went to Community Services to supervise school crossing guards and give safety talks at schools.[9]

When the incumbent chief of police at Houston's airports resigned, thirty-year veteran Navarro's name appeared at the top of Mayor Jim McConn's list of possible successors in 1979. Encouraged by Councilman Ben Reyes, Houston's first Hispanic City Council member, Navarro actively pursued the job. On January 3, 1980, he retired from HPD to become chief of the Airport Police three days later. He was responsible for both Hobby and Intercontinental Airports, commanding 259 people.

Navarro worked under mayors McConn, Kathy Whitmire, Bob Lanier and Lee Brown. When the airport police merged with HPD in November 1992, he became an assistant chief, a civilian position made official by ordinance under Mayor Lanier. He improved working conditions and morale and raised the training standards at the airports, believing that his officers had undergone more training than HPD officers at the time of the merger. By the time he retired in 1999, Wilfred Navarro had spent just a few months short of fifty years in law enforcement.

***

Officially, Mercedes Halvorsen Singleton was the first-ever academy-trained female Hispanic Houston police officer, and Emily Rimmer Vasquez was the second. They actually graduated from the same academy class. Since cadets got their badges in alphabetical order, Vasquez ranked second in history's count. Velia "Belle" Ortega, a Houston native and 1951 graduate of Sam Houston High School, was an HPD Records clerk in the early 1950s when Singleton, Vasquez, Jean Smith and Jo Bankston were the first policewomen to be academy-trained.

Everyone called Ortega "Belle," a nickname that meant "young beautiful woman," and often sought her to translate Spanish. Sergeants begin to suggest to her, "If you are going to translate for the reports, why don't you try out for the academy?" She wound up in Class 15 and was sworn in on New Year's Day 1957, the third Hispanic female officer in HPD history. As was typical, Ortega replaced a matron who retired and alternated between Juvenile and the jail before spending eleven years in Crime Analysis. She was in her thirties and let "the younger women go and be brave" when policewomen were allowed to patrol the streets.[10]

Ortega's first taste of resentment of Hispanics came when she was a cadet and a high-ranking Command Staff member was conducting a class discussion and asked the class, "Anyone here speak Mexican?" She and other Hispanics took remarks like this one in stride and tried to do the job.

Having so few female officers caused frustrating scheduling problems. If another division needed a woman for special duty, Ortega was "loaned out" from Juvenile or the jail. Shift scheduling was inflexible. A female officer's schedule stayed the same until someone quit, retired or died. Ortega worked the night shift eighteen years before she was able to work days.

After her retirement, Belle Ortega served eleven years as a police service officer (PSO), a de facto desk officer who took police reports from citizens, performing virtually every duty but riding the streets. Ortega died August 11, 2008 from gunshot wounds she suffered in a July 21 drive-by shooting at her daughter's apartment. Her death was ruled a homicide. She was seventy-eight years old.

***

When the admittedly bright-eyed and bushy-tailed Art Contreras, age twenty-two, drove in from Baytown and walked into the Houston police recruiting office in the basement of City Hall, two Anglo recruiters stood between him and the police academy. The height requirement in 1961 was five-foot-nine. The first recruiter, an older man, tersely informed Contreras that he was too short and walked out of the room. Contreras stood in the middle of the room, too angry to move.[11]

The second Anglo recruiter—an Officer Hill—came in, measured Contreras and all of a sudden the recruit had grown an inch. Contreras always credited Hill with giving him a life-changing break that resulted in a career that lasted more than four decades. In November 1961, the son of a Humble Oil and Refining Company (later Exxon) safety inspector and LULAC activist entered the Houston Police Academy at Police Headquarters at 61 Riesner by commuting from Baytown.[12]

A tough-minded sergeant, Julius Knigge, required meticulous notes and gave hard tests. Each cadet turned in his notebook every day for grading. Knigge put strong stock in a cadet's ability to pick up details in even the most basic investigation. Knigge once asked cadets how many steps were there in front of this training building. Contreras always remembered that there were thirteen.

Contreras' father was a "color blind" Baytown reserve officer who urged his son to change the policing system "from within," an outlook that inspired the new officer to conclude that only certain *individuals* had racist problems. When Contreras started in 1961, there were less than 100 Hispanic officers. Overall, in his Class No. 25, there were six—Contreras, George Rodriguez, Humberto Moreno, Abel Casas, Robert Luna and Johnny Gonzalez.

Contreras' first job in 1962 was riding a three-wheeler, working downtown to make sure traffic didn't get backed up. He made sergeant in 1968, the third Hispanic sergeant behind Raul Martinez and Richard Castillo and the first one assigned as a supervisor in Patrol. All previous Hispanic sergeants were assigned to Dispatch or the jail. Weldon Waycott, his supervisor, emphasized the fact that he ran Patrol and made Contreras the Northside sergeant on the night shift. Contreras had a few attitudinal problems with subordinates but gradually worked through them.

He became a lieutenant in 1973, serving in Juvenile and Recruiting. In the latter division he worked hard at enhancing the message to Hispanics and African-American would-be cadets that there was upward mobility available to them. He was promoted to captain in 1982 and spent time in Night Command at Northeast and took the lead in the elimination of some sexually-oriented questions on the pre-employment polygraph test. The new set of questions and guidelines required that all inquiries be job-specific and not designed to satisfy voyeuristic tendencies, including questions involving homosexuality or sodomy.[13]

Contreras drafted a bilingual pay bill during the 1987 session of the Texas Legislature, trying to use better pay as a recruiting tool to encourage bilingual men and women. The bill's passage meant officers who could speak Spanish, Vietnamese, Mandarin, Cantonese and Korean began receiving bilingual pay. Another bill provided the city with the ability to offer shift differential pay.

Contreras became HPD's first Hispanic deputy police chief in 1990 and served in that capacity until his retirement after thirty-six years in HPD. He spent only two days "unemployed" when President Bill Clinton named him U.S. Marshal for the Southern District of Texas on March 10, 1998—the first Hispanic in history to serve in this capacity. He was there four and a half years. In his HPD career, Contreras was considered as a candidate for Houston's police chief by two mayors, Bob Lanier in 1996 and Bill White in 2003.

***

Phyllis Serna Wunsche recounted her HPD career as a true calling or blessing. Her recollections flow as if out of a storybook with a happy ending despite the inevitable conflicts along the path. Wunsche's most significant "first" was *pregnant* with controversy and changed a bad tradition and policy for a department which took aim to recruit more women in the changing times of the 1970s.[14]

Wunsche was "the first Hispanic female math degree holder" to become a Houston police officer. A March 1972 graduate of the academy, her rise was meteoric—she became a robbery detective in three years and later stair-stepped up to become the first Hispanic female assistant chief. She also was the female half of the first married couple on the Command Staff. Her husband, Les Wunsche, was the first head of the Internal Affairs Division. He retired in 1986.

The University of Houston graduate began her career in November 1971, when she was looking for a government job that would take advantage of her way with numbers. HPD had four openings for women in its next cadet class, only hiring women to replace those retiring or resigning. She never had any inclination to be a police officer but ultimately "never went through any burned-out period in twenty-three years." Always motivated by changes in assignments and promotion, her longest assignment was five and a half years as a robbery detective.[15]

Wunsche scarcely passed her six-month probation when she violated an unwritten HPD rule—she got pregnant. She already had a three-year-old child at a time when motherhood was discouraged for policewomen. There were no health benefits that enabled her to take a paid leave of absence to give birth. If a policewoman wanted to have a baby, she had to take a non-paid leave of absence. Police Chief Carrol Lynn rejected Wunsche's request to use sick leave time.

It was a *city* policy that affected any pregnant employee, whether in the police department or any other city department. The young officer learned from research that some other cities granted sick leave for pregnancies. She thought it was worth fighting the city of Houston for such an entitlement and sought help from Wilfred Navarro of the Houston Police Officers Association Board of Directors.

Wunsche went down the line with the association officers and none gave her any hope. Navarro, chairman of the Insurance Committee, presented the issue to the full board and said pregnancy should be recognized as a health issue. He took Wunsche to an HPOA meeting when she was "very pregnant" and had her stand up as he made the case.

The board then got Mayor Fred Hofheinz and City Council to grant sick leave for pregnant city employees as part of the city's health insurance plan. The measured passed a few weeks before Wunsche's delivery. She was later transferred to the midnight shift at the jail for rocking the boat.

Policewomen found it hard to raise any stink about another issue that touched them almost every day of their job assignment, their blue uniforms. In the Hofheinz/Lynn years the department saw a major influx of women. But there were no uniforms designed to fit them. Women had to wear men's pants and jackets usually three or four sizes too large. Many women were reduced to tears by the way they looked in a department that could fit 300-pound men but not 110-pound women. Many women altered their own blue, and in the 1990s Wunsche ordered a Navy cap, which became part of the female assistant chief's uniform.

Wunsche became the first female detective in Texas assigned to investigate armed robberies. In 1980, she was promoted to lieutenant with another aspiring policewoman, Elizabeth "Betsy" Watson. Every week Wunsche worked as a lieutenant on all three shifts—days, evenings and nights—in what was a special "swing shift." She didn't complain.

She was a lieutenant when Watson succeeded Lee Brown as chief in 1990. Watson eliminated the deputy chief position and increased the number of assistant chiefs reporting directly to her to eleven. Newly appointed assistant chiefs hereinafter were subject to City Council confirmation. Later, under Police Chief Sam Nuchia, the Command Staff consisted of five executive assistant chiefs and eight assistant chiefs.

Watson could fill vacancies by appointment and chose Wunsche as the first female assistant chief. The appointment finally came but not without controversy, complicated by Watson's lack of political experience with City Council. Watson first sought Wunsche's appointment along with two white males in 1990 but endured political heat before a more diverse list of five appointees got through the mayor and council on July 2, 1991. Wunsche was not the Hispanic community's choice and stayed in limbo while Watson held her ground.[16]

As Watson's budget administrator, Wunsche finally got to use her talent with numbers. Bob Lanier took office as mayor in 1992 and demoted Watson in favor of Nuchia. But Wunsche remained in her "numbers job" and mastered the details of the move of police headquarters to 1200 Travis in downtown. The department didn't want to lose her knowledge and talent until the project was almost completed. She was the only chief of any rank that Mayor Lanier and Chief Nuchia asked to stay. She went on to serve on the Presidential Commission on Organized Crime as the group's only Hispanic female police officer.

***

Adrian Garcia's desire to become a police officer started to unfurl when he was hanging out at his dad's gas station on the Northside at age ten. Garcia was in awe of the take-charge men in police uniforms that performed their daily duties while riding Harleys. These "solos" hung out at a Texaco across the street from his dad's station. One day he saw them pull over a man who was driving through the neighborhood. Since this driver only spoke Spanish, the solo officers had trouble communicating with him.

One of them approached Garcia and respectfully asked, "Can you translate?" The little boy was happy to do so and his work resulted in a better understanding between the officers and a citizen who had a malfunctioning tail light. The officers cautioned him and let him go. One of them said to Garcia, "You'll make a good police officer."[17]

In 1980, when the outreach toward Hispanics was greater than ever and the height requirement all but gone, Garcia got into the Houston Police Academy Class No. 93 at age nineteen. Many of Garcia's contemporaries called him a sell-out, while memories of Joe Campos Torres and the Moody Park Riot lingered in the community.

Like Martha Montalvo, Garcia credited Whitmire's choice of Lee Brown as the first-ever black police chief as a major turning point in the attitude of Hispanics. Minority recruiting went through the roof as the department instituted academic standards. Brown also included the Hispanic community more and more in his interworking and strategies. Garcia believed the initial changes came through Harry Caldwell and were truly embraced by Chief Brown.[18]

Garcia became the first-ever Houston police officer elected to the Houston City Council in 2003. In his HPD career he worked in Patrol in downtown and the Northside, in HPD's Criminal Intelligence Division's Organized Crime Squad, and served as a special investigator for the District Attorney's Office in the Special Crimes Division. He also served in HPD's Community Services Division before his appointment to be HPD's liaison to the Mayor's Anti-Gang Office in 1994, becoming director in 1999.

Before retiring after twenty-four years as a Houston police officer, Garcia saw Hispanics come to form a much larger percentage of the force. The number of high-ranking Hispanics in HPD became too long to list completely. In 2008, Adrian Garcia, a Democrat, became the first Hispanic elected Harris County sheriff.

Creation of OSSO

Hispanic officers in the Houston Police Department set up the Organization of Spanish Speaking Officers in 1981. Victor Trevino believed the term "Mexican" was deliberately not in the title of the new group because there were other Hispanics who were not Mexican. The primary goal of OSSO was to assist minorities in special issues that they face in their day-to-day work life. Jesse Garza was the first president, Trevino the second.

OSSO celebrated its twenty-fifth anniversary in 2008. Its stated objective "is strength through united effort, guided by intelligence. Such unity is essential for the mutual protection and advancement of interests and general welfare of law enforcement officers. We believe this is the hallmark of any organization." The organization represents officers in work-related issues "for safety, equality, dignity and respect."

Richard Rodriguez, OSSO president in 2008, said in a message to membership, "In the beginning Hispanic officers issues were seen as Hispanic only. But time has changed and so has our membership. Our diversity has given this organization a new outlook and strength." Members do not have to speak Spanish to join. In its silver anniversary year, OSSO had 320 active members and eighty retirees.[19]

Notes

1. Raul Martinez, recorded interview; Thomas H. Kreneck, *Mexican-American Odyssey, Felix Tijerina, Entrepreneur and Civic leader, 1905–1965* (College Station: Texas A&M University Press, 2001) Wilfred Navarro interview.
2. Kreneck, *Mexican American Legacy.*
3. Martinez interview.
4. Victor Trevino interview.
5. Martha Moreno Montalvo interview.
6. Ibid.
7. Ibid.
8. Wilfred Navarro interview.
9. Ibid.
10. Velia Ortega interview.
11. Art Contreras interview.
12. Ibid.
13. Ibid.
14. Phyllis Serna Wunsche interview.
15. Ibid.
16. Watson, Wunsche, and Lanier interviews.
17. Adrian Garcia interview.
18. Ibid.
19. Richard Rodriguez interview.

Sources

Interviews:

Art Contreras, Oct. 18, 2004

Adrian Garcia, Dec. 15, 2004

Bob Lanier, former Houston Mayor, Mar. 7, 2005

Wilfred Navarro, June 17, 2004

Belle Ortega, Aug. 25, 2006

Victor Trevino, July 9, 2005

Betsy Watson, former Houston Police Chief, Nov. 12, 2004

Phyllis Wunsche, June 29, 2004

Reference

Kreneck, Thomas H. *Mexican American Odyssey: Felix Tijerina, Entrepreneur and Civic leader, 1905–1965.* College Station: Texas A&M University Press, 2001.

Reading 1.2

Selection from "Introduction" from *Recruiting and Retaining America's Finest: Evidence-Based Lessons for Police Workforce Planning*

Jeremy M. Wilson, Bernard D. Rostker, and Cha-Chi Fan

A CRITICAL BUT OFT NEGLECTED FUNCTION OF police organizations is management of the sworn officer force. While there is much attention to recruiting and retention, these are just tools for moving and maintaining career profiles that meet the needs and aspirations of officers and provide the rank/experience profiles desired by police departments. Police decisionmakers have little ability to assess their organization and environment to develop their own evidence-based personnel planning lessons. Likewise, they receive little empirical guidance on how best to build and maintain their workforce.

Recent economic difficulties have catapulted the issue of police staffing into the forefront of national discussion. The COPS Hiring Program, with $1 billion in congressional funding to help stabilize law enforcement positions, received requests totaling $8.3 billion to support more than 39,000 sworn officer positions (COPS Office, 2009). Those familiar with police staffing contend that larger systemic trends continue to make it challenging to staff police organizations with qualified, diverse, and effective personnel.

Some may contend that recent recessionary times, and resulting high unemployment, have solved the staffing problem by overrunning agencies with applications. But the problem is not so simple. First, the systemic issues and trends, including those in qualifications, generational preferences, and attrition, affecting police recruitment and retention transcend economic conditions—and are likely to be exacerbated when economic conditions improve. Second, agencies overwhelmed by applications must still determine which and how many applicants to recruit—that is, they must still determine which are the best qualified and most committed to law enforcement as a career. Third, some agencies report continuing decreases in applications and particular difficulty in recruiting and maintaining a workforce that reflects their community. Fourth, agencies must still determine the career profile that best meets their needs, using recruitment and retention as the tools to ensure a proper staffing distribution. Fifth, police decisionmakers typically have little time, resources, and expertise for developing their own data-driven lessons on personnel planning, and researchers have provided them few lessons on what works. Information on promising practices tends to be anecdotal, entirely qualitative, limited in scope, or centered on the experience of a single person or agency (Switzer, 2006; Scrivner, 2006), thereby limiting the extent to which any particular agency can draw meaningful lessons for itself. All of this means that recruitment, retention, and career management will remain important challenges to police decisionmakers and communities.

The Dynamic Staffing Challenge

Police agencies face many challenges in filling their workforce needs. First, they must determine the experience and rank structure of their personnel that will most cost-effectively meet their needs. Second, they must select and use recruiting and retention tools that will foster their goals, taking into account such problems as the retirement of older cohorts, changing work preferences of younger generations, and decreasing funds for a steady or even expanding scope of work.

Wilson et al. (forthcoming) uses the metaphor of a bucket to illustrate some of the problems in managing departments with an ever-changing workforce environment. In this metaphor, the size of the bucket represents the absolute demand for police officers regardless of internal personnel structure and allocation. Water inside the bucket reflects the current level of police strength able to fulfill the demand. The size of the demand "bucket" or the amount of staffing "water" to fill are being affected in three ways: The hole draining the bucket of current staffing is widening, the faucet replenishing staff is tightening, and the width of the bucket representing the scope of police work is widening.

Even in the best circumstances, police agencies often find that they cannot fill the bucket. The current level of staffing is nearly always below the allocated level of staffing. Even the allocated level may not be enough to fulfill unmet demand (Figure 1.2.1).

The current level of staffing is being drained by a widening hole with several causes (Figure 1.2.2). These include

- *"Baby-boom" generation retirements.* In Chicago, for example, an early retirement option is expected to increase from about 500 to nearly 900 the deficit of officers below the authorized level of 13,500—a problem exacerbated by the department's wait for federal funding for new academy classes (Spielman, 2009).

- *Changing career preferences of younger generations.* Lower salaries than are available in the private sector, competition from the military, negative public perceptions of law enforcement, lower levels of organizational commitment, and a lack of interest by younger Americans in policing may all be dampening interest in police work among those entering the work force (Jordan et al., 2009; Pomfret, 2006; Egan, 2005; Tulgan, 2000; Wheeler, 2008; Twenge and Campbell, 2008).

- *Military call-ups.* Many police officers serve in the military reserves. Increasing use of reserve forces in military operations overseas has depleted police forces at home. In the year ending June 30, 2003, 21 percent of local police departments had full-time personnel called to serve (Hickman and Reaves, 2006).

- *Budget constraints.* Two extreme cases of the effects decreasing financial support can have on police retention are evident in New Orleans and San Diego. New Orleans suffered particularly high losses from officers relocating to better-paying jurisdictions after Hurricane Katrina (Rostker, Hix, and Wilson, 2007; Wilson, Rostker, and Hix, 2008). In San Diego, uncompetitive wages and salary freezes led many officers to seek better opportunities elsewhere, including a detective with more than 20 years of experience who applied for a patrol position in a neighboring community (Manolatos, 2006).

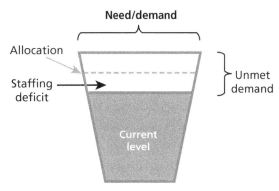

FIGURE 1.2.1   The Bucket Metaphor and the Demand for Police Officers

RAND *MG960-1.2.1*

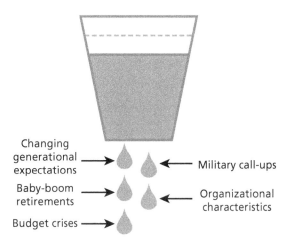

FIGURE 1.2.2   Attrition Is Widening the Hole

RAND *MG960-1.2.2*

- *Other organizational characteristics.* In addition to those noted above, officers may choose to leave a department for still other reasons, including the characteristics of their immediate supervisor, lack of career growth, unmet job expectations, inadequate feedback, insufficient recognition, or lack of training (Orrick, 2008a, 2008b; Wilson and Grammich, 2009).

There appear to be five main influences on why officers may leave an agency: (1) the pull of other opportunities, (2) actual and potential compensation, (3) personal characteristics and demographic variables, (4) organizational health, policy, and culture, and (5) employee needs (Lynch and Tuckey, 2004). Police turnover can be problematic for several reasons. Police employee success is a function of experience and ability to make sensible decisions with minimal oversight (Frost, 2006; Gottfredson and Gottfredson, 1988). Reducing the number of officers with experience inhibits effective decisionmaking and diminishes department strength and cohesion. This is similar to problems other fields experience in "brain drain" following voluntary separations that reduce performance levels and increase operational risks (Birati and Tziner, 1995; Mobley, 1982; Holtom et al., 2008). Nevertheless, the cost of training sworn police officers is substantial in comparison to other fields (New South Wales Council on the Cost of Government, 1996), although levels of turnover for police appear to be lower than that for other occupations (Cooper and Ingram 2004). The high level of organizational and job-specific knowledge that police officers require means that high turnover can impair organizational performance.

The faucet of supply that can replenish the bucket is also tightening for several reasons (Figure 1.2.3). The militaristic nature of police work may be less likely to appeal to younger generations for many of the same cultural reasons that have reduced youth propensity to join the military (Bowyer, 2007; U.S. Department of Defense, 2003; Wilson, 2000). Altogether, fewer than half of U.S. youths consider a police agency a "desirable" or "acceptable" place

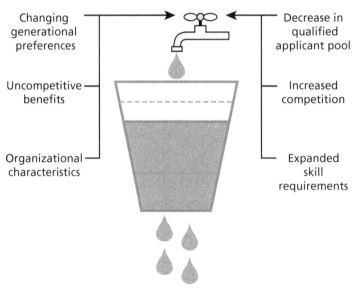

FIGURE 1.2.3   The Shrinking Supply Is Tightening the Faucet
RAND MG960-1.2.3

to work (National Research Council, 2003). Increasing proportions of younger generations are unable to meet the qualifications for police work, including a clean criminal record, little to no drug use, physical fitness, and financial stability (see Johnston et al., 2008, on drug use; Sturm et al., 2004, on fitness; and Draut and Silva, 2004, as well as Draut, 2008, on debt). Police applicants today must have a wider range of skills than those of earlier years; educated workers meeting present standards for law enforcement positions have more job prospects, making it difficult to recruit them to the field. Other agencies, including the military and the growing homeland security industry, increasingly compete for those that are qualified (Kane, 2005; Frawley, 2006; DeRugy, 2006; Kondrasuk, 2004; and Makinen, 2002). Many potential applicants perceive the financial benefits of police work to be increasingly uncompetitive with those of similar or other work (for more on officer salaries and those in the private sector, see Hickman and Reaves, 2006, and U.S. Bureau of Labor Statistics, 2009). Organizational characteristics, such as the image of a particular agency, especially for minority candidates, can discourage the flow of applicants (Wilson and Grammich, 2009; Wright, 2009).

While the hole draining current staff is widening and the faucet replenishing staff is tightening, the bucket of demand is also widening as local police agencies are asked to undertake new, more complex tasks (Figure 1.2.4). In the past two decades, most police agencies have adopted some form of community policing (Maguire and Mastrofski, 2000; Wilson, 2006; Zhao, Lovrich, and Thurman, 1999). This has changed the nature of much traditional police

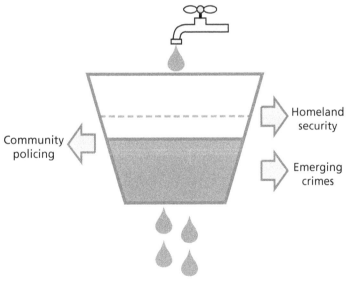

FIGURE 1.2.4 Expanding Duties Increase the Demand for Police Officers
RAND MG960-1.2.4

work, requiring police to collaborate with local citizens in maintaining order in their communities (Hickman and Reaves, 2006). Homeland security demands have required local police to perform additional patrol and surveillance, gather and analyze counterterrorism intelligence, increasingly enforce immigration laws, and participate in various task forces that coordinate such work among multiple agencies. Globalization and technological advancement are contributing to a greater awareness of still other crimes, such as human trafficking, identity theft, and cybercrime, requiring the attention of local police.

Finally, economic changes affect the ability of police agencies to fill the bucket in many, sometimes contradictory ways. Recently increasing unemployment has caused some departments to be inundated with applications from workers who come from a variety of industries. Yet this increasing applicant pool raises concerns, including those about the ability of agencies to screen higher numbers of applicants and the continuing interest of these applicants in police work once conditions in other industries improve. Furthermore, the same economic conditions that are leading to increased unemployment are also adversely affecting the ability of police agencies to hire young, talented officers—the very officers departments will need in the future for its leadership.

Even when economic conditions improve, long-term systemic changes will likely continue to pose staffing problems for local police agencies. In particular, past hiring booms and freezes will create difficulties as they ripple through the organization over time, from field training to retention, and as police agencies determine how best to replenish officers leaving the force over time and to replace the benefits of their experience.

The bucket example illustrates the problem that police departments face in recruiting and retaining officers to meet the expanding demands. This is but part of their personnel management challenge. Most departments have not been able to "shape" the age and experience profiles of their personnel. As a result, they find themselves struggling to address such issues as having too many recruits, not having enough patrol officers to provide field training, or waves of retirement for experienced career officers. Distribution of personnel by years of service also affects career opportunities, promotion rates, retention, and total personnel costs for departments.

References

COPS Office, *Community Policing Dispatch*, Washington, D.C.: U.S. Department of Justice, Office of Community-Oriented Policing Services, June 2009. As of July 7, 2009: http://www.cops.usdoj .gov/html/dispatch/June_2009/hiring_recovery.htm

Egan, Timothy, "Police Forces, Their Ranks Thin, Offer Bonuses, Bounties and More," *New York Times*, December 28, 2005. As of June 24, 2010: http://www.nytimes.com/2005/12/28/national/28police.html

Jordan, William T., Lorie Fridell, Donald Faggiani, and Bruce Kubu, "Attracting Females and Racial/Ethnic Minorities to Law Enforcement," *Journal of Criminal Justice*, Vol. 37, No. 4, July–August 2009, pp. 333–341.

Pomfret, John, "Police Finding It Hard to Fill Jobs," *Washington Post*, March 27, 2006. As of June 24, 2010: http://www.washingtonpost.com/wp-dyn/content/article/2006/03/26/AR2006032600995.html

Scrivner, Ellen, *Innovations in Police Recruitment and Hiring: Hiring in the Spirit of Service*, Washington, D.C.: Office of Community Oriented Policing Services, 2006. As of May 5, 2009: http://www.cops.usdoj.gov/RIC/ResourceDetail.aspx?RID=113

Spielman, Fran, "Early Retirement for Cops Helps Budget, Not Force," *Chicago Sun-Times*, July 23, 2009. As of October 12, 2009: http://www.suntimes.com/news/cityhall/1681991,chicago-cops-shortage-retirement-072309.article

Switzer, Merlin E., *Recruitment and Retention: Best Practices Update*, Sacramento, Calif.: Commission on Peace Officer Standards and Training, April 2006.

Tulgan, Bruce, *Managing Generation X: How to Bring Out the Best in Young Talent*, Oxford: Capstone, 2000.

Twenge, Jean M., and Stacy M. Campbell, "Generational Differences in Psychological Traits and Their Impact on the Workplace," *Journal of Managerial Psychology*, Vol. 23, No. 8, 2008, pp. 862–877.

Wheeler, Christopher H., "Local Market Scale and the Pattern of Job Changes Among Young Men," *Regional Science & Urban Economics*, Vol. 38, No. 2, March 2008, pp. 101–118.

Reading 1.3

Selections from "Recruitment: Filling the Bucket" from *Police Recruitment and Retention for the New Millennium: The State of Knowledge*

Jeremy M. Wilson, Erin Dalton, Charles Scheer, and Clifford A. Grammich

Police Recruitment Practices: Past and Present

In 1931, the National Committee on Law Observation and Enforcement (commonly known as the Wickersham Commission), appointed by President Herbert Hoover to study enforcement of Prohibition, detailed advances needed in the professionalization of policing, including the elimination of the spoils system for recruitment and hiring (Alpert, 1991; S. Walker, 1997). As police agencies moved toward merit-based hiring in the 1940s and 1950s, the dual problems of liability for law-enforcement behavior and increasing concerns over discrimination in police work fueled the use of more-scientific methods, such as psychometrics and standardized psychological testing in recruitment (Fyfe et al., 1997; Hogue, Black, and Sigler, 1994). These culminated in the formation of the Law Enforcement Assistance Administration (LEAA) in 1967, which sought to implement Equal Employment Opportunity Commission guidelines in the hiring of law-enforcement officers (Scrivner, 2006). The LEAA aligned selection methods with perceived job duties to create more-valid external analyses of demonstrated skills for police work. By the end of the 1960s, agencies nationwide used scientific and career-specific methods of testing, evaluating, and examining potential recruits on the basis of departmental perceptions of what one needed to know to be a good police officer.

This system was challenged in the mid-1970s, when Goldstein (1977) examined what police did on patrol. He found that most officer time in uniform was spent in human-service roles, such as helping citizens, negotiating disputes, or interacting with diverse community members in nonenforcement roles. The skills required for this work were incompatible with those for which recruits were screened, trained, and tested. This realization led to a reorientation of police work toward community policing. The Commission on Accreditation for Law Enforcement Agencies put forth recommendations for diversifying personnel to reflect the community (White and Escobar, 2008), although selection practices remained inconsistent with the new police role into the 1980s.

Evaluation processes might either "select out" candidates (that is, discern flaws in a candidate disqualifying him or her from a position) or "select in" candidates (that is, identify positive qualities that make an applicant an attractive candidate). Controversies over the two approaches and their merit have persisted since the advent of the community-policing era (Scrivner, 2006). It is unclear what skills agencies should identify in "selecting in" candidates, given rapid changes in community needs and demographics (Canadian Association of Chiefs of Police et al., 2000; Woska, 2006). The "selecting out" or hurdle process of recruitment remains attractive because many agencies cling to an outdated perception of the police role (Scrivner, 2006).

Nevertheless, rigidity is giving way to some experimentation and innovation. The Community Policing Consortium, through its Hiring in the Spirit of Service program, has sought to align hiring practices with individual agency needs regarding officer duties and skills. The results might help agencies attract a wider range of officers for open positions (Scrivner, 2006). The use of assessment centers and hurdle approaches might be incompatible with career needs and goals of new generations of recruits (DeCicco, 2000; Orrick, 2008a; Taylor et al., 2006). At best, the current climate of police recruitment consists of a lack of uniformity, little widespread use of data or research to guide recruitment efforts, and a fragmented approach to understanding the crisis and planning a response to it (Orrick, 2008a; Scrivner, 2006; White and Escobar, 2008).

How these fractured approaches have affected recruiting in recent years is unclear. Strawbridge and Strawbridge (1990) provided one of the first systematic efforts to describe the recruitment environment across jurisdictions, surveying 72 local police departments with 500 or more sworn officers about their recruiting, screening, and training practices. Among their findings was the need for a computerized database to facilitate communication about best practices given societal changes and resource limitations.

Langworthy, Hughes, and Sanders (1995) conducted a second survey of 60 of these agencies in 1994. They found decreasing use of television for recruiting, of maximum age requirements, of preemployment standards, and of state subsidies for training. They also found increased use of intelligence tests, psychological reviews, and duration of academy training and little change in probationary periods.

Taylor et al. (2006) conducted a national survey of nearly 1,000 agencies in 2002, including 32 of those in the earlier survey by Strawbridge and Strawbridge. They found little evidence to accept or reject hypotheses of a growing "cop crunch" but did find that some of these agencies had developed a severe shortage of officers, with more than 10 percent of their allocated slots vacant. They also found that many agencies had developed targeted recruiting strategies for minority, female, veteran, college-grad, and experienced candidates, but that they had difficulties in hiring sufficient numbers of female and minority candidates.

Determining Staffing Needs

Agencies must prepare themselves for hiring by first assessing their staffing needs (Switzer, 2006). There has been little analysis on the determination of staffing needs, despite the belief that empirical analyses of organizational needs would have widespread benefit. Police needs assessments have their roots in patrol allocation formulas of the pre–community policing era, when patrol manpower and risk formulas relied heavily on crime activity and calls for service as standard measurements of patrol saturation (Larson, 1978; Metropolitan Atlanta Crime Commission, 1977). As policing has grown more complex, staffing analyses have evolved as well. The Delaware State Personnel Office (2002) recommended the use of internal assessments prior to hiring and training law-enforcement employees. The National Institute of Corrections (Liebert and Miller, 2001) published a guidebook for corrections facilities that assisted facilities in conducting staffing analyses. Orrick (2008a) has also supported the use of needs analysis in determining hiring levels. In an applied example, the Pinal County (Ariz.) Sheriff's Office (PCSO) conducted an internal staffing analysis that examined such topics as patrol deployment, attrition rates, and scheduling policy to determine future hiring needs (PCSO, 2008). These and other strategies form a broad organizational needs assessment that can help shape the hiring process. The steps we discuss in this section, derived from organizational-assessment literature on strategic planning, might help focus and set the parameters for a strategic hiring plan. Many of these strategies can be performed internally, without external assistance.

Develop an Assessment Team. Staffing decisions and processes involve the input of community, government, and department stakeholders. Involving them in an assessment team invigorates hiring with input from those affected by hiring decisions. Departments might also wish to consider using outside agencies or private companies to assist with the needs assessment, which will come at a cost but can add expertise, objectivity, and independence. Orrick (2008a) suggests that assembling the assessment team could be as crucial in the hiring process as enacting the hiring plan itself. By choosing a team that represents all stakeholders in the hiring process, the department can assess its true needs and make more-comprehensive decisions about staffing.

Identify Budget and Source of Revenue. Analyzing available revenue is seen as a final step in conducting a needs assessment of hiring in corrections (Clem, Krauth, and Wenger, 2000) but might be better used as an initial step in police staffing assessments. Evaluating resources can help departments realistically determine their true capacities for personnel expansion (Clem, Krauth, and Wenger, 2000).

Specify Organizational Goals and Values. Hiring criteria differ by region and organizational setting (Kahanov and Andrews, 2001). There might also be variation within a single department, with upper management, training staff, and line-level officers all having different ideas. Defining candidate characteristics should be a deliberative process. It might involve the creation or reiteration of a value or mission statement communicating a department's core beliefs (Switzer, 2006). Crafting the "ideal" candidate should be tied closely to organizational goals and mission and help establish criteria the department will use to hire (Orrick, 2008a).

Use Benchmarks to Determine True Staffing Need. Despite the use of data-driven peer comparisons to determine police behavior in such areas as police growth and personnel expenditures, benchmarks determining staffing needs have not improved on informal peer comparisons (Nalla, Lynch, and Leiber, 1997). A few analyses have used hard data: The PCSO analysis used five other agencies of comparable size, patrol strength, and demography for a staffing comparison (PCSO, 2008). Similarly, a Canadian policing human-resource study used computer models to project attrition rates and models to predict police staffing requirements (Canadian Association of Chiefs of Police et al., 2000). Using benchmarks for staffing needs requires data collection and analysis, but these could be data readily available to most departments, including those on demographics, budgetary outlays, political structure, crime trends, calls for service, and community needs (Koper, Maguire, and Moore, 2001; Orrick, 2008a). The benchmarks could then be adjusted for qualitative differences, such as by emphasis on discretionary time for community policing and problem-solving projects. Additionally, a performance- or workload-based assessment can be conducted for an individual agency to estimate the number of officers required to meet workload demands (Shane, 2007; Fritsch, Liederbach, and Taylor, 2009). Such models can empirically account for discretionary and relief (e.g., authorized leave) time, as well as work schedules and minimum staffing requirements. It is common for agencies to consult with staffing experts to conduct these analyses, although various staffing software programs are available to assist those that prefer to conduct such analyses internally.

Integrate the Community in the Hiring Process. In addition to department stakeholders, including community input can better inform decisions on external issues (Switzer, 2006). Community members can help ensure that hiring reflects not only community needs but also community characteristics. Orrick (2008a) sees community input as crucial to determining standards for hiring. Scrivner (2006) recognizes the essential input of minority community members for establishing ethnic diversity in a department. The city of St. Paul, Minnesota, as part of a program to reduce racially biased policing, worked with the community to determine a list of characteristics (e.g., enthusiastic, fair, possessed of good judgment, tenacious, respectful, compassionate, unafraid to engage the community) that ideal candidates should possess (McDevitt, Farrell, and Wolf, 2008). Without a clearer picture of community character and an assessment of the needs of special populations in a department's jurisdiction, benchmark comparisons might omit community viewpoints not reflected in raw data. Community leaders, seeing that the department is inclusive of community input and needs, might "recruit" for the department by speaking positively of careers with it (Haggerty, 2009; Whetstone, Reed, and Turner, 2006).

Attracting Candidates: Considerations

Organizations must consider several issues for attracting candidates. First, they should understand the function of research and data-gathering in the personnel selection process (Switzer, 2006; Canadian Association of Chiefs of Police et al., 2000; Chien and Chen, 2008). This can inform each aspect of the process by examining it as a larger endeavor of matching individual talents to departmental goals and objectives. Second, they should craft recruitment goals that reflect an ethic that is visible to applicants (McKay and Avery, 2005; Orrick, 2008a). Decision rules about qualities of good candidates should spring from the department's climate as revealed in the earliest stages of the needs assessment and be linked to the attraction strategy. Third, when examining strategies for attracting candidates, departments should remember that the relative success of strategies might depend on budget, departmental commitment, personnel resources for recruitment, and departmental effectiveness in targeting specific subgroups that the agency seeks to recruit.

There might be synergies among these strategies (Switzer, 2006). When the community and department stakeholders have formed a partnership, identified hiring resources and needs, and used research to inform their work, the hiring process might flow more smoothly, with specific strategies that "work" for the department arising from the outflow of ideas, philosophy, and planning.

Attracting Candidates: Internal Strategies

The best recruiters for a department are often its own personnel (Baker and Carrera, 2007; Haggerty, 2009). Building professional networks within the department to support recruitment can enhance community outreach efforts by making recruitment an overall philosophy rather than a task to be performed. Internal strategies that emphasize interaction, relationship-building, and partnerships with the public can enhance perceptions of diversity and boost hiring of women and minorities (Taylor et al., 2006; COPS, 2009b). Without a climate that reflects legitimate and credible organizational beliefs, recruitment for diversity can be seen as false and might even increase turnover (McKay and Avery, 2005). Having a department-wide outlook that emphasizes recruitment potential in public interactions can help overcome negative or unrealistic impressions of what police work entails and contribute to a larger strategic recruitment plan. Recruiting can become a part of the department's everyday interactions with the public (Baker and Carrera, 2007; Canadian Association of Chiefs of Police et al., 2000).

Build Employee Referral Networks. Referrals by family, friends, and employees strongly influence individual decisions to apply for careers in public service (Baker and Carrera, 2007; Switzer, 2006; Slater and Reiser, 1988; Yearwood, 2003). Relationship-based recruiting can also dispel myths about police work and build associations across different groups (Baker and Carrera, 2007). Applicants who are referred and sponsored by an existing employee are more likely to complete the hiring process (Barber, 1998).

Two important influences on the decision to apply for police positions are department reputation and exposure to the variety of tasks that police perform; these can be solidified with employee referrals and community activism (Baker and Carrera, 2007; Slater and Reiser, 1988). Personal referrals can also provide a realistic portrayal of how a law-enforcement career affects family life (Ryan et al., 2001). To boost referrals, departments should consider compensation and other incentives for them (Switzer, 2006; Haggerty, 2009; Lachnit, 2001). Relationship-based and employee referral strategies help increase applicant pools and provide balance to other recruitment strategies, such as online processes, that lack human interaction.

Create a Department Recruitment Unit. A recruitment unit can be separate from recruitment teams that perform hiring needs assessments or linked interdepartmentally (Geis and Cavanagh, 1966; Orrick, 2008a; Whetstone, Reed, and Turner, 2006). Recruitment units oversee internal and external strategies devoted to recruitment, such as testing, advertising, coordinating outreach programs, media relations, and recruiting events (New York City Commission to Combat Police Corruption, 2008). By establishing such a unit, departments can better ensure that recruitment efforts reflect the department's needs, goals, and philosophies and enhance the credibility and openness of recruitment efforts (Breaugh and Starke, 2000). Departments should consider structuring the team and mentoring team members so as to best improve quality and efficacy; this can include integrating background investigative and personnel staff into the recruitment team (Switzer, 2006; Lim et al., 2009). Departments should also consider using incentives for recruiting-team participation and success (Switzer, 2006; Whetstone, Reed, and Turner, 2006).

Look Within the Department for Potential Recruits. Referral networks might consider a department's civilian staff for sworn positions, a strategy that would create "feeder" networks of existing employees (Ridgeway et al., 2008). Auxiliary and reserve ranks have frequently been used as an internal personnel resource (Yearwood, 2003). Because such employees are already part of the organization, this process reduces hiring costs, time, and procedures (Jordan et al., 2009).

Conduct an Internal Assessment of Employee-Engagement Strategies. Google, the Internet search-engine company, publishes a list of benefits called the "I bet you don't have that where you work" list (Sullivan, 2005). The list details Google's employee-engagement strategies, which range from perks (on-site dry cleaning, a wine club, and yoga classes) to more-traditional benefits (flexible hours, vacation benefits, and health counseling). Police agencies should ask themselves what they present that will attract the best possible officers. Police chiefs should ask themselves, "Why would I want to work for this department?" (McKeever and Kranda, 2000). Conducting an inventory of benefits can be the first step in assessing those that work best in attracting candidates, those that are weak, and how they appear from the applicant's perspective. This is a crucial step in department marketing and outreach efforts (Orrick, 2008a). An inventory of benefits can also bolster department pride in recruiters who speak to candidates. The inventory could be conducted both to attract candidates and to prevent turnover (Switzer, 2006; Jordan et al., 2009; Sullivan, 2005).

Attracting Candidates: Outreach Strategies

Departments have used myriad outreach strategies over time to attract candidates. Though there is minimal research on their effectiveness, to attract candidates, departments have used such tools as advertise-and-wait, "word of mouse" social networking, traditional job fairs, and proactive community partnerships.

Use Internet Media in a Variety of Forms. Increasing use of the Internet has lured agencies seeking to attract officers. The interactive potential of Internet media has increased beyond simple advertising, and it continues to do so in ways that outpace empirical study (Russell, 2007). Websites have been seen as the top tool in attracting qualified applicants (Switzer, 2006). Internet presence should maximize department resources. The Los Angeles Police Department (LAPD) recruitment website contributed to an increase in recruitment during a fiscal year in which advertising budgets were cut (Lim et al., 2009). The democratic properties of the Internet have helped smaller agencies compete with larger ones for candidates (McKeever and Kranda, 2000). Nevertheless, use of the Internet only to place advertisements online and without any overall marketing strategy can be ineffective (Yearwood, 2003).

Many organizations have failed to jump the digital divide to best reach new generations of technologically savvy applicants. More than two-thirds of companies responding in one survey had never used social-networking sites in recruitment efforts, although nearly half said they searched such sites for information on applicants ("MySpace," 2006).

Contemporary Internet tools (referred to as *Web 2.0*) have magnified the importance of "word-of-mouse" tactics that new generations expect in their job search (Van Hoye and

Lievens, 2007; Verhoeven, Mashood, and Chansarkar, 2009). Social-networking sites, such as Facebook, MySpace, and Twitter (along with law-enforcement networking sites, such as Officer.com and Police Link), have increased in use but represent the social cornerstone of many young persons' lives (Russell, 2007). These websites enable connections across audiences, including high-school and college students and graduates, military personnel, professionals, former and current law enforcement, police supervisors, and job searchers from other fields ("MySpace," 2006; Van Hoye and Lievens, 2007; Verhoeven, Mashood, and Chansarkar, 2009). Podcasts, blogs, and "really simple syndication" (RSS) feeds have increased job-seekers' sophistication, allowing them to process growing amounts of information and network more efficiently (Kolbitsch and Maurer, 2006; Martin, Reddington, and Kneafsey, 2009; Orrick, 2008a).

The Internet's overall effect on police recruiting varies, but agencies using it have been able to present their organizations in ways that influence applicants (Cable and Yu, 2006), dispel negative images (Ellis et al., 2005; Orrick, 2008a; Syrett and Lammiman, 2004) and transmit positive ones (Ellis et al., 2005; Verhoeven, Mashood, and Chansarkar, 2009), showcase their technological abilities (Charrier, 2000), and place recruiting efforts in contexts that resonate with new generations of applicants (Gubbins and Garavan, 2008). Despite the generational differences that might separate police command staff from young recruits, using Internet media could sell policing in messages that are heard very personally in a medium that previous generations might find impersonal (COPS, 2009b).

Use Electronic Media Other Than the Internet. Electronic recruitment techniques are not confined to blogs and websites. Gaming and other visual technology can also help attract new generations of recruits. Many simulation-based video games mimic interactive problem-solving activities, such as probing and telescoping, exploratory analysis, and critical thinking (Harrison, 2007). Beyond games, the use of emotional video clips in a structured, reality-show format can also help attract candidates (Lim et al., 2009). Interactive electronic media restructure traditional communications with workers, which could be a boon to departments with advanced technological capabilities (Ellis et al., 2005; Harrison, 2007). Yet, use of electronic media can present a paradox: If emotional vignettes of police life are used to attract candidates, specifically where department diversity and work life are represented, the department must ensure that such representations and "simulations" are consistent with the realities of police work in their department.

Brand Your Department and Your Profession. The message transmitted through advertising media constitutes the "brand" that applicants see and the identity that agencies give themselves. In the first episode of the LAPD's Internet-based recruitment video series, a variety of images designed to present information to recruits include a black female police sergeant, a diverse workforce of Hispanic and Asian officers, and fast-paced and adventurous police work (LAPD, undated). These and other branding images attempt to foster a deep, emotional attachment to the department and its supposed values (in this case, opportunities for advancement and diversity for minority populations) through the use of a reality-based film clip directed to a younger audience (Orrick, 2008a; Sartain and Schumann, 2006). Aside from marketing a department image or philosophy, branding also sells the profession of policing by aligning positive impressions of police work with applicants who might feel a "calling" to human-service careers (Ellis et al., 2005; Scrivner, 2006; Slater and Reiser, 1988; COPS, 2009b). In the LAPD video, segments display officers attempting to calm disputes, dealing with family problems, and working closely with community members in emotionally charged situations as much as they display traditional "crime-fighter" images (LAPD, undated). These reality-based images are expected to resonate with Internet-savvy and video-oriented applicants who are seen as socially aware, brand-loyal, and susceptible to cause branding (Syrett and Lammiman, 2004). Branding in this way must be sincere and emotionally consistent with police work, or the department runs the risk of appearing out of touch with its intended audience (McKay and Avery, 2005; J. Wilson and Grammich, 2009a).

Use Community Liaisons to Reach Potential Recruits. Community liaison efforts have been a cornerstone of many community-policing strategies for decades, with notable impact on recruitment of diverse populations (Skolnick and Bayley, 1988). These liaisons need not be involved in direct recruitment efforts. Liaisons could be any employees conducting community outreach, especially with targeted populations. Liaisons can be embedded in many ways. The Detroit Police Department's Recruiting Ambassadors program uses not only departmental employees but also community representatives for its recruitment effort, with incentives for community "ambassadors" to help recruit (Scrivner, 2006; Haggerty, 2009). Liaisons are often a critical part of outreach efforts to reach diverse populations but can also reflect diversity within the department in the eyes of potential candidates (Switzer, 2006). Liaison visibility and subsequent community relationships can enhance recruitment efforts with female candidates (Donnelly, 2005; Harrington, 2000) and in traditionally hard-to-reach ethnic and religious communities, such as Arab Americans (OJP, 2008), and other isolated urban populations (Cunningham and Wagstaff, 2006).

Open Department Doors and Allow On-Site Visits. Community policing can improve community visibility and, in turn, bolster recruitment efforts (Haggerty, 2009). When community partnerships are merely superficial, they risk alienating applicants who might be aware of hypocrisy in branding and advertising when such activities are inconsistent with realities of the job (Syrett and Lammiman, 2004). Outreach must be meaningful, genuine, and reflect a departmental desire to build true relationships with future employees

(Baker and Carrera, 2007; Switzer, 2006; McKeever and Kranda, 2000). Realistic job-preview strategies, by providing accurate representations of the department, can influence a candidate's interest in an organization (McKay and Avery, 2005). Making outreach partnerships sincere requires going beyond traditional public appearances and might require imaginative techniques, such as site visits, to enhance connections with targeted populations (McKay and Avery, 2006). Such tactics can enhance applicant interest beyond initial attraction stages (Breaugh, 2008; Rynes, Bretz, and Gerhart, 1991) and might be particularly important for recruiting female and minority candidates when such persons occupy important positions within the agency (Avery and McKay, 2006; COPS, 2009b). Nevertheless, site visits that expose work climate, employee demographics, and physical environments that differ from department recruitment media can reduce interest (Breaugh, 2008). Agencies should make the interactions between candidates and staff meaningful and take the time to introduce important individuals within the department to the applicants.

Attend Career and Job Fairs. Face-to-face interaction and fostering human connections can make recruitment more meaningful and personal for both the department and applicants (Whetstone, Reed, and Turner, 2006). Many of these opportunities are available through local college and university placement offices and in military and civilian settings (Orrick, 2008a). Attending job and career fairs is often an expense for the department involving travel and creative marketing techniques for mixed results, although maximizing these opportunities can pay off in departmental visibility and recruit targeting (Switzer, 2006; Whetstone, Reed, and Turner, 2006; Yearwood, 2003). One potential benefit for departments attending such events is gaining firsthand insight on employment trends and overall staffing outlook in peer agencies; one drawback is that job fairs are largely limited to applicants currently looking for work (Breaugh, 2008).

Consider the Greater Value of Youth Programs in Recruiting. Explorer programs, internships through local schools, cadet academies, and mentorships with youth foster special relationships between young adults and departments (Whetstone, Reed, and Turner, 2006; Yearwood, 2003). From the development of the Department of Justice's Police Corps in the mid-1990s through the diffusion of similar scholarship, education, and training programs nationwide, youth outreach efforts have been a tradition of law-enforcement organizations.

Nevertheless, for many reasons, these efforts often produce few results for recruiting. Most youths entering policing decide prior to their high-school graduation to do so (Switzer, 2006; Slater and Reiser, 1988). Consequently, results for recruitment efforts vary widely (Whetstone, Reed, and Turner, 2006; Yearwood, 2003). Costly and time-intensive efforts, such as Explorer programs, might misdirect resources that could be used to entice undecided youths.

Beyond identifying specific candidates, such programs brand the profession for young persons in the community (Presman, Chapman, and Rosen, 2002; Ridgeway et al., 2008). They might also acquaint the department with newer generations of applicants, including their work-life preferences, expectations, and career visions. By forging partnerships with a wide variety of youth, the value of such programs might extend beyond recruiting. At the same time, such programs help those already contemplating a police career develop qualifications within a police organization (COPS, 2009b).

Target Second-Career Applicants, but Assess and Train Them Appropriately. With the economic downturn of the late 2000s, some police departments noted an increase in applicants seeking a second career in policing, emerging from fields as diverse as automobile manufacturing, steel fabrication, marketing, and business administration (Crowe, 2009; Currier, 2009). The Virginia State Police noted a surge in applications of individuals laid off from private-sector jobs in 2009, a trend that appeared to normally follow economic downturns (Sidener, 2009). The increase in second-career applicants presents opportunities for departments to expand their workforce to include individuals with prior experience in diverse careers, but the diversity does not end with these applicants' previous career choices. Individuals with prior careers outside law enforcement might present unique challenges by having differential training needs and abilities, previous work experience, levels of commitment, competing work values, familiarity with and attachment to wide varieties of perceived job benefits and rewards, and concepts of professionalism. Many of their attitudes toward work have been learned and ingrained through previous career experience, and organizations should be cautious in measuring the advantages and challenges of such candidates (COPS, 2009b).

The professional development of second-career police-officer candidates requires transferring previous career experience in a manner that suits both the department and the candidate's unique needs. In the field of education, a profession with many second-career applicants, several principles of learning guide the transfer of outside professional experience to new career paths. Extracting appropriate practical and professional expertise from previous career experience, adapting it to new work dimensions, and integrating these new employees into the organization to maximize their expertise, poses numerous challenges (Bolhuis, 2002; Tigchelaar, Brouwer, and Vermunt, 2010). Second-career applicants have different motivations and values, which can simultaneously invigorate and strain organizations unfamiliar with their special needs, and their levels of commitment might be used to organizational advantage (Pennington, Congdon, and Magilvy, 2007). In medicine, second-career applicants have been attractive because their life experiences and successes, as well as their perceived maturity, might enhance organizational mission with other applicants (Kohn and Truglio-Londrigan, 2007). Models of career transitions have described the potential effects of integrating second-career workers as mutually transformative, with organizations offering experienced persons previously unattainable potential for actualization in exchange for experience and maturity (Cary Cooper and Torrington, 1981; Bandow, Minsky, and Voss, 2007).

One solution to the complexities of hiring individuals with diverse previous experiences is to diagnose how their values fit with the organization. Schein's model of career anchors can be used to examine values and career priorities among workers from different fields and to assess their self-perceptions of talents, abilities, and values from prior experience (Danziger, Rachman-Moore, and Valency, 2008; Schein, 1990). For example, a second-career applicant with technical competence might struggle with service-oriented components of police work. An individual who seeks challenges might thrive on constant stimulation and not fit well in smaller agencies with limited opportunities. This model might help determine where training for second-career applicants should be focused. For example, for a former social worker appearing to be strong in public-service aspects of the job, training might best be focused on technical and tactical issues.

[...]

Selecting Candidates

Often, the process of candidate selection becomes confused with the exercise of attracting applicants (Breaugh, 2008; Ellis et al., 2005). For the candidate, the selection process requires patient navigation of physical, mental, and aptitude screening examinations, interviews, and meetings and submitting to a thorough background investigation. The crucial task for agencies is to use selection methods that reveal the best possible recruits for department needs (Cavanagh, 2003; Scrivner, 2006).

Because screening and selection play pivotal roles in narrowing a large, generalized pool of interested persons to a manageable cohort of applicants, agencies often examine their selection procedures to ensure that the testing and screening process is consistent with what they seek in new officers (Searle, 2006). Efficiency, accuracy, and fairness are but a few of the concerns for departments in structuring this crucial task in the recruitment process. Yet, departments have changed their selection procedures very little since a 1973 review of police selection procedures by the National Advisory Committee on Criminal Justice Standards (Doerner, 1998; Langworthy, Hughes, and Sanders, 1995), even as departments seek to increase recruiting among women and minorities (Lim et al., 2009; J. Wilson and Grammich, 2009a).

Possible reasons for the relative stagnation of reforms of the selection process include the need for agencies to pattern their selection procedures after state mandates (Bradley, 2005), an overall practitioner attachment to more-reactive models of selection (Scrivner, 2006), and the difficulty in modifying a procedure without incentives to do so (Tuomey and Jolly, 2009). Community policing and generational differences have driven reexaminations of the selection process by forcing departments to rethink what specific characteristics they seek in their officers (DeCicco, 2000; Scrivner, 2006).

Although alternatives, such as the assessment center, to traditional hurdle approaches of selection have blossomed, evidence on them is mixed (DeCicco, 2000; Kolpack, 1991; Reuland and Stedman, 1998). Scores on assessment-center examinations are positively correlated with academy and patrol performance (Hogarty and Bromley, 1996; Dayan, Kasten, and Fox, 2002; Pynes and Bernardin, 1992) and supervisor performance (Ross, 1980) in preliminary empirical tests.

Nonetheless, when considering the challenge of recruiting qualified applicants from younger generations, departments should consider restructuring the process to account for both applicant perceptions and departmental goals. Applicants' top two reported frustrations about the selection process were the length of time and impersonality of the procedure, items that departments can correct (Switzer, 2006). Some agencies are also considering restructuring the order of selection tasks to ensure a diverse applicant pool and cut costs by eliminating unnecessary and redundant screening procedures (Haggerty, 2009). In structuring a departmental protocol for selecting the best candidates, departments should consider aligning selection procedures with what they consider to be important job dimensions (Scrivner, 2006). For example, if a department identifies residency as one of the most important job dimensions for applicants, screening for applicants' residence proximity would take place before that for most skills and abilities.

As selection procedures are subjected to closer scrutiny, predicting candidate success at various stages of the recruitment process (even in the training academy) has become increasingly important. The Las Vegas (Nev.) Police Department recently adopted a testing program designed to maximize department time and resources by processing only applicants who display a high probability (85 percent) of completing the process (J. Wilson and Grammich, 2009a). The LAPD has similarly streamlined its selection process to use predictive models (Lim et al., 2009). As agencies increasingly use predictive models, traditional hurdle approaches are slowly being infused with more–empirically based selection processes, especially for targeted populations of recruits.

Screening Processes. Since the early 1970s, the structure of police screening procedures has revolved around three basic tests: physical agility testing, psychological testing, and a medical examination (Ash, Slora, and Britton, 1990; Langworthy, Hughes, and Sanders, 1995). The exact prevalence of these screening procedures for police-candidate selection is unknown, but some studies indicate that they are used in about 90 percent of agencies (Ash, Slora, and Britton, 1990; DeCicco, 2000; Ho, 1999; Langworthy, Hughes, and Sanders,

1995). Yet, despite the dominant emphasis on these screening procedures, they have shown widely varying predictive value in determining success with a number of outcome measurements (White, 2008). Their chief effect is often to select out applicants from further consideration, meaning that tighter or more-rigorous selection processes will reduce the number of applicants.

Interview Procedures. Personal interviews are used in more than 95 percent of police agencies' selection efforts (Hickman and Reaves, 2006a). Interview processes are beginning to incorporate diverse stakeholders to examine for a broader "cultural fit" (J. Wilson and Grammich, 2009a), including values and beliefs consistent with department and community mission. Such interviews often take the form of an "oral board" protocol (Doerner, 1998). Some researchers have warned against relying heavily on oral-board interview techniques for reasons ranging from the lack of training for many interview board members to the use of ambiguous and invalid rating dimensions (Gaines and Kappeler, 1992). Nevertheless, some studies indicate that newer generations of recruits have been able to perform better on oral portions of the selection process than on written examinations, which might indicate the need for pretesting and access to practice written testing by computer (Whetstone, Reed, and Turner, 2006). The assessment-center approach has also been effective in yielding task-specific interview questions, shifting interview focus from standard question-and-answer format to interactive simulations and roleplay (Hogarty and Bromley, 1996; Dayan, Kasten, and Fox, 2002).

Background Investigations. Traditionally, background investigations and character references have formed the backbone of police selection techniques (Fulton, 2000; Langworthy, Hughes, and Sanders, 1995; Smelson, 1975). In early use, such studies correlated background problems with after-hire disciplinary issues (Cohen and Chaiken, 1972). Background investigations have proliferated in use as a screening tool, often being conducted at multiple stages by different levels of the organization (Ridgeway et al., 2008). The extent of these investigations in probing a candidate's background varies by locale and can often involve a lifetime criminal history check, a credit-bureau report, and examinations of close associates from the recent to the distant past (DeCicco, 2000; New York City Commission to Combat Police Corruption, 2008).

Younger generations pose unique challenges to such investigations. Applicants from these generations can be remarkably candid in disclosing personal information, but their impressions of what constitutes "character" might be startlingly different from those of evaluators (Russell, 2007; Verhoeven, Mashood, and Chansarkar, 2009). For instance, social-networking sites often display photographs of applicants in poses that older generations might think inappropriate. In the Internet age, conducting background investigations on candidates, especially those for whom computer use often constitutes a social reality, can be inherently problematic for law-enforcement agencies because of the sudden transparency with which younger generations are living their lives.[1] Similarly, financial background information on candidates might be of decreasing value in an era of increasing economic difficulties.

Recent research shows that biographical information gained from background investigations is of limited help in predicting subsequent officer termination (Brennan et al., 2009). As such, departments should proceed with caution and not place undue emphasis on a technique that appears to be steadily losing favor, especially for new generations of recruits, for whom transparency is assumed.

Predicting Future Success in Applicants

Closely related to the issue of electronic background investigation is electronic surveillance for the purposes of human-resource selection and its negative effect on recruiting as a whole. Recent research has indicated that a wealth of personal data about candidates can be obtained simply by searching the Internet for names, nicknames, email addresses, and addresses and looking at candidates' social-networking profiles (Searle, 2006). This power is increasing exponentially with the proliferation of electronic media and outpaces empirical study of its impact on recruitment efforts.

Yet, preliminary research shows that with such ability comes equal responsibility for the human-resource professional. Worries that such sensitive information might compromise individual freedom and privacy and adversely affect candidate selection have resonated with those concerned with civil liberties and organizational justice (Chapman and Webster, 2003; M. Harris, Van Hoye, and Lievens, 2003; Truxillo, Steiner, and Gilliland, 2004). The Internet age has changed the selection game in ways that are still unclear for both job-seekers and agencies looking for qualified applicants.

What is apparent is that traditional methods of selection might be losing reliability in the absence of more-current data analysis on new generations of applicants and their changed career expectations, conflicting notions of privacy, and sustained cynicism about invasive and lengthy application processes. Placing these new recruits in uniform based on selection techniques that might not only be obsolete but also be seen as invasive and irrelevant could be counterproductive. Recent research demonstrating that personal demographic and background information (such as age, gender, and race) can predict police academy performance

---

1 Such transparency can also affect officers on the force. In one case, a Sandy Springs, Georgia, officer was fired for his Facebook postings, including one in which he divulged the possibility of a Federal Bureau of Investigation (FBI) drug seizure. See "Cop Says Facebook Postings Got Him Fired" (2009).

(White, 2008) appears not only to be contradicted by empiricists' inability to link academy performance to patrol behaviors but also to be in widespread disagreement about what qualities might best befit "good police officers" (Sanders, 2003). A more-proactive approach for selection would use department-specific benchmarks and performance measurements for determining what specific selection processes are a good fit for the department and keeping departmental needs assessments current for staffing.

Conclusion

Many of the core problems that police agencies face in recruiting have worsened in the past decade, even as changing economic conditions have led to temporary fluctuations in the numbers of recruits. Changing generational tastes for police work, increased prevalence of disqualifications (such as drug use or physical unfitness), and greater competition from other organizations (such as the military) have helped restrict the pool of qualified applicants. Further complicating recruiting efforts is the fragmented approach many agencies take to recruiting.

Nevertheless, agencies can take several modest steps to make their recruiting more effective. First, assessing their staffing needs can help shape a more-effective recruiting approach. This can include developing an assessment team, identifying budget and sources of revenue for recruiting, specifying organizational goals and values that recruits should have, and integrating the community in the hiring process.

Both internal and external strategies might help departments attract candidates. Internally, departments can build employee referral networks, create a recruitment unit, identify potential recruits from auxiliary or reserve ranks, and assess the effectiveness of their employee-engagement strategies (e.g., identify reasons employees should want to work for the agency). Externally, departments can use Internet and other electronic media, brand the department and its work within the community, use community liaisons to reach potential recruits, allow on-site visits, attend career and job fairs, and target both youth programs and second-career applicants. Such external marketing efforts should take care to ensure that agency work is portrayed realistically; portrayals of work that do not match the reality can cause the department to appear insincere in its efforts to engage.

Departments might also wish to expand their recruitment possibilities by opening wider the "faucet" of supply for recruits. Such efforts can include relaxing age, education, or residency requirements and becoming more tolerant of experimental drug use, bad credit history, or minor arrest records. Such initiatives, however, might raise concerns about the quality of recruits. Departments might also wish to expand their supply of candidates by revamping their screening processes, interview processes, and background investigations.

At the same time, streamlined selection processes, particularly those aided by electronic media, should be cautious about applicant freedom and privacy, as well as about identifying characteristics of applicants likely to have success.

Bibliography

Alpert, Geoffrey P., "Hiring and Promoting Police Officers in Small Departments: The Role of Psychological Testing," *Criminal Law Bulletin*, Vol. 27, No. 3, May–June 1991, pp. 261–269.

Ash, Philip, Karen B. Slora, and Cynthia F. Britton, "Police Agency Officer Selection Practices," *Journal of Police Science and Administration*, Vol. 17, No. 4, December 1990, pp. 258–269.

Baker, Nicole, and Max Carrera, "Unlocking the Door to Relationship-Based Corrections Recruitment," *Corrections Today*, Vol. 69, No. 1, February 2007, pp. 36–38.

Bandow, Diane, Barbara D. Minsky, and Richard Steven Voss, "Reinventing the Future: Investigating Career Transitions from Industry to Academia," *Journal of Human Resources Education*, Vol. 1, No. 1, Summer 2007, pp. 23–37. As of June 23, 2010: http://business.troy.edu/JHRE/Issue.aspx?Volume=1&Issue=1

Barber, Alison E., *Recruiting Employees: Individual and Organizational Perspectives*, Thousand Oaks, Calif.: Sage Publications, 1998.

Bolhuis, Sanneke, "Alternative Routes to Teaching in Secondary Education in the Netherlands," *European Journal of Teacher Education*, Vol. 25, No. 2–3, October 2002, pp. 223–238.

Bradley, Patrick L., "21st Century Issues Related to Police Training and Standards," *Police Chief*, Vol. 72, No. 10, October 2005, pp. 32–39. As of June 23, 2010: http://policechiefmagazine.org/magazine/index.cfm?fuseaction=display_arch&article_id=724&issue_id=102005

Breaugh, James A., "Employee Recruitment: Current Knowledge and Important Areas for Further Research," *Human Resource Management Review*, Vol. 18, No. 3, September 2008, pp. 103–118.

Breaugh, James A., and Mary Starke, "Research on Employee Recruitment: So Many Studies, So Many Remaining Questions," *Journal of Management*, Vol. 26, No. 3, 2000, pp. 405–434.

Brennan, Adrianne M., Robert D. Davis, Cary D. Rostow, and Matrix Incorporated, "An Investigation of Biographical Information as Predictor of Employment Termination Among Law Enforcement Officers," *Journal of Police and Criminal Psychology*, Vol. 24, No. 2, October 2009, pp. 108–112.

Cable, Daniel M., and Kang Yang Trevor Yu, "Managing Job Seekers' Organizational Image Beliefs: The Role of Media Richness and Media Credibility," *Journal of Applied Psychology*, Vol. 91, No. 4, July 2006, pp. 828–840.

Canadian Association of Chiefs of Police, Canadian Police Association, PricewaterhouseCoopers, and Human Resources Development Canada, *Strategic Human Resources Analysis of Public Policing in Canada*, Ottawa: PricewaterhouseCoopers, 2000.

Cavanagh, Michael E., *Policing Within a Professional Framework*, Upper Saddle River, N.J.: Pearson Prentice Hall, 2003.

Chapman, Derek S., and Jane Webster, "The Use of Technologies in the Recruitment, Screening, and Selection Processes for Job Candidates," *International Journal of Selection and Assessment*, Vol. 11, No. 2–3, June 2003, pp. 113–120.

Charrier, Kim, "Marketing Strategies for Attracting and Retaining Generation X Police Officers," *Police Chief*, Vol. 67, No. 12, December 2000, pp. 45–51.

Chien, Chen-Fu, and Li-Fei Chen, "Data Mining to Improve Personnel Selection and Enhance Human Capital: A Case Study in High-Technology Industry," *Expert Systems with Applications*, Vol. 34, No. 1, January 2008, pp. 280–290.

Clem, Connie, Barbara Krauth, and Paula Wenger, *Recruitment, Hiring, and Retention: Current Practices in U.S. Jails*, Longmont, Colo.: National Institute of Corrections Information Center, 2000. As of June 23, 2010: http://nicic.gov/Library/015885

Cohen, Bernard, and Jan M. Chaiken, *Police Background Characteristics and Performance: Summary*, Santa Monica, Calif.: RAND Corporation, R-999/1-DOJ, 1972. As of June 23, 2010: http://www.rand.org/pubs/reports/R999.1/

Cooper, Cary L., and Derek Torrington, eds., *After Forty: The Time for Achievement?* New York: Wiley, 1981.

"Cop Says Facebook Postings Got Him Fired," *WSBTV.com*, December 8, 2009. As of June 23, 2010: http://www.wsbtv.com/news/21900267/detail.html

Crowe, Robert, "Economy Has Folks Feeling the Blue," *San Antonio Express-News*, February 8, 2009. As of June 23, 2010: http://www.mysanantonio.com/news/local_news/Economy_has_folks_feeling_the_blue.html

Cunningham, Sonia, and Melissa Wagstaff, *Reflecting London: Diversity of Police Community Support Officer Recruits Compared to Police Officer Recruits in the Metropolitan Police Service*, London: Metropolitan Police Authority, December 2006. As of June 23, 2010: http://www.mpa.gov.uk/downloads/publications/pcso-diversity-full.pdf

Currier, Joel, "Missouri Police Academies Grow Despite Budget Tightening," *St. Louis Post-Dispatch*, November 2, 2009. As of June 23, 2010: http://www.columbiamissourian.com/stories/2009/11/09/mo-police-academiesseeing-growth/

Danziger, Nira, Dalia Rachman-Moore, and Rony Valency, "The Construct Validity of Schein's Career Anchors Orientation Inventory," *Career Development International*, Vol. 13, No. 1, 2008, pp. 7–19.

Dayan, Kobi, Ronen Kasten, and Shaul Fox, "Entry-Level Police Candidate Assessment Center: An Efficient Tool or a Hammer to Kill a Fly?" *Personnel Psychology*, Vol. 55, No. 4, January 2002, pp. 827–849.

DeCicco, David A., "Police Officer Candidate Assessment and Selection," *FBI Law Enforcement Bulletin*, Vol. 69, No. 12, December 2000, pp. 1–6.

Delaware State Personnel Office, "Research Project: Phase 1," Newark, Del.: University of Delaware, Institute for Public Administration, June 2002.

Doerner, William G., *Introduction to Law Enforcement: An Insider's View*, Boston, Mass.: Butterworth-Heinemann, 1998.

Donnelly, Daniel, "Policing the Scottish Community," in Daniel Donnelly and Kenneth Scott, eds., *Policing Scotland*, Cullompton, Devon, U.K.: Willan Publishing, 2005, pp. 130–156.

Ellis, Gene, Greg Marshall, Chris Skinner, and Gary Smith, "Using Visual Technology for Recruitment," *Police Chief*, Vol. 72, No. 1, January 2005, pp. 20–24.

Fritsch, Eric J., John Liederbach, and Robert W. Taylor, *Police Patrol Allocation and Deployment*, Upper Saddle River, N.J.: Pearson Prentice Hall, 2009.

Fulton, Roger, "Recruiting and Hiring New Officers," *Law Enforcement Technology*, Vol. 30, August 2000, p. 130.

Fyfe, James J., Jack R. Greene, William F. Walsh, O. W. Wilson, and Roy Clinton McLaren, eds., *Police Administration*, 5th ed., New York: McGraw-Hill, 1997.

Gaines, Larry K., and Victor E. Kappeler, "Selection and Testing," in Gary W. Cordner and Donna C. Hale, eds., *What Works in Policing? Operations and Administration Examined*, Cincinnati, Ohio: Anderson Publishing, 1992, pp. 107–123.

Geis, Gilbert, and Elvin Cavanagh, "Recruitment and Retention of Correctional Personnel," *Crime and Delinquency*, Vol. 12, No. 3, July 1966, pp. 232–239.

Goldstein, Herman, *Policing a Free Society*, Cambridge, Mass.: Ballinger Publishing, 1977.

Gubbins, M. Claire, and Thomas N. Garavan, "The Changing Context and Role of the HRD Professional: Time to Recognize the Importance of Social Networking Competency," paper presented at the Ninth Annual Conference on Human Resource Development, Lille, France, May 2008.

Haggerty, Catherine, lieutenant, recruiting division, Austin Police Department, interview, "From the Field Experiences," Santa Monica, Calif.: RAND Corporation, July 2009. As of June 24, 2010: http://www.rand.org/ise/centers/quality_policing/cops/resources/field_experiences/catherine_haggerty.html

Harrington, Penny E., *Recruiting and Retaining Women: A Self-Assessment Guide for Law Enforcement*, Los Angeles, Calif.: National Center for Women and Policing, a Division of the Feminist Majority Foundation, 2000. As of June 24, 2010: http://www.ncjrs.gov/pdffiles1/bja/185235.pdf

Harris, Michael M., Greet Van Hoye, and Filip Lievens, "Privacy and Attitudes Towards Internet-Based Selection Systems: A Cross-Cultural Comparison," *International Journal of Selection and Assessment*, Vol. 11, No. 2–3, June 2003, pp. 230–236.

Harrison, Bob, "Gamers, Millennials, and Generation Next: Implications for Policing," *Police Chief*, Vol. 74, No. 10, October 2007, pp. 150–160.

Hickman, Matthew J., and Brian A. Reaves, *Local Police Departments, 2003*, Washington, D.C.: Department of Justice, Office of Justice Programs, Bureau of Justice Statistics, NCJ 210118, April 1, 2006a. As of June 24, 2010: http://bjs.ojp.usdoj.gov/index.cfm?ty=pbdetail&iid=1045

Ho, Taiping, "Assessment of Police Officer Recruiting and Testing Instruments," *Journal of Offender Rehabilitation*, Vol. 29, No. 3–4, December 1999, pp. 1–23.

Hogarty, Kris, and Max Bromley, "Evaluating the Use of the Assessment Center Process for Entry-Level Police Officer Selections in a Medium Sized Police Agency," *Journal of Police and Criminal Psychology*, Vol. 11, No. 1, March 1996, pp. 27–34.

Hogue, Mark C., Tommie Black, and Robert T. Sigler, "Differential Use of Screening Techniques in the Recruitment of Police Officers," *American Journal of Police*, Vol. 13, No. 2, 1994, pp. 113–124.

Jordan, William T., Lorie Fridell, Donald Faggiani, and Bruce Kubu, "Attracting Females and Racial/Ethnic Minorities to Law Enforcement," *Journal of Criminal Justice*, Vol. 37, No. 4, July–August 2009, pp. 333–341.

Kahanov, Leamor, and Lanna Andrews, "A Survey of Athletic Training Employers' Hiring Criteria," *Journal of Athletic Training*, Vol. 36, No. 4, October–December 2001, pp. 408–412.

Kohn, Paula S., and Marie Truglio-Londrigan, "Second-Career Baccalaureate Nursing Students: A Lived Experience," *Journal of Nursing Education*, Vol. 46, No. 9, September 2007, pp. 391–399.

Kolbitsch, Josef, and Hermann Maurer, "The Transformation of the Web: How Emerging Communities Shape the Information We Consume," *Journal of Universal Computer Science*, Vol. 12, No. 2, 2006, pp. 19–37.

Kolpack, Bryce D., "Assessment Center Approach to Police Officer Selection," *Police Chief*, Vol. 58, No. 9, September 1991, pp. 28–30, 44–46.

Koper, Christopher S., Edward R. Maguire, and Gretchen E. Moore, *Hiring and Retention Issues in Police Agencies: Readings on the Determinants of Police Strength, Hiring and Retention of Officers, and the Federal COPS Program*, Washington, D.C.: Urban Institute, October 2001. As of June 24, 2010: http://www.urban.org/UploadedPDF/410380_Hiring-and-Retention.pdf

Lachnit, Carroll, "Employee Referral Saves Time, Saves Money, Delivers Quality," *Workforce*, June 2001.

Langworthy, Robert H., Thomas Hughes, and Beth Sanders, *Law Enforcement Recruitment, Selection and Training: A Survey of Major Police Departments in the U.S.*, Highland Heights, Ky.: Academy of Criminal Justice Sciences, Police Section, 1995.

Larson, Richard C., *Police Deployment: New Tools for Planners*, Lexington, Mass.: Lexington Books, 1978.

Liebert, Dennis R., and Rod Miller, *Staffing Analysis Workbook for Jails*, Washington, D.C.: Department of Justice, National Institute of Corrections, 2001.

Lim, Nelson, Carl Matthies, Greg Ridgeway, and Brian Gifford, *To Protect and to Serve: Enhancing the Efficiency of LAPD Recruiting*, Santa Monica, Calif.: RAND Corporation, MG-881-RMPF, 2009. As of June 24, 2010: http://www.rand.org/pubs/monographs/MG881/

Los Angeles Police Department, "To Protect and to Serve," undated video, webisode 1. As of June 24, 2010: http://www.joinlapd.com/webisode_01.html

Martin, Graeme, Martin Reddington, and Mary Beth Kneafsey, *Web 2.0 and Human Resource Management: "Groundswell" or Hype?* London: Chartered Institute of Personnel and Development, 2009.

McDevitt, Jack, Amy Farrell, and Russell Wolf, *Promoting Cooperative Strategies to Reduce Racial Profiling*, Washington, D.C.: U.S. Department of Justice, Office of Community Oriented Policing Services, COPS evaluation brief 1, 2008. As of June 24, 2010: http://purl.access.gpo.gov/GPO/LPS115585

McKay, Patrick F., and Derek R. Avery, "Warning! Diversity Recruitment Could Backfire," *Journal of Management Inquiry*, Vol. 14, No. 4, December 2005, pp. 330–336.

———, "What Has Race Got to Do with It? Unraveling the Role of Racioethnicity in Job Seekers' Reactions to Site Visits," *Personnel Psychology*, Vol. 59, No. 2, Summer 2006, pp. 395–429.

McKeever, Jack, and April Kranda, "Recruitment and Retention of Qualified Police Personnel: A Best Practices Guide," *Big Ideas for Smaller Departments*, Vol. 2, No. 1, Summer 2000, pp. 3–15. As of June 24, 2010: http://www.theiacp.org/LinkClick.aspx?fileticket=Jn02Pt%2BKiWI%3D&tabid=407

Metropolitan Atlanta Crime Commission, *Manual on Police Patrol Manpower Resource Allocation*, Atlanta, Ga., 1977.

"MySpace, Facebook and Other Social Networking Sites: Hot Today, Gone Tomorrow?" *Universia*, May 31, 2006. As of June 24, 2010: http://www.wharton.universia.net/index.cfm?fa=viewfeature&id=1156&language=english

Nalla, Mahesh K., Michael Lynch, and Michael J. Leiber, "Determinants of Police Growth in Phoenix, 1950–1988," *Justice Quarterly*, Vol. 14, No. 1, March 1997, pp. 115–143.

New York City Commission to Combat Police Corruption, *Tenth Annual Report*, February 2008. As of June 24, 2010: http://www.nyc.gov/html/ccpc/downloads/pdf/10th_annual_report_feb_2008.pdf

Orrick, W. Dwayne, *Recruitment, Retention, and Turnover of Police Personnel: Reliable, Practical, and Effective Solutions*, Springfield, Ill.: Charles C. Thomas, 2008a.

Pennington, Karen, JoAnn G. Congdon, and Joan K. Magilvy, "Second-Career CNAs in Nursing Homes: Tapping an Underused Resource," *Journal of Gerontological Nursing*, Vol. 33, No. 6, June 2007, pp. 21–28.

Pinal County Sheriff's Office, *Police Allocation Staffing Analysis*, Florence, Ariz., March 3, 2008. As of June 24, 2010: http://pinalcountyaz.gov/Departments/Sheriff/AboutPCSO/Documents/FinalStaffingReportwithaddendums.pdf

Presman, Dylan, Robert Chapman, and Linda Rosen, *Creative Partnerships: Supporting Youth, Building Communities*, Washington, D.C.: U.S. Department of Justice, Office of Community Oriented Policing Services, September 2002. As of June 24, 2010: http://purl.access.gpo.gov/GPO/LPS24105

Pynes, Joan, and H. John Bernardin, "Entry-Level Police Selection: The Assessment Center Is an Alternative," *Journal of Criminal Justice*, Vol. 20, No. 1, 1992, pp. 41–52.

Reuland, Melissa M., and John Stedman, *Recruitment and Selection for Community Policing: An Analysis of Organizational Change*, Washington, D.C.: Police Executive Research Forum, 1998.

Ridgeway, Greg, Nelson Lim, Brian Gifford, Christopher Koper, Carl Matthies, Sara Hajiamiri, and Alexis Huynh, *Strategies for Improving Officer Recruitment in the San Diego Police Department*, Santa Monica, Calif.: RAND Corporation, MG-724-SDPD, 2008. As of June 24, 2010: http://www.rand .org/pubs/monographs/MG724/

Ross, Joyce D., "Determination of the Predictive Validity of the Assessment Center Approach to Selecting Police Managers," *Journal of Criminal Justice*, Vol. 8, No. 2, 1980, pp. 89–96.

Russell, Cristel Antonia, *Advertainment: Fusing Advertising and Entertainment*, Ann Arbor, Mich.: University of Michigan Yaffe Center for Persuasive Communication, 2007. As of June 24, 2010: http://www.bus.umich.edu/FacultyResearch/ResearchCenters/centers/Yaffe/downloads/ Advertainment_teaching_materials.pdf

Ryan, Ann Marie, S. David Kriska, Bradley J. West, and Joshua M. Sacco, "Anticipated Work/Family Conflict and Family Member Views: Role in Police Recruiting," *Policing: An International Journal of Police Strategies and Management*, Vol. 24, No. 2, 2001, pp. 228–239.

Rynes, Sara L., Robert D. Bretz Jr., and Barry A. Gerhart, "The Importance of Recruitment in Job Choice: A Different Way of Looking," *Personnel Psychology*, Vol. 44, No. 3, 1991, pp. 487–521.

Sanders, Beth A., "Maybe There's No Such Thing as a 'Good Cop': Organizational Challenges in Selecting Quality Officers," *Policing: An International Journal of Police Strategies and Management*, Vol. 26, No. 2, 2003, pp. 313–328.

Sartain, Libby, and Mark Schumann, *Brand from the Inside: Eight Essentials to Emotionally Connect Your Employees to Your Business*, San Francisco, Calif.: Jossey-Bass Publishers, 2006.

Schein, Edgar, *Career Anchors: Discovering Your Real Values*, San Diego, Calif.: University Associates, 1990.

Scrivner, Ellen M., *Innovations in Police Recruitment and Hiring: Hiring in the Spirit of Service*, Washington, D.C.: U.S. Department of Justice, Office of Community Oriented Policing Services, January 26, 2006. As of June 24, 2010: http://www.cops.usdoj.gov/ric/ResourceDetail. aspx?RID=113

Searle, Rosalind H., "New Technology: The Potential Impact of Surveillance Techniques in Recruitment Practices," *Personnel Review*, Vol. 35, No. 3, 2006, pp. 336–351.

Shane, Jon M., *What Every Chief Executive Should Know: Using Data to Measure Police Performance*, Flushing, N.Y.: Looseleaf Law Publications, 2007.

Sidener, Carrie J., "Lynchburg Police Department Sees Surge in Applications," *Lynchburg News and Advance*, May 6, 2009. As of June 24, 2010: http://www2.newsadvance.com/lna/news/local/article/ lynchburg_police_department_sees_surge_in_applications/15759/

Skolnick, Jerome H., and David H. Bayley, "Theme and Variation in Community Policing," *Crime and Justice*, Vol. 10, 1988, pp. 1–37.

Slater, Harold R., and Martin Reiser, "Comparative Study of Factors Influencing Police Recruitment," *Journal of Police Science and Administration*, Vol. 16, No. 3, September 1988, pp. 168–176.

Smelson, I. Harold, "Psychiatric Screening of Police Candidates," *Journal of the Medical Society of New Jersey*, Vol. 72, No. 3, March 1975, pp. 213–216.

Strawbridge, Peter, and Deirdre Strawbridge, *A Networking Guide to Recruitment, Selection and Probationary Training of Police Officers in Major Departments of the United States of America*, New York: John Jay College of Criminal Justice, 1990.

Sullivan, John, "A Case Study of Google Recruiting," *Dr. John Sullivan's Talent Management Thought Leadership Community*, December 2005. As of June 24, 2010: http://www.drjohnsullivan.com/articles-mainmenu-27/hr-strategy-mainmenu-33/81-a-case-study-of-google-recruiting

Switzer, Merlin E., *Recruitment and Retention: Best Practices Update*, Sacramento, Calif.: Commission on Peace Officer Standards and Training, April 2006.

Syrett, Michel, and Jean Lammiman, "Advertising and Millennials: Young Consumers," *Insight and Ideas for Responsible Marketers*, Vol. 5, No. 4, 2004, pp. 62–73.

Taylor, Bruce, Bruce Kubu, Lorie Fridell, Carter Rees, Tom Jordan, and Jason Cheney, *Cop Crunch: Identifying Strategies for Dealing with the Recruiting and Hiring Crisis in Law Enforcement*, Washington, D.C.: Police Executive Research Forum, April 2006. As of June 24, 2010: http://www.ncjrs.gov/pdffiles1/nij/grants/213800.pdf

Tigchelaar, Anke, Niels Brouwer, and Jan D. Vermunt, "Tailor-Made: Towards a Pedagogy for Educating Second-Career Teachers," *Educational Research Review*, Vol. 5, No. 2, 2010, pp. 164–183.

Truxillo, Donald M., Dirk D. Steiner, and Stephen W. Gilliland, "The Importance of Organizational Justice in Personnel Selection: Defining When Selection Fairness Really Matters," *International Journal of Selection and Assessment*, Vol. 12, No. 1–2, March 2004, pp. 39–53.

Tuomey, Lianne M., and Rachel Jolly, "Step Up to Law Enforcement: A Successful Strategy for Recruiting Women into the Law Enforcement Profession," *Police Chief*, Vol. 76, No. 6, June 2009, pp. 68–73.

U.S. Department of Justice, Office of Justice Programs, National Institute of Justice, *Policing in Arab-American Communities After September 11*, Washington, D.C., July 2008. As of June 24, 2010: http://purl.access.gpo.gov/GPO/LPS103999

U.S. Department of Justice, Office of Community Oriented Policing Services, *Law Enforcement Recruitment Toolkit*, Washington, D.C., October 16, 2009b. As of June 24, 2010: http://www.cops.usdoj.gov/ric/ResourceDetail.aspx?RID=542

Van Hoye, Greet, and Filip Lievens, "Investigating Web-Based Recruitment Sources: Employee Testimonials vs. Word-of-Mouse," *International Journal of Selection and Assessment*, Vol. 15, No. 4, December 2007, pp. 372–382.

Verhoeven, Helen, Neelofer Mashood, and Bal Chansarkar, "Recruitment and Generation Y: Web 2.0 the Way to Go?" paper presented at the Annual American Business Research Conference, New York, N.Y., April 2009. As of June 24, 2010: http://www.wbiconpro.com/8.Neelofar.pdf

Walker, Samuel, ed., *Records of the Wickersham Commission on Law Observance and Enforcement*, Bethesda, Md.: University Publications of America, 1997.

Whetstone, Thomas S., John C. Reed Jr., and Phillip C. Turner, "Recruiting: A Comparative Study of the Recruiting Practices of State Police Agencies," *International Journal of Police Science and Management*, Vol. 8, No. 1, Spring 2006, pp. 52–66.

White, Michael D., "Identifying Good Cops Early: Predicting Recruit Performance in the Academy," *Police Quarterly*, Vol. 11, No. 1, March 2008, pp. 27–49.

White, Michael D., and Gipsy Escobar, "Making Good Cops in the Twenty-First Century: Emerging Issues for the Effective Recruitment, Selection and Training of Police in the United States and Abroad," *Crime and Criminal Justice*, Vol. 22, No. 1–2, March 2008, pp. 119–134.

Wilson, Jeremy M., and Clifford A. Grammich, *Police Recruitment and Retention in the Contemporary Urban Environment: A National Discussion of Personnel Experiences and Promising Practices from the Front Lines*, Santa Monica, Calif.: RAND Corporation, CF-261-DOJ, 2009a. As of June 24, 2010: http://www.rand.org/pubs/conf_proceedings/CF261/

Woska, William J., "Police Officer Recruitment: A Public-Sector Crisis," *Police Chief*, Vol. 73, No. 10, October 2006, pp. 52–59.

Yearwood, Douglas L., *Recruitment and Retention Study Series: Sworn Sheriffs' Personnel*, Raleigh, N.C.: North Carolina Sheriffs' Education and Training Standards Commission, April 2003. As of June 24, 2010: http://www.ncgccd.org/PDFs/Pubs/NCCJAC/rrsheriff.pdf

Discuss the evolution of the treatment experienced by minority group members and women in policing in the United States.

1. Is the current treatment of women in law enforcement fair and impartial?

2. How does history influence the current treatment and perspectives of female and minority officers or agents? How can departments and agencies, in a fair and legal manner, proactively recruit more female and minority law enforcement officers?

3. Should departments and agencies recruit more female and minority law enforcement officers? Why or why not? What are bona fide occupational qualifications (BFOQs) and how do they apply to women in law enforcement? You should support any opinions with scholarly sources that are cited in proper American Psychological Association format.

Chapter 2

Ethics and Integrity in Law Enforcement

SOUTHERN ILLINOIS
PUBLIC CORRUPTION
TASK FORCE

U.S. ATTORNEY'S OFFICE

FBI

STATE'S ATTORNEY'S OFFICE

Tip Line 1-618-589-7353

FIGURE 2.1 Law enforcement organizations have internal accountability systems, like the Southern District of Illinois US Department of Justice, to deal with police misconduct and corruption. These systems are available to the public.

INTRODUCTION

In this chapter, we will discuss the importance of ethics in the law enforcement profession. Police officers and other law enforcement officials are delegated tremendous legal authority by our governments and often broad discretion to implement that legal authority. We will explore the inherent problems of corruption and abuse of authority in law enforcement that can result from that discretion. Law enforcement officials are held to a higher standard than the general public. It is important for us to understand the training and management systems in place to address any cases of misconduct and to instill a culture of ethical behavior in law enforcement. We will identify and describe various organizational strategies that can be used to mitigate unethical police conduct and identify specific examples of police corruption. The term *ethics* can be defined as moral principles that govern a person's behavior or the conduct of any activity. Ethical people have *integrity*, which is the quality of being honest and having strong moral principles. We will see how ethics and integrity are important traits for everyone in a law enforcement position.

We will also examine relative or situational ethics. While there are some ethical dilemmas that are dependent on situations, ethics in law enforcement are usually static regardless of the situation. The lack of ethics or the use of ethics that are dynamic and based on the relative situation can result in corruption. Sometimes even well-meaning law enforcement officers can be susceptible to corruption. Some officers may violate rules, policy, or even laws to create what appears to be a beneficial outcome. This is usually referred to as *noble cause corruption*. We will discuss this in more detail in this chapter. Any law enforcement officer misconduct, including ethical violations and corruption, are investigated by an internal affairs organization. This is an important accountability process that we will study in this chapter.

Figure Credit

Fig. 2.1: Source: https://www.justice.gov/sites/default/files/fieldable-panel-panes/image-panes/images/2017/05/08/public_corruption_task_force.jpg .

Reading 2.1

Organizational Ethics

Arthur Wiechmann

Topics

- Values
- Ethics
- Ethical Relativism
- Integrity
- Principle versus Preference
- Ethical Problems in Law Enforcement

Introduction

Police organizations and their employees are held to a higher ethical standard than are private organizations and their employees. But most police departments have not undertaken active programs to promote an ethical work environment. Management expects employees to behave in an ethical manner, but they do not take steps to develop this.

By their very nature and structure, many large bureaucracies tend to promote unethical and dishonest behavior. Many workers find themselves feeling they must compromise their ethical standards to fit in or to be successful:

- **Fitting in:** In a police subculture, some officers are verbally abusive to suspects, so a new officer does the same.

- **Being successful:** In a police department, if there is pressure by a supervisor to make drug arrests, an officer may invent probable cause to make vehicle stops that can lead to these arrests.

Many dynamics are involved: wanting to fit in, but also wanting to do the right thing. So, ethics can be very personal, but in this [reading] we will also look at ethics from an organizational perspective. Personal and organizational ethics can sometimes conflict, but they must be congruent. For instance, if an officer has to be unethical to get ahead in the department, the ethics of the officer and the ethics of the department are not congruent.

Example: Everyone is getting along fairly well in an organization. Then comes an announcement that there is going to be a testing process for promotion. Suddenly, a false rumor surfaces about a candidate who is a frontrunner for promotion. Rather than the organization ignoring or quashing the rumor, they perpetuate the process by conducting an investigation on the candidate. The candidate, to save himself, creates rumors about the other candidates, to take the heat off of him and spread it around a little.

Many terms and concepts are associated with organizational ethics. Understanding them will provide a good introduction into the subject.

Values

Values are the things that are important to the individual, the things that motivate them. Values are a person's *enduring preferences*, and they are the beliefs that guide the person's behavior. Values include such things as relationships, money, success, honesty, appearance, and health, just to name a few.

Values vary between social classes. Criminal justice personnel generally have middle-class values, which are conservative. *Conflicts can develop when these values are pushed onto those who have different values.* Research has even shown that there is a link between hostile, even prejudiced activity, and conflicts in value systems.

Example: A police officer may be so disgusted by a homeless person's lifestyle or by someone on welfare that it may lead to an insensitive or hostile confrontation.

So, personnel must make a conscious effort to maintain a neutral stance on imposing their values onto others, which could lead to a negative encounter. The goal of this effort is providing unbiased and fair treatment of all people.

Values are developed during a person's formative years, but they can change as time goes by. People choose their values and prioritize them.

Example: A teenager smokes pot, hangs out with his friends, and takes advantage of his parents. But as he gets older, his values change; he gets a job, cleans up his habits, and helps out his family.

Example: A young man enjoys the company of different women. He always has something going, and gains a reputation as a player. As he gets older, he no longer values the next conquest, but rather wants to settle down with one woman and have a family.

Many work-related problems are the result of value conflicts. Managers must be aware of their values and the values of others. A good manager will realize that his values may not be the same as those he manages and will take steps to prevent conflict.

> **Example:** A supervisor does not get promoted into that position by accident; it is because he values success and achievement and has worked hard to get that position. The supervisor has an employee who has no aspirations of supervision or management; he is one of those people who just wants to do the job they were hired for and go home at the end of the day. (And there is nothing wrong with that; there are not enough positions at the top of the hierarchy for everyone anyway. Organizations need people like this.)
>
> But this supervisor, who values success and achievement highly, views this employee as being lazy and lacking motivation, rather than having different values. If this supervisor fails to recognize the distinction, the relationship between him and this employee will suffer, and undoubtedly lead to poor performance by the employee who is now encountering a hostile work environment.

> **Example:** [... T]he emerging workforce culture values recreation time, which makes alternative scheduling so desirable to them. The older workers, many of them supervisors to the younger ones, did not have it as well in their day; they worked five days a week and were not allowed to use vacation time except once a year.
>
> These new employees are constantly asking for vacation time off, even when they have three or four days off every week. An old school supervisor, who is not aware of changing values from generation to generation, may take a very negative approach to these requests, resulting in hostility between supervision and employees.

So, it is very important for managers and supervisors to recognize that these differences can lead to conflict in the organization. If there is a conflict, it will likely result in a negative outcome for the organization. (In the above example, if the employee is not allowed to take a vacation day because the supervisor does not think he needs it, the employee will most likely just call in sick.)

Ethics

Ethics are the rules that ought to govern human behavior. There are not a lot of them: honesty, truth, the Golden Rule, hard work, equality, justice. These are the things that we know are right. Ethics involves a process of clarifying what is right and wrong, and acting on what is right.

The real concern about ethics is not in what one does value, but what one should value. Our ethics do not change. We have a choice about following them, which is a choice about who we are.

Remember, *it is our values that guide us, not our ethics.* Ethics are the "rules" that we are supposed to follow, but that does not mean that we follow them.

> **Example:** A thief knows that it is wrong to steal (ethic), but he has a stronger personal value which creates this choice to be a thief (easy money).

So, knowing the right course of action does not necessarily mean that an individual will follow it. But true leadership instills a desire in others to be ethical. A true leader does this through leading by example.

An ethical person has values that are congruent with ethical standards; they know what the right thing is, and they do it.

Police organizations are very concerned that the employees they hire have high ethical standards. One way to assess for ethical standards is by conducting a background investigation on candidates. The purpose of this investigation is to determine if the candidate has led an ethical life. This is done by examining the candidate's *pattern of behavior.*

> **Example:** A candidate was arrested for shoplifting when he was 14, but there have been no other similar incidents. Therefore, this would not be a pattern of behavior that the investigator would be concerned about.
>
> However, if the candidate was also terminated from a job when he was 16 for stealing the petty cash and a neighbor tells the investigator that at age 18 the candidate went joyriding in his car, this would be a pattern of unethical conduct that would be of concern.

Another step that police departments take to determine the ethical standards of potential employees occurs during the oral interview process. Generally, a scenario-type question is posed to the candidate, geared toward determining what the candidate values as higher, honesty or loyalty (maintaining membership in the informal group versus telling the truth).

The question will be along the lines of a fellow employee (with seniority and in good standing with the organization) doing something obviously wrong or illegal. The candidate is asked to explain what he will do about it.

Many times, the value of loyalty is so strong that the candidate actually does not know the right answer to the question. He values loyalty so highly that he assumes the organization does, too. Often, the candidate with this conflict will dance around the issue, and usually stop short of actually reporting it to a supervisor. Unfortunately for this candidate, he has shown the interview panel that to him there is a gray area when it comes to honesty.

Ethical Relativism

Ethical relativism is the belief that some actions are moral in some circumstances and immoral in others; that is, that they are *relative to the situation*. According to this approach to ethics, there is no absolute right or wrong and no universal rules of conduct.

An example of ethical relativism is *utilitarianism*. According to this concept, an action is right, compared to other actions, if the result is the greater good for the greatest number of people.

> **Example:** Here is a scenario commonly used to stimulate discussion in ethics workshops: five people are on a life raft, and there is only enough food and water for four. If the group kills one person, the rest will live; otherwise, everyone will die. The question is: Would it be ethical to kill someone in this situation?

You can take this even further. What if it is a family of five? Most people would rather face death than live the rest of their lives knowing they had killed a family member so that they could live. But what if none of the people on the boat knew each other? What if one of them was as escaped child molester, who was already injured, and would probably die in a few days anyway?

Many public-sector decisions are based on this approach, such as fund allocations. Other decisions that can have a negative effect on some people are also based on utilitarianism, such as a decision to put a freeway through a neighborhood, causing many families to be displaced.

Another area of management, the disciplinary process, is based on the concept of utilitarianism. When a supervisor or manager is considering discipline for an employee, a guideline that is followed is, "The good of the organization must supersede the good of the individual." What this means is that although the discipline hurts the employee, maintaining discipline benefits the organization.

Integrity

An ethical person has *integrity*. A person with integrity consistently follows an ethical standard that does not compromise his values, because his values are ethical ones. If someone does the right thing only because they are afraid of being caught, that is not integrity.

Principle Versus Preference

Organizations lose effectiveness when preference is chosen over principle when making decisions. Preference is the imposition of personal values over doing what is right. Often, this occurs because it is easier, safer, or because of personal benefit or satisfaction.

This conflict between principle (doing the right thing) and preference (doing what you want to do) happens a lot when employees have to follow orders. Line-level employees have often been faced with dilemmas involving individual morality versus obedience and loyalty. It is common for employees to succumb to this pressure because it is easier to just follow orders than to be personally accountable for actions.

> **Example:** During the Vietnam War, the My Lai incident involved soldiers killing innocent civilians because they were ordered to. During World War II, Nazi soldiers facing war crime charges said they were just following orders. In both instances, soldiers had to commit crimes disguised as orders or face a potential firing squad for insubordination during wartime.

So, we can either *excuse* the individual from personal moral decisions when they are following orders or we can *condemn* the behavior in support of *disobedience* of laws or orders that conflict with ethical principles.

These are difficult positions for employees. They raise difficult questions: Where does personal accountability begin? Is this accountability absolute, or is someone absolved if they are following orders?

> **Example:** A police sergeant is dealing with a belligerent subject outside of a bar. The sergeant orders an officer to arrest the subject for being intoxicated even though he is not.
>
> If the officer makes the arrest, he is committing an act completely contrary to the standards he has sworn to uphold. If he refuses, the sergeant will make his work life miserable, because if this sergeant is unethical enough to order an unlawful arrest, he is likely unethical enough to retaliate against this officer for his lack of loyalty.

These are the most difficult choices people must make in their careers, choosing personal values that conflict with colleagues or supervisors, which could lead to complete alienation from the work subculture. To add to this difficulty, organizations do not create an atmosphere that helps people to make the right choice.

Ethical Problems in Law Enforcement

No other occupation possesses greater control over personal destiny than law enforcement officers, because of the elements of *authority*, use of *physical force*, and *discretion* inherent in the job. Unethical behavior in the field of law enforcement is usually an abuse of one of those three elements:

- **Authority:** This refers to the authority that police officers have to detain and arrest people. Officers have the ability to control others due to their position. Even when officers obtain consent from people to talk to them (consensual encounters), most people are too intimidated by the uniform to refuse. An abuse of authority amounts to a violation of individual rights.

- **Physical force:** This refers to the use of physical control granted by law to affect arrests, prevent escape, and overcome resistance. Abuse of physical force takes the form of excessive use of force. This occurs when an officer uses more force than is reasonable for the level of resistance that he is encountering.

- **Discretionary power:** This refers to the ability to choose between two or more courses of action, with none of the alternatives potentially being wrong. This is the power that officers have when they decide when and how to enforce laws, how to handle disputes, and how much and what kind of force to use.

Discretion differs from standard decision making, because decision making generally is making a choice between almost right and probably wrong, whereas discretion is choosing between a right course of action and another right course of action. *Abuse of discretion occurs when an officer bases his behavior or actions on personal feelings or prejudice rather than doing what is right.*

There is a potential for abuse in such a volatile and dynamic occupation that requires critical and immediate decision making. Officers must remain calm in hostile and dangerous situations without succumbing to the temptation to abuse these elements of authority, force, and discretion. Because of this, the selection process for police officers is exhaustive because it is so important to hire people who will not abuse their position.

During the testing process, the oral interview will generally contain an "ethical dilemma" question, which will give the interview panel clues as to whether this candidate will uphold the ethics of the organization, or whether he will weaken under pressure or frustration.

Conclusion

None of us are perfect. Sometimes we will choose what we know is not right, because of immediate rewards, convenience, or lack of courage. That just makes us human. But, when we choose that course of action consistently, where it becomes a "pattern of behavior," we choose to be unethical.

Law Enforcement Ethics 101

Howell Wright

Why Study Ethics?

Most law abiding people consider themselves moral beings, and when asked if they feel they are ethical, the overwhelming answer will be yes. In law enforcement, we often define ourselves as moral and ethical and the bad guys as amoral and unethical. This makes for an easy distinction between good and bad. It is as if the good-guy group has either been annointed by God or simply had a superior upbringing by knowledgeable, loving, and enlightened parents. In either case, the thought is instilled in us that we are truly ethical.

I have had the opportunity to arrange ethics programs in federal government (don't laugh), and private organizations. In each case, when I conducted a needs assessment in preparation for designing an organizationally specific program, I interviewed both employees and managers. Frequently, conversations included statements such as, "I don't need anyone to try and make me ethical because I am already ethical" or "Do you really think you can make someone ethical? If they aren't ethical by now, they are not going to get that way in a classroom." Actually, there is an element of truth in both of these statements.

The problem is that most of us <u>feel</u> we are ethical—we just have not thought through <u>why</u> we are ethical or even what being ethical means. This places our ethics at a very superficial or conversational level and not at a deeply understood emotional level. Let's play this out a bit. Could we approach firearms training only from a classroom perspective? Even if we give you the best firearms training in the world, could you accept the fact that we would teach it once and never retrain? The answer to both of these situations is obviously NO. We know that training someone when and how to use a service weapon is an involved process, and that the skills obtained are perishable. Consequently we train hard and periodically retrain just as hard. Mastering the use of a firearm in a tactical situation not only involves physical skill; it is a thinking/decision-making game.

Now consider the topic of ethics. Because we already feel we are ethical, there is very little interest in even thinking about the topic. It is part of our every day rhetoric but not our everyday thinking. However, the one thing that we do every day is make decisions, even more often than we fire our weapons, practice arrest control, or drive rapidly. Many of the decisions we make are moral decisions with no obvious right or wrong answer. They can be emotionally charged, gut wrenching decisions, and if we do not have a strong, practiced ethical platform we are less likely to make good decisions on a consistent basis. The bottom line is that, if we want to be prepared to make good decisions either considered or in the blink of an eye, we must learn and practice an ethical decision-making process.

What is Ethics

Before we can make ethical decision-making part of our lives, we must understand the terminology and basic concepts that make up ethics as a field of study. We can start with a concept called the "worldview."

Worldview is the lens that people use to interpret their reality and assign meaning to events, experiences, and relationships in their world. Basically, it represents a person's beliefs and assumptions about how the world fits together. On a cultural level, it is the accumulation of beliefs, ideologies, and knowledge maintained by people that helps define an overall perspective on life for members of that culture. For many of us, our worldview directs our lives because we simply respond to situations based on what we learned growing up. Worldviews change and sometimes not for the better. A simple test here would be for those of you old enough to remember Rhett Butler in the movie *Gone With the Wind* saying "I don't give a damn." Consider that phrase, which was considered scandalous in the day, to what is on TV screens today. It was not long ago that the most hardened criminal would hesitate to fire at a peace officer. Today, it is becoming a right of passage for some groups. In America our world view has changed. We may not like to think about it, but it has. Only when we begin to challenge our thinking can we begin to truly understand why our worldview is what it is.

Morals and Ethics. Most people use the terms morality and ethics interchangeably. Many philosophers, however, infer that morality refers to the actual content of right and wrong, and ethics refers to the process of determining right and wrong. Another way of considering these terms is that morality refers to the standards of behavior that should be followed by everyone. Ethics, on the other hand, is concerned with how individuals should conduct themselves. Still another way of looking at these terms is that morality is the end result of ethical deliberation, the substance of right and wrong, and ethics is the study of choices people make concerning right and wrong. Being ethical means doing the "right thing." The focus of ethics is on behavior involving human values which are those qualities that are considered good and desirable.

One way of describing a person as being ethical is, "If no one is watching, will they to do the right thing?" Being an ethical being is not always easy and it can, in fact, cost a person dearly.

An **ethical dilemma** is a problem that forces a decision between two ethical values. Technically, there can be no dilemma if one option is right and one is wrong. You must always go with what is right. We have laws, rules, and policies that help define right and wrong but, unless we have a strong ethical and moral foundation, we have nothing that helps us resolve an ethical dilemma. A typical scenario that is discussed in ethics classes which covers this situation is, "Does one kill a person in order to save ten?"

Normative ethics is the study of what is reasonable and thus what people should think. **Metaethics** is the study of ethical systems and how they are formed and to what degree they have internal consistency. I mention these two terms because it is important to realize that there are ten or more ethical systems that have significant followings around the world. Several systems have religious underpinnings and are built on the idea that who we are comes from God. Other systems are based on cultural parameters. It is important for philosophers and ethicists to identify the definitions and origins of ethics. It is also important for each of us to study their work because it does help discover how we think. Metaethics can easily become a life's study. For most of us in law enforcement, normative ethics is a more practical approach.

A **belief system** is what one accepts as truth. Values are based on one's beliefs; as we attach meaning to our values, we can interpret the way we live. We think based on values, beliefs, and our world view. All values are not necessarily ethical values. You can have ethical, unethical, or non-ethical values. The fact that you may really want to drive a Cadillac and you really admire those who do is a value but it is not ethical or unethical. The realization that not all values are ethical or unethical is important when you begin to analyze what first appear to be ethical situations.

Character is an ethical trait that is expressed in our outward behavior and can best be defined as the motivation to do what is right. Character is expressed in countless behavioral qualities many of which cut across cultures. Unfortunately, many of us are morally weak and, even knowing the right thing to do, will not guarantee that we will choose the right course of action. Character involves the courage and conviction to make difficult and unpopular decisions.

Integrity is often placed, by some authors, as a trait under the umbrella of character. I, however, place it on equal footing with character because I define integrity as the glue that binds the qualities of character together. If you are a person of integrity the qualities of character become integral, not just to certain parts of your life, but to all parts of your life—both public and private.

I have emphasized the above terms both because they are the ones most often used, but also because they are the ones that are most often used without a clear understanding of their meaning. Without a basic understanding of terminology, it is not likely that we will ever be able to foster ethical thinking.

Looking Through the Gaps: A Critical Approach to the LAPD's Rampart Scandal

Paul J. Kaplan

Introduction

The Los Angeles Police Department's (LAPD) Rampart Scandal of the late-1990s involved allegations of outrageous misconduct, led to the overturning of over 100 criminal convictions and resulted in the firing or resignations of nearly 20 officers, several of whom were convicted of criminal charges (Burcham, 2001). The cost to the city of Los Angeles has been estimated to be as high as one billion dollars (Pomerantz, 2000),[1] and the LAPD is currently under federal oversight from the Department of Justice (*pbs.org*, 2007). The Rampart Scandal raises serious questions about the Los Angeles justice system at many levels. In light of recent allegations of brutality by the LAPD,[2] it is important to understand what happened in Rampart in the 1990s. Unfortunately, no entity has systematically investigated the alleged misconduct at the heart of the Rampart Scandal (although the Los Angeles District Attorney's office has investigated a few allegations). Instead, justice system investigators have analyzed the LAPD organization in an attempt to discover organizational problems that may have contributed to a context for misconduct. These efforts address only a few incidents and leave open questions about the type, frequency, and causes of misconduct in the LAPD.

In this vacuum of knowledge, the LAPD developed a version of the story suggesting that a very small group of Black and Hispanic officers were responsible for all of the misconduct (LAPD, 2000). This familiar "bad apples" framing contradicted whistleblower Rafael Perez's[3] version of the story, which described widespread misconduct. Perez claimed that a large number of officers were "in the loop," meaning they regularly planted evidence, manufactured probable cause, beat citizens, and generally abused citizens' due-process rights.

Which version of the story is correct? It is impossible to say because neither version can be confirmed with publicly available information. Nevertheless, evidence suggests that there are elements of truth in both versions of the story. It seems clear that something like a "loop" exists within the LAPD,[4] and it is obvious that Rafael Perez, and at least a few of his officer friends, were "bad apples."

What are we to make of this explanatory stalemate? Considering the LAPD's history of scandals, and the failure of previous reforms to prevent misconduct, it might make sense to try to develop some ideas that go beyond the "bad apples" or the "rotten barrel." My goal is to suggest critical lines of inquiry that have been ignored by official investigators and media commentators so far. Specifically, I hope to draw attention away from individualist or organizational approaches to the LAPD's troubles, and toward an approach attending to the justice system institution. Specifically, I propose two alternative causal factors: (1) the ideological "war on crime," and (2) the privileged position of police narratives in criminal trials. These factors operate both within and outside the police organization, and illuminate the influence of racist and essentialist ideological discourse on the patterns and practices of justice system organizations and the individuals who constitute them. Police misconduct influenced by these factors cannot be addressed through organizational reforms unless those reforms reflect larger-scale changes in discourses about the justice system institution.

One way to discover factors such as "the war on crime" and "privileged police narratives" is to look for their absence in official analyses and media representations of the scandal. This method seems counter-intuitive—"looking for an absence"—but if we theoretically contextualize the roles and apparatuses that produce the mainstream discourse on Rampart, we can see how ideology operates to foreground individual (and to a lesser extent, organizational) level analyses at the expense of institutional-level analyses. This foregrounding is evident in the official and media representations that lay the blame for Rampart on the bad character of Rafael Perez and a few other Black and Hispanic officers. This framing occurs, I argue, because media apparatuses operate from a similar ideological location vis-à-vis the justice system as official apparatuses such as the police department and police commission. That is, due to their similar ideological position in society's power relations, both official and media accounts of Rampart focus on individual (and to a lesser extent, organizational) factors and thus *preclude* inquiry into factors at the institutional level. This prevents a deep critique of racist and essentialist ideologies that permeate the justice system. Ultimately, it hinders deep change in the LAPD organization, resulting perhaps in more misconduct and scandal. Indeed, the events in MacArthur Park on May Day of 2007 indicate it may already have.[5]

Methods and Sources

This research is an interpretive analysis of official and media documents, including: LAPD Board of Inquiry and Police Commission Reports on Rampart, LAPD Board of Rights Hearings, Law Professor Erwin Chemerinsky's independent analysis of the LAPD Board of Inquiry Report, Rafael Perez statement transcripts, *People* v. *Perez* trial transcripts, transcripts of

Secret Grand Jury hearings investigating allegations of misconduct, and various Rampart-related legal pleadings (e.g., police union lawsuits against the LAPD).

As for the media, I focus specifically on Rampart articles in *Rolling Stone* (Sullivan, 2001) and *The New Yorker* (Boyer, 2001). I chose these, rather than broadcast or daily newspaper accounts, because each magazine produced a totalizing story about the scandal, purporting to be authoritative on the topic. This is important because although the *Los Angeles Times* produced dozens of articles covering the Rampart Scandal, the paper did not produce a *narrative* of the scandal. Put another way, the *Los Angeles Times* coverage of the scandal is *discursive*, while the *New Yorker* and *Rolling Stone* versions of the scandal are *narrative*. The former coverage is a scattershot pastiche of information related to the scandal, while the latter stories each have a narrative structure. This article is thus a form of narrative analysis, relying on an understanding of what Bruner (1991: 1) calls the "narrative construction of reality," meaning the human process of interpreting experience through the structural conventions of narrative. Invoking narratologists such as Roland Barthes and Hayden White, Ewick and Silbey (1995: 199) point to narrative's constitutive function in human reality as evidence of the epistemological advantages of narrative analysis:

> It is argued that narratives have the capacity to reveal truths about the social world that are flattened or silenced by an insistence on more traditional methods of social science and legal scholarship. According to this view, social identities and social action, indeed all aspects of the social world, are storied. Consequently, narrative is not just a form that is imposed upon social life ... [but is] constitutive of that which it represents. To attempt to examine lives, experiences, consciousnesses, or action outside of the narratives that constitute them, it is argued, is to distort through abstraction and decontextualization, depriving events and persons of meaning.

If the reality of the Rampart Scandal is being constructed through narratives, it is my goal to analyze those narratives. Thus, this is not an investigation into causes of police misconduct or the Rampart Scandal. Rather, it is an interpretive, critical analysis of the major accounts of the scandal.

A Sketch of the Rampart Scandal

The origin of the Rampart Scandal can probably be traced to the arrest of LAPD Officer David Mack in December 1997 for bank robbery. Mack was a veteran LAPD officer who convinced a girlfriend who worked at a bank in Los Angeles to help him rob over $700,000 in November

1996 (Boyer, 2001). When he was arrested the next year, he refused to cooperate with the LAPD (*Ibid.*). As investigators looked into the case, they learned that Mack had gone to Las Vegas for a weekend two days after the robbery with two friends on the police force: Rafael Perez and Sammy Martin (*Ibid.*). When investigators interviewed Perez, he claimed Mack told him nothing about the bank robbery (Perez, 1999), but the suspicions of LAPD investigators were raised. Investigators focused on Perez when in March 1998 three kilograms of cocaine were checked out of the LAPD's evidence storage office and never returned (Boyer, 2001). In August 1998, Perez was arrested and charged with several felonies, including possession of cocaine for sale, grand theft, and forgery (Cannon, 2000). Perez was later tried in a criminal case that resulted in a hung jury. When the prosecution came up with more evidence for a second trial, Perez agreed to a plea agreement.

The ensuing discourse between Perez and Assistant District Attorney Richard Rosenthal (as well as several LAPD detectives) spawned what has become known as the Rampart Scandal. According to Rosenthal, he anticipated that Perez was going to discuss various sensational unsolved crimes (including the murder of rap star Biggie Smalls) that officials believed were associated with David Mack and other friends of Perez (Boyer, 2001). But Perez surprised the authorities by denying any knowledge of his friends' misconduct, instead describing widespread LAPD corruption and due process abuses against civilians. According to Perez, many officers in special units such as Rampart CRASH ("Community Resources Against Street Hoodlums") were corrupt; at the least, many officers regularly manufactured probable cause, and some regularly beat citizens, planted evidence, and perjured themselves. In the rambling discussions spanning from September 1999 to July 2000, Perez repeatedly referred to an understanding among officers called "being in the loop," which describes a willingness to participate in, or condone, misconduct. For Perez, being in the loop was essential to success as a CRASH officer. Officers in the loop were "solid," while those who were not could not be trusted and were described as "weak links" (Perez, 1999).

In all, Perez named 70 LAPD officers that he claimed were in the loop. The most common type of misconduct was apparently the regular fabrication of probable cause to arrest suspects. The unspoken sentiment of officers appeared to be that most of the people they encountered were actually guilty of something, even if they happened to be innocent in a particular encounter—a "we may be framing, but we're framing the guilty" attitude. Beyond fabricating probable cause, Perez's primary accusation was of planting evidence to obtain arrests or to justify officer-involved shootings. According to Perez, this practice was so deeply embedded in CRASH culture that new officers were trained to hide misconduct from superiors (*Ibid.*).

In addition to his story about the loop generally, Perez delineated several incidents in which he directly participated. Two of these became sensational: his theft of cocaine from the LAPD property office and his participation in an illegal shooting of an unarmed alleged gang member, Javier Ovando. The missing cocaine ultimately resulted in Perez's arrest, and the LAPD eventually connected him to approximately eight pounds of missing cocaine from previous thefts (Boyer, 2001). The Ovando shooting, in which Perez and his partner Nino Durden shot and seriously wounded the unarmed man, did not result in a criminal conviction for Perez, but the city of Los Angeles settled a civil suit with Ovando for several million dollars (*Ibid.*).

From the beginning, then, the Rampart Scandal was a story about outrageous criminal acts by at least three officers, as well as a culture wherein corruption and abuse were commonplace. How should we interpret this story? Rather than taking Rafael Perez at his word, or deciding that official or media accounts represent "the truth," we might benefit by theoretically contextualizing the ideological position of the producers of these accounts and identifying lacunae in them. By "looking through the gaps" in these accounts, we can raise the possibility of alternative sources of misconduct that go deeper than the bad character of individuals or organizations.

Official Accounts

There are two major official accounts of the Rampart Scandal, the LAPD's (2000) *Board of Inquiry into the Rampart Area Corruption Incident*, and the Independent Review Panel of the Los Angeles Police Commission's (2000) *Report of the Rampart Independent Review Panel.*[6] Each is a lengthy, detailed report compiled by an impressive team of dedicated professionals. In essence, the LAPD report frames the cause of the scandal as the bad character of a small group of Black and Hispanic officers who should never have been hired by the department, while the Police Commission report locates the cause of the scandal in a variety of LAPD organizational problems.

The LAPD Board of Inquiry Report

The word "Incident" in the title of the LAPD's official response to the Rampart Scandal reveals the Board of Inquiry's contention that the alleged misconduct was isolated and aberrational. In the discourse, the only voice to describe the Rampart Scandal as an "incident" is the LAPD leadership. This perspective makes it more logical to narrow the focus of blame to a few individuals, which is precisely how the LAPD framed the scandal. In its conclusion, the Board of Inquire declares: "After careful consideration of the information developed during the Board of Inquiry's work, it is the Board's view that the Rampart corruption occurred because a few individuals decided to engage in blatant misconduct and, in some cases, criminal behavior" (LAPD, 2000: 331).

This perspective pervades the report and is made clear from the beginning with an extensive focus on the organization's failure to screen out the "bad apples." For example, the report declares "of the 14 officers [Perez and 13 others the LAPD decided to scrutinize], four had questionable issues in their pre-employment background which strongly indicate they never should have been hired as Los Angeles Police Officers" (*Ibid.*: 9). This failure is blamed on bureaucratic problems and pressures to hire more officers. This view is essential to the LAPD's fundamental argument that misconduct is not consistent with their standards:

> The fact that these men were hired with egregious information in their packages leaves only two explanations: 1) Recognize that erosion has occurred and shore up the systems to prevent it from recurring; or, 2) Insist that the application of our standards did not erode, which means that criminal conduct, drug dealing, financial irresponsibility and violent behavior are consistent with our standards. Clearly there has been erosion ... (*Ibid.*: 14).

Considering Rafael Perez's allegations, as well as verifiable evidence (see [en.]. 2) in support of the "loop" explanation, one might argue that the second explanation is at least as plausible as the first. The LAPD's frame exhibits a dissatisfying circular logic: "eroded hiring policies lead to the scandal because eroded hiring policies is the only acceptable explanation."[7]

In any case, the bottom line for the LAPD is that Rampart was caused by the misbehavior of a few individuals who should never have been hired. The implication of this frame is that the problem lies outside the LAPD organization and within the character of certain types of individuals. The policy solution is thus simply to prevent such individuals from entering the organization. This is a classically *individual*-level analysis.[8]

The Rampart Independent Review Panel (RIRP) Report

The LAPD police union's response to the LAPD Board of Inquiry Report was to ask Law Professor Erwin Chemerinsky to analyze the report in detail. The result was a scathing critique that pointed to the LAPD's bias and failure to address organizational and cultural problems (see Chemerinsky, 2000: 5). Since Chemerinsky's role was simply to analyze the LAPD report and not the scandal generally, he suggested the formation of an independent review panel to conduct a comprehensive investigation, along the lines of the Christopher Commission after the Rodney King beating.

The subsequent Police Commission's Independent Panel was comprised of many dozens of attorneys, advisors, and investigators who interviewed a great many people involved with criminal justice in Los Angeles, including LAPD officers, police commissioners, attorneys, and community leaders. The result was an extensive description of organizational problems in the LAPD, delineated into several problematic domains: civilian oversight, ethics, culture and community policing, community outreach and relations, discipline, officer-involved shootings and other uses of force, risk management, personnel, and specialized units (see Chemerinsky, 2000, Appendix 1: 1–6).

Taking one of these categories as an example, we can see how the LAPD's technique of investigating officer-involved shootings (OIS) creates barriers to detecting and investigating misconduct. According to the report, the LAPD's method is flawed in a number of ways, including the practice of conducting "run-throughs" with field supervisors before the appearance of investigators from Internal Affairs. Essentially, the LAPD's practice is for Robbery Homicide Division (RHD) officers to arrive at the scene of a shooting before any other authority and conduct a preliminary investigation. According to the report, these investigations are often lax and fail to treat these shootings as potential criminal matters. This is exacerbated by one of the great peculiarities in California's criminal justice system: the effects of *Lybarger* v. *City of Los Angeles* (1985). As the RIRP describes it:

> Under the California Supreme Court's decision in *Lybarger* v. *City of Los Angeles,* police officers may be threatened with dismissal for refusing to provide statements about the conduct of their official duties to supervisors or internal investigators. But a statement given after such a warning—colloquially known as a *Lybarger* admonition—is inadmissible in any criminal prosecution of the officer, as is evidence that investigators obtain through use of the statement (p. 112).

Obviously, then, anything an officer says during the investigation of a shooting can result in nothing more than his dismissal. Although administrative action is a serious deterrent, it is not as serious as the prospect of criminal prosecution for murder. Of course, it may appear that *Lybarger* admonitions would induce officers to "spill the beans" immediately so as to inoculate themselves against criminal actions. According to the RIRP, however, the actual result is usually an ineffective interview of the officer by an attorney from the police union, consisting of leading questions such as "You feared for your life, right?" (p. 117).

Another problematic mechanism in the LAPD's OIS policy is that the initial discussions between RHD investigators and the involved officers are not documented in any way; no recordings or even notes are made of these "pre-interview walk-throughs." The potential for error or blatant misconduct is obvious enough, as the RIRP acknowledges in its lengthy criticism of this area of LAPD policy (see p. 118). However, according to Rafael Perez, even stringent oversight after OIS incidents may not have prevented some of the misconduct in Rampart (although such improvements may have made it easier to detect it). In the following discussion, Perez describes what transpired after the Ovando shooting:

Q: Okay. So, Officer Durden takes the rag, drops the gun next to the body. … At that point, you call for your C.R.A.S.H. officers, you call for the rescue ambulance. What happens then?
A: Uh, myself, Durden, Rios, Montoya, and Ortiz, we—again, we sent somebody out to be a—a diversionary person out in the front. Because there is some people that—that either worked C.R.A.S.H. before, or have some insight that once we use certain codes, and you hear, you know, requesting an R.A. at 1209, they know something's gonna be up. So, we don't want other officers coming in.

Q: Okay.
A: And we set up—or we send an officer, get at the front door, if somebody wants to come in—I don't care if it's the Captain, you tell him that we're a building search, there could be possible suspects still around, whatever. The reason we do that is, so that we can sit there and discuss what happened, how it happened, what occurred—everything that needs to be explained.

Q: When you met with Ortiz, Montoya, and Rios, did Ortiz and Montoya and Rios know that Durden had planted the gun on the suspect?
A: No.

Q: So, you and—and Durden had told them he had this—this is the gun. He had the gun.
A: Yes.

Q: Okay. And did you and Durden have any conversations prior to Ortiz, Montoya, and Rios showing up?
A: Yes, we did.

Q: And what were your conversations?
A: Exactly what they were, I don't remember. I do know one thing that we never discussed is how it all went down. You know what I mean, how, uh, you know, you sort of don't even want to talk about it amongst yourselves. You know what I mean. It's—it happened. And, you know, you look at each other like, okay. You just need to fix this. You know, it's—it's one of those things where you don't go, man, we just shot a guy who was unarmed. You don't discuss that. You know, you say, okay, well, let's get this straightened-out. Let's fix this.

Q: Okay. And then, later in a separate interview, you would have said what he said?

A: And—and, right. And, you know, how they send you back to the station. You're supposed to sit in separate rooms. And when you go back, they sit you in the same room and you discuss it more, talk about it more, get your story straight more, or whatever. That's what happens (Perez, 1999, Vol. 1: 70–72).

By this account, obviously, even a careful intervention by Internal Affairs investigators immediately after the incident probably would not have uncovered the gun planting. However, since Perez contended that he and Durden were not separated for interviews properly, adherence to at least one official policy may have lead to detection. The implication here is twofold: first, some officers successfully circumvented OIS policies, and second, supervisors did not follow OIS policies. In any event, it appears that the LAPD OIS policies are significantly flawed.

All in all, the RIRP refutes the LAPD's framing of the scandal's cause as the bad character of a few individuals who slipped through the screening process, and instead frames the scandal as the result of a long list of organizational problems. The policy implication is that the LAPD could prevent misconduct by instituting a number of bureaucratic changes. In this sense, the RIRP is similar to previous analyses of the LAPD (such as the Christopher Commission) that listed organizational sources of misconduct and proposed LAPD policy changes intended to eliminate or minimize these problems. In this frame, then, the source of the problem is the *organization* (not the individual).

Both the LAPD Board of Inquiry Report and the RIRP succeed in identifying important causal factors related to Rampart. It is undeniable that individual and organizational problems are related to misconduct, but neither report accounts well for *why* these types of problems have come into existence. This is because these accounts begin from the position that the police and the justice system "do" justice, but that sometimes "bad" people or bureaucratic structures contradict the system's "just" project. Both of these frames assume that the *criminal justice system institution* is off limits for criticism. By operating under this assumption, the individual and organizational approaches deflect deeper, potentially destabilizing critiques of racist and essentialist ideologies that influence and constitute the justice system. To avoid such deflection, it is necessary to critically explicate the relationship of the producers of these accounts to the justice system institution.

Institutional Theory

The LAPD and the LA Police Commission are both components of the criminal justice system institution, which describes a collection of organizations (such as police departments and courts) and individual roles (such as law enforcers and judges) involved in social processes of "doing" justice. According to Jepperson (1991: 143–163), institutions are "socially constructed, routine-reproduced (*ceteris paribus*) programs or role systems. They operate as relative fixtures of constraining environments and are accompanied by taken-for-granted accounts." Furthermore, according to Crank (2003: 137) (discussing Friedland and Alford, 1991):

> Institutions are carried by formal organizations, regimes which convey a central authority system, and by culture, which gives meaning to the customary and the conventional in daily life. Institutions are also carried by individuals, and provide accounts of the social and legal constructions of individual identity.

Institutions thus lie between the analytical level of the organization and the level of the society, and operate as locations of meaning production both for and by the roles and organizations that constitute them. In other words, institutional constituents influence one another in the quotidian production of meaning about roles, norms, objectives, imperatives, conceptions of right and wrong, what is taken for granted, etc.

Importantly, the structure and operation of organizations within an institution reflect the values that permeate the institutional environment (Crank, 2003). Thus, organizations within the criminal justice system (such as police departments) reflect values that dominate discourses relating to the justice system institution (such as "the war on crime"). Furthermore, according to Crank (2003: 188), "a logic of good faith pervades organizational practices, impeding critical evaluation and supervision. Organizational members believe in the essential rightness of what they do." Under this logic, the influence of dominant justice system discourses is virtually invisible to organizations and their constituent members.

Considering the LAPD's and LA Police Commission's position within the justice system institution, their framing of the Rampart Scandal as either the result of "bad apples" or a "bad organization" is not surprising. Both organizations are participants in the social construction of the justice system, and are thus heavily influenced by dominant discourses therein. Maintaining a logic of good faith, both are relatively unreflexive about their role in perpetuating racist and essentialist ideologies that underlie these dominant discourses. In light of this situation, we can look to other major accounts of Rampart—namely, media representations—in hopes of finding analyses that go beyond the "bad apples" or "rotten barrel." However, as we shall see through the following analysis, we find a similar lack of reflexivity in these media representations.

Media Accounts of Rampart: The Story of Javier Ovando's Wrongful Conviction

The two media representations are narratives by Randall Sullivan (2001) in *Rolling Stone* and Peter Boyer (2001) in *The New Yorker*. Each article frames the scandal as the result of the LAPD's infiltration by criminals or even gang members, rather than due to the LAPD's flawed organizational practices or deeper ideological factors, such as the war on crime or the privileging of police narratives. For example, Boyer (2001: 66–67) delineates rather vague circumstantial evidence to suggest that David Mack (the bank robber) was an associate or perhaps member of the Bloods gang, including the fact that Mack grew up in a tough Compton neighborhood and allegations by jail workers that Mack began to wear red clothing once he was incarcerated. More explicitly, Sullivan (2001: 81) closes his first paragraph with a quote from an LAPD deputy chief: "This isn't about cops who became criminals, it's about criminals who became cops." Beyond noting the importance of this general framing of the scandal evident in both articles, we can briefly analyze one prominent Rampart story, the Ovando case, to further explicate how these media workers' framing foreclosed institutional level questions.

According to Rafael Perez, Javier Ovando was an unarmed 18th-Street gang member who was shot by Perez and his partner Nino Durden during a confrontation in 1996 (Perez, 1999). Perez claimed that Ovando had startled Durden and him in an abandoned building that the officers were using as a stakeout. Apparently, Durden shot Ovando first, and then Perez fired four rounds. After Ovando collapsed with serious wounds to his chest and head, the officers discovered that Ovando did not possess a weapon. According to Perez, Durden hurriedly planted a machine gun they had previously recovered from the field and were carrying for the purpose of planting on an unarmed suspect (*Ibid.*). In the few moments before other officers and an ambulance arrived, the partners invented the story that Ovando was attempting to kill them when they shot him (*Ibid.*). This representation became the prosecutor's theory in the subsequent trial (in which Perez testified) against Ovando, which resulted in a 23-year state prison sentence. Ovando's case was later overturned when Perez admitted to the gun planting. Beyond the sensational stories about Perez's cocaine thefts, David Mack's bank robbery, and the Kevin Gaines shooting,[9] the Ovando case became central in media representations of the Rampart Scandal. Indeed, Ovando's case is the primary example journalists evoked when discussing Perez's allegations of officers "putting cases on people."

In the *New Yorker* and *Rolling Stone* articles, discussion of the Ovando case focuses on two themes: Perez's convincing job as a witness in Ovando's criminal trial, and Perez's act of perjury (the facts of the gun-planting that Perez later described in statements that led to Ovando's release). Both themes demonstrate how journalists frame the *source* of Ovando's wrongful conviction as the work of "bad apple" Rafael Perez, The *Rolling Stone* passage on Ovando is worth quoting at length:[10]

> Public defender Tamar Toister recalls feeling helpless as she watched Perez testify against her client Javier Ovando in early 1997. Toister figured that both the judge and jury might feel sympathy for her client. ... Ovando had to

be wheeled into court on a gurney at his preliminary hearing and would be confined to a wheelchair for the rest of his life. But after Perez described how Ovando (whose gang name was Sniper) had attempted to ambush him and his partner with an assault rifle, Ovando's fate was sealed. "He was better on the witness stand," Toister says, "than any police officer I've ever cross examined: smooth, sincere, articulate, with just the right amount of emotion." Duly impressed, Judge Stephen Czuleger sentenced Ovando to twenty-three years in state prison—even more time than the prosecutor had asked for. "That was entirely due to how good Perez had been on the stand," Toister said. "I have to admit, I believed him myself (Sullivan, 2001: 98).

This framing of the story places the responsibility for Ovando's wrongful conviction squarely within the character of Rafael Perez. Ovando was framed because Perez was an evil, smooth-talking bad guy. This representation of Ovando's wrongful conviction directly mirrors the LAPD's conception of the scandal—interloping criminals duping the "just" system.

Why do these media representations so closely reflect the LAPD version of the Rampart Scandal? As cultural critic Stuart Hall (1980: 117) has argued, the media is a "major cultural and ideological force, standing in a dominant position with respect to the way in which social relations and political problems [are] defined and the production and transformation of popular ideologies in the audience addressed." Moreover, Hall describes how mediaworkers operate within what he calls a "professional code," which works to legitimize hegemonic ideologies through its adherence to the value of objectivity. According to Hall, the "professional code" is *relatively* autonomous from what he calls the "dominant code" (hegemonic ideological discourses) in that it reconfigures the dominant code through its technical apparatuses. Yet this code is ultimately one of the chief reproducers of dominant stereotypes and definitions:

> The professional code, however, operates *within* the "hegemony" of the dominant code. Indeed, it serves to reproduce the dominant definitions precisely by bracketing their hegemonic quality and operating instead with displaced professional codings which foreground such apparently neutral-technical questions as visual quality, news and presentational values, televisual quality, "professionalism," and so on (Hall, 1980: 136).

The professional code is hegemonic in its reproduction of dominant ideology precisely because it purports to be unbiased. Fundamental questions about ideology, race, class, etc., are bracketed and thus forgotten. The foregrounding of "the objectivity ideal" by the professional media obscures the position of the media within the dominant code, and thus hegemonically perpetuates it. The operators of this code are reporters, editors, news producers, etc., agents that sociologist Darnel Hunt calls "newsworkers."

In *O.J. Simpson, Facts and Fictions,* Hunt (1999: 42) describes the cultural performances of the media as occasions through which "much of the meaning of contemporary life is (re) negotiated and (re)enforced—'authenticated.'" Hunt argues that the selection of "media events" is connected to hegemonic ideologies (*Ibid.*: 42–43). Newsworkers select events in terms of their ideological potentialities (e.g., the story about a famous black athlete's alleged murder of a white woman, or, in the case at hand, a gang of Black and Hispanic criminals who infiltrated the LAPD) and frame them within the dominant-hegemonic code. The ritualization of media events, which sanctifies them as preferred locations for meaning production, inevitably "talks" in the dominant-hegemonic code; and, furthermore, this talk is conducted "professionally" (purportedly without bias), which masks its connection to the dominant code.

Specifically, according to Hunt[11] (1999, and echoing Hall), the process of "newswork" (p. 90) is shaped by (among other factors) "the objectivity ideal" (p. 91), which describes the status and power of journalists to codify stories as "facts": "objectivity as a newswork ideal had become a professional cornerstone that could be identified, taught, and (re)affirmed—'facts' exist and newsworkers are uniquely qualified to uncover, verify, and report on them." Very often—and exemplified by the *New Yorker* and *Rolling Stone* articles—journalists covering crime stories get their stories directly from law enforcement and official agencies involved in the investigation, rather than from investigating the events independently or consulting nonofficial sources (Hunt, 1999). As Regina Lawrence (2002: 53) makes clear, this "official dominance" model of the media demonstrates how "objectivity" perpetuates the ideologies of the "dominant code":

> According to [the official dominance] model, news "objectivity" is bounded by the ideas that are acceptable to the power structures within which news organizations themselves are embedded. … This meaning of "objectivity" tells reporters that in a world full of competing sources making competing claims, it is best to report information that can be officially verified and make less use of sources and claims that are most likely to invite charges of bias. "Objectivity" thus becomes reporting "what happened" in a way that is least likely to be criticized by those in power.

However, the relationship between newsworkers and officialdom is complex. It would be an oversimplification to say that newsworkers slavishly parrot official sources on problems such as police misconduct. Rather, newsworkers may rely on official sources for a complex array of reasons, including uncertainty or fear about "street people," concerns about the potential loss of access to official sources, or perhaps their own internalized beliefs in the dominant order:[12]

> People who accuse police of brutality are often non-white, are often relatively poor, and often have criminal records. ... These are not the kinds of people reporters feel most comfortable relying on for "news." Nor are they the audiences for whom many reporters envision producing the news (Lawrence, 2000: 55).[13]

Despite the narrowness of the media narratives of Rampart I have described, one might wonder why, in the first place, the judge was so impressed by Perez's testimony, why the public defender felt helpless, or how and why Perez and Durden framed Ovando. In addressing these questions, we can look through the gaps in these major accounts of Rampart, and raise the possibility of deeper causal factors at work in the justice system institution.

The War on Crime Discourse

Although the authors of the *New Yorker* and *Rolling Stone* articles acknowledge that the CRASH units at the heart of the Rampart Scandal emerged in the context of discourses about curbing crime (Boyer 2001; Sullivan, 2001), neither satisfactorily accounts for the influence of these discourses. As police scholars Skolnick and Fyfe (1993: 116) have argued, the war on crime, which puts officers in the position of soldiers, creates two problems: (1) as soldiers, officers must identify an enemy, and (2) it positions officers on the front lines of an unwinnable war against the people they supposedly serve:

> When any soldiers go to war, they must have enemies. When cops go to war against crime, their enemies are found in inner cities and among our minority populations. There, in a country as foreign to most officers as Vietnam was to GIs, cops have trouble distinguishing the good guys from the bad.

Thus, as soldiers in the war on crime, officers break the law to satisfy the imperative to produce arrests. Indeed, much of the misconduct alleged in the Rampart Scandal seems to reflect the difficult position the war on crime puts officers in; they are supposed to uphold the law, but they are also supposed to produce arrests. Indeed, Perez and Durden were originally lauded for taking a "dangerous gang-banger," Ovando, off the street. From the perspective of supporters of the war on crime, Javier Ovando was the enemy, and soldiers

Perez and Durden did the right thing by shooting and arresting him. In light of the war on crime, Ovando's wrongful conviction can be read as resulting from two officers resolving the dissonance inherent to that war. Perez and Durden solved the confusion by abandoning the law and obeying the demands of their war.[14]

Chambliss (1994) develops a similar line of reasoning. Conservative political movements that began in the 1960s (and continue today), he argues, created moral panics over crime as smokescreens from politically threatening issues (e.g., the Vietnam War, budget cuts, etc.). Such "moral panics'" engendered a "crime industry" (including the police), which perpetrated injustices against Black and Hispanic young men. Chambliss vividly describes due process abuses committed by the elite Rapid Deployment Unit in Washington, D.C. A consequence of such aggressive tactics was a prison explosion of overrepresented minorities who were incarcerated for drug crimes, which was accompanied by a concomitant decrease in public spending on education and welfare. For Chambliss (*Ibid.*: 186–189), common explanations for increased spending on criminal justice—"crime has increased," "crimes have become more serious," or "the public thinks crime is important"—are false. Police due process abuses, he argues, can be attributed to moral panics and the crime industry. Such abuses exist because the police need something to do; once the crime industry was in place (after the 1960s), its soldiers needed a crisis to handle. The war on crime became that crisis.

With the politicization of crime functioning to distract the public from politically dangerous issues (such as poverty), we can see Chambliss' project as a critical theory of the police. His societal-level analysis is analogous to critical theories of popular culture. Just as prime-time television interpellates us toward consumerism, the crime industry invites us to believe that young nonwhite men are synonymous with crime (*Ibid.*). The false consciousness of the crime industry distracts us from our own subordination, and inscribes young, nonwhite men as criminals.

Importantly, this inscription is a component of what Etienne Balibar (1991: 21) calls "neo-racism," in which "difference" is identified through discourses of culture rather than biology:

> It is a racism whose dominant theme is not biological heredity but the insurmountability of cultural differences, a racism which, at first sight, does not postulate the superiority of certain groups or peoples in relation to others but "only" the harmfulness of abolishing frontiers, the incompatibility of lifestyles and traditions. ...

The war on crime's ideological work of inscribing young nonwhite men as criminals achieves neo-racism precisely because race is never officially mentioned in the war on crime—the officially relevant factor in the war on crime is not race, but *criminality.* As Balibar points out, neo-racism, such as we see in the war on crime, is difficult to identify because of its purported allegiance to contemporary values such as "color-blindness." Yet, *"culture can also function like a nature,* and it can in particular function as a way of locking individuals and groups a priori into a genealogy, into a determination that is immutable and intangible in origin" (*Ibid.:* 22).

In thinking about the war on crime and neo-racism, it is important to remember that the LAPD's CRASH units were *manifestations* of the war on crime. CRASH units can be construed as neo-racist agents, carrying out the prerogatives of the war on crime. Framed this way, the misconduct of CRASH officers may not seem so surprising. Unfortunately, due to their respective locations vis-à-vis the justice system institution (and their role in the construction of the war on crime) official commentators and newsworkers have not approached the Rampart Scandal from a theoretical position that includes concepts such as "neo-racism."

Privileged Police Narratives

Why did our adversarial system of jury adjudication fail to catch the errors that produce miscarriages of justice such as in the case of Javier Ovando? The judge and jury in the Ovando case believed Rafael Perez's lies. It seems intuitive that judges and juries would take the word of police officers over defendants in criminal trials (although, as a result of Rampart, this is probably changing). But why is this so? White (1990: 4) contends that "familiar cultural images and long-established legal norms construct the subjectivity and speech of socially subordinated persons as inherently inferior to the speech and personhood of dominant groups." Courts talk like upper-class white men and subordinate those who do not. The police narrative in a criminal trial is the epitome of white male speech, *especially* when uttered by nonwhite officers. Public Defender Toister's comments on Perez's talk—*smooth, sincere, articulate, with just the right amount of emotion*—suggest that such a presentation was unexpected. Would she have had the same impression if Perez were white? Toister's comments give the impression that she was disturbed by Perez's appropriation of the white juridical subject's talk. His perjury seems to have been, for Toister, something like a desecration of the law. Perez's "white talk" was especially powerful in juxtaposition to Ovando. The Honduran native Ovando—brown, tattooed, head shaved, and labeled with the gang moniker "Sniper"—was unable to understand well the language of the proceedings. In sharp contrast, Rafael Perez, a Hispanic man speaking the language of the juridical subject the court and jury believed represented "the truth," sparkled.

Susan Bandes (1999: 1317) elaborates on White's insights in her discussion of biased assumptions in appellate courts that cause judges to treat cases of police misconduct as fragmented aberrations, rather than components of "a grand narrative of official misconduct." This "anecdotalizing" reproduces police misconduct because it misses the ideological and systemic nature of the problem. Bandes identifies biases such as "the assumption that the status quo is essentially coherent and just," which describes the pervasive view among judges that the current governmental order is not based on political and social choices, but rather is "neutral, natural, and nonpolitical" (p. 1319). Further, "selective empathy" describes judges' natural tendency to comprehend and empathize with "those who share their defining attributes, such as class, gender, race, and prestige" (*Ibid.*), while "the fear of destabilization and chaos" captures the concern over identifying deep, systemic problems due to the potentially costly and destabilizing effects of contending with them (p. 1320). Biases such as these are manifestations of the subordinating assumptions White (1990) describes. Although one might argue that Bandes' analysis focuses on the level of the organization (e.g., "the courts"), her critique is of the justice system institution:

> To the extent that low-level police officers, unhindered or condoned by supervisors, the chief, the local political structure, and the courts, are brutalizing minority residents of poor neighborhoods, it may be that these actions are a part of an implicit bargain with society—at least that part of society that has political and economic power. Such brutality is often implicitly approved by majority residents of stratified, segregated societies who value law and order, who want the boundaries between black and white neighborhoods policed, and who will put up with the infliction of a substantial amount of brutality on others as long as it is not made impossible [to] ignore. The treatment of police brutality as aberrational and anecdotal is an essential though largely invisible part of the bargain (Bandes, 1999: 1340–1341).

This discussion, like that of Chambliss, is a variety of conflict theory. Central to a "conflict approach" to police misconduct is the belief that inequality leads to misconduct. Such theories argue that powerful, majority groups perpetuate biases and discourses that produce and reproduce police misconduct, which, in turn, reproduces inequality. Although Bandes does not explicitly make the connection, her perspective (along with Chambliss') conforms to the Althusserian notion of the police as a repressive state apparatus, as described by Resch (1992: 213–215):

> Althusser contends, following Gramsci, ... that we must see the political power of a ruling class as consisting not only of their monopoly of the repressive apparatus of the state (the army, police, and so on), but also of their ideological

hegemony over society. ... The role of the repressive state apparatus consists essentially in securing by force (physical or otherwise) the political conditions of the reproduction of production.

This political-economic view of the police (as components of the superstructure, operating to protect capitalist modes of production) clearly underlies the analyses discussed above, regardless of whether they say so explicitly. The upshot of such analyses is that the "cause" of police misconduct is to be found in the ideology of political economy (in the United States, free-market capitalism). Interestingly, this perspective is supported by Paul Chevigny's (1995: 249) comparative analysis of police violence in several industrialized nations (including the U.S.), which found that there is a "correlation between the sociopolitical structure of the places and the level of violence by the police; the departments reproduce and represent the relations in the social order."

These different theoretical themes show that "invisible," ideological factors may have contributed to misconduct such as the wrongful conviction of Javier Ovando. As such, they are unrelated to the individual character of Rafael Perez or others (or the LAPD organization). These other factors are entirely absent from authoritative representations (both official and media) of the Ovando case and the scandal in general. In their narrow focus on Perez's perjury, official and media representations mask the privileging of the white juridical subject in criminal trials (and the war on crime). The consequence of these representations is that institutional-level causal factors are bracketed out of the discussion about Rampart.

Conclusion

My intent has been to bring a critical perspective to the scholarly discourse on the Rampart Scandal. Investigators and commentators have focused mostly on the character of a few individuals at the heart of the scandal, although the RIRP and some law professors have discussed the LAPD's organizational problems as well. There has been very little investigation into specific acts of misconduct. The LAPD's internal investigation placed the blame squarely on the shoulders of a few Black and Hispanic officers. Media representations have mirrored the LAPD's version of the story, focusing exclusively on "bad apples" such as Rafael Perez and David Mack. The danger is that this version of the story will become "the truth," and thus shut down inquiry into the influence of ideology on the justice system institution. By looking through the gaps of official and media representations of Rampart, I suggest two invisible ideological causal factors, namely the war on crime and the privileging of the white juridical subject, as manifested in police narratives in criminal trials. My argument is not that individual or organizational level factors are totally meaningless. Rather, I wish to suggest that scholars interested in the Rampart Scandal and other instances of police misconduct consider analytical levels beyond the individual or the organization in hopes of identifying the role of ideology in such social problems.

Is this likely? Probably not, considering that policy suggestions based on an institutional approach would require changing the justice system institution—a level policymakers are not in a position to contend with. Bluntly, institutional-level theories of police misconduct suggest that police misbehavior will probably persist as long as the conditions of our political economy (and its related apparatuses) remain essentially the same. Policy recommendations based on such approaches would involve creating conditions of material equality and significantly altering conceptions of the police. This is probably not something that much of the audience for policing theories (or at least those with the power to change or make policy) would welcome. (Here I echo Bandes' arguments about appellate judges' resistance to challenging the status quo.) Even when scholars do identify institutional-level factors related to police misconduct, they are not likely to offer policy proposals that go beyond the organizational level. For example, Kane (2002: 891), in his study of the social ecology of police misconduct, finds that structural disadvantage predicts police misconduct, but none of his recommendations address this society-level variable. Kane's suggestions mostly call for bureaucratic changes in the New York Police Department.

Unfortunately, the conflict paradigm that underlies institutional approaches to police misconduct is probably thought of as radical among official and media commentators (not to mention mainstream criminologists). But the truth is that one need not be radical to think that material equality, decriminalization of victimless crime, and a different vision of policing would probably significantly reduce police misconduct (especially police violence and due process abuses). Yet this level of thinking has been bracketed out of the discourse because mainstream policymakers and newsworkers are not in a position to widen their theoretical frame. In the case of Rampart, the unfortunate result is a body of texts that either ignores or minimizes the relationship of ideology to police misconduct.

Notes

1. Other cost estimates put the total well below $100 million; see, for example, Lait and Glover (2003).
2. On May Day 2007, LAPD officers injured at least one person while aggressively disrupting a rally in MacArthur Park (see Marquez, 2007).
3. This officer, caught stealing cocaine, made a deal with prosecutors and spawned the scandal.

4. See, for example, the cases of officers Gustavo Raya (LAPD Board of Rights, 1997), Dennis O'Sullivan (Stearns, 2001), William Ferguson (Glover and Lait, 2001b), and Ruben Palomares (Glover and Lait, 2001a).

5. See Marquez (2007).

6. Two other documents are important to note: (1) Law Professor Irwin Chemerinsky's detailed analysis of the LAPD's Board of Inquiry Report, and (2) the Los Angeles County Bar Association's *Recommendations for Improving the California Criminal Justice System in the Wake of the Rampart Scandal*. Each of these (in different ways) addresses organizational problems in the Los Angeles justice system. Since they were not publicly sponsored, neither is "official."

7. This defense might be interpreted as an attempt to avoid legal action by the Department of Justice (DOJ) based on "bad patterns and practices" under *Monell* v. *Department of Social Services of the City of New York* (1978) (case law allowing legal action against government organizations that maintain policies and practices that violate civilians' constitutional rights). This defense has failed, however, as evinced by the current Consent Decree between the LAPD and the DOJ (see *pbs.org*, 2007).

8. This individualist, "bad apples" approach is familiar from past official accounts of police scandals, such as those involving "rotten apple" cops in the New York Police Department (see the Knapp Commission, 1972: 6–13, for a discussion of the NYPD leadership's insistence on the "bad apples" framework after Frank Serpico's revelations about systemic corruption), and scandals involving state abuses of power subsequent to Rampart, such as the initial official explanations of the Abu Ghraib torture and prisoner abuse scandal (see Whitney, 2004: *viii*, for a discussion). What stands out about Rampart is the added dimension of racism.

9. Gaines was a Black off-duty LAPD officer shot and killed by a white undercover LAPD officer during a road rage incident (see Sullivan's *Rolling Stone* article for details).

10. This passage closely reflects the *New Yorker* representation of the Ovando story.

11. Hunt's analysis relies heavily on Dayan and Katz (1992).

12. Thanks to an anonymous *Social Justice* reviewer for pointing this out.

13. See Huspek (2004) for an interesting analysis of one component of the media that sometimes *does* rely on nonofficial, nonwhite sources—the Black press.

14. The point here is not that the war on crime required Perez and Durden to deal drugs, but that this war created the legal space for the lack of oversight over CRASH units and fostered subcultures in the LAPD in which alleged gang members were thought to be subhuman and exploitable.

References

Balibar, Etienne and Immanuel Wallerstein

1991   *Race, Nation, Class: Ambiguous Identities.* London: Verso.

Bandes, Susan

1999   "Patterns of Injustice: Police Brutality in the Courts." *Buffalo Law Review* 47.

Berry, Steve, Scott Glover, and Matt Lait

2001   "D.A. Says No New Charges Expected in Rampart Probe." *Los Angeles Times* (November 8).

Boyer, Peter

2001   "Bad Cops." *The New Yorker* (May 21).

Bruner, Jerome

1991   "The Narrative Construction of Reality." *Critical Inquiry* 18.

Burcham, David W. and Catherine L, Fisk

2001   "Symposium on the Rampart Scandal: Policing the Criminal Justice System, Introduction." *Loyola of Los Angeles Law Review* 34.

Cannon, Lou

2000   "One Bad Cop." *New York Times Magazine* (October 1).

Chambliss, William J.

1994   "Policing the Ghetto Underclass: The Politics of Law and Law Enforcement." *Social Problems* 41, 2.

Chemerinsky, Erwin

2000   "An Independent Analysis of the Los Angeles Police Departments' Board of Inquiry Report on the Rampart Scandal." Unpublished manuscript, available from the author.

Chevigny, Paul

1995   *Edge of the Knife: Police Violence in the Americas.* New York: The New Press.

Crank, John P.

2003   "Institutional Theory of the Police: A Review of the State of the Art." *Policing: An International Journal of Police Strategies and Management* 26, 2.

Dayan, Daniel and Elihu Katz

1992   *Media Events: The Live Broadcasting of History.* Cambridge: Harvard University Press.

Ewick, Patricia and Susan S. Silbey

1995   "Subversive Stories and Hegemonic Tales: Toward a Sociology of Narrative." *Law and Society Review* 29, 2.

Friedland, R. and R. Alford

1991   "Bringing Society Back in: Symbols, Practices, and Institutional Contradictions." W. Powell and P. DiMaggio (eds.), *The New Institutionalism in Organizational Analysis.* Chicago: University of Chicago Press.

Glover, Scott and Matt Lait

2001a   "Ex-Rampart Officer Held in Cocaine Sting." *Los Angeles Times* (June 14).

2001b   "L.A. Police Haunted by '99 Incident." *Los Angeles Times* (August 7).

Grogan, Jim

2001   "Fairness Delayed: LAPD Belatedly Agrees to Review All Arrests Made by Two Troubled Cops." *LA Weekly* (July 20).

Hall, Stuart

1997   "Representation and the Media." Video recording. Media Education Foundation.

1980   "Introduction to Media Studies at the Centre." *Culture, Media, Language: Working Papers in Cultural Studies, 1972–1979.* London: Hutchison.

Hunt, Darnell

1999   *O. J. Simpson Facts and Fictions: News Rituals in the Construction of Reality.* Cambridge: Cambridge University Press.

Huspek, Michael

2004   "Black Press, White Press, and Their Opposition: The Case of the Police Killing of Tyisha Miller." *Social Justice* 31,1–2.

Independent Commission on the Los Angeles Police Department

1991   "Christopher Commission Report."

Independent Review Panel of the Los Angeles Police Commission (RIRP)

2000   *Report of the Rampart Independent Review Panel.*

Jepperson, R.

1991   "Institutions, Institutional Effects, and Institutionalism." W. Powell and P. DiMaggio (eds.), *The New Institutionalism in Organizational Analysis.* Chicago: University of Chicago Press. Quoted in: John P. Crank, "Institutional Theory of the Police: A Review of the State of the Art." *Policing: An International Journal of Police Strategies and Management* 26, 2 (2003).

Kane, Robert J.

2002   "The Social Ecology of Police Misconduct." *Criminology* 40, 4.

Knapp Commission

1972   *Commission Report of the Commission to Investigate Allegations of Police Corruption and the City's Anti-Corruption Procedures.* New York: George Braxiller.

Lait, Matt and Scott Glover

2003   "Secret LAPD Testimony Implicated Nine Officers." *Los Angeles Times* (February 27): A1.

Lawrence, Regina G.

2000   *The Politics of Force: Media and the Construction of Police Brutality.* Berkeley: University of California Press.

Los Angeles County Bar Association

2003   *Recommendations for Improving the California Criminal Justice System in the Wake of the Rampart Scandal.*

Los Angeles Police Department (LAPD)

2000   "Board of Inquiry into the Rampart Area Corruption Incident."

Los Angeles Police Department Board of Rights Hearing

1997   In re Gustavo Raya, #30322.

Los Angeles Police Protective League v. *Gil Garcetti*

2001   Case No. BC 240 300.

Marquez, Jeremiah

2007   "LA Mayor to Address Rally Violence." *Associated Press Online.*

pbs.org

2007   At *www.pbs.org/wgbh/pages/frontline/shows/lapd/later/decree.html.*

People of the State of California v. *(Secret) Grand Jury*

2000   Control No. 99-00/011.

People of the State of California v. *Rafael Perez*

2000   Superior Court of the State of California for the County of Los Angeles. No, BA173281.

Perez, Rafael

1999   "Statement." In re: Case BA 109900.

Pomerantz, Dorothy

2000   "Final Cost of Rampart: $1 Billion?" *Los Angeles Business Journal* (February 28).

Resch, Robert Paul

1992   *Althusser and the Renewal of Marxist Social Theory.* Berkeley: University of California Press

Sherman, Lawrence W.

1979   *Scandal and Reform: Controlling Police Corruption.* Berkeley: University of California Press.

Skolnick, Jerome H. and James J. Fyfe

1993   *Above the Law: Police and the Excessive Use of Force.* New York: The Free Press.

Stearns, William Boyd

2001   Habeas Corpus Petition, Case No. LA033682-01.

Sullivan, Randall

2001   "Who Killed B.I.G.?" *Rolling Stone* (June 7).

White, Lucie E.

1990   "Subordination, Rhetorical Survival Skills, and Sunday Shoes: Notes on the Hearing of Mrs. G." *Buffalo Law Review* 8, 1.

Whitney, Craig R.

2004   "Introduction." Steven Strasser (ed.), *The Abu Ghraib Investigations: The Official Reports of the Independent Panel and Pentagon on the Shocking Prisoner Abuse in Iraq.* New York: Public Affairs Books.

Reading 2.4

Selection from "Police Discretion Police Misconduct and Mechanisms to Control Police Misconduct" from *Community Policing: A Police-Citizen Partnership*

Michael J. Palmiotto

Police Discretion

America is a nation of laws. Our laws are passed by the legislative branch of government and enforced by the executive branch. Cox and McCamey write that:

> The law explicitly grants some discretionary powers to police officers and creates a framework within which other discretionary judgments may legitimately be made. It is one measure of the importance of discretion in police work that these are among the first items that become incorporated into the officer's working knowledge of the law.
>
> (2008, 36–37)

Laws are passed to keep the peace and maintain order. Political scientists often claim that the purpose of laws is to "keep the underclass under control" for the benefit of the middle and upper classes. These groups could not remain affluent if chaos and disorder became rampant. Therefore, laws are passed and are enforced, not only for public safety purposes, but also to keep our society functioning well economically.

Individuals in our society, including those responsible for enforcing the law, do not always specifically follow the letter of the law. In addition, legal norms are constantly changing (Aaronson et al. 1984, 4). For example, a few years ago, it was acceptable to discriminate against homosexuals, but today this discrimination would be a violation of the law. Also, several decades ago it could be appropriate behavior to smack a youngster who talked back to a police officer and send him home to his parents, where he could expect to be smacked again. Today, this would be considered misconduct on the police officer's part.

Police discretion is the authority of police to decide how much effort they will apply to enforcing specific laws and which laws they will or will not enforce. According to Reiss (1984), the concept implies several things:

> One is quite simply that an officer who has discretion has the power to choose among alternatives. A second and closely related aspect is that a choice made by an officer in the exercise of his discretion must be permitted by law. A third is that an officer who has discretion exercises individual judgment in making a choice.
>
> (89–90)

Although the police are sworn to enforce all the laws all the time, they enforce only the laws they choose to enforce, and even when they choose to enforce specific laws, they often will enforce these laws only some of the time. In many situations, they will warn, reprimand, or release an individual rather than make an arrest. Often they decide not to arrest for crimes they do not consider to be violent or a serious threat, such as traffic violations, petty gambling offenses, and simple assaults between acquaintances. When the police decide not to arrest someone who qualifies to be arrested, it can be said that they are using discretion.

Joseph Goldstein (1960) argued that full enforcement would be difficult, if not impossible, to achieve. Police officers take an oath on the day they officially are sworn in as police officers that they will uphold and defend the U.S. Constitution, their state constitution, and federal and state laws. They are expected to respect individual rights of all people as outlined with the Bill of Rights of the U.S. Constitution, including the rights of those suspected of committing a criminal offense; to know and follow all the various court decisions establishing legal police procedures; and to protect the due process rights, as guaranteed by the Fifth and Fourteenth Amendments, of everyone that they arrest, search, or interrogate. Given the ambiguities in criminal law and due process boundaries, the conflicts between requirements, the time constraints, and the limitations of personnel and investigative techniques, full enforcement is simply not feasible. Therefore, actual enforcement of the law is inevitably selective enforcement (554–561).

Selective enforcement emphasizes the "spirit of the law" rather than the letter of the law. The unwritten selective enforcement policy of police departments enables police to enforce only the most serious laws and the laws the community wants enforced. Although legislation is written as if full enforcement is expected, lawmakers do not really expect it, and police agencies do not really expect it either. Kenneth Culp Davis (1971) argued that the police should not be expected to enforce all laws when prosecutors do not prosecute all cases. Prosecutors pick and choose what to prosecute, and police officers who observe them soon know what it takes for a prosecutor to take a case to trial. Further, insufficient funds allocated to police departments allow only for selective enforcement. Finally, law makers frequently pass laws that are difficult to obtain evidence to enforce (79–97).

The recognition of police discretion can be traced back to the early twentieth century, when the Supreme Court of Michigan, in Gowan v. Smith, 122 N.W. 286 (1909), asserted that

> the police commissioner is bound to use the discretion with which he is clothed. ... To enable him to perform the duties imposed upon him by law, he is supplied with certain limited means. It is entirely obvious that he must exercise a sound discretion as to how those means shall be applied for the good of the community.

Although police discretion has been recognized by the courts since the early 1900s, it was not until the late 1950s that the police began to officially claim that officers possess discretion in performing their policing duties. The legitimating of police discretion was aided by an American Bar Association survey on the administration of justice in the mid-1950s. The survey found that criminal laws were frequently used for a variety of purposes other than their specified purposes—for example, to deal with numerous social problems, such as family problems, mental illness, and alcohol abuse. Thus, it was acceptable practice for police officers to use their own judgment about when to arrest and for what purpose (Walker 1993, 10). The 1987 U.S. Supreme Court ruling in McClesky v. Kemp, 411 crL 4107, further upheld the use of police discretion. Although police administrations under the professional model of policing have held onto the claim that the police fully enforce all the laws, progressive police administrators and personnel know that selective enforcement is the norm.

Discretion in when and whether to arrest or to use force against an individual places police officers in an extremely significant position in our society. Michael Brown (1988) went so far as to claim that "police discretion—the day to day decisions of policemen—is tantamount to political decision making, for the role of the police is based upon the legitimate use of coercion" (3–4). Brown further argued that

> the police have crucial policymaking powers by virtue of their power to decide which laws will be enforced and when. At issue is not simply the legality of these decisions, but the routine use of the legitimate means of coercion in society. The day-to-day choices of policemen affecting the meaning of law, order, and justice within American society.

(5–6)

Fairness issues necessarily arise when race or class biases influence who is arrested or apprehended and who is not. Kenneth Culp Davis (1971) provides a realistic example:

> A statute, an ordinance, and a police manual all provide that a policeman "shall" arrest all known violators of the law. A policeman lectures a boy from a middle-class neighborhood, but he arrests a boy from the slums, although he knows that both are equally guilty of violating the same statute. Because the evidence against both boys is clear, the policeman's decision is the only one that counts, for the release of the first boy is permanent and the conviction of the second follows almost automatically.
>
> (218)

Further, police discretion can be abused. One common form of abuse is the dispensing of street justice. Street justice occurs when the police believe that someone should be punished for what he or she did or is about to do. The police usually have no qualms about using street justice on an individual who defies their authority or insults them. They feel that if they are to function effectively, they must be in control, and that if they are insulted and allow an individual to get away with it, then they have lost control of the situation. The Rodney King beating by the Los Angeles police officers could be considered an example of street justice. Rodney King gave the police a high-speed chase. He refused to stop when the police were in pursuit. According to police culture, when the police want you to do something, you do it. If you refuse to follow police orders, you may have to pay the price. Rodney King was beaten to teach him a lesson—and also to teach a lesson to the passengers in the vehicle King was driving.

Some police officers see nothing wrong with street justice. They consider it to be a part of their right and duty to teach an individual a lesson. However, when police officers dispense street justice, the individual has been denied due process and judicial review. By using street justice, a police officer has violated the law. Assaulting an individual is a crime, and police officers should not be immune from criminal charges if they have violated the criminal law or denied someone his or her constitutional rights.

The nature of the role assigned to the police by the community may be a factor contributing to the use of street justice:

> Studies of police discretion largely reinforce the view that street decisions to intervene, arrest, use force or issue traffic citations are primarily a function of situational and organizational factors that reflect interpretations of community needs and expectations by police. "Street justice" in this sense is a

response to a community mandate that something be done about situations where formal institutions cannot or will not respond for a variety of reasons.

(Sykes 1986, 498)

Sykes argued that the liberal reformers fear police repression and overlook the functional role of "street justice" in creating a sense of community. They choose to emphasize justice defined as due process over the community-based idea of justice as righting a wrong and protecting the physically weak from the powerful. Police accountability remains a problem, and order maintenance continues to create the potential for abuse of power. However, the answer provided by the professional model, which emphasizes the enforcement role, leaves many citizens without the means to civilize their community. The trade-off must be recognized and provides an ongoing moral dilemma in liberal society (507).

The dilemma here is that street justice is used by police officers to enforce the moral code of the community they police but that the use of street justice pushes justice aside.

According to Carl Klockars (1986), the police, for practical reasons, do not use street justice all that frequently. If an individual given street justice has been beaten severely, the police officer has to transport the individual to the emergency room and file a report explaining how the individual received his injuries. Because of the threat of departmental charges and the reactions of the community, which may not know the context of the officer's use of force, street justice is kept to a minimum (515–516)—although this may be hard to believe at a time when publicity has surrounded the Rodney King fiasco and the case of Brooklyn police officers accused of shoving a broom handle up a suspect's rectum. The next section will discuss the various forms of police misconduct in detail.

As Joseph Goldstein (1960) pointed out, police, unlike the other actors within the criminal justice process, generally operate without being seen, so their actions are not reviewed. If police officers assigned to investigate a disturbing event report the complaint as unfounded, in most cases their report will be accepted and not visible to the public. Even the records maintained by the police are usually too incomplete to be used to evaluate nonenforcement decisions (543–553). Because of concerns over fairness issues in police discretion, police abuses of discretionary powers, and the public invisibility of much police practice, many commissions and agencies have recommended that police departments establish rules to guide police discretion. In 1967, the President's Commission on Law Enforcement and Administration of Justice recommended such guidelines, stating that

in view of the importance, complexity, and delicacy of police work, it is curious that police administrators have seldom attempted to develop and articulate clear policies aimed at guiding or governing the way policemen exercise their discretion on the street.

(103)

In 1973, the National Advisory Commission on Criminal Justice Standards and Goals reiterated this theme. It recommended that

> every police agency should acknowledge the existence of the broad range of administrative and operational discretion that is exercised by all police agencies and individual officers. That acknowledgment should take the form of comprehensive policy statements that publicly establish the limits of discretion, that provide guidelines for its exercise within those limits, and that eliminate discriminatory enforcement of the law.

1. Every police chief executive should have the authority to establish his agency's fundamental objectives and priorities and to implement them through discretionary allocation and control of agency resources. ...
2. Every police chief executive should establish policy that guides the exercise of discretion by police personnel in using arrest alternatives. ...
3. Every police chief executive should establish policy that limits the exercise of discretion by police personnel in conducting investigations, and that provides guidelines for the exercise of discretion within those limits. ...
4. Every police chief executive should establish policy that governs the exercise of discretion by police personnel in providing routine peacekeeping and other police services that, because of their frequent recurrence, lend themselves to the development of a uniform agency response.
5. Every police chief executive should formalize procedures for developing and implementing the foregoing written agency policy.
6. Every police chief executive immediately should adopt inspection and control procedures to insure that officers exercise their discretion in a manner consistent with agency policy.

(21–22)

In 1974, the American Bar Association argued that

> police discretion can best be structured and controlled through the process of administrative rule making by police agencies. Police administrators should,

therefore, give the highest priority to the formulation of administrative rules governing the exercise of selective enforcement, investigative techniques, and enforcement methods.

(8)

Internal rule making gives police agencies a means of limiting the control of external agencies that can regulate police decision making. The courts, state legislatures, city councils, and county commissioners can all influence police policies and discretion. The numerous United States Supreme Court decisions have dictated police policies and have limited police discretion in many situations. State legislatures and city councils have directed the police to arrest the abuser during a domestic violence call. When the police observe or believe that a person has been assaulted by a spouse or live-in companion, they are legally required to make an arrest. This requirement to arrest during a domestic dispute is an example of how the legislative branch has taken away the power of the police to exercise discretionary decision making in certain situations. Rule making exists to increase predictability, fairness, and efficiency in daily policing activities. It should also contribute to more effective and responsive policing by minimizing procedural errors, improving police–community relations, establishing uniform policy, and centralizing accountability for decision making (Aaronson et al. 1984).

Although rule making has been advocated as a means of controlling police discretion and police behavior, most police departments have not followed the recommendations to implement rule making for the police officers. For the most part, departments initiate rules for their officers as a reaction to predicaments or in response to lawsuits, political pressure, or some other crisis. Rule making by police departments reflects a reactive approach rather than a proactive approach (Walker 1986, 362–363). But when police departments have failed to implement rules to control police discretion, the judicial branch has taken over this function. For example, the United States Supreme Court in Delaware v. Prouse has taken a strong stand against random traffic stops by the police. The Supreme Court in 1979 ruled that police officers could not randomly stop motorists without probable cause to suspect crime or illegal activity, to check the driver's license and auto registration (24CrL 3089). In 2000 the United States Supreme Court ruled in Indianapolis v. Edmond that police check points aimed at discovering drugs and other illegal activity are illegal and in violation of the Fourth Amendment rights of citizens (N99–1030).

Enlightened police leaders have realized that when police activities have intruded on the liberty of citizens, policies and procedures are required to give police officers guidance on:

1. The use of physical and deadly force.
2. Arrest and alternatives to arrest.
3. Stopping, questioning, and frisking citizens.

4. The handling of disorders and/or minor nuisances short of arrest.
5. The use of all intrusive investigative techniques including informants, infiltrators, and electronic surveillance.

(Walker 1986, 388–389)

How does police discretion fit into community policing? The community policing philosophy emphasizes a closer police–community working relationship. Traditional, or professional-model, policing requires that police respond to citizen complaints that are telephoned in to a dispatcher. When patrol officers have free time and are not responding to citizen calls or investigating a traffic accident, they are expected to look for crime on their beat—for example, by patrolling areas that are known to have a high rate of burglaries or a high rate of automobile accidents. Under the community policing philosophy, all police officers are community-policing officers. If this concept becomes operationally successful, the use of discretion by patrol officers may be more carefully thought out. As the beat patrol officer and the neighborhood develop a closer working relationship, breaking down barriers and sharing a stake in crime prevention and control, police discretion may become more attuned to community needs, and police misconduct may decrease.

Police Misconduct

According to organizational scholars, most occupations provide their members with the opportunities for behavioral misconduct, and police departments are no exception. Three elements of occupational misconduct are: "(1) opportunity structure and its accompanying techniques of rule violations, (2) socialization through occupational experiences, and (3) reinforcement and encouragement from the occupational peer group, i.e. group support for certain rule violations" (Barker 1977, 356).

The quality of work performance varies considerably from one police department to another. Most police departments employ police officers who generally function in a fair and impartial manner. However, some police officers become involved in police misconduct. Despite the publicity that police misconduct receives, police departments or even state or federal agencies keep few records of misconduct. It is not uncommon for departments to allow officers involved in police misconduct to resign their position rather than to be fired or prosecuted so that both the officers and the department can avoid publicity. In some states, policy agencies that do this may be violating state training standards that certify police officers. By these standards, an officer involved in police misconduct can lose his certification so that he is no longer employable as a police officer. But when a department allows a police officer to resign, this individual can obtain employment in another police department.

When the police are involved in misconduct, or even when the community believes that the police have committed acts of misconduct, the community loses confidence in the police. To obtain and maintain the community's backing, the police must refrain from wrongdoing. The community expects its police officers to be beyond reproach. When the police lose the community's respect and trust, the department cannot be an effective tool in criminal apprehension and in controlling crime. Without the community's support, victims and witnesses will not come forward. This is crucial because victims and witnesses willing to participate in the legal process contribute to the arrest and prosecution of offenders.

Forms of Police Misconduct

Since the formal organization of policing in the United States, police misconduct has inundated police departments. The police in the early decades of the twenty-first century are no closer to removing the misconduct problem than they were in the twentieth century. The police are in a position of authority and power. Their authority can lead to confrontation with citizens who challenge that authority. Often, police–citizen confrontations create the appearance that the police overstep their boundaries. It is important to recognize that the police have the duty to protect the constitutional rights of all citizens. It is not unusual for police officers to be accused of not fulfilling this role (Palmiotto 2001, 32).

Police misconduct may be either a criminal violation or a violation of departmental rules. It may be unethical or amoral without being criminal, and it does not have to result in personal gain, such as monetary rewards. It may be a reflection of the community, the police department, or an individual police officer. Misconduct of police officers include not only lying, protection of illegal activities, accepting of bribes, and theft occurring during investigations (Hyatt 2001, 75) but also the following misconduct actions:

> Sleeping on Duty—Sleeping on duty usually occurs on the midnight shift during slow periods when there are few calls for service. Although this violates police policies, there are officers who attempt to take catnaps during working hours. Some police officers have second jobs and work during the day and need to rest during their midnight tour of duty.
>
> Use of Illegal Drugs—In the modern era of policing, the use of drugs by police officers can be added to the police misconduct list. Police officers who were exposed to drugs growing up and who in all probability experimented with drugs do not necessarily see anything wrong in using drugs. With drugs easily available in our society, it can be expected that some police officers will use illegal drugs.

Police Brutality

Police brutality is an ambiguous term that has had different meanings depending upon who uses it. Does police brutality include verbal abuse? To some people, it does. A number of police actions, including profane and abusive speech, commands to move or go home, field stops and searches, threats, prodding with a nightstick or approaching with a pistol, and the use of "physical force," may be called police brutality (Barker 1986, 71).

Citizens should recognize that police have the right to direct citizens' behavior. For example, if a person is double parked and blocking traffic on a city street, the police officer has the responsibility to require that person to move his or her vehicle. Also, if a group of teenagers are blocking access into a store and intimidating adults from entering the store, the police officer has the right to tell the teenagers to move. In these situations, the police officer should be civil and courteous but should expect the citizen or teenagers to comply with his or her request.

Many citizens are unaware that when police are patrolling their beat they are expected to conduct field stops and searches. The stops are to determine if the person or group stopped has legitimate business in the area. Generally, stops will take place during the evening hours. Citizens not versed in the law may not know that police officers have the legal right to conduct searches to protect themselves or others from potential harm. Whether police misconduct occurs during a field stop or search depends upon the specific situation and the police officer's behavior.

The use of physical force by police officers is not illegal or a violation of a departmental policy if it is justifiable. Every situation where physical force has been used must be judged on its own merit. Generally, acts of police brutality are known only to the police officer and a few witnesses, normally fellow police officers, who observe excessive force being used. Segments of the American population, especially minority members, who have the largest number of brutality complaints against the police, consider police brutality to be more of a serious problem than politicians or police administrators care to admit. Police brutality is usually discovered when the victim of police brutality reports it to police authorities or to other governmental agencies. Most states provide for a state investigative agency to investigate police brutality by local police officers. On the federal level, the Federal Bureau of Investigation has the authority to investigate police misconduct that can be in violation of federal laws.

Today, with the prevalence of video cameras, cases of police brutality can be videotaped and shown later. The videotaping of acts of police brutality is evidence that a specific officer or officers were involved in the use of excessive force. One case in which an act of police brutality was brought to the world by a citizen's videotaping was the beating of Rodney King on March 3, 1991, by Los Angeles police officers. George Holliday, the citizen who videotaped the

Rodney King beating, brought the tape to the Los Angeles Police Department, who refused it. Upon the department's refusal, Holliday brought the tape to a local Los Angeles television station, which aired it. Eventually, CNN received a copy of the videotaped beating of Rodney King and gave it national and international coverage.

Another well-publicized case of police brutality took place on August 9, 1997, when a Haitian immigrant, Abner Louima, was taken into custody by police while sitting in a Brooklyn music club. The police took him to the 70th Precinct station house, where they strip-searched him and beat him. A New York City police officer allegedly shoved a toilet plunger into his rectum and then forced the toilet plunger into his mouth, breaking his front tooth. Louima asserted that while this was occurring, the officers taunted him, saying, "That's your shit, nigger," "We're going to teach niggers to respect police officers," and "This is Giuliani time, not Dinkins time" (Farley 1997, 38). Later, Louima recanted these comments. Eventually, Louima was hospitalized after a one and one-half hour ordeal in the station house. His injuries included a ripped bladder and a punctured lower intestine. The New York City police Commissioner Howard Safir called the incident a "horrific crime" and stated "We're going to make sure the perpetrators ... go to jail." He also pointed out that a police officer who had been present had come forward to implicate his colleagues (Farley 1997, 38). One police officer was arrested and charged with sexual assault and sexual abuse, and 12 police officers were transferred, suspended, or demoted to desk duty.

When the public becomes aware of acts of police brutality in incidents such as the Rodney King or Abner Louima cases, they cannot have much confidence that the police will refrain from using excessive force. As acts of police brutality keep coming to the attention of the public before they can forget the last act of brutality brought to their attention, the police forfeit the community's trust more and more. The gap between police and minority communities grows wider or at least cannot be lessened while such inhumane acts are being committed.

Police brutality cannot be condoned. For community policing to be successful, police brutality must be eliminated. Why would citizens want to cooperate with the police when police are abusing community residents? The negative publicity from the Rodney King beating and the Abner Louima abuses will take decades for the police to overcome.

Throughout the 1990s, there have been numerous documented incidents of police brutality in American police departments of all sizes and in all parts of the country, rural and urban. But very little statistical information is available to document the overall extent of police brutality. Obtaining reliable data on police brutality is extremely difficult. To correct this deficiency, the U.S. Congress passed the Violent Crime Control and Law Enforcement Act in 1994, requiring the Attorney General to collect data on the use of excessive force by the police and to publish an annual report of the findings. The President's Commission on Law Enforcement and Administration of Justice (1967) reported in its task force report that physical abuse by police officers was not a serious problem but did exist. Commission researchers observed patrol officers in a number of cities and did observe instances where excessive force was used when none was necessary. Those abused were poor, drunks, sexual deviates, or youngsters considered hoodlums. The key ingredient discovered by the task force members was that those abused had verbally challenged the police officer's authority (181–182). If police officers are willing to use excessive use of force in the presence of the president's task force, what can the community expect when officers are not in the presence of witnesses?

In order to deal with the "use of force" misconduct issue the Community-Oriented Policing Service (COPS) national office with the New England Regional Community Policing Institute developed a curriculum on how to deal with the "use of force" in the community-policing environment. The training program was designed for police chiefs and senior managers with the authority and responsibility for overseeing, reviewing, and revising the department's use of force approaches. This training program makes the assumption that the administrators attending the "use of force" training will have experience in implementing policies, familiarity with internal affairs, and a commitment to community policing. The goal of the attendees for this "use of force" training is to identify and implement "the use of force" model for their department (Sweeney, n.d.).

Specific "use of force" training curriculums that are designed specifically for senior police administrators should go a long way in curtailing police brutality and excessive use of force by police officers.

Corruption

Police corruption is the abuse of police authority to obtain personal gain. This gain may be either monetary or nonmonetary. In committing acts of corruption, police officers gain financially by failing to perform services they are required to perform or by giving services that they should not be giving. Thirty years ago Barker and Wells characterized acts of corruption, which are still valid today, in three ways: "(1) They are forbidden, by some norm, regulation or law, (2) they involve the misuse of the officer's position, and (3) they involve a material gain, no matter how insignificant" (1981, 4).

Police corruption, according to veteran police officers, is always around and comes to life whenever the police department's vigilance subsides. For example, New York City police officers have been charged with selling protection to drug dealers and sometimes trafficking in drugs themselves. A report by the Mollen Commission investigating corruption in the New York City Police Department asserted that the department's internal affairs unit routinely buried corruption cases. The report also stated that police officers routinely made false arrests, tampered with evidence, and perjured themselves in court ("Policing the Police," 1994, 16).

Stoddard (1995) found that the police culture has an informal code that protects police misconduct and tolerates corruption. Recruits are indoctrinated into the police culture and soon come to the realization that they need the support of their fellow police officers, because their personal safety may depend upon a fellow officer being there when they need assistance. Further, recruits quickly learn that they themselves are bound to make mistakes, which may result in violations of departmental policy or criminal law, so that it may be best "not to see anything" if they observe misconduct by other officers.

Corruption has been found in many police departments—among them Atlanta, Miami, Houston, New Orleans, Philadelphia, Savannah (Georgia), and Los Angeles. Further, suburban and rural areas are not free from corruption. For example, a number of rural sheriffs from Georgia have been sent to prison for protecting drug dealers. Scandals involving police officers in corruption cannot benefit the police–community relationship. Police departments must check corruption if they hope to develop a successful community policing program.

Commission of Criminal Acts

A police officer lying in a court of law to obtain a conviction of a suspect has committed a crime. Lying in court has been termed perjury and is considered a criminal offense. Other violations of criminal law by police officers include murder, bank robbery, burglary, domestic violence, child abuse, and rape. In New Orleans, an off-duty police officer committing a robbery killed her partner, who was moonlighting as a security guard. Four Detroit police officers were charged with the murder of a black motorist who was beaten to death. In Galesburg, Illinois, a police officer was charged with bank robbery, and in Chatham County, Georgia, a police officer was caught robbing a convenience store on his own beat. In Wichita, Kansas, a police officer was charged with child molestation. In Savannah, Georgia, a police officer placed his own child in scalding hot water.

Although few police officers commit criminal acts, the few that do create a negative image for all police officers. Police departments must recruit people of integrity and investigate all complaints of improbity. Also, they must be proactive in their investigations and emphasize eliminating not only police crime but all police misconduct.

Mechanisms to Control Police Misconduct

For police misconduct to be controlled, mechanisms must be in place to control police behavior. These mechanisms can be either internal or external to the police agency. There are strong arguments for both approaches. Groups and individuals that distrust the police claim that the police cannot clean their own house, so that outside mechanisms are necessary to control police misconduct. On the other hand, police personnel find it offensive that "outsider" civilians who do not understand police work will be reviewing their behavior. This controversy is a hot topic in policing. If community policing is to be accepted by both the community and the police, this dispute will eventually have to be settled to the satisfaction of both.

Internal Affairs Units

Since the 1950s, midsized and large police departments have established internal affairs units to investigate citizen complaints of police misconduct. The size of an internal affairs unit can range from one officer to several hundred officers. The norm for staffing internal affairs is to have a ranking officer, captain or lieutenant, involved in investigating the conduct of police officers.

The ideal would be for every complaint against a police officer to be investigated impartially. When the internal affairs unit conducts an investigation, it interviews all witnesses and examines all pertinent evidence. The internal affairs unit commander reports directly to the chief of police. A report is made of the unit's findings to the chief, who then makes a decision for the appropriate action to be taken.

Civilian Review Board

The notion of a civilian review board can be traced to the 1930s. A civilian review board is "an independent tribunal of carefully selected outstanding citizens from the community at large" (Bopp and Schultz 1972, 146). Today, civilian review boards are often referred to as civilian oversight of the police. Although there may have been a name change, the two terms have similar meaning.

Every time there is a situation where the police are suspected of police misconduct, we hear the call for implementing a civilian review board if one does not already exist. Many of the same arguments made for a civilian review board in the late 1990s are similar to those made by supporters for civilian review boards in the 1960s and 1970s.

Civilian review boards review citizens' grievances against the police and are made up of only civilians, without any police representative. In 1967, the President's Commission on Law Enforcement and Administration of Justice recommended the adoption of such an external grievance system, stating that

> the primary need is for the development of methods of external control which will serve as an inducement for police to articulate important law enforcement policies and to be willing to have them known, discussed and changed if change is needed.

(32)

Police acceptance of such an external grievance mechanism is a way of showing that their operations are open for inspection. The police can only create doubt and suspicion by rejecting an external grievance mechanism. In keeping with the community policing philosophy, with its emphasis on community-police interaction, it is a friendly gesture on the part of the police to accept civilian review boards, or civilian oversight bodies, as they are referred to today. Civilian oversight bodies have several characteristics in common. First, civilian oversight has been legally approved, either as an amendment to the city charter or by city ordinance. Second, civilian oversight bodies function independently of the police agency (Terrill 1990, 80).

Many of America's largest cities have some type of civilian oversight of police actions. In addition, many of America's midsized cities have adopted civilian oversight boards (Snow 1992, 51). The implementation of civilian oversight bodies does not necessarily mean that the police officer will always be found guilty. In all probability, the police officer will be exonerated. Civilian oversight boards are not in conflict with the community policing philosophy. In fact, civilian oversight boards indicate to the community the seriousness of police intentions to develop alliances and a cooperative spirit. The City of Wichita, Kansas, Police Department, which has a civilian oversight board, rarely has a recommendation of its internal affairs unit overturned by the civilian oversight board.

References

Aaronson, D.E. et al. 1984. *Public policy and police discretion: Processes of decriminalization*. New York: Clark Boardman.

American Bar Association. 1974. *The urban police function*. Gaithersburg, MD: International Association of Chiefs of Police.

Barker, T. 1977. Peer group support for police occupational deviance. *Criminology* 15(2): 356.

———. 1986. An empirical study of police deviance other than corruption. In *Police deviance* ed. T. Barker and D.L. Carter. Cincinnati, OH: Anderson.

Barker, T. and R.O. Wells. 1981. Police administrators' attitudes toward the definition and control of police deviance. Paper presented at the Academy of Criminal Justice Sciences, Philadelphia.

Bopp, W.J. and D.O. Schultz. 1972. *A short history of American law enforcement*. Springfield, IL: Charles C. Thomas.

Brown, M.K. 1988. *Working the streets: Police discretion and the dilemmas of reform*. New York: Russell Sage Foundation.

Cox, S.M. and W.P. McCamey. 2008. *Introduction to criminal justice*, 5th ed., Durham, NC: Carolina Academic Press.

Davis, K.C. 1971. *Discretionary justice: A preliminary inquiry*. Urbana: University of Illinois Press.

Farley, C.J. 1997. A beating in Brooklyn. *Time*, August 22, p. 38.

Goldstein, J. 1960. Police discretion not to invoke the criminal process: Low-visibility decisions in the administration of justice. *Yale Journal* 69: 543–561.

Hyatt, W.D. 2001. Parameters of police misconduct. In *Police misconduct* ed. M.J. Palmiotto, Upper Saddle River, NJ: Prentice-Hall.

Klockars, C.B. 1986. Street justice: Some micro-moral reservations: Comments on Sykes. *Justice Quarterly* 3(4): 515–516.

Nahmond, S.H. 1986. *Civil rights and civil liberties litigation*. New York: McGraw-Hill.

National Advisory Commission on Criminal Justice Standards and Goals. 1973. *Police*. Washington, DC: Government Printing Office.

Palmiotto, M.J. 2001. Police misconduct: What is it? In *Police misconduct* ed. M.J. Palmiotto, Upper Saddle River: NJ: Prentice-Hall.

Policing the police [editorial] 1994. *New York Times*, May 1, section 4, p. 16.

President's Commission on Law Enforcement and Administration of Justice. 1967. *The challenge of crime in a free society*. Washington, DC: Government Printing Office.

Reiss, A.J. 1984. Consequences of compliance and deterrence models of law enforcement for the exercise of police discretion. *Law and Contemporary Problems* 47 (Autumn): 89.

Snow, R. 1992. Civilian oversight: Plus or minus. *Law and Order* 40(12): 51.

Stoddard, E.R. 1995. The informal "code" of police deviancy: A group approach to "blue-coat crime." In *The police and society: Touchstone readings*, ed. V.K. Kappeler. Prospects Heights, IL: Waveland.

Sweeney, Joan, n.d. "Use of Force Issues in a Community Policing Environment," U.S. Department of Justice: COPS.

Sykes, G. 1986. Street justice: A moral defense of order maintenance policing. *Justice Quarterly* 3: 498–507.

Terrill, R.J. 1990. Alternative perceptions of independence in civilian oversight. *Journal of Police Science and Administration* 17(2): 80.

Walker, S. 1986. Controlling the cops: A legislative approach to police rulemaking. *University of Detroit Law Review* 63: 362–389.

———. 1993. *Taming the system: The control of discretion in criminal justice 1950–1990*. New York: Oxford University Press.

DISCUSSION QUESTIONS

Discuss the evolution of the police code of ethics or conduct in the United States.

1. Are ethics especially important in the law enforcement profession? Why or why not? Explain.
2. Discuss strategies that law enforcement managers can take to encourage ethical decision making.
3. Find the written code of ethics or code of conduct for a local law enforcement agency on the Internet. Compare the local code to the code established by the International Association of Chiefs of Police. In your opinion, is the code enforceable? Why or why not? Explain. Cite scholarly sources to support your opinion.

Chapter 3

Trends in Data Driven Law Enforcement

FIGURE 3.1   The image is a logo highlighting the Federal Bureau of Investigation's two major data collection programs: the Uniform Crime Reporting Program and the National Incident-Based Reporting System.

INTRODUCTION

In the last 50 years, technology has continued to change rapidly, the Internet becoming an invaluable communication and information resource. Dramatic changes in means and methods of data collection and the utilization of data have been innovating policing. In this chapter, we will look at how data and intelligence drives policy and actions in law enforcement today. We will also envision the future of law enforcement in the United States based on an analysis of current trends in the field. The global policing community is increasingly complex due to the rise of terrorism and transnational crime. Therefore, future police organizations may not resemble today's police forces. The 21st century has put policing into a whole new milieu, one in which the causes of crime and disorder often lie outside the immediate community, and thus demand new and innovative approaches in law enforcement. We will summarize the variety of ways that computers have affected policing and identify the issues surrounding the increased use of video cameras by police. There are also many constitutional issues that confront the judicial and legislative bodies in our government with the growth of surveillance technologies. In

FIGURE 3.2   A Federal Bureau of Investigation (FBI) image of a cyber classroom demonstrates the importance of continuing education in the law enforcement fight against cybercrimes.

this chapter, we will discuss these rapidly changing issues that involve the collection and use of data and intelligence by police organizations.

Figure Credit

Fig. 3.1: Source: https://www.fbi.gov/services/cjis/ucr/nibrs.
Fig. 3.2: Source: https://leb.fbi.gov/image-repository/cyber-classroom-stock.jpg/view.

Selection from "Policing in the New Era of Public Safety and Law Enforcement" from *Risk-Based Policing: Evidence-Based Crime Prevention with Big Data and Spatial Analytics*

Leslie W. Kennedy, Joel M. Caplan, Eric L. Piza

Develop Spatial Risk Narratives

Crime events occur within spatial and situational contexts. In Atlantic City, NJ [...] stakeholders created risk narratives from RTM results: they believed shootings are probably connected to drug sales and related turf conflicts whereby convenience stores are the places where drug buyers are solicited; nearby laundromats are locations where drug transactions are made; and vacant buildings nearby are used by drug dealers as stash houses for drugs and weapons, or by drug buyers to use drugs after purchase. When community stakeholders used the data-driven evidence to surmise that drugs, prostitution, retail businesses, and vacant properties are related in this way to shootings, they were more likely to agree with police that certain places will probably experience shooting incidents in the future. This led to conversations about how to effectively target and remediate the problems in these locations. In this example, policing interventions aimed at reducing shooting events focused preemptively on factors beyond the shooting incidents, the offenders, or their victims. Areas around laundromats received directed police patrols; police officer "meet-and-greets" with convenience store managers were implemented at frequent intervals every shift; and the city's Planning and Development Department prioritized remediation of vacant properties and installation of new LED street lights (to replace dimmer halogen lamps) at the highest-risk places.

Risk narratives such as this aid police in articulating crime problems in diverse ways, beyond those entailed in established paradigms, practices, or procedures. This supports reasoning with hypotheses, whereby preconceived notions held by police or other stakeholders about the crime problem and its relationships to space and time are tested and addressed accordingly. Police and policy-makers have evidence from RTM to articulate explanations for the occurrence of crime events at any moment in time in ways that diminish assumptions based on high-profile cases or the reinforcement of personal biases accrued from personal experiences or gut feelings. Risk terrain models serve as a foundation for discussions to form and advance risk narratives, to identify new data inputs for inclusion in future analyses, and to propose solutions that can be tested with actions that are planned and implemented to address or disrupt the risk narratives in meaningful and measurable ways. Risk narratives enable effective risk governance led by police and supported by other stakeholders.

Solicit and Value Input from Multiple Stakeholders

Risk-based policing uses the diagnostic and predictive outputs of RTM to moderate reactive law enforcement actions and maximize resource deployments to places where public safety needs are greatest. It emphasizes problem-solving, evidence-based decision-making, and regular assessments of actions and impacts. Police target offenders for the crimes and harms they commit, and they continue to conduct investigations and clear cases. But police realize they cannot arrest their way out of crime problems; nor should they be expected to try. Many examples of high-crime cities persist with voluminous law enforcement actions, but where the public does not routinely feel safe. Conversely, some cities have seen a drastic cutback on aggressive street-level enforcement without experiencing any significant upticks in crime. New York City, for example, experienced a 93% reduction of stop-question-frisk events from 2011 to 2015 (Ferrandino 2016) without experiencing significant crime increases as a result (see e.g. Pyrooz et al. 2016, fig. 2; Smith 2018). Similar findings have been observed elsewhere, as well (e.g., Shjarback et al. 2017; Towers and White 2017). Thus, it does not appear that aggressive law enforcement on a day-to-day basis inherently equates to public safety. Repeat offenses at the same places label areas "problematic" and garner police attention. But the seizure of an offender (or two, or three, etc.) from a hot spot area rarely diminishes the overall stability of the hot spot in the long term. Policing focused solely on seizing or incapacitating offenders located at hot spots often fails to cool hot spots because unaffected offenders adjust to these inconveniences (i.e., arrests) inflicted on others and continue to be attracted to these settings. Solving crime problems requires a concerted effort not only to focus on the individual offenders or their (potential) victims present there at any given moment in time, but to assess the mechanisms that enable hot spots to emerge and persist. Innovative police leaders recognize this and, through risk-based policing, redefine the missions of their police departments from "policing people in communities" to "governing crime risks while also enforcing the law."

"Our earth is round and, among other things, that means that you and I can hold completely different points of view and both be right," wrote June Jordan (1970), a poet, teacher, and essayist born in Harlem in 1936. "The difference of our positions will show stars in your window I cannot even imagine." Risk-based policing works best when police officials acknowledge the difference of their perspectives on crime relative to various other community stakeholders and all parties realize that their points of view can contribute to achieving the shared goal of public safety. When police share the burden of ensuring public safety with other city agencies and community stakeholders, these people become partners to help solve existing crime problems and to identify and address emerging public safety threats. This keeps police officers safer, too. And it goes a long way toward making policing and related activities effective, sustainable, and less susceptible to bias. Additionally, with an appraisal of risk narratives by police officers and other stakeholders, public safety efforts remain grounded in the nuanced social, cultural, economic, and political atmospheres in which crime is happening. The most vocal or politically connected constituents, for instance, don't get intervention efforts in their neighborhoods first if these places are not the highest-risk. This articulable and justifiable response prioritization is a valuable commodity for elected officials who must allocate limited resources in transparent ways.

This was demonstrated at a community meeting in Jersey City, NJ, when discussions centered on gas stations, identified by the risk terrain model as one of the highest risk factors for violent crimes. RTM confirmed experienced police officers' gut feelings about these locations. But a community stakeholder (from a local youth organization) added context to the conversation that warranted further analysis before interventions were planned. She argued that "service stations," "gas-only stations," and "gas stations with food marts" should not be lumped together in one category (as was originally done). The reasoning, she explained, derived from her awareness of youth hanging out after school around convenience stores, where they can easily congregate and get food and drinks. A city ordinance requires closing time for these business to be 10 p.m., but gas stations with food marts are exempted. The 24-hours-a-day, 7-days-a-week gas stations provide space for youth to congregate late at night, creating unique contexts for victimization. Her well-articulated opinion was reasonable to other stakeholders, and so new data were collected and analyses rerun before decisions about intervention strategies were made. In this example, the social relevancy of environmental features affected their spatial influences on behaviors at different times and under particular circumstances.[1] That is, the attractive qualities and related risks of convenience stores are very different at 10:30 a.m. compared to 10:30 p.m.; school days and weekends can also vary. Interactions among people and their geographies are deeply fluid and something that must be considered by multiple stakeholders with regard to risk governance. RTM diagnoses environmental risk factors, whereas risk narratives help convey their contextual nuances to plan risk reduction strategies that disrupt the criminogenic qualities accordingly.

Make Data-Driven Decisions

With risk-based policing, police review RTM reports and define the focus and intent of responsive actions. They record productivity data accordingly and then measure success by clear standards. Ideally, the risk reduction activities suppress a risk factor's attractive qualities completely, rendering it empirically absent from the subsequent risk terrain model altogether. Reported crime rates and the quantification of arrests and citations continue to be important performance measures for some police agencies. But RTM removes the need for a sole dependency on them, and it adds new options. Policing has an important role to play in affecting the risk terrain. Police officers can deter offenders, embolden victims, and assist in the hardening of targets. These products can have the overall impact of reducing crime occurrence. But an effective and sustainable risk reduction strategy requires identifying the environmental conditions in which crime is likely to appear, based on diagnostics from RTM. Then the next step is to propose strategies to address these conditions and interrupt the interactions that lead to illegal behavior settings and crime outcomes. Risk reduction often includes activities related to (1) reducing the spatial influence of one or more environmental risk factors that were identified by RTM; (2) target-hardening, situational prevention, or community awareness; and (3) police patrols or other operations to deter motivated offenders at high-risk places.

Police agencies implementing risk-based policing have been able to emphasize situational approaches to crime prevention in lieu of more traditional law enforcement tactics, such as stop-and-frisk. Thus, risk-based policing presents opportunities to build processes for systematically collecting data relevant to risk-based interventions. As previously discussed, police have traditionally collected data on crime occurrence and police enforcement activity when measuring the success and fidelity of targeted efforts. Given that risk-based policing routinely diagnoses underlying attractors of crime hot spots, this approach lends credence to evaluation efforts incorporating a wider range of data sets. Process and outcome measures are typically operationalized as part of evaluations conducted by outside academic researchers. However, recent research suggests that such data can be readily collected and analyzed by police agencies themselves through the increased use of police "pracademics," active police officers who have received academic research training that they can apply to in-house analytical efforts (Huey and Mitchell 2016). In addition, Piza and Feng (2017) have argued that crime analysis units offer a particularly rich source for evidence-based policing, as demonstrated by the increased reliance on crime-analysis products in the design and implementation of contemporary police practices. Piza and Feng further explained that police would benefit from empowering crime analysts to conduct in-house evaluations of agency programs and practices; provide recommendations related to training; reconfigure CompStat processes; and design researcher–practitioner partnerships around the core components of the action research methodology.

The cumulative effect of risks allows police leaders to develop a reliable probability of crime occurring at certain places over time, during and after interventions. This is accomplished through a comparison of various outcome measures and/or through an analysis that considers treatment and control areas during the same time periods. Sparrow (2015) argues that reported crime rates will always be important indicators for police departments. However, substantial and recurrent reductions in crime figures are only possible when crime problems have first grown out of control. A sole reliance on the metric of crime reduction, Sparrow explained, would "utterly fail" (5) to reflect the very best performance in crime prevention practices when police actions are successful at keeping crime rates low and nipping emerging crime problems as they bud. Beyond looking at crime-rate changes, a risk governance approach to solving crime problems points to success when factors in addition to crime counts improve.

Balance Strategies for Crime Risk Reduction

Police leaders, such as in Fayetteville, NC, and Atlantic City, NJ, have embraced risk-based policing for their agencies to balance law enforcement activities with strategies for crime risk reduction. As Captain Nolette of the Fayetteville Police Department explained, with RTM and smart policing concepts, police can identify factors that contribute to attracting criminal behavior and develop thoughtful responses to their city's unique circumstances (Nolette 2016). The Fayetteville Police Department reported reduced violent crime citywide by 11 percent. This occurred with minimal disruption to regularly expected patrol functions; no additional resources; and improved rapport with community stakeholders. There was more satisfaction all around. In Atlantic City the value of RTM derives from the fact that it shifts the focus of crime reduction away from people and onto places by using hard data showing that people tend to commit crimes in certain kinds of environments. This is according to Henry White, an old-school cop who started on foot patrol in 1985 and rose through the ranks to become chief of the Atlantic City Police Department. "That's why I like this model so much," White told the attendees of a business luncheon in 2016 (Strenger 2016). It improves community relations and does not define people as the problem, nor does it focus on people as the crime problem's sole fix. "We were able to reduce crime without contributing to mass incarceration," Chief White said (Melamed 2017).

In the Fort Worth area of Texas, police are working in partnership with Cook Children's Hospital to identify risky situations for children in homes during calls-for-service (such as the presence of an infant child but no crib or safe place to sleep in the house) and making referrals to outreach services that can directly provide free cribs and other needed resources (Rice 2017). "It's about changing the context, changing the features of the environment, so the people living there are safe," explained Dr. Dyann Daley (Blackburn 2017). In addition to police efforts toward this goal, non-profits like One Safe Place (an organization that helps abuse victims) are using risk terrain maps to target ad buys and put boots on the ground in high-risk places to help potential victims get out of dangerous situations before abuse occurs. Risk-based policing complements police and other community leaders who have already established programs that bring together police officers and other stakeholders by adding options to what would otherwise be law enforcement responses to people in crisis. Risk-based policing needs the preconceived notions about police being a force of community warriors pitted against bad people to be replaced with a sense of job satisfaction when emergency calls for police services diminish, juxtaposed with positive and strategic police–community interactions increasing at high-risk places.

Risk narratives about the dynamic interactions among people that occur at places can be shared with multiple stakeholders as a way of determining effective strategies for responding to threats and crime outbreaks. In the interactions that take place between crime incidents and context, constantly changing risk dependencies emerge from the actions of all persons and features at locations. It is here that risk-based policing integrates law enforcement, public safety, and community engagement—all focused on risk governance for the purpose of crime prevention—with great effect. "We've had certain neighborhoods in town that have been hot spots since I was on patrol," explained Chief White. "We made a ton of arrests. But, you know what? They were still hot spots until recently. Before, we would clean up an area temporarily but all we were doing was displacing crime" (Melamed 2017). The sustainability of risk-based policing comes from reduced crime plus many other benefits that propagate ground-swelled buy-in and further engagement among police officers and other stakeholders at all levels of the community.

Conclusion

The imperatives of risk-based policing require broadening policing practice to go beyond law enforcement and include consideration of the contexts in which crimes occur. In an era where there is alarm that police tactics are overly aggressive or out of touch with community concerns, risk-based policing offers alternative ways of informing police decisions, targeting officer deployments, and engaging with community stakeholders (for mutual benefits) that leads to greater success in crime prevention compared to traditional practices. The need for transparency and accountability is intense at this juncture in policing. Civic leaders are calling for new tools and new insights to provide a new openness to policing practices. So, the willingness to move forward with risk-based policing exists among some key constituencies. But effectively adopting these new ideas and approaches requires local police leaders to be willing to ask new questions, collect new data, and find value in the empirical (but contextualized) results to aid in achieving public safety. Information and analysis must guide decisions about where to police, and also about what to do beyond law enforcement actions when resources get to particular places. Risk-based policing requires more than technological changes or software upgrades. It requires police leaders to adopt a mission that differentiates the practice of law enforcement from the promise of public safety and to deliver on both of these needs in coordinated and complementary fashion. People are not only seen in the equation as either potential victims or offenders to be guarded or captured but as stakeholders to partner with and learn from.

Risk-based policing responds to the demands of problem-oriented policing by offering a way to measure the contextual effects of environments on behavior and then establish how effective interventions are implemented to reduce the risk that may occur at these places. Risk-based policing is problem *solving*, not merely problem orientation. It offers an extension of the previous attempts at focused policing, [...] that is evidence-based and actionable. Risk-based policing agencies that engage with community members to share information and solicit new insights on public safety further succeed at reducing the long-term risk of crime and its rate of occurrence. Members of the public who are directly or indirectly affected by crime problems engage with police as problem-solvers to promote processes and outcomes intended for the community. Public engagement enables evidence-based decision-making and increased transparency of policing while still keeping sensitive law enforcement information confidential or undisclosed. With all this in mind, and with a goal of crime prevention, the most effective risk-based policing leaders follow the central tenets in ways that are consistent with the goals of both public safety and law enforcement. They incorporate them into the three steps of risk-based policing [... .]

Notes

1. Spatial influence serves as the measurable link between features of a landscape and their impacts on people and the ways they use space. Spatial vulnerability to crime will not change unless one or more factors that comprise the risk terrain are mitigated. The secret, then, is that spatial vulnerabilities are mitigated by focusing efforts

on reducing or eliminating spatial influences, and not necessarily just the risky features themselves. The effect of spatial influence is not a constant but one that can be altered to reduce risk. So, it is sensible to consider a risk reduction strategy that focuses on mitigating spatial influences. If the spatial influences of risky features increase the chance of crime and its patterns over time, then it should be equally the case that reducing these spatial influences would reduce the incidence of crime (Caplan and Kennedy 2016).

References

Blackburn, B. (March 3, 2017). New research in Tarrant County targets abuse. WFAA 8 ABC. Retrieved from http://www.wfaa.com/article/news/new-research-in-tarrant-county-targetsabuse/419071412.

Caplan, J., and Kennedy, L. (2016). *Risk terrain modeling: crime prediction and risk reduction*. Oakland, CA: University of California Press.

Ferrandino, J. (2016). The effectiveness and equity of NYPD stop and frisk policy, 2003–2014. *Journal of Crime and Justice* 41(2):119–35. doi: 10.1080/0735648X.2016.1249385.

Huey, L., and Mitchell, R. J. (2016). Unearthing hidden keys: why pracademics are an invaluable (if underutilized) resource in policing research. *Policing: A Journal of Policy and Practice* 10(3):300–07.

Jordan, June. (1970). "Corners on the Curving Sky." In J. Jordan (ed.), *Soulscript*. New York: Harlem Moon.

Melamed, S. (August 10, 2017). Can Atlantic City's bold experiment take racial bias out of predictive policing? *Philadelphia Inquirer*.

Nolette, J. (2015). Using research to move policing forward. *NIJ Journal* no. 276, 1–5.

Piza, E., and Feng, S. (2017). The current and potential role of crime analysts in evaluations of police interventions: results from a survey of the International Association of Crime Analysts. *Police Quarterly* 20(4):339–66.

Pyrooz, D., Decker, S., Wolfe, S., and Shjarback, J. (2016). Was there a Ferguson Effect on crime rates in large U.S. cities? *Journal of Criminal Justice* 46(1):1–8.

Rice, S. (May 3, 2017). What new Texas moms should know about those free baby boxes. *Dallas News*.

Shjarback, J., Pyrooz, D., Wolfe, S., and Decker, S. (2017). De-policing and crime in the wake of Ferguson: racialized changes in the quantity and quality of policing among Missouri police departments. *Journal of Criminal Justice* 50:42–52.

Smith, K. (2018, January 1). We were wrong about stop-and-frisk: crime in New York City fell even as the policing tactic was abandoned. *National Review*. Retrieved from http://www.nationalreview.com/article/455035/new-york-city-stop-and-frisk-crime-decline-conservatives-wrong.

Sparrow, M. (2015). Measuring performance in a modern police organization. National Institute of Justice, U.S. Department of Justice.

Strenger, E. W. (December 21, 2016). Caplan's crime-reduction model expected to make AC a safer place. *Voice at the Shore*.

Towers, S., and White, M. (2017). The "Ferguson Effect," or too many guns? Exploring violent crime in Chicago. *Significance* (April), 26–29.

Selection from "Introduction" from *Intelligence-Led Policing*

Jerry H. Ratcliffe

What is Intelligence-Led Policing?

When first proposed, intelligence-led policing was an operational tactic that would reduce crime through proactive policing targeted by criminal intelligence. Kent Police (UK), under the leadership of Sir David Phillips, moved resources from reactive, crime investigation departments to proactive units, began tactical operations that were directed by criminal intelligence analysis, and promoted greater intelligence gathering. As a whole department, they were among the first to practise 'genuine' intelligence-led policing (John and Maguire 2003). This information-based strategy focused heavily on active and prolific offenders.

Some began to see that the business model required to manage crime analysis and criminal intelligence would also work as a broader management model for policing in general. From these early UK developments in intelligence-led policing grew the National Intelligence Model, which has evolved into a business and management model for resource decisions affecting a wide range of police activities. As a result, the interpretation of intelligence-led policing appears to be broadening in scope, and has evolved into a management philosophy that places greater emphasis on information sharing and collaborative, strategic solutions to policing problems at the local and regional level.

While it now appears clear that intelligence-led policing is evolving into a framework to encompass most operational police activity, police departments are at varying stages of development. Furthermore, the paradigm of intelligence-led policing is being interpreted differently in some places. While there is certainly a lineage that can be traced, a single unifying definition may prove elusive under these circumstances. In case the reader is seeking a quick answer, I will endeavour in this book to argue that intelligence-led policing is a business model and managerial philosophy where data analysis and crime intelligence are pivotal to an objective, decision-making framework that facilitates crime and problem reduction, disruption and prevention through both strategic management and effective enforcement strategies that target prolific and serious offenders. This definition (explained and expanded on in Chapter 4) recognises the evolution from whack-a-mole policing that arrests offenders with no overarching strategy, to one that places significant emphasis on data and intelligence analysis as the central component of police strategic thinking. This requires a wider interpretation of the information resources that police can draw upon. In this book, 'crime intelligence' is used as a collective term to describe the result of the analysis of not only covert information from surveillance, offender interviews and confidential human sources (informants), but also crime patterns and police data sources as well as socio-demographic data and other non-police data. It also centralises the role of the crime intelligence analyst (or police analyst) at the core of police decision-making.

What Makes Intelligence-Led Policing Unique?

[Related literature goes] into greater depth in attempting to clarify what intelligence-led policing is, and how it compares with other crime-control strategies. However, at this point, it is necessary to state what it is not. This [reading] is about intelligence-led policing. It is not about intelligence-led police. The police are a specific institution common across the world, whereas 'policing' is a term that suggests a set of processes within society that fulfil specific social functions related to regulation and control (Reiner 1997). As such, it is theoretically possible to conduct intelligence-led policing without involving the traditional public police force. Policing is now being widely offered by institutions other than the state, including private companies and community volunteers (Bayley and Shearing 1996). To understand the role of analysis in this expanding security field, it may be necessary to pay as much attention to 'knowledge and power, information and action' (Ransom 1980: 148) as to the formal structures of the policing environment.

Some of the perceived problems with intelligence-led policing lie with the name. Some people have a tendency to see the word *intelligence* and assume it has negative connotations, suggesting activity that is secretive, subversive and possibly illegal. There is an implication of dubious and immoral activity used to protect a police state. When the word is used in conjunction with the police, they fear the worst. However, intelligence-led policing actually develops data and information analysis into crime intelligence processes to the point where, 'as opposed to being a marginalised, subordinate activity, mythologically and furtively pursued by a caucus of officers, the collection and analysis of intelligence has become central to contemporary policing' (Christopher 2004: 117). When practised properly, intelligence-led policing provides an objective mechanism to formulate strategic policing priorities. The difficulty is that few outside law enforcement are aware of this broader interpretation of the term. As Grieve notes, 'The word intelligence needs to be reclaimed from the secret world, made less threatening to communities and used in their service' (2004: 26). Within the conceptual framework of intelligence-led policing, intelligence has a meaning more similar to competitive or business intelligence as commonly used in the business world.

For most of the history of policing, criminal intelligence was used to support individual, reactive investigations. Informants penetrated the organisational structure of criminal groups, and wiretaps and other forms of surveillance were employed against known, recidivist offenders. The aim was always to gather evidence to support a criminal prosecution. This is not the model of intelligence-led policing. Although achieving a prosecution against a serious repeat offender is rarely discounted, intelligence-led policing seeks to use crime intelligence for more than just individual cases. Intelligence-led policing uses crime intelligence for strategic planning and resource allocation, so that investigative action is used to target the right offenders and predict emerging areas of criminality. One of the unique aspects of intelligence-led policing is this use of crime intelligence—what was once a case-specific and myopic tool of crime control—as a strategic resource for better targeting and managerial decisions. In an intelligence-led policing model, crime intelligence drives operations rather than operations dictating intelligence-gathering priorities. This move from investigation-led intelligence to intelligence-led policing is revolutionary for modern policing.

The development from an investigative ethos to a strategic 'business model' (John and Maguire 2003: 38) to address a wide variety of policing problems provides police and analysts with a real opportunity to have a greater impact on crime. Instead of tackling crime one laborious investigation at a time, never truly having an impact on the more expansive criminal opportunity structure, the capacity to step back and place threats and risks into a holistic perspective that assesses the social harm of criminality may allow policing to prevent crime across a wide area rather than solve a single event that has already occurred. A further intriguing aspect of intelligence-led policing is the concentration on prolific and persistent offenders. This focus stems from the realisation that a relatively small percentage of the population is responsible for a significant percentage of crime [...]. Intelligence-led policing is also a realisation of the need to better integrate the information systems available to police so that a wider array of data and information sources can be brought to bear when creating a picture of the criminal environment. As Osborne (2006) points out, some of the information analysts require is inaccessible not just because of technological failures or lack of computer literacy but also as a result of interjurisdictional rivalries or a simple lack of understanding by police management and analysts. While we are now operating in an information-rich environment, it is not necessarily easier to translate that information into action; we are, in effect, information-rich but knowledge-poor.

Intelligence-led policing is quite different from the meaning of intelligence common in a military or national security context. Unlike in the military, law enforcement analysts are rarely a recognised feature of the managerial sphere, and across policing there is a lack of understanding of the role and applicability of crime intelligence analysis to strategy. Crime intelligence techniques and applications are seldom institutionalised, even with the supposed introduction of intelligence-led policing to some jurisdictions. There is so little research in the area of crime analysis that even an agreed establishment of analysts to population ratio, sworn officer count, or crime rate does not exist. For example, Cope (2003) found that the ratio of analysts in different UK police forces varied considerably. In the US, while about three-quarters of police departments with more than 100 sworn personnel employ at least one person in a crime analysis function, only 23 per cent of smaller departments have a dedicated crime analysis person (O'Shea and Nicholls 2002). The large departments (100 or more sworn officers) range from employing no crime analysts to one department that makes use of over 10 per 100 sworn officers (O'Shea and Nicholls 2002: 13).

A Holistic Approach to Crime Control

Crime control has been the central tenet of most police models in recent times. Some have questioned the wisdom of the police returning to crime control or administration of justice as their dominant function, suggesting that the community or social components of policing remain the central focus. Tim Newburn and Rod Morgan have argued that a significant policy shift away from other activities that police perform towards crime-fighting as a way to prevent crime is a 'dangerous illusion' (Morgan and Newburn 1997: 9), and they advocate a balance between police functions:

> We do not doubt the value of 'intelligence-led policing'. On the contrary, we also think there is a powerful case for concentrating a good many police resources on identifying and bringing to book persistent offenders. However, we do not think this is a policing panacea. And the key question is: how many police resources are to be devoted to this as opposed to other, in our opinion, *equally important* police objectives? (Morgan and Newburn 1997: 203, emphasis in original)

Embracing the crime-fighting image may indeed threaten the legitimacy of the police, and it may see the police move away from what is perceived to be a more traditional service ethos. Yet, this crime-fighting role is precisely what police expect to do and why officers usually join the police, at least initially. Importantly, it is also the role that the public usually ascribe to them. If criminal intelligence really is, according to John Abbott—former Director General of the National Criminal Intelligence Service—'the future of policing' (Johnstone 2004: 409), then 'By effective use of analysed intelligence the traditional dichotomy between crime fighting and problem solving may be resolved to the benefit of the community' (Amey *et al.* 1996: 32–33). One potential solution, proposed elsewhere and in this book, is to move to a strategic social harm approach that integrates the benefits of objective analysis with a greater appreciation for risk as perceived by the community. A strategic social harm approach works to 'establish priorities for strategic criminal intelligence gathering and subsequent analysis based on notions of the social harm caused by different sorts of criminal activity' (Sheptycki and Ratcliffe 2004: 204).

While a number of police departments are experimenting with intelligence-led policing, some claims to be intelligence-led are rather dubious and often just based on the police department making arrests in a big case rather than demonstrating any proof that the case was a priority resulting from managerial decisions based on a strategic assessment of the criminal environment. Unfortunately, many such approaches tend to stress the *intelligence* aspect of *intelligence-led policing* rather than emphasising *policing*; in doing so, they relegate the value of crime intelligence to a sideshow rather than as central to forming organisational goals (Ratcliffe in press).

This book does not present the concepts of intelligence-led policing as a *fait accompli*. As Brian Flood explains, 'It has been a journey of adaptation: from the lingering, attractive certainties of the pre- and post-war years to the uncertain, information rich, intelligence-led, 21st century world of multi-agency law enforcement' (Flood 2004: 37). That process of adaptation continues today.

Are police leaders ready to be more flexible in their view of both the criminal environment and their own working environment? Are analysts able to conceptualise the organised crime world with a view to prevention? Are managers ready to allow civilian crime intelligence analysts to sit at the big table? How much are decision-makers prepared to allow risks identified in strategic documents to trump their personal biases, pressure from the media, and expectations from the rank and file? The answers to these questions may predict the future of intelligence-led policing.

References

Amey, P., Hale, C. and Uglow, S. (1996) 'Development and evaluation of a crime management model', Police Research Group: Police Research Series, Paper 18: 1–37.

Bayley, D. H. and Shearing, C. D. (1996) 'The future of policing', *Law and Society Review*, 30(3): 585–606.

Christopher, S. (2004) 'A practitioner's perspective of UK strategic intelligence', in J. H. Ratcliffe (ed.), *Strategic Thinking in Criminal Intelligence*. Sydney: Federation Press, pp. 176–192.

Cope, N. (2003) 'Crime analysis: principles and practice', in T. Newburn (ed.), *Handbook of Policing*. Cullompton: Willan Publishing, pp. 340–362.

Flood, B. (2004) 'Strategic aspects of the UK National Intelligence Model', in J. H. Ratcliffe (ed.) *Strategic Thinking in Criminal Intelligence*. Sydney: Federation Press, pp. 37–52.

Grieve, J. (2004) 'Developments in UK criminal intelligence', in J. H. Ratcliffe (ed.), *Strategic Thinking in Criminal Intelligence*. Sydney: Federation Press, pp. 25–36.

John, T. and Maguire, M. (2003) 'Rolling out the National Intelligence Model: Key challenges', in K. Bullock and N. Tilley (eds.), *Crime Reduction and Problem-oriented Policing*. Cullompton: Willan Publishing, pp. 38–68.

Johnstone, P. (2004) 'Director General, National Criminal Intelligence Service (NCIS) of the United Kingdom (recently retired), John Abbott', *Police Practice and Research*, 5 (4/5): 407–414.

Morgan, R. and Newburn, T. (1997) *The Future of Policing*. Oxford: Oxford University Press.

Osborne, D. (2006) *Out of Bounds: Innovation and Change in Law Enforcement Intelligence Analysis*. Washington DC: Joint Military Intelligence College.

O'Shea, T. C. and Nicholls, K. (2002) 'Crime analysis in America', Final report. Washington, DC: Office of Community Oriented Policing Services.

Ransom, H. H. (1980) 'Being intelligent about secret intelligence agencies', *American Political Science Review*, 74 (1): 141–148.

Ratcliffe, J. H. (in press) 'Intelligence-led policing', in L. Mazerolle, R. Wortley and S. Rombouts (eds.), *Foundations of Environmental Criminology and Crime Analysis*. Cullompton: Willan Publishing.

Reiner, R. (1997) 'Policing and the police', in M. Maguire, R. Morgan and R. Reiner (eds.), *The Oxford Handbook of Criminology*. Oxford: Clarendon Press, pp. 997–1049.

Sheptycki, J. and Ratcliffe, J. H. (2004) 'Setting the strategic agenda', in J. H. Ratcliffe (ed.), *Strategic Thinking in Criminal Intelligence*. Sydney: Federation Press, pp. 194–216.

Reading 3.3

Selection from "Are Fusion Centers Achieving Their Intended Purposes?" from *State Fusion Centers: Their Effectiveness in Information Sharing and Intelligence Analysis*

Renee Graphia Joyal

FUSION CENTERS, IN GENERAL, WERE ESTABLISHED for the primary purpose of bridging the communication and collaboration gaps between agencies at all levels of government via streamlining the collection, analysis and dissemination of information and criminal intelligence. It was presumed that developing and improving the nation's domestic information and intelligence capabilities would improve the overall flow of information, as well as the ability for separate entities and sectors to coordinate better. The 9/11 Commission clearly concluded that the outdated structure of the U.S. intelligence infrastructure and the failure of timely information dissemination were major contributing factors to the success of the September 11, 2001 terrorist attacks, and future efforts to bridge this gap were imperative. Moreover, subsequent events, such as Hurricane Katrina in 2005, have reaffirmed the federal, state, local and tribal government's inability to share vital information and reliably coordinate emergency response activities.

By improving communication and coordination capabilities, government entities would be better able to *collect* the dots—that is having the abilities to collect disparate data and circulate it to particular communities of interest (Libicki and Pfleeger, 2004). These circumstances were compelling catalysts for the construction and operation of a majority of fusion centers. To achieve this, a number of physical, technical and cultural barriers must be minimized or removed not only vertically between the layers of government, but also horizontally across jurisdictional and disciplinary boundaries, so that all public safety entities would be better able to *collect* the dots, figuratively speaking. Moreover, since fusion centers conceptually are founded on the principles of intelligence-led policing, fusion centers were established to reprioritize and formalize the collection and use of information away from a tactical, reactive, investigative use towards supporting a more proactive, prevention-oriented approach to law enforcement capable of identifying threats before they become pervasive. To accomplish this goal, the development of a robust analytical capability would also be necessary then to *connect* the metaphorical dots.

In an effort to surmount such physical, technological and cultural barriers, a number of arrangements were implemented, specifically the collocation of partners into one location with onsite access to multiple state and federal databases. The collocation of people should not only minimize the physical barriers between people, and thus agencies, but also curtail some of the long-standing cultural barriers. Thus, fusion centers have been organized in such a way that should redefine the nature of a number of interagency relationships, including those between the federal, state, local and tribal levels of government; between agencies within a single state; and between the fusion center and its host organization. The fusion center structure should also be redefining working relationships between sworn and civilian staff, particularly those who regularly work together within the fusion center setting.

Not only were fusion centers tasked to improve information sharing both vertically and horizontally, but they were also envisioned as hubs equipped with an analytical capability that is both sufficiently organized and sophisticated to enable the center to develop both tactical and strategic intelligence products and threat assessments—that is, to connect the dots. It was presumed that by prioritizing the analysis of information, and the subsequent dissemination of intelligence products, users would then use those products to make informed decisions, which in turn would theoretically influence their operating environments.

The findings from this research suggest that fusion centers are fulfilling their intended purposes partially. Specifically, fusion centers appear to be helping reduce the barriers addressed above, which in turn is improving information sharing and communication both between and within the levels of government, as well as influencing professional relationships (see Table 3.3.1).

However, the findings also indicate that they are not yet successfully achieving a robust analytical function at this time. Moreover, participant's responses imply that while a fusion

TABLE 3.3.1 Perceptions of Fusion Centers Fulfilling Primary Purposes (N=49)

Fusion Centers' Purposes	%
Collocation Minimizing Physical & Technological Barriers	82
Collaborative Arrangements Minimizing Subcultural Barriers	57
A Deficiency of Robust Analytical Capabilities	80
Moderate Role of Counterterrorism	45
Marketing Fusion Centers	51

center must always remain cognizant of the terrorism-related threats, terrorism does not consume the majority of their daily activities, nor should it, if they are to be regarded as valuable and relevant to their customers. Finally, the participants included in this research indicated that their centers continue to market themselves to solicit buy-in from different user groups. It appears that there is considerable variation in the degree of buy-in not only between, but also within, the local, state and federal levels of government.

Increasing Information Sharing by Minimizing Physical and Technological Barriers

Approximately 82% of participants agreed that fusion centers' presence and structural arrangements are instrumental in improving and facilitating information sharing between agencies by minimizing several barriers, particularly physical barriers. Collocating multiple agency personnel and access to their respective information systems has improved agencies' abilities to communicate and coordinate by minimizing the physical proximity between people, and thus entities. Fusion centers appear to be bridging the historical information gap in law enforcement, or at least demonstrate having the capability to do so. A sworn supervisor from Site B stated, "there is talk of a virtual fusion center, [but] to me that would be garbage. If you are going to do fusion, you need to put everybody together. You are establishing these contacts, knowing how they tick." Various participant perspectives support this finding, including those assigned to and working directly in fusion centers, as well as those persons with peripheral involvement in the fusion centers' day-to-day functioning.

A number of participant perspectives indicated that fusion centers are increasing information sharing, namely by collocating various agencies into a single facility and/or workspace. Several commissioned officers assigned to the fusion center addressed how fusion centers have facilitated information sharing. According to a Captain in Site A, the fusion center is viewed as a major participant in statewide communications:

> More and more I am finding that state government and the federal government are looking to the fusion center. They are especially in [Site A]. Everything seems to be falling to 'what is [the fusion center] saying about it?' Right to the point, we are going to a meeting on Thursday on H1N1 and its impact on the state. Now, that's a Health and Senior Services issue. But, they are also looking at the fusion center from an emergency management standpoint, from a mitigation standpoint, from a COOP and COG, so we can get out to the private sector information to push things out so we can help, again, that continuity

of business, continuity of government ... they look to us to be that very synthesized information source.

The following *partner* participant responses illustrate how Site A's fusion center, specifically, facilitates information sharing. A Special Investigator from the state-level Office of Homeland Security and Preparedness explained:

> The other aspect of it is the sharing, the talking to all the partners. To be able to just say 'hey, can you check on such-and-such a thing?' It's definitely the luxury of having the partners there, the other agencies, like right there, to be able to call them and go see them. As opposed to not having the DHS rep there, it delays getting that immediate information you are trying to get. When she was there, you would get information immediately, and if she didn't know, she would get it and it was an immediate thing. So, the strength, I think is the ability to truly all work together for public safety.

A Senior Parole Officer assigned to the same fusion center reiterated the same sentiment:

> I don't know how much you know about law enforcement, but it's a lot of people, especially with gangs and investigations and intelligence, nobody likes to share; it's difficult. Have fusion centers helped? Absolutely, you see it first hand as opposed to someone just telling you we are sharing or getting a phone call. The two different agencies are actually meeting and speaking in one location, and the analysts' kind of being the intermediate to get us together. So, in that regard, yes, at least it's helping in that sense; you are seeing it. [Information] coming in here, we are getting the information, they are supplying it to us and we bring it back to our respective agency.

A Detective from a large local police department assigned to the fusion center also depicted the fusion center as a conduit for information sharing since it enables partner agencies and other users to network with additional professionals with whom they might otherwise not come into contact. He felt that:

> The good thing is that is it [i.e. the fusion center] opens up a field of networking with other agencies, so information is shared a little bit more fluently. There is not that territorial boundary of intelligence. It's more shared information nowadays, which is good.

Furthermore, the three participants representing the national perspective on fusion centers confirmed that in general fusion centers have contributed to increased information sharing. A senior policy advisor to the Department of Justice, Bureau of Justice Assistance explained, "[fusion centers] have opened up communication. Even if it's not perfect, they have opened up silos that historically have been there and may not have been overcome unless there was this type of structure in place." His contemporary from the DHS supported this statement, arguing that:

> Certainly, there was an inability to make informed decisions prior to 9/11. I think it has certainly got much better since, and I think fusion centers are a major reason why ... For the first time in U.S. history, there is the capability to pull or push classified information to state, local, tribal, private sector decision-makers, and this is largely based on the national network of fusion centers. Whether or not we are always passing the right information or that we have perfected what we are passing, but the fact that we are willing to use fusion centers as that facilitation in and of itself is a very important step.

Finally, an FBI agent who was heavily involved at the national level with the National Fusion Center Initiative confirmed that:

> Prior to 9/11, the only real means we had, the FBI, for sharing information with sate and locals was primarily through our task forces—JTTF, Safe Streets, Fugitive, Organized Crime, etc. After 9/11, it became apparent, even within the federal government, we weren't sharing information ... Post-9/11, fusion centers have become one of the primary means for us to share information with the state, local and tribals. I know there has been some intelligence generated at the local level that has been put into the President's daily briefing. Does it happen all the time? No, but it does happen.

Collaborative Arrangements Minimizing Subcultural Barriers

Over half of participant responses indicated that to some degree subcultural barriers have been reduced, namely between commissioned officers and civilian analysts. However, this change seems to be occurring primarily within the fusion center environment and potentially, albeit to a lesser degree, in specific contexts outside of the fusion center walls. A Detective Sergeant offered his observations on how the subcultural differences between analysts and commissioned officers assigned to the fusion center have changed since the fusion center's inception, stating:

> You are talking about two different cultures coming together. A quasi-military organization coming into, I guess, a free-flowing, free-thinking mind-set of the analysts. In the beginning, there was cultural divide. With time it has been, you know, an understanding of the two cultures coming together and really working together and fusing together and willing to achieve the goals that have been established. The underlying differences still exist, but there is a better understanding, and things are totally different than they were before.

Addressing the changing roles of analysts within the fusion center setting, another Detective Sergeant assigned to Site A explained how analysts within the fusion center have the access to a greater range of law enforcement information and how they engage in the over-all process more than they would in a traditional policing environment. He explained that:

> I don't think there is anywhere, definitely here in the state police, where civilian members have the access and the opportunities that they have here [in the fusion center]. It just doesn't exist; briefings to senior level, not only government folks, law enforcement folks, across the spectrum, [civilians have] access to information that was once law enforcement only. The civilian-sworn issue is blurred here, and it has to be just because of the tempo. The mindset is that we are out there in the mix. I have to take off my trooper hat ... That was a personal adjustment I had to make that was not easy to do, but [I do] in the spirit of fostering this civilian-sworn cooperation, and I think its working here pretty well.

When probed to distinguish how analysts are perceived by commissioned officers working within the fusion center compared to those in the law enforcement community who do not have the same daily interaction with analysts, the Detective Sergeant admitted that:

> A lot of times you get that initial skepticism or kind of quizzical, 'who are these people? Why are they talking to me and who allowed them in here?' Ok, that's fine, but once presentations are made, and the [information] coming out of their mouth and the impact they are able to make, that credibility factor goes up. Once again the proof is in the pudding, and a lot of these folks out there in

law enforcement, while initially skeptical and wanting to only talk to a cop, hey at the end of the day you are getting stuff you can use and it's working for you, and that makes these people very happy. Law enforcement executives for the most part, but right down to detectives working a squad, working an investigation, we have seen that here too, the initially skepticism and some reticence to get involved with a civilian as opposed to a law enforcement person. But the proof is in the pudding, and if the information is good and its helping an investigation, you know what, they get over it.

A sworn supervisor from Site B conferred that the relationship between analyst and officers does well in-house but subcultural divides persist outside of the fusion center environment, stating:

It goes very well here because I can see you are involved, you are busy, [and] you do good work. I think there is a good repertoire in the field, but every once in a while I have to step in. Someone might talk to me in a condescending manner about what they [i.e. analysts] do. I do my role, [and] stick up for my people. It pisses you off, but still. Most of these people are former dispatcher so they know a lot of people.

A state police analyst from Site A working within the fusion center offered his observation on the issue of civilian analysts working with commissioned officers:

I have seen troopers come into this situation were there are analysts and immediately say, 'oh, you are a civilian.' As we work together longer that attitude starts to fall by the wayside because they see the analytical skills and they see analytical talents they just don't have. These guys spend six months being trained how to use a gun, how to wrestle people down, and how to be the man in the middle of the night. Those skills don't necessarily translate well into, 'hey, lets all sit around the talk and discuss; let's brainstorm' ... So, when you are within the four walls, that kind of evolves and dissolves.

I have called other units [within the state police] and said, 'hey, I need certain information from your unit,' and gotten 'Are you civilian?' You do get that. As recently as last week I called someone and got that question, 'why should I waste my time with you? Have your Sergeant call me.' When I have called locals ... well, I haven't got that as much. With federal agencies, they are used to working with civilian co-workers, [so] federal agencies not so much. Local agencies not so much, but part of that is when I introduce myself, I just give name and my organization [i.e. state police] [not my status as a civilian or commissioned officer].

A commissioned officer from Site A with an investigative background, who was recently assigned to the fusion center at the time of the interview, addressed how he feels coming into a fusion center setting where the boundaries between civilians and officers are less clear. It is evident from his comment that while the working relationships between the two subcultures have improved within the fusion center environment the status quo largely persists outside of the fusion center. He explained that:

> I am still in the middle because again, I am going on twelve years [in the state police], and this is the first time I have worked this closely with civilians. For me, it was almost a little bit of a learning curve since you kind of, when you come into a room of troopers you kind of know where everybody stands. And here it's a little bit … its not the same dynamic, I guess, and its kinds of hard figuring out where people fall in, I guess, the food chain so to speak.

The FBI analyst assigned to the fusion center offered a partner perspective on this dynamic, one that corroborated the investigators perspective:

> I think there is a little bit of a barrier [between analysts and troopers] … I would have to say that the wall, in my opinion, has not come down yet between analysts and trooper. The troopers are still held in a little bit of a rung up, a little higher on the rung, which was always that way in the federal, in the FBI, also up until 9/11. So, I do not think they have shattered their wall, yet.

When addressing the relationship between sworn and civilian personnel, the Director from Site D explained:

> The commissioned guys think sometimes when they get information or a request, the analysts are telling them how to do their job. Its gotten better since the Captain and I have taken over, but this is something from years ago that has gone on.

As evidenced by the participants' comments, it seems that physical proximity directly influences the working relationships between civilian and commissioned staff.

A Deficiency of Robust Analytical Capabilities

While the participant interviews revealed that fusion centers are positively influencing inter-agency communications and coordination both vertically and horizontally, approximately 80% of their responses also indicate that fusion center's analytical capabilities have yet to be developed internally or utilized externally. While there may be exceptions to this finding, a robust and reliable analytical component with *estimative* or *predictive* capabilities has yet to be fostered and institutionalized. Two sub-themes emerged regarding the absence of a robust analytical capability. First, intelligence analysis as a profession and analysts collective skill sets have yet to mature at the subfederal level. Developing a robust analytical capability is partially influenced by the resources a fusion center is able to secure, namely a sufficient number of analysts with the experience and skills necessary to engage in analyses that are more sophisticated. However, it is greater than the set of skills and experiences analysts collectively bring to the table.

Secondly, a robust analytical capability also requires a shift in external user's mindset of how to use information and intelligence in policing. The study's findings suggest that users have yet to fully understand and appreciate the value an analytical function can contribute to their occupational duties. While the role of analysis, and thus analysts, have seemingly improved since 9/11, at least within the fusion center setting, it appears that a significant portion of analysts' activities remain focused on providing an investigative, case support function and continue to be peripheralized by the larger law enforcement community.

While reactive policing practices are important and should not be abandoned, fusion centers are theoretically founded upon the principles of proactivity and prevention, rather than case support and prosecution. It seems that rather than providing decision-makers with strategic, future-oriented information, a significant portion of fusion centers' analytic activities remain tactically and operationally focused. An analyst subcontracted by DHS and assigned to Site A asserted that the fusion center is "not producing products with predictive capability, they are getting to that. The end result will be products that they can use and take action on." The assistant supervisor within the same fusion center's analytical unit also affirmed that while the fusion center does provide products that are tactically useful, he notes that "the biggest thing we *want* to do here is provide current and warning intelligence." A Detective Sergeant assigned to Site C similarly stated that, "they [i.e. analysts] have good ideas, and they put out good products, but we are still doing more case support here than we are putting intel products out."

Continuing maturation of the analytical profession

Analysts' collective skill sets have yet to fully develop and achieve a level of sophistication that is necessary in strategic analytical work as envisioned within a fusion center environment.

The collective deficit in analysts' skill set appear to be due to several co-occurring issues, such as inexperience, lack of training, and the diversity of customer's needs to which a fusion center's analytical component should be catering. Carrying the job title of *analyst* does not necessarily entail having an analytical skill set; rather, that skill set is developed with experience.

Analysts appear to be inexperienced primarily in two ways—they are either young or older. Younger analysts, while more likely formally educated, are disadvantaged in that they are more likely to have recently graduated from college, and therefore have limited occupational experience performing analysis. Older analysts, on the other hand, have largely been recruited internally from other areas within the state police, largely clerical workers, dispatch and civilian administrators. It seems they are less likely to be college educated and are less likely to have developed critical thinking skills than their younger counterparts. As the director from Site D explained:

> Only three of my analysts have degree[s], but that is because they were hired prior to the fusion center. They are good tactical people, its just their writing is weak and their critical thinking is not there … I think it's because they didn't go through the process of writing papers etc. You take information, gather it, and come up with a product, and that is something they need to be trained on and it's going to take time.

Moreover, older analysts have largely supported an investigative, case support function during their tenure with the state police, and it is difficult for some to shift from a tactical orientation to a strategic orientation. The Director from Site C explained that the majority of his analysts have been with the state police, "For quite some time doing case support, so trying to move through that transition. And to be totally honest with you, I think there is a lot of trying to figure out what is analysis and what the heck are they talking about." As the Site A's analytical supervisor stated, "We have a burgeoning work force that is … young, not necessarily in age but in experience level of analysis. As that grows, it will certainly strengthen out ability to provide value out to folks, to get more involved in predictive type of analysis." The Director from Site D similarly explained:

> The newer fusion centers are going to hire people with a college [education], and they are going to be able to do more critical thinking and analytical work on their own, opposed to us pushing them and telling them exactly what they need to be asking and why and really, unfortunately, us taking their hand and walking them through it.

Another issue to emerge regarding analyst shortcomings is the lack of standardized training. While this problem is clearly known at all levels of government, rectifying it is a substantial challenge. A number of separate agencies provide analytical training, and typically, analysts travel to receive the training. Not only is funding analytical training a major issue, but standardizing analytical training curriculum is a daunting task. Federal entities and professional associations are reviewing their current training programs and consolidating their resources so analysts at the local, state and federal levels will receive identical analytical training and so that a greater number of analysts can receive training more cost effectively. For example, the FBI interviewee from headquarters explained that the ODNI is trying to develop a mobile training program with three different levels: basic, intermediate and senior. He explained that the ODNI:

> [Is] looking at a combination of instructor and web-based training, but the goal is to make the difference between a state or local analyst and a federal analyst indistinguishable. They are all writing the same way, products look the same way, and they all know what they are supposed to be doing, but it's a challenge.

While not explicitly identified as problematic by the participants, the scope of analytical responsibility and the diverse arrays of (potential) customers, and thus their needs, appear challenging to fusion center's analytical elements. For example, analytical products are requested for both strategic, proactive purposes as well as tactical and investigative reasons. Furthermore, a customer may be from the either the federal or subfederal community or even the private sector. Even within the state police, a user may be from the executive leadership, the uniformed division or investigations. It is difficult to be everything to everybody, particularly when there are so many uncertainties.

The participant interviews indicated that the analysts' status has improved over the years; however, they are not yet fully perceived as equals to their law enforcement counterparts. Until recently, the term *analyst* was used inappropriately to classify employees who did not conduct analysis. Rather, those labeled as an *analyst* often fulfilled administrative and clerical support. This trend was not restricted to state, local and tribal agencies, but was also evident in the federal government. In fact, many analysts were employed originally in clerical and administrative positions prior to being 'promoted' to an analyst title. An FBI Supervisory Special Agent explained:

> When I first got to the FBI, what we were calling analysts weren't analysts. They were file clerks, secretaries that worked their way up. They were called analysts, but they weren't analyzing anything. The analyst has really come

into being in the Bureau, at least at the field level, real true analysts, probably three to four years ago when we started hiring from the Intelligence Community. People who actually looked at raw intel and developed a product ... we did not have the cadre of analysts that we do now—analysts in the true sense of the word.

His counterpart from DOJ addressed how he believes that law enforcement officers at all levels of government do not uniformly accept analysts as legitimate professionals, explaining that:

The biggest issue is state, local and tribal governments, and federal governments to some degree, recognizing the analyst is a professional and that, you know, they are not second-class citizens or any longer just a secretary who was moved up there because she ran out of promotional opportunity. These are people with a legitimate career and with additional levels of analytical skills and other intuitive skills that can really be positive.

A law enforcement executive in the top brass of the state police reaffirmed the FBI agent's previous comment stating:

That is historical, although it's much better that what it used to be. Analysts before 9/11 were glorified secretaries; now they are viewed for their analytical skills, but they are still run by sworn [officers] ... in my opinion, there should be more analysts there and law enforcement should give more credit to the analytical field. In other words, analysts are not viewed at the same level than police officers.

A Detective Sergeant in the state police assigned to the fusion center also addressed how:

Initially, the state police used analysts as data entry people, not as analysts to analyze information. There was a total misunderstanding, and again it comes down to a lack of understanding of the intelligence process and how different components plug into that process. That is what has caused a lot of the issues, but the analysts here, engaging in the process and coming up with the products and really being able to make an impression, saying, 'based on the information you have provide[d], this is what we have come up with. They [i.e. consumers] have been impressed and really their [i.e. analysts] stature has really been elevated. I can speak for the analysts here at the fusion center. I can't really speak for the analysts at other sections.

Not only is the analytical profession relatively young, particularly at the local and state level, but the profession of law enforcement is also young with regards to using information in a proactive capacity. The policing mindset is largely ad hoc and reactive, and changing this mindset takes time. The fusion center's users must not only understand the analytical process, but also adequately value it in order to use it in an anticipatory capacity. As a Director within a state's Attorney Generals Office explained:

> Fusion centers have another important mission, which we are all involved in hoping to craft. Information used to *conduct* operations is one thing, but using intelligence to *define* those operations is another ... it's not just providing the tool, it's providing for an operating environment or philosophy that transforms the thinking as to how we use that product.

The Role of Counterterrorism in Fusion Centers

Since the concept of fusion centers originated in the states' desire to develop an intelligence capability due to the failures identified post-9/11, it is important to address how those individuals working in and with fusion centers perceive the importance of counterterrorism activities, and what role counterterrorism activities are perceived to have in the fusion center's day-to-day functions. While many centers were founded initially on the concept of countering terrorism, different centers have developed with a range of missions, some of which have changed over recent years.

The majority of fusion centers that were established solely focused on counterterrorism have since shifted their mandates to include all crimes and/or all hazards focus. This has occurred for several reasons, primarily the rarity of terrorist events, the related difficulty of financially justifying a narrowly focused, new, undeveloped and seldom-used capability, and the FBI's statutory authority to investigate terrorism-related cases. Moreover, since DHS provides the primary source of federal funding to fusion centers, a fusion center must demonstrate its ability to allocate money in ways that align with and support DHS' mission, which is the broader all-hazards mandate.

Almost half of the respondents indicated that the threat of terrorism and law enforcement's activities to counter the threat of terrorism do not dominate fusion centers' day-to-day activities. Moreover, this conclusion is considered common knowledge among those working in or associated with fusion centers. While the threat of terrorism does not dominate fusion centers' primary foci, the respondents largely agreed that it should not be removed from their center's purview either, primarily due to the pervasive belief that there is a nexus between crime and terrorism. Thus, law enforcement, and fusion centers specifically, have both good reason and a responsibility to address terrorism-related threats. As a former Attorney General noted:

> I agree with the all crimes-all hazards approach. I think it makes sense because there is a continuum. The 9/11 highjackers violated all kinds of laws to get where they got. They overstayed visas, submitted fraudulent documentation; so, if a fusion center were looking for that kind of information—precursor crimes— it would have picked them up.

The federal policy advisor for Department of Justice mirrored the previous sentiment stating:

> You have to be aware because of precursor issues, that's my sense on it. It always has to be in the background, it shouldn't be in the foreground, in terms of that you have to be looking at … the gang issues, the bootleg sales and asking the next question, 'where are the proceeds going? And is this supporting just the local Bloods or Crips? Or is it supporting [terrorism], going overseas to Hizbullah or something else in terms of that issue?' I think when you do that you can combine both.

Nevertheless, law enforcement is, and will continue to be, primarily responsible for preventing and responding to crime and its perpetrators, and fulfilling this responsibility is what the public primarily expects. As such, the law enforcement community is responsible for ensuring that they meet their constituencies' expectations. To do this, the police will value information from the fusion center that better enables them to address the community's needs and concerns; thus, the fusion center must be sensitive to their customer's needs if they are to remain valuable and relevant. This issue was reiterated many times from a number of perspectives. As an FBI agent stated:

> I think that the reason many fusion centers went to all-crimes is because terrorism is just a small piece of what is going on out there. I know, I have sat in a lot of conferences where smaller police departments are saying, 'you guys are talking about car bombs and all this stuff, and I have meth labs and biker gangs. We got prostitution rings. That terrorism stuff—great, but that's not

what my constituencies are worried about.' I think that is what drove the big push to the all-crimes segment of it. And through there, I think there is a good amount of information being developed. Terrorism should not be taken off the table because you never know what is going to be out there

An academic and consultant affirmed that:

> Crime is what the public expects the police to be dealing with. I think the focus on counterterrorism was well meaning, but it is hugely limiting ... places like [Site A] were always set up to be all crimes-all hazards to start with. If they [i.e. fusion centers] adopt that approach, they really do a nice job of filling in a huge problem in American policing, which is the gulf between the different levels [of government].

As the fusion center's analytical unit supervisor, a Lieutenant in the state police from Site A, further explained:

> I think the answer has to be an all-crimes approach because if you are going to keep the customer interested, the customer primarily focuses on things that are in their lane. Osama bin Laden is not in the lane of [city x] police department, crime is. If you want to engage our customers into terrorism products, then we better develop the credibility in crime products because that is what they [i.e. the customer] do everyday.

A Captain managing Site A cleverly summarized the role of counterterrorism in fusion centers' day-to-day activities, highlighting the severe limitations and risks of embracing and supporting a strictly counterterrorism focus:

> When you really start rattling that counterterrorism saber, you are missing the mark. The people you are serving don't get it. They look at you as Chicken Little—the sky is falling. They don't listen; it becomes white noise to them. So, when it does happen they are not going to listen to you anyhow because you have been rattling that saber so long ... If you keep trying to rattle that monster-under-the-bed of counterterrorism that could come out of the closet at any time, and it could, the American public won't stand for it. They don't have the ability to wrap their heads around it. We don't live our life that way. It's not what this country is built on, so I don't know that they will stand for

the kind of spy vs. spy mentality, living within their own state ... [So,] if that [i.e. terrorism] is all you are going to be looking at, I think you have a very small seat at the table. I think you are missing the mark. I think you are not serving your public fully; I think you are almost self-serving your own nature.

Moreover, since threats of terrorism are not equally distributed geographically, many participants felt that a fusion center's prioritization of terrorist threats would be a function of several factors. These factors may include their geographical location; the presence of sensitive infrastructure within and near their jurisdictions; presence of terrorism disaggregated by type of terrorist threats that currently are or have been present within the state and/or region; population density; and population diversity.

Reference

Libicki, M. and Pfleeger, S. (2004). *Collecting the Dots: Problem Formulation and Solution Elements*. Santa Monica, CA: RAND Corporation.

DISCUSSION QUESTIONS

The post-9/11 environment in the United States, the *era of homeland security* for American policing, has led to increasing partnerships and data sharing among various agencies to combat crime and terrorism. Some believe that the 9/11 terrorist attacks could have been prevented if not for intelligence failures. The difference between intelligence-led policing (ILP) today and earlier intelligence roles is that intelligence is no longer considered a specialized function of crime analysts or intelligence units. The implementation of CompStat and community policing served as a foundation for ILP. "COMPSTAT (short for COMPuter STATistics or COMParative STATistics) is the name given to the New York City Police Department's accountability process and has since been replicated in many other departments. CompStat is a management philosophy or organizational management tool for police departments, roughly equivalent to Six Sigma or TQM, and was not a computer system or software package in its original form. Through an evolutionary process, however, some commercial entities have created turnkey packages including computer systems, software, mobile devices, and other implements collectively assembled under the heading of CompStat" (Retrieved from http://dictionary.sensagent.com/CompStat/en-en/). Although there are substantive differences in the concepts, the similarities can serve us as reliable prior-policy experience in the field. This experience will allow ILP to be implemented in the immediate future here in the United States (Ratcliffe, 2006).

Contemporary ILP doctrine blends problem solving, environmental design, community policing, and public-private partnerships. ILP is envisioned as a tool for information sharing both within law enforcement agencies and between all participants in the community, private sector, intelligence community, and public government. ILP is a multidisciplinary tool that, when used correctly, will have major societal benefits which we are yet to realize today. Although regional intelligence centers (also known as fusion centers) focus on terrorism, each fusion center has a criminal analysis function as well as terrorism analysis components (Taylor and Davis, 2010; Riebling, 2006).

Please discuss these questions:

1. What is ILP?
2. How does this concept of ILP relate to fusion centers?
3. What are some of the challenges in the United States regarding collection of data necessary for effective ILP?
4. In your own opinion, discuss the future role you see for data-driven law enforcement or intelligence-led policing in the American law enforcement community. Does it have a role in the future of law enforcement? Please support your statements with relevant references.

REFERENCES

Ratcliffe, J. (2006). *Intelligence-led policing*. Routledge.

Riebling, M. (2006). *The new paradigm: Merging law enforcement and intelligence strategies*. Center for Policing Terrorism.

Taylor, R. and Davis, J. (2010). *Intelligence-led policing and fusion centers*. Waveland Press Inc.

Chapter 4

Community Policing and Problem-Solving Policing

FIGURE 4.1   An image showing positive and routine interaction between a community policing unit and the public.

INTRODUCTION

In this chapter, we will study community policing: what it might be expected to accomplish, and why it might work where other strategies have failed. Contemporary community-oriented policing (COP) can be more complex than traditional police–community relations programs. COP is an inclusive term that covers many programs. Some common goals of these programs include: police–community reciprocity, areal decentralization of command, reorientation of patrol, and civilianization of some police operations.

In a community policing program, the term *police–community reciprocity* refers to the concept that police are a part of the community, and that the public they serve can contribute to policing, too. The police communicate this idea to the public, and they learn from public input in turn. The police are accountable to the community they serve. The police, along with the citizens and residents of the community, are responsible for overall success in crime prevention.

Areal decentralization of command refers to the establishment of substations, store front stations, and other practices that increase interaction between police officers and the public they serve in a geographic area.

Reorientation of patrol involves a transition from vehicle patrols to foot patrols to increase police interaction with other people in the community. Positive contact between officers and other citizens and residents is just one benefit of foot patrol that contributes to crime prevention.

Civilianization refers to employing more civilians in positions within police departments, increasing the number of civilians in research, intelligence, training, forensics, and as community service officers.

COP requires adopting both philosophical and operational changes that lead to a paradigm shift in traditional policing operations. Community policing is proactive, with the goal of improving the quality of life for police officers in addition to the community. These efforts are especially important in addressing issues of the most vulnerable in the community, including the poor, the elderly, and the homeless. Modern technology is important in community policing as well. However, community policing does not work without innovation and increased human interactions. Community policing can only be successful if it is adopted by the members of the police department as well as citizens and residents of the community. It is important to understand advantages and disadvantages in the implementation of any new policing policies and practices. We will discuss the strengths and weaknesses of community policing in this chapter.

Figure Credit

Reading 4.1

Community-Oriented Policing

Arthur Wiechmann

Introduction

Until the 1970s, American law enforcement was very much a *closed system*, in which the police did not seek a great deal of interaction, assistance, or cooperation from the public. This was intentional as it provided a means for avoiding corruption and political control. Prior to this period, law enforcement was a very open system—open to corruption, bribery, and political influence. *In an effort to professionalize the field of law enforcement, police administrators separated their organizations from public influence.*

This closed-system approach worked fine until the 1960s, which is when the *social environment of the country changed dramatically.* Crime was on the rise, law enforcement responsibilities were becoming more complex, and there was a great amount of civil unrest. Much of this unrest was focused on the police themselves, and the police found that they did not have support, understanding, or cooperation from the public; this meant that they ended up fighting a war in which they were badly outnumbered.

This was when the *community policing era* evolved. Police work became more than just fighting crime, and law enforcement had to become more of an open system in order to gain public support in helping them to deal with a much more complex society. Additionally, with crime on the increase, the police realized that they could not do it alone; they needed the public's help. They also had to figure out a way to be more efficient.

Many requests for police service were repeat requests, which was draining manpower. With a weaker economy than in the past, police resources were at an all-time low. Something had to be done to reduce the cycle of calls. So, what the police needed to do to reduce these cycles of calls, which reduce resources, was to look at ways to *eliminate the source of the problem.*

The police had to ask themselves, "Can traditional, reactive policing really put enough people in jail and keep them there so as to effectively reduce crime and the fear of crime?" The answer was "no," there will always be another criminal to take their place, and criminals will always outnumber cops, so the war will always be in favor of the criminals.

But one of the things they realized they had to do was to even the odds a little. This did not mean hiring tens of thousands of cops; that would never happen. It meant that they had to enlist the help of volunteers—the public. They needed to gain back the support, understanding, and cooperation they had in a previous era. With that support of the public regained, perhaps the police would be able to get a handle on the war.

So now, because of the changes in society, resulting in increased responsibilities given to law enforcement, the police have to view themselves as *agents of social change*. They are in an excellent position to improve the quality of life in their communities, in fact more so than any other criminal justice occupation.

One of the reasons for this is because the police are considered the *agency of last resort*, in which they are available 24/7. There is virtually no other public service agency in which someone can call the agency at any time of the day or night and speak to a member of that profession and have a member of that profession respond to their location and handle their problem.

And with this unique characteristic of the profession, police officers end up handling situations that are not really crimes. This is the primary reason that police work has evolved into more than just law enforcement.

Goal and Components of Community Policing

The goal of the police, when using a community policing approach, is to develop a cooperative effort between the police and the community to achieve three things: repress crime, reduce fear of crime, and maintain public order.

Repress Crime

This will always be a goal of law enforcement, no matter what philosophy, style, or strategy the police are using. Repressing crime usually involves the use of *traditional policing strategies*, such as making arrests and maintaining heavy patrols in problem areas. This approach is often the best way to solve a problem and is often used in a community policing approach.

Reduce Citizen Fear of Crime

In the community policing approach, the police make a concerted effort to reduce fear of crime. This is because studies have shown that people are more concerned about their fear of crime than they are concerned about crime itself. (Perhaps because the fear of crime directly affects more people than actual crime.)

There can be an *ethical dilemma* if the police attempt to reduce the fear of crime without also attempting to reduce crime at the same time. Because if the police make physical changes in the environment that cause a reduction in the fear of crime, but they have not actually reduced crime in the process, it can create a *false sense of security* with the people who live in the area, and this can make people more vulnerable to criminal activity.

> **Example:** In a particular neighborhood, the residents are afraid to go out at night because of the roving gangs. New graffiti shows up every morning, signaling the ongoing presence of the gangs. The police take action: as part of their community policing strategy, they start a graffiti removal program, in which graffiti is removed within 24 hours of it appearing. Soon, all the graffiti is gone, and to the residents, it gives the appearance that the police have run the gangs out of the area.

With this newfound security, residents then venture out at night. The problem is, the gangs never left, and the residents become victims of gang crimes. So, if the police are going to take steps to reduce fear, they must also take steps to reduce the crime associated with it.

Maintain Public Order

Maintaining public order becomes an important issue when it comes to what is called *marginal criminal activity*, which experts also describe as "disorder," which is a breeding ground for serious crime. This is because when there is continual disorderly activity in a particular area it sends a signal that the residents have lost control over their neighborhood.

The two components to the public order issue are deterioration and disorder. *Deterioration* refers to the physical appearance and decay of areas, which sends a signal to outsiders (including potential criminals) that the people who live there are apathetic about their surroundings and do not care about what goes on around them.

> **Example:** If an apartment complex needs painting, the landscaping has been neglected, graffiti adorns the walls, and there are other maintenance issues, it looks like anyone can do just about anything there and get away with it, because, obviously, no one who lives there cares about anything either.

Disorder is the marginal criminal activity that, if left uncontrolled, can lead to more serious crime.

> **Example:** If kids are allowed to loiter, drunks are left alone in the alleys, impromptu parties are allowed to spring up, and a variety of noise issues are left unresolved, it creates a potential breeding ground for serious criminal activity.

The individuals causing these problems or others who observe the lack of social control, or both, evolve this nuisance behavior into crimes—it is just human nature; borderline deviates turn into full-time deviates, petty criminals turn into serious criminals.

In the past, the police did not really concern themselves much with disorder issues, and certainly not with deterioration issues. These issues only became important to law enforcement when studies showed the connection of these two issues to serious criminal activity.

The California Attorney General's Office identifies three components that make up the concepts of community-oriented policing:

1. Community policing is a change in philosophy. Rather than trying to constantly play catch up all the time by always reacting to things that have already happened, *the police must work smarter* than before. They can save time by doing their job right the first time that they respond to an incident (or when they discover a cycle of repeated calls) by eliminating the problem, rather than allowing a continuing strain on their limited manpower.

Another part of the philosophy involves *a cooperative effort between the police and the community*. By taking an open systems approach, the police embrace community input and interest in law enforcement activities, rather than keeping the public at arm's length.

This cooperative effort extends beyond community members; it also involves a cooperative effort with other resources. Part of the community policing philosophy necessitates that the police make *maximum use of both internal and external resources* to help them in their problem-solving efforts.

Rather than trying to do everything themselves, the police should call upon other city departments and public agencies for tasks that the police are unable to do, such as the health department, probation and parole agencies, social services, and code enforcement, just to name a few. Because of this interaction and involvement of outside resources, much of the time that an officer spends on problem-solving projects involves lengthy coordination of activities with these other agencies.

2. Community policing is a change in management style. Law enforcement organizations have traditionally used an *autocratic management style*, which is very task oriented, with little consideration given to the personal needs of employees and void of line-level input in the management decision-making process.

This power-oriented style of leadership has been necessary for the type of work activities that the police are traditionally involved in. *Strict control* is often necessary because of the dynamic and volatile nature of police work, which is provided with this leadership style.

Additionally, *quick decision making*, which is a defining characteristic of autocratic management, is often necessary in the life-and-death situations that law enforcement constantly face.

When employees are armed with guns and have an enormous amount of power and responsibility, a controlling environment is often required.

When officers are involved in crisis situations, which is commonplace, time is of the essence to save lives and protect property. Therefore, it is of paramount importance that decisions be made quickly for immediate action.

But, community policing activities require autonomy at the line level, which makes an autocratic management style a less-than-optimal choice. A *democratic (or participative) style of leadership* must be used as much as is feasible for effective community policing activities.

This preferred style of leadership is people oriented. That is, leaders of the organization are concerned with involving the officers in important decisions that affect them. *This style is characterized by power sharing and participation in the decision-making process, which provides for the line-level autonomy necessary for community policing to be successful.*

Community policing places more responsibility on officers, so the management style must relinquish some power to them, because *management must give authority when they are increasing responsibilities.*

A basic tenet of participative leadership is that when a subordinate is given added responsibility, the authority that accompanies that responsibility must also be relinquished. To withhold the power but still make the employee accountable for the results is manipulation and coercion thinly disguised as delegation.

3. Community policing is a change in organizational strategy. Two of these changes are decentralization and despecialization.

Decentralization refers to a *decentralization of power* throughout the organization. Generally, in a typical autocratic structure, most of the formal power in the organization is "centralized" at the top of the organizational chart; that is, the upper managers have most of the power, with less and less power making its way down the hierarchy to the officers.

When power is decentralized, it is disbursed to others in the organization, usually to the lower levels of the agency. This is the concept of power sharing.

[... O]ne police organizational strategy is to make investigators accountable for specific geographic locations rather than a specific type of crime. With despecialization, specialists become generalists and work all types of crime in a particular area rather than only one type of crime throughout the city.

So, these generalist work groups are designed for geographic responsibility, which is believed to improve problem-solving efforts, rather than only having a sense of responsibility for a specific block of time (patrol officers) or a specific type of crime (investigators).

Traditional Versus Community Policing

The most important thing to realize when analyzing the differences between traditional policing and community policing is that it is not a choice between one and the other. Traditional police work, which is making arrests, responding to calls, and handling disputes and problems, will always be a critically important role in law enforcement, serving as the foundation of everything that the police do to protect their communities.

As long as there are people who do not conform to a peaceful and homogenous society, or are unable or unwilling to resolve differences in a civilized and mature manner (which will likely run concurrent with the existence of the human race), these work activities will always be a part of police work.

But there are distinct differences between the two ways of doing the job, and by understanding the differences, we can embrace them and realize that a combination of these two approaches can create a synergistic effect of sorts, in which the best of both worlds are combined to (hopefully) reduce crime to levels that would not be possible by using a singular approach to crime control and prevention.

Traditional Policing

The traditional policing approach is very *incident driven*, which means that the police leap into action only after something has already happened. In this regard, the police are very much like firefighters—they run all over town putting out fires (but in a figurative sense). By dealing with problems after they have already occurred, it is always a game of catch up, in which the police try to resolve a problem that has already happened, rather than preventing the problem from occurring in the first place.

By being a *reactionary force*, the police are limited by previous events, events that have injured or killed people, events that have resulted in damaged or stolen property, and events that have forever changed the courses of people's lives. In always trying to perform damage control, the police, at best, will be able to stem the tide against the tidal wave of man's inhumanity against man—a battle that can never be won. When winning means placing a sizable percentage of the population in cages for a long period of time, winning becomes a shallow victory—one that is neither morally satisfying, nor practically productive.

In their traditional role, the police are handcuffed (okay, a cheap and easy analogy). They can only take action after something has happened, often at great expense to others. Quite literally, if someone were to call the police and explain that someone was trying to kill them, the only response that the police would be able to provide would be, "Well, call us back when he kills you." As sad and pathetic as this example is, it is all too real. The way the law is written a crime must occur before the police can take action against it. What community-oriented policing attempts to do is to prevent some crimes from occurring in the first place.

And this is what traditional policing lacks. With traditional policing, officers are constantly trying to fix things, some of which cannot be fixed because they have already happened; it is like trying to put a spilled glass of water back into the glass, it just is not going to happen, no matter how dedicated and willing the participants are.

This is the primary impediment for efficiency in law enforcement: all of their activity (in a traditional role) is reactionary, which means it is little more than damage control. And damage control is little more than fixing things that are already broken—some of the things can be fixed, and some cannot. Stolen property can be recovered, but someone who has been murdered cannot be brought back. It is a sad state of affairs when a society is at the mercy of its laws, rather than the laws providing society with guidelines that are there to protect and strengthen it.

With the traditional approach to law enforcement, police agencies are closed to the public; that is, they do not seek input or support from citizens, because they know what they are doing and do not need help from outside. *Under the closed system approach*, the police view their activities as battles that they must face alone, because they have no allies. They have no reserves, no comrades who will muster their courage and resolve to take on the daunting task of reducing crime and the fear of crime in their community.

With the traditional approach, the police seek little input or assistance from the community. However, *the goal of both the traditional approach and community policing are the same—to reduce crime.*

Community Policing

The primary focus of this modern approach to police work is in addressing the underlying problems that cause crime. Rather than simply reacting to past events, the police analyze patterns of crime and use an evaluation process to attempt to identify *the root problem* of the crime pattern, rather than just addressing the symptom, which is the traditional approach.

> **Example:** A large apartment complex suddenly experiences a rash of auto burglaries. Using a traditional approach, the police would increase their presence in the area and possibly conduct surveillances in hopes of catching a suspect in the act.
>
> With the community-oriented approach, the officers who work that area spend a lot of their time talking to residents and apartment managers when they are walking around, as opposed to strictly patrolling by car. They learn from the manager that there is a rumor that a new tenant is selling drugs from his apartment, and that he takes stolen property as well as money in exchange for drugs.
>
> The officers notify the narcotics unit and, working together, develop a case against the drug dealer. A warrant is issued, and when the drug dealer is arrested the auto burglaries stop, because it was the dealer's customers committing the thefts to trade for drugs.

With the community-oriented approach, police departments rely on *the expertise of the police officers* to develop tactics and methods to solve problems. In addition to efforts of the police to identify root causes of problems, another important characteristic of the community-oriented policing approach is *involving the public* in the law enforcement effort. Police officers develop relationships with community members with the goal of the public taking responsibility for what happens in their neighborhoods.

It is important that the police be able to get the public to take on at least some of the law enforcement responsibilities, because the police cannot do it alone. Taking on responsibility does *not* mean that the police expect citizens to patrol their streets and confront suspicious characters, but it does mean paying attention to what is going on around them and calling the police when they see something that needs police attention.

When the police initiate a major community policing project, they commit a large number of officers. The officers saturate the area around the clock in order to learn what the problems are and who the troublemakers are, to introduce themselves to community members, to attend neighborhood meetings, to conduct foot patrols, and to perform a number of other activities that are designed to improve the level of trust between the police and the community members to prod them into taking on some responsibility.

But the police cannot do this for a long period of time. This type of activity is manpower intensive and is too expensive to maintain for a long period of time. Also, the police need the officers for other activities; most police departments do not have the luxury of having enough police officers to maintain a high presence in one area for an extended time. The strategy here is to get the community to take on some responsibility, then to quietly back of out the area and let the community take over some responsibility for their own neighborhood.

The *goal of community policing* will always include the ever-present goal of reducing crime, but it is taken one step further—to *reduce the fear of crime*. As mentioned earlier in this chapter, studies have demonstrated that people are as concerned about their fear of crime as they are about crime itself.

Differences between COP and POP

In addition to the community-oriented policing approach, there is a companion approach known as *problem-oriented policing*, or POP. Both of these approaches to law enforcement evolved at roughly the same time. Different experts in the field of criminology have variations in their theories as to how the police should modify their work activities. Along with these differences came differences in what the approach was called.

The approach discussed so far in this [reading] has been community-oriented policing, or COP. But the other popular approach—problem-oriented policing—is equally important as a modern law enforcement approach. Very often, these two terms are used interchangeably, and over a period of time many lay people fail to realize that there is a difference between the two approaches.

COP is generally identified as a *philosophy*, whereas POP is generally identified as a *strategy*. The philosophy, which was described earlier in this chapter, has more to do with the attitude and general outlook that the police have about how they accomplish their goals. The strategy is much more specific, in that police officers follow prescribed tactics and procedures to address tangible law enforcement problems.

The COP approach generally uses the POP approach (i.e., problem solving), but the POP approach does not always subscribe to community policing. The choice of which approach to use depends on the needs of the individual police department and the problems of each community.

Community-Oriented Policing

The primary component of COP is the concept of *shared responsibility* between the police and the community. This sharing of responsibility ideally should evolve to the point that these two entities develop a *partnership* in which the community does not rely on the police to do everything by themselves.

What everyone must realize is that for this to occur *there must be a great deal of commitment by community members.* This will likely only occur if the police instill this feeling of commitment into community members, which is a daunting challenge, to say the least. Police officers are generally very committed to their job; this is the easy part of developing a partnership. The difficult part is getting ambivalent citizens as energized as the police are.

Another significant component of community policing focuses on *community priorities.* That is, the police focus their law enforcement efforts and activities on what the community believes is important.

> **Example:** If the police think that the priority is to locate a serial killer in a community, but the community members think that the priority is a parking problem (which is very likely, because the parking problem affects more of the residents than a serial killer), then the police should focus on the parking problem.

Obviously, this can lead to problems, especially with the relationship of trust and respect that the police and the community have managed to develop over a long period of time. This is because often the police think that they are in a better position (and are more objective) about what the focus of their activities should be.

The final significant component of COP focuses on what has been previously presented in this chapter—deterioration and disorder. This focus has more to do with crime prevention than fighting crime, in the traditional sense.

Problem-Oriented Policing

The primary focus of POP is successfully identifying the *underlying root cause* of the problem rather than a symptom of a problem. This requires the police to have an in-depth understanding of crime causes, as well as an equally deep understanding of crime patterns and activities in the location being evaluated.

> **Example:** If a particular area or location is a constant target for crime, rather than just beefing up patrols and taking reports the police take steps to evaluate what it is about the area or location that makes it more susceptible to being victimized. They may take a target-hardening approach, perhaps with a community watch program.
>
> Using the POP approach, the police take a proactive stance toward their responsibilities. Rather than just using the traditional, reactive approach to policing, police activities also include efforts that prevent crimes or apprehend suspects before additional crimes are committed.

Example: Officers stake out locations where a pattern of crimes are being committed so that they can catch the suspect in the act, or before he is about to commit a crime, rather than the traditional approach of taking a report and having detectives investigate the case and identify the suspect.

Example: Sometimes, using a proactive approach, the police can actually arrest someone before they commit a crime. For instance, the police receive information from an informant that a certain person, who is on parole, is planning a major crime. The police surveil the subject, and when they see him in contact with known gang members, they arrest him for a parole violation and send him back to prison.

The POP approach also includes a focus on a specific problem. Rather than focusing on partnerships, shared responsibility, and other traditionally "nonpolice" activity, the police activities are directed toward a tangible crime problem by taking traditional and nontraditional steps to solve it.

Example: Rather than attending community meetings to discuss how to approach a particular problem, the police are staking out a liquor store or saturating a problem area with patrol officers and gang investigators. POP is serious police work.

There has been much focus on solving problems, so it is only fitting to discuss *what the police consider as being a true problem.* Three specific characteristics cause something to become a police problem:

- **Recurring incidents**: This is an *identifiable pattern* to the problem. If there has not been a recurrence of a specific crime at a specific location, it is not going to be viewed as a problem. It only becomes a problem when the same thing keeps happening at the same location.
- **Community concerns**: When evaluating the situation, the police must ask themselves if the situation is important enough, whether it is important enough that citizens are concerned about it. If the community is not concerned about whatever is going on, then the police do not need to concern themselves with it either. (The police have enough to do without fighting battles that no one cares about winning.)
- **Police business**: Before it becomes a true police problem, the police must determine if the situation is within the scope of law enforcement responsibilities.

Example: If an apartment complex is having problems with tenants using the community pool after hours, that is not a police problem. If the complex is having problems with nontenants sneaking in and using the pool, that is a police problem.

The COP approach to law enforcement asks a lot of police officers: they are expected to continue to fight crime in the traditional sense, as well as take on extraordinary responsibilities that were never expected of them in the past. To help these officers in the pursuit of organizational goals, the creators of COP have created a four-step process to help police officers identify and solve community problems.

Sara Model

The creators of COP created a four-step process modeled after a decision-making process to help officers identify and solve problems. *SARA* is an acronym for this process that provides police officers with tangible guidelines for identifying and solving police problems in their communities. SARA stands for scanning, analysis, response, and assessment.

This simplistic process was an effort by the experts to turn the *theory* of problem solving into the *practice* of problem solving.

Scanning

Officers monitor their area for crime problems. For the officers to do this effectively, they must remain in an assigned area for a longer period of time than they have traditionally stayed. Typically, most officers remain in a specific area for about six months, sometimes less, depending on the agency. Experts in community policing recommend that officers remain in a specific area for 18 months or more. This is because it takes a considerable amount of time just to get to know the people in an area—the apartment managers who know everyone, the business owners and their unique problems, the street people who know everything that is going on, the troublemakers and their proclivities, as well as the crime problems and other police-related matters.

Analysis

In this step, *the police define the problem and the underlying causes.* They make sure that they identify the root cause of the problem, *rather than a symptom* of the problem. This is where the expertise of the field officers is important—administrators sitting in an office cannot do this.

During this step, *the officers develop a method to solve the problem and identify the alternatives.* There is no limit to what these alternatives can be and are limited only by the imagination and ingenuity of the officers dealing with the problem.

The following are some examples of alternatives.

- **Zero-tolerance enforcement:** This is a very traditional approach to law enforcement, which can be very effective and is a vital aspect of community policing. If there is a serious crime problem in a certain area, the police will not give warnings to violators; that is, there with be no tolerance—zero—for violations of the law. This means that any violations will result in full prosecution under the law. Once the violators figure out that they will get slammed every time they break the law, they will either stop doing it or will move on to a location where there is less heat.

- **Evictions:** This is a great way to get rid of troublemakers and undesirable individuals. Whether a tenant is a drug dealer or just plays his music too loud all the time, a few telephone calls from the police to the property owner will usually result in the eviction of people and elimination of the problems that the landlords want no part of.

- **Target patrols:** This approach is also a very traditional approach to police work, and one that is also very effective at solving problems. Remember, traditional approaches to police work are often the best way to solve serious crime problems and will always be an important part of the crime-fighting arsenal. With target patrols, the police become aware of a particular problem in a particular area, and focus their patrol time in that area. In other words, when they are not handling calls for service they saturate the particular area with patrols. The sudden presence of many patrol cars can be very effective at reducing certain crimes that rely on defenseless victims and reluctant witnesses.

- **Neighborhood watch:** In conjunction with other police activities, the police may want to involve community members to be additional eyes and ears for them. The police cannot be everywhere all the time. The ratio of police officers to citizens is usually less than 1 police officer for every 1,000 citizens, with only a small portion of them on duty at a time. If the police take the approach that they must do it alone, there will only be 25 people (the police) watching over a community of 150,000 during the wee hours of the night, which is when a lot of really bad stuff can happen. But by enlisting the assistance of enthusiastic members of the community, the police can increase the number of eyes and ears to detect and report criminal activity. The police have figured out that they cannot fight crime alone; they must rely on the people who live in the community to take on some of the responsibility of protecting and preserving their community.

- **Stakeouts:** Stakeouts are undercover surveillances of certain locations that police have received information about, such that a crime was going to occur there or there has been a pattern of recurring crime in a specific area, that justifies the extensive use of police manpower to covertly observe and monitor activities that, hopefully, will lead to the identification and apprehension of offenders who were observed committing crimes.

- **Other resources:** During the analysis stage, police officers should consider the services available by other agencies and city departments. Rather than continuing with the mentality that the police must do everything on their own, they should seek out the assistance of other private and public agencies that could take on some of the responsibilities that have traditionally been the sole domain of law enforcement.

- **Gang intelligence:** If a particular crime problem involves gangs, it is important for the police to get as much information as possible about its leaders and their activities. Anything less is traditional, reactive policing. The police have specialized units that focus solely on gang activity—their command structure, their goals, their enemies, and anything else that could result in crimes that harm innocent citizens. If gang intelligence can provide the police with information which enlightens them as to the various dynamics going on in a particular area, it can improve their chances of solving the problem, because they will know who is causing the problems, and why they are causing them.

Response

In this third step of the process, officers select one or more of the alternatives that they have developed. The officers, often with the help of other resources, *put their plan into action*. It is at this point that the police work closely with the community and other agencies to solve the problem.

Assessment

In this step, the police evaluate the progress and effectiveness of the alternatives. They may need to make changes or modifications. Actually, it is inevitable that some changes will be necessary. By realizing from the beginning that no plan will ever be perfect, the police build flexibility into their plan, which is a fundamental component of the decision-making process that SARA is modeled after.

During this step, the police also try to determine if the problem was eliminated, reduced, or displaced:

- **Eliminated**: If a problem is eliminated, that obviously means that the problem has stopped occurring, rather than just being moved to another location. This is the optimal result.

- **Reduced**: A problem is reduced if it is not as serious or not as frequent as it was in the past. A reduced problem is better than no change, but not as optimal as being eliminated.

- **Displaced**: A displaced problem only means that it has been moved. When the police put the heat on, often the problem-makers move elsewhere, usually to a more vulnerable area where there is not as much police attention or presence. This is not optimal, because it will probably require the police to follow the problem and work on it at its new location.

Three-Step Problem-Solving Process

Remember, community-oriented policing is a philosophy, and problem-oriented policing is a strategy—the tactics, methods, and processes that the police use to prevent, reduce, and eliminate crime. Just as the SARA process is a problem-solving approach, there is a three-step problem-solving process that is useful in giving direction to the police when they are trying to develop alternatives and work activities to solve problems.

This three-step process is generally used during the analysis step in the SARA process, which is when the police are evaluating the problem and developing a list of alternatives for consideration in the response stage.

A crime always has three components. Depending upon the crime, one of these three components will be the optimal focus for the police to solve the problem. *The three components are the location, the victim, and the suspect.* Once the police have figured out what their focus should be, they will have a clearer outlook on developing alternatives to solve the problem:

- **Location**: A crime has to occur someplace, so there will always be a specific location where it occurs. If there are many crimes occurring at the same location, the police would focus on that location.

  Example: There is a rash of auto burglaries occurring at a certain location. The focus would be on that location. The alternatives that the police would consider could include surveillances, video cameras, improved lighting, and increased patrols in the area.

- **Victim**: Obviously, every crime involves a victim. If a series of crimes show similarities between the victims, then this could be an appropriate focus for the police as they develop the alternatives.

  Example: There is a date rape trend with the use of drugs, so the focus may be on the victim. The police would make notifications of the problem to potential victims, and provide information and education to prevent further crimes. Also, the police could focus their interviews with the victims to determine any similarities, such as parties they attended, people they know, or activities they are involved in.

- **Suspect:** For there to be a crime, there must be a person who commits it. If the location varies, and there is no pattern regarding the victims, the focus will usually be on the suspect. And if there is a pattern to the crimes, such as a method of operation, the police will develop alternatives which focus on the suspect.

   Example: If there is a problem involving a gang that is terrorizing a neighborhood, or there is an active serial killer or rapist, the focus will be on the suspect.

Effectiveness of Patrol Efforts

So, what is the best use of resources, traditional policing or community-oriented policing? One of the reasons that community policing is being used is because there is some doubt about the effectiveness of traditional patrol activities (driving around and looking for bad guys).

However, critics of community policing say that taking officers away from patrol duties to attend meetings and other community policing activities prevents them from doing real police work. So, we have to look at the true value of patrol versus community policing activity to determine the best use of limited resources.

The effectiveness of patrol activities was examined in the following well-known study, which concluded that *preventive patrol, response time to calls, and follow-up investigations did not reduce crime.*

The 1971 Kansas City Study

In this study, Kansas City was divided into three demographically similar areas. One area had very heavy police patrols, the second area had the same level of patrol that it always had, and the third area had no patrols. If there was a call for service in the third area, the police would respond, handle the call, and then go back to one of the other areas.

After two years, a survey was conducted and crime statistics were analyzed. The results of the study were that the three areas showed no difference in reduction of crime, reduction in the fear of crime, or in the level of satisfaction that the community had with the police. These results were in conflict with the preventive patrol doctrine, which is that the police must have a visible presence to prevent crime and to make people feel safe.

The point of this study as it relates to community policing is this: community policing is manpower intensive, and officers leave their assigned areas to handle nontraditional duties, such as attending community meetings, coordinating work activities with outside agencies, and many other problem-solving duties, but the Kansas City study showed that patrol time was an ineffective use of resources.

It boils down to this: *preventive patrol does not reduce crime, so if officers are busy with problem-solving activities that prevent them from patrolling their area more, it really does not matter, because visible patrol is a waste of time.*

However, one must also consider the activity generated by patrol officers while they are patrolling their areas. On a daily basis, they encounter individuals who are involved in crimes, and are arrested for them. Perhaps just driving around and being visible is a waste of time (according to the study), but *officers on patrol still do a lot to reduce and prevent crime by arresting violators that they encounter during their patrol duties.*

Problem-Solving Considerations

Four concepts need to be considered to understand the concept of community policing and problem-oriented policing. These fundamental concepts provide the layperson with a foundation for understanding the complex and changing philosophies and strategies of these modern methods of law enforcement.

Target Hardening

A *target*, in police terminology, is a location that is potentially desirous or inviting to criminals; it is a location or individual that is either easy to get to or that offers a high reward. *Hardening* refers to making the target "harder" for the offenders to get to. Hence, *target hardening* refers to making physical modifications to locations (or individuals) so that those locations are more difficult for offenders to get to.

This is more than just telling citizens to get stronger locks; *officers evaluate crime areas* to determine what can be done to make the area less desirable for criminals. A variety of strategies can be used to harden a target:

- **Lighting:** Oftentimes when lighting is added to a high-crime location, it acts as a deterrent for future criminal activity, because criminals want to conduct their nefarious actions without fear of detection.

But sometimes, adding lighting is not the best solution; if disorderly or marginally criminal activity relies on lighting, such as games in the streets or gambling in an alley, the best solution would be to remove lighting. [...]

- **Modifying areas:** Much of the evaluation of problem areas done by the police requires that they consider modifying areas where troublemakers congregate, so as to make it less attractive for them to stay there.

  Example: Public telephones are used by drug dealers to receive calls for drug sales. By modifying the telephones so that they only allow outgoing calls, or by removing the telephone booths completely, the drug dealers will move on.

  Example: Bus benches are a desirable spot for homeless individuals to bed down for the night, because they get them off the ground and they are the right size for sleeping. By placing a center armrest on the bench, people cannot use the bench for other than its intended purpose, and the transients seek out other sleeping arrangements.

- **Adjust or limit traffic patterns:** If the police can make changes in the physical environment to control pedestrian and vehicle traffic, it can have an effect on crime.

  Example: If walkways in apartment complexes are designed so that pedestrians can more easily get close to doors or windows of apartments without looking out of place, it will make the area more desirable for criminals to commit crime.

Crime prevention through environmental design (CPTED) is an entire field of study devoted to the concept of making physical changes to specific locations to prevent the location from being attractive to criminals. The field of CPTED studies how the design of landscaping, walkways, and walls, among many other things, can have a major impact on crime reduction and resident responsibility. [...]

  Example: A short row of hedges around the perimeter of a front yard is enough to keep people out.

Shared Responsibility

One of the primary objectives of community-oriented policing is for the police to get *community members involved in the law enforcement effort*. This objective of community interaction with the police in solving police related problems is to get the citizens to take responsibility for their homes and neighborhoods through actions such as the following:

- **Improve the appearance of their homes**. If potential criminals get the feeling that the people who live in the area care about their neighborhoods, the criminals are more likely to find a more vulnerable location.

- **Call the police.** Residents should call the police when they see something that the police need to address. The police do not expect nor do they want private citizens to take police action. They only want to turn ambivalent residents into responsible citizens, who want to defend their turf and are willing to be concerned enough about what is going on around them to make a simple telephone call to the police while something is happening, rather than being a reluctant witness long after a crime has occurred.
- **Join groups.** If the police can manage to get residents to join neighborhood groups, such as Neighborhood Watch, whose goals are to be vigilant and watchful, it will go a long way toward developing the objective of shared responsibility.

When this responsibility is established, *the police can let the residents take over much of the policing effort*. It will not be as necessary for the police to maintain a high level of patrol, because the people who live in the area will be doing that for them by being vigilant and watchful.

When true shared responsibility has been achieved, residents will be more willing to report crimes as they occur and confront suspicious persons in the area, because they have become empowered. Too often, residents have come to rely on the police for too much. This reliance can reach a point of dependence on an overburdened, overworked, and understaffed agency that does not have the same personal stake in a particular area that the people who live there have, or should have.

Environmental Change

Another objective of community-oriented policing is to *reduce the atmosphere of crime* by changing the *physical appearance* of an area from looking like a high crime area to a peaceful, orderly area. This is in furtherance of the goal of reducing fear of crime, which also uses a psychological approach to crime prevention, which is a fundamental component of CPTED.

One of the most basic objectives of the environmental change approach is the *redevelopment of rundown areas*. Using this tactic, the police work with and encourage property owners of apartments to improve the appearance of the structures and landscaped areas and to ensure they abide by health and safety regulations.

The police also try to rid neighborhoods of *establishments that generate or attract criminal activity*. Some of these businesses, and sometimes residences, are a constant source of calls for service, and a constant source of crime.

> **Example:** A certain bar, because of its location and clientele, attracts a high level of crime, which results in many calls for service from the police, draining manpower resources, which causes other parts of the community to suffer.

Crimes such as drug transactions, assaults, street robberies, fights, and public drunkenness, as well as many other alcohol-related crimes can quickly turn a quiet, peaceful neighborhood into a skid-row type of environment. The decent people move away, and all that is left is the degenerates who perpetuate the criminal activity and decay of the area.

A very visible sign of urban decay and lack of community control over a neighborhood is graffiti. Gang graffiti is a constant reminder to the people who live in the area that criminals are walking their streets at night, which means the streets belong to them, not to the people who live there.

Police departments that are involved in community policing and are dealing with a gang problem will inevitably have a graffiti removal program. This type of program allows residents to call a "graffiti removal hotline" number to report new graffiti that has shown up overnight. Within 24 hours, a work crew will arrive and paint over the graffiti. (The idea is that if the gang members who put up the graffiti see that it is immediately removed, it will discourage repeat offenses to occur at the same area, because it will be a waste of their time and paint to embark on something that is so temporary.)

Another example of preventing neighborhood deterioration is something as simple as *trash removal.* Many, if not most, of the high crime areas that the police must deal with are high-density, low-income apartment areas. As low-income individuals move into these areas, many more people than are designed to live in the apartments share living quarters to reduce their living expenses.

This results in way too many people living in an area than it was originally meant for. What happens then is that there are too many cars for the area (which causes many parking problems), but, more important, it creates a serious trash problem.

When double or triple the amount of people live in a location than was intended, there is a doubling or tripling of the amount of trash. When the dumpsters in the alleys overflow, which is within a day or two of the trash pickup day, it creates a deteriorating environment, along with health concerns.

What the police must do in this situation, which is far from their traditional responsibilities of fighting crime, is to create ordinances or other requirements that force the property owners to increase trash pickup respective to the volume of trash accumulated. This simple tactic can have a positive visual and health impact on the neighborhood.

This entire concept of the neighborhood deterioration approach is supported by the *broken windows theory.* A broken window is used as a metaphor for deterioration and disorder. The theory is that *if a window in a building is broken and is left unrepaired, the rest of the windows will soon be broken because the broken window is a signal that no one cares.* As the property deteriorates, it becomes fair game for additional damage or loitering. *This lack of caring can spread through the neighborhood, and soon no one cares about the appearance of their houses, and the neighborhood deteriorates, inviting criminal activity.*

A supporting study demonstrated the social and psychological effects of deterioration on the attitudes and actions of residents. A theorist tested this theory by placing an unattended automobile in different neighborhoods and then monitored it with cameras. An intact vehicle remained unmolested, whereas a vehicle with a smashed-out window was quickly vandalized and stripped.

Demographics

The people who live in a particular area play a part in the success or failure of community policing. The police can only get the ball rolling; the residents must eventually take over. If the predominant population of a neighborhood is predisposed to distrust the police or have an inherent apathetic attitude about their surroundings, then the best efforts and intentions of the police will be futile.

Low-income areas are inherently transitory; that is, most of the residences are rental units, and renters are much more transient than property owners. Also, renters do not have as much control over the appearance of the area as homeowners do. (A tenant of an apartment cannot get the building painted nor have the landscaping improved. They can apply pressure to the landlord, but most tenants in low-income areas are not likely to make such requests.)

Because the low-income, high-density area is less than desirable for long-term living, *once residents can afford to live someplace nicer they leave the area*. Because of this, these people have little or no personal stake in the community, which results in a *lack of community*.

This means that neighbors are not as close to each other as in the past. In the past, neighbors interacted more, which improved their sense of community. One of the things that caused more interaction in the past was a lack of other modes of entertainment and distraction. But with electronic sophistication in this modern era, conveniences such as television, computer games, and the Internet have replaced neighborliness.

Television has replaced neighborhood social life. People living next door to each other do not know each other near as well as they did decades ago. Hence, the feeling of solidarity and neighborhood responsibility has diminished substantially over time. This makes it much more difficult for the police to get residents to care.

Additionally, in today's real estate market, many people live where they do because it is what they can afford, not because it is what they view as home. When people move to less expensive housing areas, they do not necessarily embrace that area as their community—it is just where they live. Consequently, *they have little or no desire to be a part of that community*.

What this means to the success of community policing is that when the police back off as the community takes over (which is a tactic of shared responsibility), it is only temporary in these areas because most of the residents are gone after a while, and the neighborhood goes back to the way it was as new residents move in. Unless the police come back and maintain a high-visibility presence (which means they start all over again), there will be no shared responsibility, and the area will deteriorate again.

When this is the case, most likely during the assessment stage of the SARA process, the police will view their efforts as a failure. Rather than trying to do the same thing over again (because it did not have any long-term success), they will likely try something different, such as a problem-oriented approach.

Finally, *demographics have changed with respect to an increase in minority populations*. Different minority and immigrant groups may have different social values and attitudes. Getting involved in police problems and issues may not be something they are comfortable with. For example, *many immigrant groups are reluctant to trust the police*, which is understandable given the countries they came from and the corruption and brutality common with the police in those countries. Because the police in their native countries were corrupt, these immigrants may likely assume that the police cannot be trusted.

Also, because these immigrants do not trust the police, they are less likely to call upon the police for help or to report when they are victims of crimes. *This makes these people very attractive victims to offenders*, because if they are assaulted or robbed, and they do not report the crime, the offenders do not have to fear being sought by the police.

Because of these different values and attitudes of minorities and immigrant groups, their reluctance to trust the police, and their vulnerability as victims who do not report crimes, it becomes very difficult for the police to develop a sense of shared responsibility with them.

Management Changes

For community-oriented policing to be successful, law enforcement leadership must make many changes in their management approach and expectations. Rather than relying on traditional autocratic management styles and authoritative supervisory roles, police managers and supervisors must reassess and reevaluate their responsibilities in the work environment.

Some leaders can accept this change and adapt to it, whereas others will not or cannot. This ability to change with the changing culture of the police environment will mirror the success in the abilities of these organizations to implement community- or problem-oriented policing.

Police supervisors and managers must consider several different areas, and modify their behavior and expectations accordingly.

Redefine the Role of the Officer

It is the responsibility of police supervisors and managers to ensure that the officers are fully aware of their role in the police department and in the community. They must understand that their normal duties associated with traditional policing have not been eliminated. Rather, they have additional duties of identifying problems and developing innovative methods to solve them.

Redefine Productivity and Quality

Officers must be made to realize that traditional police activity (i.e., arrests, patrolling, and citations) will continue to be recognized, but that the officer's problem-solving efforts will be the greatest measurement of their worth and contribution to the organization. (It will behoove them to make an effort to demonstrate problem-solving skills if they want to be recognized as being good officers, and if they aspire to supervisory and management roles in the future.)

Reassess Officers' Management Expectations

Police managers must realize that noncritical response time, arrest and citation volume, and other traditional measurements of performance must be replaced with individual and team problem-solving efforts. Management and supervision cannot expect that the officers will maintain the same level of traditional productivity when they are given additional responsibilities of community- and problem-oriented policing.

Time Management

As police officers spend more time with nontraditional policing situations, availability of police resources will be limited. This will result in higher response times for calls in nonemergency services. When there are few officers available, calls for service get backed up, and consequently, there is a longer delay in getting an officer to respond to a call.

Both management and the public must be aware of this, and accept that it is a better way of doing business. If they cannot accept this, than the community-policing approach is not an appropriate approach for that community.

Many communities have come to expect a short response time for all types of calls, and the police managers rest their success on short response times. If neither can get past this, there will be conflicts that will result in dissatisfaction—the managers' dissatisfaction with patrol performance, and dissatisfaction of the community with the police response.

New Leadership Style

As quasi-military organizations, it is difficult for police departments to revert from an autocratic to participative or collaborative type of leadership style. But if community- or problem-oriented policing is going to work, officers must be given autonomy and trust to make their own decisions, which is not possible in the traditional autocratic environment.

Revised Reward System

Police managers must make changes in the organizational reward system. Special assignments and commendations must be based on officers' problem-solving efforts rather than just traditional enforcement-generated activity.

Revised Performance Criteria

When police supervisors and managers are completing performance evaluations on their officers, they must not only assess the officers' abilities in their traditional roles, they must also assess each officer in his ability and willingness to become involved in the problem-solving process. The evaluation form itself must be modified to include areas of evaluation that focus on problem-solving.

Training

Police managers and supervisors must understand the importance of training when their personnel are made accountable for additional responsibilities and duties. All officers must be well trained in the problem-solving process. A lack of training will lead to a lack of commitment by the officers, and the process will be in the form of lip service only; that is, they will go through the motions but will not really try, because they will not understand the process.

New Sources of Information and Knowledge

Community- and problem-oriented policing have been around for several decades now, but they are still relatively new concepts. As studies and research results begin to accumulate, police managers must be flexible in their approach. What worked for one agency may not work for them. What worked 10 years ago may not work in a new social environment.

The organization must be flexible and willing to change as new information becomes available. Without this attitude, an organization could easily lock themselves into a community-oriented policing approach that is not suitable for the organization or appropriate for the crime problems of their particular community.

Reading 4.2

"Don't Drink the Kool-Aid": On the Resistance to Community Policing

Steve Herbert

I N THE 1990S, THE SEATTLE POLICE Department attempted an ambitious reform effort. Under the leadership of Chief Norm Stamper, who had been brought to Seattle from San Diego, the department tried to reorient all of its operations around the philosophy of community policing. For Stamper, this meant making the police an agency through which myriad efforts at neighborhood betterment could be channeled. The police would listen closely to a wide range of citizen complaints, and would address as many of them as possible. This might mean soliciting assistance from other branches of the state's bureaucracy on matters outside the police's expertise. But the mandate of the police was deliberately broad: it was to be the linchpin agency in neighborhood efforts in self-improvement.

Stamper recognized that such a thoroughgoing effort at organizational change would require the support of the rank and file. Given the amount of discretionary authority low-level police operatives possess, and given the well-documented pattern of effective resistance to similar efforts at police reform,[1] Stamper's commitment to devoting attention to ensuring "buy-in" from lower levels of the hierarchy was clearly well-advised. To this end, he regularly invited officers to short seminars on the philosophy of community policing. The goal was clear: to encourage officers to accept community policing as their principal vocational orientation.

These seminars remain the butt of frequent sarcastic jokes inside the SPD. Commonly, officers refer to invitations to the seminars as requests to "drink the Kool-Aid." The reference here is to the 1978 Jonestown Massacre, when more than 900 followers of Jim Jones drank cyanide-laced Kool-Aid rather than surrendering their territory in Guyana. Some officers ridicule the language used at the seminars, in which leaders allegedly discussed "the rivers of community policing" to emphasize the breadth of the reform movement. The persistence of such sarcasm illustrates the hostility with which many view the project of community policing.

Why such hostility? Why would officers refuse to re-orient themselves as Stamper advocated? Why resist efforts to deepen the police's connection to neighborhoods, to broaden their mandate in ameliorating the problems citizens enumerate? Why is organizational reform akin to committing suicide?

[... P]olice impulses toward subservience to the citizenry are tempered by the projects of separation and generativity. The importance of these latter two projects limits the police's ability to envision citizens as co-equal partners. This reality has telling implications for the success of community policing. Why is the calibration of the police's mission in this fashion so difficult for officers to accept?

My arguments [...] further [open up] the "black box" of the state and outline the internal dynamics most critical to police resistance to community policing. In the first section, I explore the importance of the capacity to exercise coercive force to particular tendencies within the police subculture, tendencies that reinforce the police's sense of themselves as members of an authoritative agency sharply distinct from the citizenry. I follow this by exploring how this authority gets expressed organizationally. I focus particularly on how different actors within the bureaucracy work in relative isolation to attain an independent measure of prestige. These emphases on specialization and discretion lessen the organization's capacity to coordinate officer efforts to solve problems identified by the public. I then explore the common narrative officers employ to understand criminality. This hegemonic story describes crime as acts of a few "bad apples" within a given area. By extension, the project of policing is to excise these bad actors through arrest and incarceration. Importantly, such a narrative implicitly reinforces the power of the police as the agent of expulsion. Citizens are thereby viewed largely in terms of their ability to provide information about those who need to be expelled. The public is not understood as the police's co-equal partner.

Collectively, these internal dynamics help thwart the project of subservience in everyday practice; they prevent more equitable partnerships between the police and neighborhood groups. Officers' collective sense of themselves as capable, authoritative actors extracting evildoers limits the extent to which they can embrace community policing. By encouraging each other to resist change, the officers reinforce their sense of separation from the public. They thereby obstruct the democratic thrust central to the legitimation of community policing.[2]

This sense of separation frustrates many citizens [...]. For now, my goal is to explain how dynamics within the police organization motivate the effort to ensure that officers do not "drink the Kool-Aid."

Coercive Force and the Cultural Fundamentals of the Police

Any explanation for why the police tend to keep the public at arm's length must take seriously several components of police culture and organization. Like all social organizations, the police never enact themselves in a simple, uniform fashion. It is far too limiting to consider the police solely as one component of some abstract entity called the state whose direction can be determined or directed by normative political theory. Instead, we need to understand the internal dynamics of the police—the key components of their culture, and the central narratives they use to understand themselves, their work, and their relations with the public.

Of course, these internal dynamics are critically shaped by external forces. The most significant of these is the designation of the police as the state's primary agent of coercive force. As Bittner long ago recognized, what unites the disparate actions police are asked to undertake is their capacity to compel a response, forcibly if necessary.[3] Police are summoned to such a wide array of scenes because someone believed that coercive force might be necessary to resolve a problematic situation.

One critical implication of the police's capacity to exercise force is its influence on the subcultural world officers construct. Dominant features of that culture can be traced to the coercive role officers are equipped (literally) to play.[4] I focus here on three main components of that culture.[5] One is an emphasis on a masculinist notion of adventurousness embraced by many officers. A second is an understandable preoccupation with safety. The third [...] is the widespread belief that police authority needs to be asserted effectively. Each of these subcultural components can be traced back to the coercive authority of the police. And each underlies officer resistance to a robust role for the citizenry in shaping police practice.

Adventure/Machismo

As the state's principal agency of coercion, the police are regularly summoned to potentially dangerous situations. Citizens call the police when under physical threat, and ask officers to deal with those who pose such a threat. The police are thereby obligated to insert themselves into situations where the possibility of violence looms, and to use violence themselves if necessary to protect the vulnerable. As Bouza describes the transformation that accompanied his initial entry into the police fraternity: "Once I put on the badge and uniform, I was expected to run toward things I'd formerly run away from."[6]

Many officers embrace this challenge. Such officers quickly volunteer to handle calls that represent risk; they seek opportunities to turn on lights and siren in pursuit of a particularly notorious perpetrator. They use discretionary patrol time to unearth chances to exert their authority; they cruise in higher-crime areas hoping to encounter foes of the police against whom they can test their mettle. The valorization of this approach to policing means that officers assess one another in terms of their willingness to handle dangerous calls. Those who seem reluctant to do so are disparaged as something less than full-fledged police officers. Some police, for example, joke about older officers with ebbing energy for proactive work as being "retired on duty." Another officer, after a conversation with a colleague who wished not to pursue a suspect who had fled a scene, derided him by saying, "Obviously, he has a motivation problem."[7]

This cultural celebration of adventurousness generates two important implications for community policing. One is that many officers ridicule the slow-paced, heavily interactive work of engaging the citizenry. There is little adventure in community meetings, during which the conversation predictably drags through minutiae and includes performances of pettifogging. Nor is there much excitement in trying to coordinate with other city agencies to improve poor lighting or prevent the dumping of unwanted material in an alleyway. Indeed, such aspects of community policing are commonly dismissed as "social work," and are implicitly feminized as such. These are not matters for the strong, masculinist, adventuresome officer. Further, officers who work patrol rarely stoop to associate themselves with those involved in community policing efforts. Rather, community policing is regularly denigrated as a refuge for those who seek to avoid hard work and danger, a place to "work banker's hours" and avoid the rough and tumble that "real police work" necessarily entails. I explore this bureaucratic isolation of community policing in more detail later in this [reading]. For now, I note that an important contributor to that isolation is the association between community policing and the more feminized work of relationship building.[8]

This is not lost on community police team members themselves. On several of my ride-alongs with members of this team, I witnessed officers jumping at opportunities to respond to radio broadcasts concerning potentially violent situations. In some cases, the officers turned on their lights and sirens to respond to calls from locations that were several miles away. Because the intervening streets were heavily trafficked, their response time was likely to be slow, a factor that called into question their willingness to respond. Similarly, an officer serving as the community policing officer for Blufftop rejected a suggestion by the project's manager that he schedule regular hours in a publicly accessible office so that residents could approach him with their concerns. The officer indicated that he would not waste his time "sitting in an office and playing solitaire." Instead, he patrolled the streets in search of street-level drug dealers. The lure of a major arrest trumped the boring work of community interaction.

This desire to remain connected to the adventuresome side of policing helps explain enthusiasm for a short-lived "power community policing" model with which their unit experimented during the period of the research. Instead of leaving the officers to their own devices to address the problems in their areas, the "power" model coalesced the several members of the unit. As a group, they could engage in concentrated anti-crime activity in areas of ongoing concern. On occasion, for example, officers created a "buy-bust" operation to arrest street-level drug dealers. The community police officers enjoyed this taste of proactive, adventurous policing and were displeased when the experiment was terminated.

So, even for those officers ostensibly committed to the slow, patient work of community building, the call of adventure continues to beckon.[9]

A second important implication of the embrace of adventurousness is its tendency to legitimate brusqueness. If officers seek to encounter and overcome the more dangerous members of the citizenry, they recognize the need to establish their greater power. Unfortunately, tools for isolating those in need of such displays of power are crude. As a consequence, the police sometimes assert their superiority against those who present no appreciable threat. And when officers, in the words of one resident, "act all macho," it can erode public trust in the police. The possibility that adventurousness will erode the tenor of police-citizen interactions also holds true for officers' embrace of safety.

Safety

The centrality of safety to the cultural world of the police is understandable. Given that the police's coercive capacity compels them to enter dangerous situations, it is hardly a surprise that officers do a great deal to protect themselves. Safety is reinforced in a host of ways, from formal training in tactics to gentle admonitions to one another to "stay safe out there." Officers are encouraged to make safety a paramount concern and to approach situations carefully to maximize their own protection.

One important manifestation of this is officers' treatment of suspects, particularly those officers believe might pose some threat. Officers are likely to engage such suspects verbally only after first ensuring that they are not dangerous. The typical means for doing so is a "pat down" of the citizen in question. Because officers are legally permitted to conduct such "pat downs" as long as they can demonstrate concern for their safety, they regularly employ them.[10] Unfortunately, such suspicion is not always directed accurately.

To illustrate this point, let me return to a scenario I discussed briefly in chapter 3. An officer I observed spent about an hour one morning trying to track down an African-American man, Ethan, who had allegedly barged into the apartment of his girlfriend and taken $500. According to the woman's son, the suspect had knocked on the door of the apartment, brushed past the boy when the door was opened, found $500 in the woman's bedroom, and dashed away. The officer got a statement from the boy and began scouring the neighborhood for information about Ethan's whereabouts. He visited several apartments and gathered a rough picture of the suspect's physical characteristics and clothing. At one point in the process, he looked up the block and noticed an African-American man walking down the sidewalk. The officer quickly jumped into his car, surged up the block, parked, jumped out and commanded the man to place his hands on the hood of the car. The officer conducted a hurried pat down, brushing off the man's questions. The officer said, "I'll explain everything in a moment," then proceeded with some questions about Ethan. After gaining little insight from the man, the officer briefly explained that he was looking for Ethan because he "assaulted a ten-year-old kid." Unsatisfied by the explanation, the recipient of the search asked the officer, "Do you do this to everybody?" The unstated message was clear: the man believed he received such rough attention because of his skin color.

For his part, the officer later justified the search because he thought the man matched the description of Ethan and thus represented a potentially dangerous suspect who might elude capture. The officer believed his safety was sufficiently at risk to legitimate the pat-down. Regardless of this logic, the result in this case appeared to be a diminution of police legitimacy in the eyes of at least one citizen. When this scenario is repeated in Seattle and other cities, even in the name of the much-vaunted goal of safety, it can compromise the closer police-community connections community policing promotes.

Concerns for safety also lead some officers to resist efforts to reduce the physical distance between themselves and citizens. These include, most prominently, efforts to get officers to patrol via some mechanism other than a patrol car. Because such alternate modes of transport—foot, bicycle, horse—create less of a barrier between officer and citizen and thus ostensibly promote a stronger flow of communication, they are frequently touted as important facets of community policing. But the patrol car is tied to officers' sense of safety. It enables officers to enter and exit a scene quickly, which might be important tactically. It can provide an actual shield between officers and potential assailants. And it contains an in-car terminal that allows ready access to a database from which officers can retrieve information about a suspect and a situation. This helps officers to assess the dangerousness of a scene they are about to enter. Even community police officers, whose mission revolves around citizen contact, express reluctance to eschew the patrol car, for fear of compromising their safety.

Concerns for safety also help to explain why officers are preoccupied with ensuring that their authority is unquestioned in their interactions with the citizenry.

Authority

The potential dangerousness of police work, then, underlies both the masculinist embrace of adventure and the pervasive concern for safety. It also influences the cultural emphasis on police authority. To exercise their coercive power legitimately, police officers need to understand quickly the nature of the scenes to which they are summoned and to determine whether and what kind of threat exists. This is especially important in chaotic situations, because danger may lurk. It is thus unsurprising that police officers place tremendous importance on their capacity to assume authority. This is obviously connected to safety, and is witnessed most clearly by the tactical training officers receive on how to approach and stabilize scenes of potential danger. The best way to avoid force, and to use it wisely if necessary, is to approach a scene properly and to quickly dictate the flow of action.

This felt need to assert authority becomes ingrained.[11] Even in situations with minimal danger, officers often conduct pat-down searches or request that citizens position themselves in particular ways. For example, one officer I observed demanded that a teenager with whom he was conversing stand up. This made it easier for the officer to look the young man in the eye during an interrogation about goings-on in a nearby park. In another instance, a sergeant decided to act authoritatively after a long interaction with a young man during an on-street investigation of an apparent gang-related shooting. The young man was one of three passengers in a car that matched a description of one near the scene of the shooting. After establishing that the young man had been less than truthful, the sergeant pointed his finger toward the young man's face and declared, "This is what happens to people who don't tell the truth to the police." The sergeant handcuffed the young man and escorted him to the back seat of a patrol car.

In these and many other instances, officers seek to establish their authority, to dictate how a situation will unfold. This capacity to establish authority is obviously functional to the core police task of exercising force, and can be of considerable public benefit in many situations. In cases of domestic violence, for instance, the safety of all involved is contingent on the rapid establishment of order amid chaos. Of course, overly brusque assertions of authority can exacerbate chaos. On a call involving an obviously drunken woman who physically resisted a sergeant's effort to prevent her from entering her home, some fifteen officers responded, and sought to handcuff the woman. The fervent activity and loud admonishments only served to fuel the woman's resistance. Finally, a female officer stepped forward, talked calmly to the woman, and convinced her to relax sufficiently to allow the arrest.

So, even in situations of some disorder, crude assertions of authority can produce more chaos, not less. In terms of making the police more consciously subservient to the public, the cultural assumption of police authority poses obvious problems. If this authority is simply presumed, then police officials, by definition, do not consider the public as coequal partners. The challenge for the police is to distinguish between emergencies where their authority is necessary and situations like community forums where open discussion can be welcomed. What is a defensible cultural response to potentially violent situations becomes a liability when the police are legitimately asked to open their practices to debate. To an extent, one can empathize with the patrol officer who lamented to me that the public does not fully comprehend how he "can't be Officer Friendly" when he believes his first priority is to assert his authority. But this cultural response to the street-level realities the officer faces can reduce the space for the political efficacy of the citizenry.

In sum, the police's core coercive function is translated into cultural emphases that drive the imperative to not "drink the Kool-Aid." As officers reinforce masculinist notions of adventurousness, of safety, and of deference to their authority, they implicitly reduce the political agency of the citizenry. To build more truly co-equal partnerships involves a feminization of police work and erodes the police's self-construction as authoritative actors who ensure their safety by commandeering the scenes they enter. If community policing represents a threat to such self-understandings, it must be resisted, and strongly.

The police's sense of themselves as authoritative is important not just for how they define themselves vis-à-vis the citizenry, but also for how they define themselves to each other. Like workers everywhere, police officers seek to show their capabilities to their peers. But their efforts take on a particularly individualist cast. Officers hope to demonstrate their worth through their own idiosyncratic exercise of discretionary judgment. These organizational emphases on discretion and specialization are reinforced regularly, with considerable consequences for how officers act on issues of public concern. In such fashion, the project of community policing is further thwarted.

"I Need to Take Ownership": Specialization, Autonomy, and Organizational Disarray

One of the community police team members with whom I rode was still learning the ropes after just a few months on the job. This became apparent when I asked about his relations with other police units. He told a story about a memo he wrote to the detective unit in his first weeks. He used the memo to outline what he saw as the major problems in his area. He asked for information about any individuals the detectives suspected of creating these problems. There was no response. The officer said he interpreted this to mean that he needed to "take ownership" of these problems. He inferred that the detectives regarded the memo as evidence that he was shirking his responsibilities. He heard them communicate, albeit passively, a powerful message that he was on his own.

On another afternoon, I rode with a patrol officer whose beat included Blufftop, the large-scale public housing facility. The streets of the facility were frequently dotted with abandoned and improperly parked cars. As we cruised the meandering streets, he noticed an abandoned car he had previously ticketed for a tow. He was frustrated that the tow had not yet occurred. I asked him about his strategy for the broader problem of abandoned cars. He told me that he issued tickets when he could. He said nothing about coordinating any such strategy with other patrol officers who worked the beat or with the facility's community police officer. This was particularly striking because this officer formerly worked in the community policing unit and was a devout believer in the theory of "broken windows." In other words, this officer saw abandoned cars as important symbols of neighborhood decline that would invite more serious crime. He was also presumably well versed in the importance of coordinated action to address an intractable problem. Yet he, too, was flying solo.

Recall that community policing includes an emphasis on solving these more entrenched problems. Police-citizen partnerships should develop both a deep understanding of ongoing concerns and a thorough set of strategies for resolving them. As we have seen, the police are reluctant to surrender the prestige and moral standing they associate with authoritative and professional crime fighting. But they are equally reluctant to come together to address issues like abandoned cars in a coherent and comprehensive way. Implicit here is a valorization of individual autonomy and capability, a respect for any given officer's discretionary authority, a recognition that one must "take ownership" of one's responsibilities. A consequence is a frequent lack of coordinated action. As one officer told me, "Around here, one hand does not know what the other is doing."[12]

One obvious manifestation of this organizational disarray is the strained relation between the patrol operation and the community policing team. I saw little evidence that productive communication occurred across this bureaucratic division. Some patrol officers said they carried business cards of the community police team officer assigned to their beat and distributed them to residents who complained of an ongoing problem. Others said they often acted upon requests by community police officers to engage in extra patrol of a particular block or street corner suspected of hosting criminal activity. But never did any officer—from either patrol or the community police unit—describe any thoroughgoing, cooperative effort to address the underlying causes of an intractable problem. Indeed, a few patrol officers could not even name the community police officer who worked their beat.

One patrol sergeant with whom I rode had previously worked in a community police unit. He described the community police operation as a "garbage can" into which patrol officers dumped various nuisances they considered not worth their time. Patrol officers wished to focus on "serious crime," and saw community police work as trivial. One patrol officer with community police experience complained that a typical patrol officer did not understand what community police officers actually did. As a consequence, he acknowledged, there was very little sharing of information between the two units.

For their part, patrol officers operated largely as autonomous units. An exaggerated instance of this was the patrol officer who spent much of the time I rode with him outside the beat to which he was assigned. He focused on one particular house he believed was the site of ongoing drug activity. He knew many of the residents and talked regularly with the landlord. He obviously wanted to show me his in-depth understanding of the house and to document his efforts to reduce its capacity to host criminal activity. But he also made clear that his efforts were wholly his own.

Another patrol officer told me that he might refer a matter to the community police unit, such as long-term tensions between apartment residents and their landlord. However, if he gathered any intelligence about a hub of suspected criminal activity, he did not share it.

This would amount, in his terms, to "passing the buck." He strongly preferred to investigate on his own. That was the best way, he said, to "learn things" and to take effective action.

Part of the issue here is the bureaucratic division of labor, and the manner by which it limits officers' focus. For instance, veteran officers often complain that younger officers are much less group-oriented than their predecessors. Gone, they suggest, is a greater sense of collective responsibility for monitoring and solving problems. They attribute this to the progressive parceling of responsibilities into specialized units. Indeed, community policing is cited as one instance of this. Some veterans believe that the creation of a separate community police unit has reduced the sense of responsibility patrol officers feel for their beats.

Beyond these bureaucratic barriers, however, lies a belief that credit and competence are individually earned, and that officers should spend their discretionary time as they wish. This was most obvious during my ride-alongs with three different officers with less than a year's experience. Two officers patrolled their beats with little discernible purpose; they displayed minimal knowledge of their beats, they articulated no explanation for how they spent their time. They lacked direction, both figuratively and literally; they cruised without a goal, and they frequently got lost trying to reach the locations to which they were dispatched.

By contrast, the third rookie officer possessed a strong focus. He spent much time parked at a gas station in a poor neighborhood. As cars came in for fueling, he focused on those that were particularly run down. If he spotted such a car, he would input its license plate into his in-car data terminal. He searched, in particular, for information that the car's operator possessed a suspended driver's license. Such an offense in Seattle is subject to an immediate fine and an impounding of the car. The officer enjoyed this activity because he was often able to ticket and tow one or more vehicles during each shift. Regardless of his sense of accomplishment, the striking fact was that he acted on his own; no sergeant either endorsed or supervised his work. No apparent effort had been made to determine if this was, in fact, the most productive and effective use of his time.[13]

Indeed, officers had their own idiosyncratic preferences for how to handle time not devoted to responding to calls. One officer took a great interest in juveniles. He learned the names of many of the teenagers in his area and tried to determine if any of them were in trouble or headed for it. Occasionally, he got other officers involved in these efforts, once during a night when I accompanied another officer. The officer with the juvenile focus wanted to visit a home where he thought he might locate a runaway girl. The officer with whom I rode told me that his colleague frequently requested such assistance. He used this incident to describe the extent to which he and the other officers were given free rein. He listed other officers working that night and described their tendencies. These ranged from a pair of women who patrolled in high-crime areas to a senior officer who looked for places to nap. Another officer with whom I rode informed me that he enjoyed proactive police work. However, he could name only a few locations where he concentrated any such efforts. He visited none of them during the four hours I spent with him.

In sum, the police define authority and competence in largely individualist terms. Despite the tight sense of fraternity within the organization, fueled by collective concerns about outside meddlers and by the need to protect one another when danger arises, officers demonstrated an inability to develop collective strategies to address longstanding problems. Patrol officers rarely interacted with their community police team colleagues, and individual officers largely acted as lone wolves in whatever proactive strategies they did adopt. There was a striking lack of concerted, coordinated effort to confront the full complexity of those instances of crime and disorder that generated consistent complaints.

In short, perhaps the best place for the police to build community is among themselves.

The "Bad Apple" Narrative and the Marginalization of the Citizenry

Various emphases within the culture of the police, then, help explain why officers resist public input and oversight, and why they act with minimal cohesion in addressing ongoing problems. The narrative officers employ to explain criminal behavior is an additional factor that helps minimize police-community interaction. The police tend to explain crime as acts committed by a select number of "bad apples." This narrative reinforces the police's image as authoritative law enforcers and helps downplay any significant role for the community in meaningfully assisting with problem-solving efforts.[14]

[A related reading introduced a] lieutenant who chastised the justice system for not dealing aggressively with young car thieves. His solution to crime was obvious: find the bad actors and punish them through ostracism. Such thinking is hegemonic within the organization. When asked to explain why one neighborhood experienced a high number of calls for service, an officer asked me: "Do you want the actual reason, or the politically correct reason?" The "actual reason" was that the area was home to an unusually large number of people who received federal housing assistance through the Section 8 program. The officer believed that these impoverished people were more likely to offend, and thus that their clustering generated a localized crime problem. The way forward, for him, was simple—remove them from the midst of the otherwise peaceful community. Or, as another officer summarized it, "Crime disappears when the bad guys are in jail."

Indeed, catching "bad guys" is the principal motivation of many officers. This informs their geographies. One officer, for example, explained that he looked for places to patrol that were "target rich." He sought locales where he could find criminal behavior and acquire enough evidence to justify an arrest. One of his favorite places was a strip of cheap motels where small-scale drug dealing and prostitution were commonplace. Because these activities were often visible, the officer usually acquired enough probable cause to investigate further. This often yielded an arrest. This same desire for an easy citation motivated the officer described earlier who set up in the gas station looking for drivers with suspended licenses. Another officer described the street on which that gas station was located as an "easy" place to find evidence of criminal wrongdoing, and thus to secure an arrest.

This desire to isolate and remove bad apples from an area comports with the moralistic understanding officers develop to understand their work. Police work involves a cleansing of communities, a removal of the polluting stain of criminality. For this reason, officers often celebrate an arrest; for many, a day's work is incomplete without one. This helps explain why the community police officers embraced the short-lived "power community policing" model: it enabled them to experience the moral victory of an arrest, a far more satisfying prospect than an ongoing series of inconclusive meetings. And this narrative of morally necessary expulsion coheres with the "broken windows" ideology frequently employed to justify a range of police tactics. In practice, broken windows are people, and fixing broken windows means arresting them.[15] For instance, many officers focus on those who loiter around areas of suspected drug activity. Enforcing statutes on loitering is easier than enforcing statutes on drug delivery, so officers favor the loitering statutes.[16] These statutes also comport with the bad apple narrative and its emphasis on expulsion.

Two implications of this narrative deserve stress. One is the manner by which it leads officers to discredit other components of the criminal justice system, primarily the courts. If expulsion is necessary, then detention must be lengthy. Because the police can only arrest, they depend on courts to impose stiff sentences. They seethe when this fails to occur.[17] When one officer was asked what members of the community could do to help reduce crime, his message was simple and forceful: elect politicians who will require judges to send criminals up the river for a long time.

This officer's statement illustrates the second implication of the bad apple narrative: a diminished role for the citizenry in helping reduce crime and disorder. Notice that the officer suggests that community members act most critically as voters who only indirectly affect the police through the political officials they elect. The officer seems not even to entertain the possibility that a more direct connection between citizen and police is possible. The role he envisions for the community is rather passive.

Implicit in the bad apple narrative is an infected community. While one could potentially attribute a role to community dynamics in allowing or promoting the infection, officers downplay this possibility. Instead, an emphasis on the moral stain of evildoers leads officers to stress the need for expulsion. This valorizes police action over community action, because only the police—with their tactics, bravery, and coercive tools—can surgically extract the bad actors. The community is thus demoted to a mere information provider, as the "eyes and ears" of the police.[18] Even the patrol officer with prior work on the community policing team indicated that the most critical role for the citizenry is to provide complaints. Such complaints, he argued, make evident where a problem is emerging, thereby helping to galvanize a police response. The role for the citizenry is thus to help officers isolate wrong-doers, and then to step back when the cavalry arrives.

In this way, a notion of citizen agency—of citizens as co-equal partners in developing and enacting overarching strategies—is diminished. Once again, police superiority emerges as the dominant narrative, even if presented as the virtuous extraction of cancerous evil. Perhaps the public can point out the bad apples, but shaking them out of the tree is strictly a police matter. And even if the bad apple narrative possesses some verity, there is little consideration of any wider dynamics that explain their presence in a particular area, and little role for working with the citizenry to comprehend and address these dynamics. When the police employ this narrative of crime and its possible eradication they downplay the robust role for citizen involvement that community policing potentially represents.

Conclusion

Bittner correctly emphasized the centrality of coercive force to the structure and organization of the police. The capacity for such force is largely what makes the police a public institution of such symbolic significance. It also helps explain why the tensions between subservience, separation, and generativity are so vividly exemplified through an analysis of the police-community relation. Given their coercive authority, it is necessary that the police fall under public sway; the risk of an emergent police state ensures that the narrative of police subservience to citizen oversight will forever retain power. However, the capacity for coercive force also means that excessive subservience might leave the police susceptible to unwarranted uses by a particular social group. The liberal preoccupation with state neutrality, and its attendant emphasis on the regulation of the police through law, is quite understandable. Such legally produced neutrality should help ensure that the police do not suppress a disfavored minority group. But the capacity for coercive force also helps generate the moral framework in which the police operate, and through which they construct their epistemologies of community and their preferred relation to the citizenry.

My discussion here explicates further why the projects of separation and generativity stand in general tension with the ideal of subservience. This tension is exemplified in ongoing officer resistance to community policing. The ability to exercise coercive force is implicated in the cultural world officers construct, specifically in their emphases on masculinist adventurousness, safety, and authority. Each of these reinforces a notion of police separation from the citizenry, although not in keeping necessarily with liberalism's stress on state neutrality. Their sense of separation derives instead from their self-construction as competent professionals. Police understand themselves as superior to the untrained public and arrogate to themselves the right to act forcefully and authoritatively. In so doing, they obscure notions of a citizenry with a robust degree of political agency. The police also obstruct a more active role for the citizenry via their heavy reliance on a morally laden narrative of crime causation that emphasizes the ill effects of selected bad apples. This narrative implicitly trumpets the police as the agency of extraction. The citizenry is diminished as mere providers of information for police-generated tactics.

Even when the police are made aware of issues that community members wish to see addressed, they are unlikely to develop a coordinated strategy in response. A cultural emphasis on individual discretion and autonomy, and a bureaucratically constructed sense of specialized authority, work to keep officers in general isolation from one another. Collective efforts by the police to formulate a comprehensive approach to any problem are uncommon.

All of these police dynamics help shape how police relate to the citizenry. They also shape how the citizenry understands and evaluates the police. [...]

Notes

1. A good example is the resistance officers mounted to "team policing," an attempt by many American police departments in the 1970s to introduce many of the principles—decentralization of police authority, collective problem solving—later included in community policing. See Jack Greene, "Police and Community Relations: Where Have We Been and Where Are We Going?" in *Critical Issues in Policing,* ed. Roger Dunham and Geoffrey Alpert (Prospect Heights, Ill.: Waveland Press, 1989), 349–68; Mark Harrison Moore, "Problem-Solving and Community Policing," in *Modern Policing,* ed. Norval Morris and Michael Tonry (Chicago: University of Chicago Press, 1992).

2. This is not to suggest that all officers rebuff community policing. There is support for it within the Seattle Police Department and in other police departments. Eugene Paoline, for instance, found that the strongest differentiating attitude between the police officers he surveyed was their orientation toward community policing. Paoline, "Shedding Light on Police Culture: An Examination of Officers' Occupational Attitudes," *Police Quarterly* 7 (2004): 205–36. Yet resistance remains strong, such that little change seems evident as a consequence of its alleged institutionalization. See William Lyons, *The Politics of Community Policing: Rearranging the Power to Punish* (Ann Arbor: University of Michigan Press, 1999); Edward Maguire, "Structural

Change in Large Municipal Police Organizations during the Community Policing Era," *Justice Quarterly* 14 (1997): 701–30. This resistance deserves explanation, in no small part because it has enormous consequences for the prospect of improved police-community relations.

3. Egon Bittner, *The Functions of the Police in Modern Society* (New York: Jason Aronson, 1975).

4. It is a mistake, of course, to posit that there is a single, unified entity called "police culture." As with any system of meaning, police culture is differentiated. See Steve Herbert, "Police Subculture Reconsidered," *Criminology* 36 (1998): 334–70. Further, as with all social actors, police officers vary in the extent to which their actions are shaped by elements of that culture. For instance, officers take different stances toward community policing; some embrace it, while others are hostile. See Eugene Paoline, Stephanie Myers, and Robert Worden, "Police Culture, Individualism, and Community Policing: Evidence from Two Police Departments," *Justice Quarterly* 17 (2000): 575–605; and Janet Chan, *Changing Police Culture: Policing in a Multicultural Society* (Cambridge: Cambridge University Press, 1997). That said, hostility to community policing is quite common, and is palpable in Seattle. Indeed, this hostility leads some commentators to argue that police culture is the biggest impediment to the wider implementation of the community policing philosophy. See Malcolm Sparrow, Mark Moore, and David Kennedy, *Beyond 911: A New Era for Policing* (New York: Basic Books, 1990); Susan Sadd and Randolph Grinc, "Innovative Neighborhood Oriented Policing: An Evaluation of Community Policing Programs in Eight Cities," in *The Challenges of Community Policing: Testing the Promises,* ed. Dennis Rosenbaum (Thousand Oaks, Calif.: Sage Publications, 1994), 27–52.

5. I provide a more complete account of police culture elsewhere: Herbert, "Police Subculture Reconsidered." My goal here is to isolate elements of that culture that are particularly relevant to the resistance to community policing.

6. Anthony Bouza, *The Police Mystique* (New York: Plenum Press, 1990).

7. In Los Angeles, officers make the contrast between bold and cowardly officers by employing two terms—"hard charger" and "station queen." The former's willingness to embrace danger is valued, the latter's desire to lay low is ridiculed. See Steve Herbert, "Hard Charger or Station Queen? Policing and the Masculinist State," *Gender, Place and Culture* 8 (2001): 55–71.

8. Ibid.

9. Sadd and Grinc note that the community police officers they interviewed felt compelled to argue continually with their colleagues that they were engaged in "real" police work. Sadd and Grinc, "Innovative Neighborhood Oriented Policing."

10. A pat-down is legally distinguishable from a full search. The former is acceptable as long as the officer can demonstrate a plausible concern about safety. The latter can only occur if the officer possesses either probable cause that a crime has occurred or a court-sanctioned search warrant.

11. David Bayley suggests that this process begins when the officer suits up for work. As he puts it, "Police officers especially in the United States go to work as if they were going to war." Bayley, *Police for the Future* (New York: Oxford University Press, 1994), 70.

12. Oberweiss and Musheno, in a study contrasting police officers and vocational rehabilitation counselors, noticed an important difference in the way the two groups justified the discretion they valued. Counselors defended discretion because it enabled the flexibility they thought they needed to generate positive outcomes for their clients. By contrast, the police legitimated discretion because it preserved their freedom to exercise their authority as they wished. Trish Oberweiss and Michael Musheno, *Knowing Rights: State Actors' Stories of Power, Identity, and Morality* (Aldershot: Ashgate, 2001).

13. The lack of supervision here was especially surprising because the suspended license policy was the subject of a public controversy initiated primarily by members of minority groups. These activists argued that the policy disproportionately punished poor people and worked to exacerbate their economic challenges by making transportation more difficult. The officer thus contributed, albeit probably unwittingly, to an erosion of police legitimacy in the eyes of those who suspect officers of racial profiling. Because of this controversy, a greater supervisory hand might have been expected.

14. The police's propensity to explain crime in largely individualist terms is noted, as well, in Adam Crawford, *The Local Governance of Crime* (Oxford: Clarendon Press, 1997), and Stuart Scheingold, *The Politics of Street Crime: Criminal Process and Cultural Obsession* (Philadelphia: Temple University Press, 1991). Scheingold notes that this individualist approach leads officers to favor deterrence as their preferred punishment approach and to eschew more societal explanations for crime.

15. The broken windows logic holds that visible signs of "disorder" send a signal to would-be criminals that a place suffers from inadequate informal social control and thus represents an opportunity for misdeeds. See James Q. Wilson and George Kelling, "Broken Windows," *Atlantic Monthly,* March 1982, 29–38; George Kelling and Catherine Coles, *Fixing Broken Windows: Restoring Order and Reducing Crime in Our Cities* (New York: Free Press, 1996). Although the title of the theory emphasizes the built environment, in actuality its focus is upon people. As Wilson and Kelling put it in their seminal essay, they are concerned specifically with "disreputable or obstreperous or unpredictable people: panhandlers, drunks, addicts, rowdy teenagers, prostitutes, loiterers, the mentally disturbed." Not surprisingly, they endorse a

strong police response to such street denizens, including close surveillance and frequent arrests. The theory has spawned a movement within policing, referred to as either broken windows or order-maintenance, that has been used to legitimate stringent crackdowns on activities associated with the "disreputable" people that concern them, most notably in the "zero tolerance" strategy advocated in New York City in the 1990s. For a defense of this by the police chief who supervised it, see William Bratton, *Turnaround: How America's Top Cop Reversed the Crime Epidemic* (New York: Random House, 1998). For critiques, see Bernard Harcourt, *The Illusion of Order: The False Promise of Broken Windows Policing* (Cambridge: Harvard University Press, 2001); Steve Herbert, "Policing the Contemporary City: Fixing Broken Windows or Shoring up Neo-Liberalism?" *Theoretical Criminology* 5 (2001): 445–66.

16. [... A] community police officer in Blufftop [...] sought authority to make arrests for trespassing. He sought this authority because he suspected that the loiterers were delivering drugs. To arrest them for drug delivery, however, would require a high level of probable cause. It would be much simpler for him to arrest them for trespassing.

17. It seems to have escaped the notice of the typical patrol officer that the United States now has the highest rate of incarceration in the world.

18. Ralph Saunders, "The Space Community Policing Makes and the Body that Makes It," *The Professional Geographer* 51 (1999): 135–46.

DISCUSSION QUESTIONS

1. Compare and contrast the basic tenets of both traditional and community-based styles of policing. How is traditional policing different from community-based styles of policing?

2. Describe some of the strategies associated with problem-oriented policing.

3. COP does have its problems and challenges. What are some of the criticisms of community policing today?

4. Community policing has resulted in innovations in police information, resources, environment, organization, technology, policy and processes. How have these innovations affected policing in your state and the region or county that you live in?

5. Most police departments have webpages devoted to community policing. List some specific local examples of community policing in your geographic area.

6. Which form of policing do you believe to be the most effective, traditional policing or community policing? Why? Support your discussion with appropriate sources.

Chapter 5

Transnational Crime and Terrorism

FIGURE 5.1   The FBI has deployed chaplains to crime scenes to provide support to employees since 1991. An FBI special agent (left) speaks to two FBI chaplains at Ground Zero in New York in 2001. Photo courtesy of the Federal Emergency Management Agency.

INTRODUCTION

In this age of international organized crime, terrorism, and homeland security priorities, the police community can no longer afford to ignore criminal activities that were once only the purview of federal law enforcement or international agencies. The FBI defines organized crime as "any group having some manner of a formalized structure and whose primary objective is to obtain money through illegal activities." Organized crime groups use actual or threatened violence, corrupt public officials, or extortion to control economic activities in their community.

They can have a substantial impact on some local communities and even entire countries as they continue to globalize their operations. Because transnational organized crime (TOC) is driven by financial gain instead of political power, their operations do not recognize any international borders. Transnational criminal organizations have become less centralized with smaller cell-like structures that are similar to terrorist groups. The most important categories of transnational organized crimes are: migrant smuggling, cybercrimes, hazardous waste dumping, maritime piracy, and trafficking in firearms, humans, drugs, counterfeit goods, and endangered wildlife products. The FBI believes that Russian mobsters, groups from African countries like Nigeria, the Chinese Triads, Japanese Yakuza, and Eastern European transnational criminal organizations are currently well represented inside the United States.

In this world of increasing terrorism and transnational crime complexity, the police find themselves challenged to improve upon their traditional roles and accept new responsibilities to deal with the globalization of crime. To keep up with these new developments, the police require new resources critical to effective policing of transnational crime and terrorism crimes. In this chapter, we will discuss the economic, social, and political impact of both domestic and transnational crime. It is necessary to understand, to some degree, the global conditions that can result in acts of terrorism. We will also identify some recommendations for improved law enforcement and citizen responses to terrorism and TOC. Finally, we will delve into the challenges of determining what roles should be played by state and local police agencies in response to TOC and terrorism.

REFERENCES

McConnachie, K. (2006). [Review of the book *Transnational & comparative criminology*. edited by J. Sheptycki & A. Wardak]. *The British Journal of Criminology, 46*(3), 536–538. https://www.jstor.org/stable/23639369

Sheinis, D. (2012). The links between human trafficking, organized crime, and terrorism. *American Intelligence Journal, 30*(1), 68–77. http://www.jstor.org/stable/26201986

Figure Credit

Fig. 5.1: Source: https://www.fbi.gov/news/stories/fbi-chaplains.

Reading 5.1

Deciphering the Linkages Between Organized Crime and Transnational Crime

Jay S. Albanese

IN 2011, ONLINE AUCTIONS INVOLVING EXPENSIVE items such as cars, motorcycles, and recreational vehicles were on listed websites, including eBay, Craigslist, and AutoTrader.com. Buyers (mostly from the United States) transferred funds for their purchases using Western Union and bank transfers; however, the items for sale never existed. The conspirators behind this scheme moved from city to city and used false identification to open new bank accounts, while the victims never received the items they had purchased. The case led to a Romanian man pleading guilty to fraud.[1]

This case is a classic example of transnational crime: it is a law violation that involved more than one country in its planning, execution, or impact. Unlike traditional crimes that occur within a single country, transnational crimes are distinguished by their multinational nature and cross border impact.

This article will discuss six aspects of transnational crime that help clarify misconceptions, and will also help establish a path for the future. These six aspects include: a comprehensive classification of transnational crime; transnational crimes as a form of organized crime; transnational criminal activities remaining the same over the years; focus on criminal markets rather than groups or networks; theoretical perspectives on transnational crime prevention; and finally, effective implementation of international agreements.

Classification of Transnational Crime

Transnational crimes are separate from international crimes, which involve crimes against humanity that may or may not involve multiple countries. Examples of international crimes include genocide and terrorism, as well as violations of human rights, often without a profit motive—a central objective of virtually all transnational crimes. In a recent case in New York City, four men who had met in prison concocted a plan to bomb Jewish synagogues. They wanted to carry out what they believed were Osama bin Laden's wishes. The plan was never executed because an informant infiltrated the group and police were able to defuse the bombs.[2]

TABLE 5.1.1 Classification of Transnational Crimes

Provision of Illicit Goods	Provision of Illicit Services	Infiltration of Business or Government
Drug trafficking	Human trafficking	Extortion & racketeering
Stolen property	Cybercrime and fraud	Money laundering
Counterfeiting	Commercial vices (e.g., illegal sex & gambling)	Corruption

Developed by Jay S. Albanese (2012)

The underlying motive in this case was political or religious hatred without any apparent profit motive. This distinguishes international crimes from the more frequent transnational crimes, which are characterized by motives of personal gain and profit.

Transnational crimes can be categorized as having three broad objectives: provision of illicit goods, provision of illicit services, and the infiltration of business or government operations. As summarized in Table 5.1.1, transnational crimes are grouped according to these three objectives and encompass a total of nine types of offenses.

As an example of the cybercrime and fraud category, three individuals were charged with hacking into the telephone systems of large corporations simply so they could make calls around the world and sell this telephone time to others. More than 12 million minutes of telephone calls, valued at $55 million, were fraudulently charged to the corporations in this case. Suspects in this scheme were arrested in the United States, the Philippines, and Italy.[3] This case represents a modern example of an old crime (fraud), using cyberspace, intercontinental telephone capacity, and billing schemes to operate transnationally.

Transnational Crimes as a Form of Organized Crime

A careful examination of the offenses listed in Table 5.1.1 illustrates that most forms of transnational crime center on organized crime activity rather than on traditional, individual, or politically motivated crimes. It is usually a requirement for groups of two or more to form a rational, ongoing conspiracy to plan these crimes and the objective is almost always to make a profit. The vast majority of these offenses simply cannot be carried out effectively by lone offenders, by those who are not organized, or by those without contacts in other countries, given the aims and scope of transnational crime.

A consensus definition of organized crime, using the common elements of multiple scholars, is "a continuing criminal enterprise that rationally works to profit from illicit activities that are often in great public demand. Its continuing existence is maintained through the use of force, threats, monopoly control, and/or the corruption of public officials."[4] The enterprise might be two people engaged in a small scale conspiracy or it might be a multinational crime as described in the previous example.

Therefore, transnational crime is a form of organized crime given its multinational aims and the extent of organization required for success. Transnational organized crime (TOC) can be considered the modern extension of organized crime in the globalized era.

Transnational Criminal Activities Have Not Changed Much Over the Years

It sometimes seems that new kinds of transnational crimes are occurring all the time, given press accounts of new criminal schemes unearthed, but it is difficult to name an entirely "new" kind of transnational crime. For example, sea piracy is not mentioned in Table 5.1.1, because it is an example of extortion and racketeering—a very old category of transnational crime.[5] Indeed, trafficking in weapons, migrants, and drugs are also very old crimes. Reports of intellectual property theft as a "new" form of crime are instead most often a form of the older crimes of counterfeiting or fraud. These "new" forms of transnational crimes have been made possible by changes in technology and communication, ease of travel, and political unrest—all consequences of globalization and government prohibitions.[6]

As Table 5.1.1 suggests, there is not an unlimited number of transnational organized crimes, but a limited number of criminal activities that characterize nearly all organized crime. The specific crimes change depending on local conditions (e.g., types of drugs trafficked, types of frauds committed, or nature of stolen property trafficked), but the underlying activity remains of comparatively few distinct types.

Organized criminal activity shifts in its method of execution, but its underlying nature has changed little over time. Table 5.1.2 illustrates the changes in the nature of organized crime from older, traditional forms, to newer, modern manifestations that often cross national borders. The contemporary forms are simply newer versions of organized criminal conduct that have been altered in their commission due to changes in opportunity, technology, and in the likelihood of apprehension. Transnational organized crime has characterized the last twenty years, beginning with the collapse of the Soviet Union and the rise of vulnerable emerging democracies around the world. It has evolved with the growing ease of international travel and the ability to move products and invest money around the world accompanied by corresponding adjustments made by profit-minded opportunists who have simply changed their methods to increase their gain and decrease the likelihood of apprehension.

By focusing on criminal markets rather than groups or networks, TOC can be described either by the activities in which these markets engage or by the groups they involve. The continuing criminal conspiracies that comprise TOC often require both insiders and outsiders

TABLE 5.1.2 Shifts in Organized Crime Activity over Time

Original Activity	Modern Version
Local numbers and lottery gambling	Internet gambling at international sites outside national regulation
Heroin, cocaine trafficking	Synthetic drugs (less vulnerable to supply problems)
Street prostitution	Internet prostitution and trafficking in human beings
Extortion of local businesses for protection money	Extortion of corporations, kidnappings, piracy for profit
Loansharking (exchanging money at interest rates above the rate permitted by law)	Money laundering, precious stones, commodities
Theft and fencing stolen property	Theft of intellectual property, Internet scams, trafficking globally available goods (e.g., weapons, natural resources)

Developed by Jay S. Albanese (2012)

to connect suppliers with customers and protect the enterprise from law enforcement. Therefore, organized crime groups need to obtain the product (e.g., drugs, stolen property) and make it easily available to customers (e.g., movement from source to destination), while obtaining some "insurance" when members are caught or convicted (e.g., the need for corruption of public officials to protect the enterprise from disruption). These elements help ensure that organized crime groups survive and make a profit.

Most risk or threat assessments in organized crime have focused on groups. These assessments are often carried out by law enforcement agencies to determine which groups pose the greatest threat. The methods used to determine risk involve identifying the universe of known crime groups in the country and then ranking them by their attributes and potential seriousness. Sample attributes used in these assessments include violence, corruption, infiltration, sophistication, discipline, insulation, stability, and group cohesiveness.[7] In a similar way, the FBI's organized crime investigation program is divided into specialized programs focused on African, Asian, Balkan, Italian, and Middle Eastern criminal enterprises.[8] This illustrates a primary focus on crime groups as an area of key concern in relation to TOC.

A selection of "groups" as the criterion to be targeted is based on the premise that law enforcement agencies place apprehension of criminals at the center of their mission. Experience shows, however, that the arrest of organized crime figures usually does not eliminate the group, because it simply recruits new members or promotes existing members after a successful prosecution.[9] The expectation is that prosecution of individuals involved in organized crime groups will disrupt the operation of the group as well as the illegal market for the illicit products in question. This is problematic, however, because successful prosecutions of organized crime figures impact groups for only a short period, and customer demand for the illegal products or services is not diminished by a prosecution. Therefore, existing or new groups continue to exploit these illicit markets. A UN assessment concluded that, "While organized crime groups can become problems in themselves, eliminating these groups is unlikely to stop the contraband flow."[10]

A focus on organized crime activities and their markets, rather than on groups, is useful for purposes of assessment and analysis in order to produce an objective basis for investigative priorities and prevention initiatives. There is growing concern around the world about how best to address TOC. In an era of scarce and declining resources it is imperative that attention is targeted at the most significant organized crime problems as determined by their threat and harm. In New Zealand, for example, a report on organized crime identified twelve different illicit markets that pose both domestic and international organized crime threats. The markets identified include illicit drugs, organized burglary and theft, violence, kidnapping, illicit firearms, illegal migration, identity crime, financial crime, electronic crime (e-crime), environmental crime, intellectual property theft, and corruption.[11] This list of organized crime problems is not unlike those identified in other countries, although there are some notable differences in the range of illicit markets among countries.[12] The U.S. Department of Justice's International Organized Crime Threat Assessment called for four areas of action, two of which include: "prioritize and target the most significant IOC threats" and employing all available tools to disrupt IOC activity.[13] The National Institute of Justice sponsored an expert working group (EWG) on international organized crime in 2010 to assess the state of and promising directions for organized crime research. The EWG acknowledged that "the state of knowledge on IOC has developed to the point that researchers can proceed to conduct more advanced studies," and specifically recommended that "studies should analyze their findings in an international context, exploring how studies conducted in one country might still apply to other countries," emphasizing "the importance of researcher-practitioner collaboration to produce good research."[14]

The international need is for tools to assess these illicit markets to determine their relative threat and harm so that a risk assessment can be carried out to provide a rational, empirical basis for the targeting of investigative and prevention resources in the highest-risk markets. Government agencies are not able to address all problems equally given their available resources, so a risk assessment approach provides an objective way to allocate effort. When carried out periodically, empirical risk assessments permit the ongoing adjustment of public resources to the areas of greatest need in a manner that will be most effective and defensible to the public and those controlling budgetary resources.

There are some encouraging examples of international efforts in this regard. For instance, Finland, Hungary, Italy, and the Netherlands reported on an in-depth analysis of fifteen major cases of organized crime, looking for "red flags" that suggested possible intervention and preventive measures. These cases involved trafficking in women, smuggling of illegal immigrants, and drug trafficking. The analysis found three factors common to these cases: demand for illegal products and services from the legal environment, abuse of facilitators in the legal environment (e.g., public officials, landlords, taxi drivers), and the availability of legal "tools" (e.g., forged documents, money laundering).[15] This study provides the beginnings of a risk assessment. Both EU and North American countries have examined a series of individual and structural measures associated with organized crime, including money laundering control measures and forged document prevention, making it more difficult to manufacture synthetic drugs and smuggle stolen art, restricted timber, and contraband cigarettes.[16] In addition, there have been efforts to exclude certain individuals and organizations from participating in different markets, such as construction and public works, due to past associations with organized crime activity.[17] These efforts are noteworthy because they are not primarily aimed at the perpetrators of organized crime but rather at the circumstances that facilitate organized crime activity in particular markets. In this way, enforcement efforts can also become prevention efforts when they aim at goals (i.e., reducing organized crime presence in specific markets) beyond development of individual criminal cases against known suspects.

Theoretical Perspectives on Transnational Crime Prevention: Enterprise versus Situational

The theoretical grounding of efforts to reduce the risk of organized crime groups and their activities in various markets has been based largely on the principles of situational crime prevention. By focusing on the circumstances of crime, this perspective examines the availability of opportunities to commit specific crimes using the principle of routine activities. Routine activities assume that levels of organized crime are determined by facilitating factors: availability of attractive targets, a low level of supervision, and low risk of apprehension. Rather than focusing on distant causes of crime (e.g., poverty, poor education, peer groups), the focus is shifted to practical ways to reduce the opportunities for crime or to minimize their harm.[18] Situational crime prevention has been used primarily in addressing high volume traditional crimes, such as burglary and theft. Nevertheless, there is emerging evidence that this approach can be useful in reducing organized crimes by limiting criminal opportunities and minimizing harm.[19] Efforts have been made to apply the situational crime prevention perspective to TOC, including the manufacture of methamphetamine, automobile theft, open-air drug markets, prostitution, and crime displacement.[20] All these empirical efforts have shown at least partial support for the situational perspective in preventing organized illicit activity.

A limitation of the situational crime prevention perspective is that the precise strategies needed for reducing criminal opportunities are not always evident. The theory requires that crime prevention techniques be directed at five areas: increase the effort for offenders (e.g., target hardening, controlling crime facilitators), increase the risks (e.g., surveillance of offenders and victims, screening entrances and exits), reduce the rewards (e.g., removing targets, controlling markets), reduce provocations (e.g., reducing temptations, avoiding disputes), and remove excuses (e.g., setting rules, alerting conscience).[21] The precise methods to be taken to achieve these goals depends on the specific crime to be prevented and its underlying preparatory behaviors (called "scripts"), but empirical efforts have shown that it is not always clear which specific methods can be expected to have an impact on organized crime activity.[22]

The addition of a second theoretical perspective to situational crime prevention, which focuses on enterprise, helps to resolve this problem of selecting the most effective crime prevention measures for a particular type of crime and location. The enterprise model of organized crime emerged from the observation that organized crime operates as a business. Dwight Smith explained the economic origins of organized crime in a systematic manner in his book *The Mafia Mystique*. In subsequent publications he developed a "spectrum-based theory of enterprise," which applied general organization theory to criminal activity. Smith concluded that organized crime develops from "the same fundamental assumptions that govern entrepreneurship in the legitimate marketplace: a necessity to maintain and extend one's share of the market."[23] This perspective sees the formation and operation of organized crime groups as more similar than different from legitimate businesses. In both instances, they respond to the needs and demands of suppliers, customers, regulators, and competitors in delivering their products and services. According to Smith, the primary difference between organized crime and legitimate business is that organized criminals deal in illegal products, whereas legitimate businesses do not.

Empirical studies of specific organized crime activity support this enterprise perspective. Patricia Adler studied illicit drug sales as a participant-observer and discovered the drug markets she observed consisted of "individual entrepreneurs and small organizations rather than massive, centralized bureaucracies," and that they were "competitive" rather than "monopolistic" in structure and operation.[24] Peter Reuter examined bookmaking, loansharking, and numbers gambling in New York City and observed that they were "not monopolies in the classic sense or subject to control by some external organization." He found that "economic forces arising from the illegality of the product tend to fragment the market," which made it difficult to centralize or control these illegal activities on a large scale.[25] Letzia Paoli's research concluded that the supply of illegal goods did not lead toward the development of large-scale criminal enterprises due to the illegal nature of the product.[26] Smaller, more flexible and efficient enterprises were more characteristic of this type of organized crime. An analysis of organized crime in post-Soviet Russia pointed to overlaps with white-collar crime (the need for "insiders" who become part of the criminal scheme) and the utility of "enterprise" as a central concept to explain this relationship.[27] The use of "enterprise" to guide organized crime investigations has been shown to be effective in addressing a "full range of criminal activities," rather than a particular suspect, and "determining which components allow the criminal enterprise to operate."[28]

Studies such as these typify the enterprise model of organized crime. Rather than viewing organized crime from a hierarchical or ethnic perspective, the enterprise model views it as the product of market forces, similar to those that cause legitimate businesses to flourish or die in the legal sector of the economy. When separated into its component parts, it is clear that "business" influences affect organized crime activity. All enterprises, both legal and illegal, exist to survive and make a profit. Whether the product is drugs, stolen property, sexual services, counterfeiting, or other crimes, the criminals must account for supply (of materials needed), the nature and location of demand (by potential customers), the regulators who might put them out of business (e.g., law, police), and competitors (comprised of other criminal groups and products) that might reduce their profitability or even their survival in the market.

Figure 5.1.1 provides a diagram of the pressures on criminal enterprises. In order to survive and make a profit, the changing nature of supply, demand, regulators, and competitors must be accounted for.

In each category it can be seen that specific indicators can be developed to measure the comparative nature of supply (availability, ease of movement), demand (the level of demand, and whether it is elastic or inelastic), competition from other groups and products (profitability, history of organized crime in that market, and impact the resulting harms), and regulators (ease of entry into the illicit market or product based on existing regulations and any special skills needed, the capacity and effectiveness of law enforcement in that jurisdiction, and government corruption levels). When indicators for each of these variables are gathered for different illicit products, it is possible to assess the comparative risk of organized crime involvement for different types of products and illicit markets. A UN global assessment of organized crime concluded that, "most organized crime problems today seem to be less a matter of a group of individuals who are involved in a range of illicit activities, and more a matter of a group of illicit activities in which some individuals and groups are presently involved."[29] The result of this situation is that "strategies

Regulators

- Ease of entry into market (regulation/skills)
- Law enforcement capability
- Government corruption level

Supply

- Objective availability of product of service
- Ease of movement/ sale

→

TRANSNATIONAL ORGANIZED CRIME AS ENTERPRISE

Goal: Survive and make profit

→

Customers

- Current demand for product
- Elastic/inelastic nature of demand

Competition

- History of OC in market
- Profitability compared to other illicit products/services
- Harm compared to other illicit products/services

FIGURE 5.1.1   A Model of Transnational Organized Crime Operation in Illicit Markets
Developed by Jay S. Albanese (2012)

aimed at the groups will not stop the illicit activities if the dynamics of the market remain unaddressed."[30]

A proper understanding of the structure and operation of transnational criminal enterprises is required in order to carry out effective prevention and control of these activities. The international response is recent, and its strengths and limitations are described next.

Effectively Implementing International Agreements

The United Nations drafted the Convention against Transnational Organized Crime in December 2000 in recognition of the central role of organized crime with transnational crime in general. The Convention provides model laws, policies, enforcement techniques, and prevention strategies against transnational criminal groups. The Convention had to be ratified by forty countries in order to become binding, and this occurred in 2003. As of this writing, 171 of the 193 UN member countries had ratified this agreement, representing nearly 90 percent of the world's nations. Countries that are party to the Convention must adopt laws that prohibit participation in organized criminal groups, money laundering, corruption, and obstruction of justice. The Convention directs participating countries to engage in mutual legal assistance, training, extradition agreements, joint investigations, and witness protection.

Three separate protocols were added for countries to ratify on the related issues of trafficking in persons, smuggling of migrants, and illicit manufacture and trafficking in firearms. Similar to the Convention against Transnational Organized Crime, these three protocols direct countries to criminalize these behaviors and take affirmative steps to investigate and prosecute suspects, as well as to devote resources to training and prevention efforts.[31] UN mechanisms include a conference of parties to the Convention that meets annually and a series of working groups, consisting of representatives from participating countries, which have been established to work on compliance issues. These efforts have resulted in legal tools, legislative guides, and other technical assistance and support to help countries implement and activate legislation, enforcement, and prevention initiatives in their respective countries.[32]

UN efforts are important, because they demonstrate that a multinational response is required to effectively address the problem of transnational crime. Efforts in a single country cannot succeed due to the nature of the criminal market, as producers, transporters, sellers, and buyers often cross national boundaries. Furthermore, obstacles arise in securing compliance with binding agreements that raise questions about state sovereignty. How does a binding international agreement on TOC become implemented in a reasonable way, knowing that significant changes in national laws, policies, and priorities will have to take place in sovereign countries? Another way of asking this question is, "Are we carrying out what we intended?" And the follow-up question is, "Are we having any impact on the problem of transnational organized crime?"

As Table 5.1.3 illustrates, the implementation of the Convention against Transnational Organized Crime is being carried out on several fronts: the establishment of extradition agreements, mutual legal assistance, new criminalization and liability for conduct within countries, new confiscation and forfeiture provisions, the prosecution of TOC cases, increasing public awareness on the impact of organized crime on the community, and the provision of assistance to victims and witnesses of organized crime activity. In effect, these efforts bring to life the words of the Convention. Practical implementation of these efforts have begun and consist of self assessments by individual countries and peer and expert reviews

TABLE 5.1.3 Transnational Organized Crime: Distinguishing Objectives and Outcomes of Government Action Versus Improving the TOC Situation

Implementation of Government Actions	Improving the Transnational Organized Crime Situation
Question: How does an international agreement become implemented?	**Question: How does a government know the impact of implementation?**
1. Extradition 2. Mutual Legal Assistance 3. Criminalization and liability 4. Confiscation and forfeiture provisions 5. Making significant TOC cases for prosecution 6. Public awareness 7. Victim and witness assistance	1. Changes in level of specific organized crime activities in a city or region (e.g., extortion, trafficking in humans, stolen property, drugs, firearms, migrants, cultural property, body organs, counterfeit medicines, natural resources, money laundering, piracy) 2. Changes in organized crime groups (e.g., disruption of groups, level of involvement in targeted markets)
Assessing implementation of law, policy, procedures	**Assessing the effects of interventions on Transnational Organized Crime activity**
Question: How to conduct a process evaluation?	**Question: How to conduct an impact evaluation?**
1. Self-assessment 2. Peer review 3. Expert review	1. Victimization surveys (especially business). 2. Changes in risk of specific TOC activities over time (periodic assessment of correlates and harms of selected TOC activities). 3. Changes in TOC groups and networks: interviews with OC investigators, offenders, and public in affected areas.

Developed by Jay S. Albanese

provided by qualified (and mutually agreed upon) experienced professionals from other countries. Similar to the way in which we accredit universities and inspect businesses, the implementation of the Conventions provisions is measured by internal and external reviews and assessments.[33]

The larger question, represented by the second column in Table 5.1.3, is assessing the impact of these changes in law, policy, and operations on the actual incidence and seriousness of TOC. The determination of these impacts is a more difficult problem, because it requires research and evaluation, which is time consuming and expensive (though not as expensive as wasting money on implementing policies that are ineffective). The methods to assess these impacts are suggested by some of the research work cited earlier in this article and carried out by analyzing changes over time in the levels of particular TOC activities and changes in TOC groups and networks. In the same way that most countries measure trends in homicide, robbery, and other serious crimes, measuring changes in the transnational crimes classified in Table 5.1.1 can also be carried out, although they require more effort. Changes in the incidence of these crimes can be assessed using victimization surveys of businesses about their experiences with organized crime, which has been done with some success already on a limited basis.[34] Assessing changes in the risk of specific types of TOC can be carried out with periodic assessments of the correlates and harms of selected organized crime activities. Table 5.1.1 suggests a model for doing this, as well as efforts to assess the risk of specific organized crime activities that have occurred. These efforts have been carried out on a limited basis given the difficulties of funding and the failure of most governments to see the importance of this work.[35] Changes in the nature of TOC groups and networks can be assessed using periodic interviews with experienced organized crime investigators, captured offenders, and public awareness surveys in affected areas. Canada provides a good model for using investigator input to structure the assessment of changes in the comparative threat posed by different crime groups and networks over time.[36]

In summary, the fact that the last decade has seen international recognition of transnational crime in the form of a binding General Assembly resolution which adopted the Convention is a positive sign. The ongoing Conference of the Parties to the UN Convention, which includes most member states, also shows international resolve to develop the legal tools and institutional capacity to improve national and international responses to this kind of criminal activity. On the other hand, the research and assessment required to determine that these efforts are having any impact on the problem of TOC have only been carried out on an ad hoc basis thus far. Few nations have invested in assessing the extent to, and manner in which laws, policies, training, and awareness efforts are making a difference. This investment is the key challenge that remains in addressing the problem of transnational organized crime.

Notes

1. U.S. Department of Justice Press Release, "Romanian Man Pleads Guilty for Role in International Fraud Scheme" (17 February 2011).
2. Peter Grier, "New York Plot Shows 'Bunches of Guys' Can Become Terrorists in Post-9/11 World," *Christian Science Monitor* (21 May 2009), http://www.csmonitor.com/USA/2009/0522/p02s01-usgn. html; Marc Sageman, *Leaderless Jihad: Terror Networks in the Twenty-First Century* (Philadelphia: University of Pennsylvania Press, 2008).

3. U.S. Department of Justice Press Release, "International Telephone Hacking Conspiracy Busted" (12 June 2009).

4. Jay S. Albanese, *Organized Crime in Our Times* (Burlington, MA: Elsevier, 2011), 4.

5. The typology of offenses in Table 5.1.1 was developed by the author in an effort to capture the full scope of organized crime without an unnecessarily extended list of offenses that reflect only subcategories of these offenses (e.g., sea piracy is a type of extortion and racketeering).

6. Mats Berdal and Mónica Serrano, eds., *Transnational Organized Crime and International Security: Business as Usual?* (Boulder, CO and London: Lynne Rienner, 2002); Louise Shelley, "The Unholy Trinity: Transnational Crime, Corruption, and Terrorism," *Brown Journal of World Affairs* 11 (Winter/Spring 2005), 101–11.

7. Drug Enforcement Administration, Federal Bureau of Investigation, and Royal Canadian Mounted Police, "2006 Canada/U.S. Organised Crime Threat Assessment" (2006), http://www.publicsafety.gc.ca/prg/le/_fl/2006_Canada-US_OC-TA_en.pdf; Serious Organized Crime Agency, "The United Kingdom Threat Assessment of Serious Organized Crime," http://www.soca.gov.uk/assessPublications/downloads/threat_assess_unclass_250706.pdf. Serious Organised Crime Agency, "Annual Report 2008–2009" (May 2009), http://www.soca.gov,uk/about-soca/library?start=20; Criminal Intelligence Service Canada, "Integrated Threat Assessment Methodology" (April 2007), http://www.cisc.gc.ca/products_services/ita_methodology/document/ita_methodology_2007_e.pdf.

8. Federal Bureau of Investigation, Organized Crime, http://www.fbi.gov/about-us/investigate/organizedcrime/.

9. President's Commission on Organized Crime, "Organized Crime Today" (Washington, DC: U.S. Government Printing Office, 1987); Stephen Schneider, "Organized Contraband Smuggling and Its Enforcement in Canada: An Assessment of the Anti-smuggling Initiative," *Trends in Organized Crime* 6 (December 2000), 3–31; Kristin M. Finklea, *Organized Crime in the United States: Trends and Issues for Congress* (Washington, D.C.: Congressional Research Service, 2010).

10. UN Office on Drugs and Crime, "The Globalization of Crime: A Transnational Organized Crime Threat Assessment" (Vienna: UNODC, 2010), http://www.unodc.org/documents/data-and-analysis/tocta/TOCTA_Report_2010_low_res.pdf, 6.

11. New Zealand, "Organised Crime in New Zealand 2010" (Wellington: New Zealand Government, 2010), 7–20.

12. Australian Crime Commission, "Organised Crime in Australia 2009" (Sydney: 2009), http://www.crimecommission.gov.au/publications/organised-crime-australia/organised-crime-australia-2009-report; Criminal Intelligence Service Canada, "Report

on Organized Crime" (Ottawa: 2010), http://www.cisc.gc.ca/annual_reports/annual_report_2010/document/report_oc_2010_e.pdf; Europol, OCTA 2009: EU Organised Crime & Threat Assessment" (The Hague: 2010), https://www.europol.europa.eu/sites/default/files/publications/octa2009_0.pdf; Annette Hubschle, "Organised Crime in Southern Africa: First Annual Review" (South Africa: Institute for Security Studies, Pretoria, 2010), http://www.issafrica.org/uploads/OrgCrimeReviewDec2010.pdf.

13. U.S. Department of Justice, "Overview of the Law Enforcement Strategy to Combat International Organized Crime" (April 2008).

14. John T. Picarelli, "Expert Working Group Report on International Organized Crime—Discussion Paper" (Washington DC: National Institute of Justice, 2010).

15. H.G. van de Bunt and C.R.A. van der Schoot, *Prevention of Organised Crime: A Situational Approach* (The Netherlands: WODC, 2003).

16. Ibid.; Boorsma, "Forged Official Documents," in *The Identification and Prevention of Opportunities That Facilitate Organised Crime*, eds. H.G. van de Bunt and C.R.A. van der Schoot (The Hague: WODC, 2003), 63–67; Blythe A. Bowman, "Transnational Crimes Against Culture: Looting at Archeological Sites and the 'Grey' Market in Antiquities," *Journal of Contemporary Criminal Justice* 24 (August 2008), 225–42; A. Graycar and M. Felson, "Situational Prevention of Organized Timber Theft and Related Corruption," in *Situational Prevention of Organised Crimes*, eds. K. Bullock, R.V. Clarke, and N. Tilley (Devon, UK: Willan Publishing, 2010); P. Reuter and E. Truman, *Chasing Dirty Money: The Fight Against Money Laundering* (Washington, DC: Institute for International Economics, 2004); Klaus von Lampe, "Preventing Organised Crime: The Case of Contraband Cigarettes," in *Situational Prevention of Organised Crimes*, eds. K. Bullock, R.V. Clarke, and N. Tilley (Devon, UK: Willan Publishing, 2010).

17. R. Goldstock, et al., *Corruption and Racketeering in the New York City Construction Industry: The Final Report of the New York State Organized Crime Taskforce* (New York: University Press, 1991); H. Nelen, "Situational Organised Crime Prevention in Amsterdam: The Administrative Approach," in *Situational Prevention of Organised Crimes*, eds. K. Bullock, R.V. Clarke, and N. Tilley (Devon, UK: Willan Publishing, 2010); W.K. Rashbaum, "Use of Mob-Linked Firm Shows M.T.A. Problem Vetting Subcontractors," *The New York Times*, (19 May 2010); E.U. Savona, "Infiltration of the Public Construction Industry by Italian Organised Crime," in *Situational Prevention of Organised Crimes*, eds. K. Bullock, R.V. Clarke, and N. Tilley (Devon, UK: Willan Publishing, 2010).

18. Paul Eckblom, "Organised Crime and the Conjunction of Criminal Opportunity Framework," in *Transnational Organised Crime: Perspectives on Global Security*, eds.

A. Edwards and P. Gill (Abingdon, UK: Routledge, 2003), 242–63; K. Bullock, R.V. Calrke, and N. Tilley, "Introduction," in *Situational Prevention of Organised Crimes,* eds. K. Bullock, R.V. Clarke, and N. Tilley (Devon, UK: Willan Publishing, 2010).

19. A.C. Bouloukos, G. Farrell, and G. Laycock, "Transnational Organised Crime in Europe and North America: The Need for Situational Crime Prevention," in *Crime and Criminal Justice in Europe and North America 1995-97: Report of the Sixth UN Survey on Crime Trends and Criminal Justice Systems,* eds. K. Aromaa, S. Leppa, S. Nevala, and N. Ollus, (Helinski: European Institute of Crime Prevention and Control, 2003); M. Felson, *The Ecosystem for Organized Crime* (Helsinki: European Institute for Crime Prevention and Control, 2006); K. Aromaa and T. Viljanen, *International Key Issues in Crime Prevention and Criminal* Justice (Helsinki: European Institute for Crime Prevention and Control [HEUNI], 2006); C.R.A. Van der Schoot, *Organized Crime Prevention in the Netherlands* (Den Haag: BJU Legal Publishers, 2006).

20. R.K. Shukla and E. E. Bartgis, "Responding to Clandestine Methamphetamine Manufacturing: A Case Study in Situational Crime Prevention," *Criminal Justice Policy Review* 21 (2010), 338-62; R.T. Guerette and K.J. Bowers, "Assessing the Extent of Crime Displacement and Diffusion of Benefits: A Review of Situational Crime Prevention Evaluations," *Criminology* 47 (November 2009), 1331-68; T.J. Holt, K.R. Blevins, and J.B. Kuhns, "Examining the Displacement Practices of Johns with On-line Data," *Journal of Criminal Justice* 36 (November 2008), 522–528; M.P. Levy and C. Tartaro, "Repeat Victimization: A Study of Auto Theft in Atlantic City Using the WALLS Variables to Measure Environmental Indicators," *Criminal Justice Policy Review* 21 (September 2010), 296–318; W.H. Sousa and G.L. Kelling, "Police and the Reclamation of Public Places: a Study of MacArthur Park in Los Angeles," *International Journal of Police Science & Management* 12 (Spring 2010), 41–54.

21. R.V. Clarke, "Seven misconceptions of situational crime prevention," in *Handbook of Crime Prevention and Community Safety,* ed. Nick Tilley (Portland, Oregon: Willan Publishing, 2005), 46–47.

22. James O. Finckenauer and Ko-lin Chin, "Sex Trafficking: A Target for Situational Crime Prevention?" in *Situational Prevention of Organised Crimes,* eds. Karen. Bullock, Ronald V. Clarke, and Nick Tilley (Devon, UK: Willan Publishing, 2010), 58–80; Edward R. Kleemans, Melvin R.J. Soudijn, and Anton W. Weenink, "Situational Crime Prevention and Cross-Border Crime," in *Situational Prevention of Organised Crimes,* eds. Karen Bullock, Ronald V. Clarke, and Nick Tilley (Devon, UK: Willan Publishing, 2010), 17–34; Klaus von Lampe, "Preventing Organised Crime: The Case of Contraband Cigarettes," in *Situational Prevention of Organised Crimes,* eds. Karen Bullock, Ronald V. Clarke, and Nick Tilley (Devon, UK: Willan Publishing, 2010), 35–57.

23. Dwight C. Smith, Jr., "Paragons, Pariahs, and Pirates: A Spectrum-based Theory of Enterprise," *Crime and Delinquency* 26, no. 3 (July 1980) 358–386; D.C. Smith, Jr., *The Mafia Mystique,* Revised Edition, (Lanham, MD: University Press of America, 1990).

24. Patricia A. Adler, *Wheeling and Dealing: An Ethnography of an Upper-Level Drug Dealing and Smuggling Community* (New York: Columbia University Press, 1985).

25. Peter Reuter, *The Organization of Illegal Markets: An Economic Analysis* (Washington, DC: U.S. Department of Justice, 1985), 10.

26. Letizia Paoli, "The Paradoxes of Organized Crime," *Crime, Law and Social Change* 37 (2002), 51–97.

27. Jurg Gerber, "On the Relationship between Organized and White-Collar Crime: Government, Business, and Criminal Enterprise in Post-Communist Russia," *European Journal of Crime, Criminal Law & Criminal Justice* 8 (2000), 327–342.

28. R.A. McFeely, "Enterprise Theory of Investigation," *FBI Law Enforcement Bulletin* 70 (May 2001), 19–26.

29. UN Office on Drugs and Crime, *The Globalization of Crime: A Transnational Organized Crime Threat Assessment* (Vienna: UNODC, 2010), 5.

30. Ibid.

31. UN Office on Drugs and Crime, *Organized Crime,* http://www.unodc.org/unodc/en/organized-crime/index.html (accessed 5 August 2012); Conference of the Parties to the UN Convention against Transnational Organized Crime, "Activities of the UN Office on Drugs and Crime to promote the implementation of the provisions on international cooperation in the UN Convention Against Transnational Organized Crime" (Vienna: 18–22 October 2010), Fifth Session, https://www.unodc.org/unodc/en/treaties/CTOC/CTOC-COP-session5.html.

32. UN Office on Drugs and Crime, "The UN Convention against Transnational Organized Crime and the Protocols Thereto" (New York: 2004), http://www.unodc.org/unodc/en/treaties/CTOC/index. html.

33. See UN Office on Drugs and Crime, "Open-ended Interim Working Group of Government Experts on Technical Assistance," (Vienna: 19–20 October 2010) http://www.unodc.org/unodc/en/treaties/CTOC/working-group-on-technical-assistance-2010.html (accessed August 7, 2012).

34. Nick Tilley and Matt Hopkins, "Organized Crime and Local Businesses," *Criminology & Criminal Justice: An International Journal* 8, no. 4, (2008), 443–459.

35. Tom Vander Beken, "Risky Business: A Risk-based Methodology to Measure Organized Crime," *Crime, Law and Social Change* 41, no. 5 (2004), 471–516; Ernesto U. Savona, "Initial Methodology for the Crime Proofing of New or Amended Legislation at the EU Level," *European Journal on Criminal Policy and Research* 12, no. 3–4 (2006), 221–228;

Jay S. Albanese, "Risk Assessment in Organized Crime: Developing a Market and Product-Based Model to Determine Threat Levels," *Journal of Contemporary Criminal Justice* 24, no. 3 (August 2008), 263–273.

36. Criminal Intelligence Service Canada, 2010 *Report on Organized Crime* (Ottawa: CISC, 2010), http://www.cisc.gc.ca/annual_reports/annual_report_2010/document/report_oc_2010_e.pdf; Lansdowne Technologies Inc., *Developing and Applying an Organized Crime Harm Index: A Scoping and Feasibility Study Final Report to Public Safety Canada* (Ottawa: Public Safety Canada, 2010).

Reading 5.2

Global Vice: The Expanding Territory of the Yakuza

Ania Calderón

An Interview with Jake Adelstein

As the world furthers its interconnectedness, some criminal organizations formerly operating within a regional jurisdiction are now benefitting from transnational growth. Similar to international corporate expansion, members of organized crime in Japan, also called yakuza, have proven to be "innovative entrepreneurs," increasing their profits by extending their reach.[1] Based on his reporting on crime in Japan for more than twelve years, investigative journalist and author of *Tokyo Vice: An American Reporter on the Police Beat in Japan*, Jake Adelstein, has uncovered compelling insights from the operations of modern yakuza and their reaction toward legal constraints. In an interview with Ania Calderón of the *Journal*, Adelstein discusses how the yakuza are transitioning into powerful organizations and becoming increasingly international.[2]

Journal of International Affairs: You have worked closely with the police in Japan on organized crime syndicates, and have been an investigative reporter with the U.S. State Department on the subject. How do the United States and Japan differ in their approaches to organized crime?

Jake Adelstein: The Japanese police are extremely limited in their investigative powers: they can't plea bargain, wire-tapping is so restrictive that it is almost useless and rarely applied, and now they are not supposed to have direct contact with members of Japanese organized crime—also called yakuza—making intelligence collection nearly impossible. There is no witness protection program and little incentive for a lower ranking yakuza to provide intelligence on those above him.

In fact, the negative incentives are huge: if he keeps his mouth shut, he gets a cash reward when released from jail, his family is looked after, and he will probably get a promotion. Since yakuza organizations usually provide lawyers to their members, if the member under arrest makes a confession or statement implicating his superiors, the organization will know. So if he cooperates, he doesn't get a lighter sentence, his organization will know he talked, and he loses financially. When he gets out of jail, he may lose his life or a finger, since there is no witness protection or witness relocation program. Who would cooperate in a case like that?

There is one interesting quirk in Japanese law: after the 2008 revision to the Organized Crime Countermeasures Act, it became possible for victims of a yakuza crime to sue senior bosses for the crimes of their subordinates. Tsukasa Shinobu, head of the Yamaguchi-gumi, the largest yakuza organization, and Goto Tadamasa, former Yamaguchi-gumi member and still a crime boss, was sued for the murder of Kazuo Nozaki, a real estate broker, in 2006. The case was settled out of court in October of 2012 for 1.4 million dollars to the family of the victim and Goto expressed his condolences.

Japan doesn't have a Racketeer Influenced and Corrupt Organizations Act, so the police use a hodge-podge of laws to arrest and suppress the yakuza. A criminal conspiracy act, which would allow the police to arrest senior yakuza for the crimes of their subordinates more easily, has been opposed by the ruling coalition for years. It doesn't help that one of the most powerful members of the Democratic Party of Japan (DPJ) and leader of the party from 2005 to 2006, Maehara Seiji, was bankrolled and supported by Shinohara Jun, an advisor to the Yamaguchi-gumi, who is registered in the police files as a Yamaguchi-gumi member. The DPJ was officially backed by the Yamaguchi-gumi in 2007. Yes, that's correct: a group of 40,000 yakuza supports a political party. Recently, the Minister of Justice, Keishu Tanaka, resigned from the job after his ties with yakuza were exposed. The top ninety senior members communicated their support to the sub-bosses orally in meetings in the spring and summer of 2007. The Inagawa-kai, another yakuza organization, did the same. In return, someone in the DPJ promised to keep a criminal conspiracy law off the books and also to get voting rights for Korean-Japanese since many of the Yamaguchi-gumi Kodo-kai (the ruling faction of the Yamaguchi-gumi) are Korean-Japanese.

Journal: As a foreigner having to learn to negotiate between the yakuza and the police, were there different rules or codes, formal or informal, that needed to be followed? If so, what are the different ways control and deterrence operate in Japan?

Adelstein: The rule is very simple: you can share information you get from the yakuza with the police, but you can never share information from the police with the yakuza. The flow of the information has to be tightly controlled. The obvious question is: why would yakuza share information with a reporter when it may go to the police? The answer is that sometimes it benefits them, because the information damages a rival organized crime group, or an internal enemy. Sometimes, because yakuza are people as well, they are horrified by the acts of their fellow yakuza and hope someone will stop them. For example, Ive had yakuza tip me off about people in their own greater group who were engaged in human trafficking or child pornography. The organization may turn a blind eye to it and take the money, but yakuza who still live by their traditional code cannot stand for some of the crimes the modern yakuza are involved with.

Journal: You have mentioned that "Tokyo is impossible to penetrate." What underlying factors have helped organized crime break into this city as well as into other areas of Japan?

Adelstein: Tokyo is impossible to penetrate in the sense that it was originally designed as a city with a lot of dead ends and streets that were windy so as to make it hard to invade. Kyoto, the old capital city, was laid out on a grid, according to some general principles of Chinese geomancy.

In the chaos after the Second World War, organized crime was able to gain a strong foothold in the country. At that time, joining the mob was appealing particularly to those pushed to the fringes of society. This included disenfranchised returning soldiers and many Korean-Japanese who had been taken to Japan as slave laborers. The U.S. occupying forces declared the slave laborers as "third party nationals," and for a period of time the Japanese police were not allowed to arrest them. They soon took over the black markets and for a short time, were a force to be reckoned with. The soldiers who returned from the war and had been involved with organized crime in Japan, reformed their groups and with tacit police approval, functioned as a second police force. Of course, they took the black markets over for themselves, but they did keep the peace.

In an effort to restore order and to limit the power and reach of the Korean gangs, the police sometimes backed the yakuza. During the post-war years, the Japanese syndicates fighting Koreans for black-market turf incorporated several Korean-Japanese into the ranks of the old yakuza structure. Rather than engage in a direct war, a successful policy of assimilation was put into place. Also, the yakuza have a reputation for keeping conflict between them and not harming citizens. The prevailing rule of thumb for yakuza—although it may not be written—is *"katagi ni meiwaku wo kakenai,"* which translates into, "not causing ordinary citizens trouble." Violating this "noble way" results in expulsion. Although they are criminals, they observe standards and procedures that keep them out of public ire and police attention. In the end, this is in their best interest; if people don't feel secure around areas where the yakuza does business, including sex shops, illegal gambling parlors, strip and hostess clubs, the yakuza will lose money. Today, the yakuza are embedded into Japanese society. The major gang bosses are almost well-known celebrities. Bosses for the second and third largest crime group, the Sumiyoshi-kai and the Inagawa-kai, grant interviews to publications and television. Politicians are seen having dinner with them.

One thing worth noting is that for years the local organized crime groups—the Kanto yakuza, the Inagawa-kai, and the Sumiyoshi-kai—kept the Yamaguchi-gumi, today's largest crime group, out of Tokyo. "Thou shall not cross over the Tama-river," was the lofty agreement that was in place. But after the third-generation leader of the Yamaguchi-gumi died in 1981, the Inagawa-kai was rocked by internal conflict, and a succession issue was partially settled with Yamaguchi-gumi aid. In November 2005, the Yamaguchi-gumi merged with the Tokyo-based Kokusui-kai and then had a legitimate foothold in Tokyo. It has been slowly taking over the Tokyo area as well. The de facto ruler of the Inagawa-kai, Kazuo Uchibori, is a full-blood brother of a high-ranking member of the Yamaguchi-gumi Kodo-kai. The Kodo-kai is the ruling faction of the Yamaguchi-gumi. Thus, the Inagawa-kai is more or less under the thumb of the Kodo-kai at present. If you consider alliances, the Yamaguchi-gumi has close to 64,000 members, and with Japan's yakuza population at roughly 79,000, according to the National Police Agency, the Yamaguchi-gumi is clearly the majority shareholder.

Journal: As global economies have become increasingly interconnected, how has this affected the reach of the operations of the yakuza? Does this type of mafia 'jump' to global scales, crossing international boundaries? If so, are the logistics that they operate under, be it national transnational borders, distinct?

Adelstein: The yakuza are good at working in Korea, China, Macau, Hong Kong, and Singapore. The Cayman Islands and Singapore have become some of their favorite places to set up front companies for financial crimes. The meth supply from North Korea isn't what it used to be, so a lot of it is being brought in from Canada now. Yakuza operating outside of Japan, due to the old guard having limited language skills, usually try to recruit local talent. They are also more likely to resort to extreme violence, because it is unlikely to hurt their image in Japan as "humanitarian organizations." In April 2011, a former member of the Goto-gumi (another yakuza organization), Kondo Takashi, was shot to death in Thailand. Police believe his former boss, Goto Tadamasa, now head of a new organized crime group, ordered the assassination. Incidentally, Kondo was the subject of an international arrest warrant for the 2006 murder of a real estate broker in Tokyo. The real estate broker had been opposing Goto's attempt to take ownership of a building worth about $20 million.

Journal: Considering the history of the yakuza, do you think they have recently gone through any major transitions in their operations?

Adelstein: Yakuza are recognized as legal entities in Japan. They have the same rights as any corporate entity and their members have the same rights as ordinary citizens. Even in cases where they do not own their office property and are simply renters, the yakuza are very well aware of how the law protects their rights to live and operate where they wish and they will not easily be removed. The modern-day Yakuza is an innovative entrepreneur. Rather than a bunch of tattooed nine-fingered thugs in white suits wielding samurai swords, as I have mentioned elsewhere, a more appropriate description would be "Goldman Sachs with guns."

According to "An Overview of Japanese Police," an English document by the National Police Agency that was distributed to foreign police agencies in August 2008, "Boryokudan (yakuza) groups pose an enormous threat to civil affairs and corporate transactions ... They are also committing a variety of crimes to raise funds by invading the legitimate business community and pretending to be engaged in legitimate business deals." In general, I think what happened in Japan, when the government introduced the toughest antimob legislation in a generation in 1992, is that the initial crackdowns failed. They simply encouraged the yakuza to go underground. This forced them to set up front companies that hide their activities rather than simply work out in the open, collecting protection money, doing small-scale loan-sharking, or running gambling dens. Ironically, the weak laws Japan put in place, rather than dismantling the yakuza, simply pushed them into new business arenas. An examination of the front companies of the three major crime groups in Japan—the Inagawa-kai, the Sumiyoshikai, and the Yamaguchi-gumi—by the National Police Agency in 1998, listed construction, real estate, finance, bars and restaurants, and management consulting as the top five types of yakuza front companies.

The war on the yakuza, which began in 1963, has been less successful than the war on terror and has lasted longer. The number of yakuza between 1992 and 2011 has remained around 80,000. Recently, the police have used a combination of contract laws, civil laws, ordinances, and criminal laws to arrest the yakuza more frequently, and, now that many banks, auto-dealers, and real-estate agencies have organized crime exclusionary ordinances in their contracts, life is harder for the typical yakuza. If he signs up for a credit card and checks the box stating, "I'm not a member of an organized crime group"—bam! That's fraud. Off to jail.

At the same time, a number of nontraditional gangs are now gaining power in Japan because they do not fall into so-called designated violent groups category and skirt some of the more serious regulations and penalties applied to the twenty-two designated organized crime groups. A designated crime group has a certain number of members with a criminal record and the Japanese government determines the designation. A designated crime group is regulated but not outlawed. But the state still hasn't made membership of a criminal organization illegal or given the police the antimob tools long considered crucial in other countries: wiretapping, plea bargaining, and witness protection. It seems unlikely that such radical tools to dismantle the yakuza will be given to the Japanese police forces soon. In many ways, the yakuza are stronger than ever despite almost thirteen years lapsing since the first laws targeting them went on the books.

As the yakuza continue to evolve and get into more sophisticated crimes, the police will have a tough time keeping up. The so-called *marubo* cops, who are organized crime control division detectives, are used to dealing with simple cases of extortion and intimidation, not massive stock manipulation or complicated fraud schemes. The old days when there was give-and-take between the police are gone. Cops used to go have tea at the yakuza offices, chit-chat, and exchange information. Not anymore.

The yakuza have more money and more power than they ever had before, and the consolidation of the Yamaguchi-gumi has made them a huge force to be reckoned with. In many ways, the Yamaguchi-gumi is the Liberal Democratic Party of organized crime, operating on the principal that "power is in numbers." They have capital, they have manpower, they have an information network that rivals anything the police have, and they are expanding into every industry where money is to be made. Today, the Yakuza are increasingly international, working with Chinese organized crime groups, expanding into casinos in the Philippines and Macau, setting up front companies in Singapore and the Cayman Islands, hiring bilingual henchmen, manipulating the Japanese stock markets from overseas accounts, and working with foreign banks including Citibank, Credit Suisse, and possibly HSBC.

Notes

1. Jake Adelstein, *Tokyo Vice: An American Reporter on the Police Beat in Japan* (New York, Random House Inc., 2009), 88.
2. Japanese names in this article follow the Japanese convention: family name (surname) followed by a given name.

Reading 5.3

An Introduction to Terrorism

Philip B. Heymann

T HE FEDERAL BUREAU OF INVESTIGATION REPORTS that in the decade after 1985 there were only two terrorist incidents on U.S. soil with substantial foreign involvement (i.e., "international terrorism"): the bombing of the World Trade Center in February 1993, and an all-but-ignored occupation of the Iranian Mission to the United Nations by five opponents of the regime in 1992. During the first half of the 1990s we had 32 domestic incidents of terrorism, of which 9 occurred in a single night in 1993 when small incendiary devices were placed in department stores by one of the most active domestic terrorist groups, animal rights activists. The number of attacks on U.S. individuals abroad has fallen to less than a third of what it was in 1986, with 66 attacks in 1994, a year in which there were no domestic terrorists incidents in the United States.

Why then the immense attention to terrorism in the later 1990s in the United States? It is true that U.S. citizens have been among the leading victims of international terrorist events, including the downing of Pan Am Flight 103 in 1988 over Lockerbie, Scotland; the 1985 hijacking of the *Achille Lauro*; the machine gunnings in the same year of the airports of Rome and Vienna; and the 1983 suicide bombings of U.S. marine headquarters in Beirut. Still, home felt safe. That feeling of security at home was shattered by the bombings of the World Trade Center in 1993 with nearly 1000 injured and of the Oklahoma City federal building in 1995 with 169 killed. These events, terrible enough in themselves, raised the possibility of a sustained campaign of violence on U.S. soil. This side of the Atlantic suddenly seemed to be exposed to political violence of the sort that the United States had escaped while other democracies had not. Germany, Italy, and Spain, for example, lived through sustained terrorist campaigns in the 1970s and 1980s; France, Great Britain, and Israel had suffered the same in the 1990s as well.

Added to this was a fear that a terrorist repertoire that had been limited to assassination, conventional bombing, hostage-taking, and hijacking might be dangerously expanded. American apprehensions, reflected in dramatic Congressional hearings, grew with the use of poison gas in Tokyo subways by the Aum Shinrikyo cult in Japan. The possibility that the use of nuclear, biological, or chemical weapons might be added to the terrorist arsenal is chilling. At the end of 1995, John Deutch, then the new director of the CIA, described terrorism as one of the major threats facing the United States.[1]

Such events, the fears they excite, and the reactions they invite are the subject of this book. It is about violent activity designed to create grave public apprehension in order to convey, with awesome force, the terrorists' message. And it is about governmental responses. Deep and broad national fears of terrorism create grave political problems for a government. Immense popular concern makes acts of terrorism exceptionally tempting occasions for political opponents of the administration in power to make the evil appear far clearer and the danger far greater than they are. The Iranian taking of 52 U.S. citizens as hostages in 1979 and the futility of efforts to free them may have cost U.S. President Jimmy Carter an election. In the context of a terrorist act or campaign, the political risks to an administration of inaction or even caution are very grave. But wise policy may counsel restraint. In terms of national well-being, the gravest national dangers from a terrorist act (short of an immense escalation of terrorist tactics) are that the interplay of terrorism, public reaction, and governmental response may sharply separate one significant group from the rest of the society or severely undermine the nation's democratic traditions.

Violence as politics has been a subject of great concern in many other democracies for generations. Although the word "terrorism" dates only from the time of the French Revolution, the acts it embraces go back to biblical times. Nor is political violence new to the United States. We have lost four presidents and two senators to assassination. We have also had our share of famous bombings, including the Haymarket Square bombing in 1886; the *Los Angeles Times* bombing in 1910; the San Francisco Preparedness Day bombing in 1916; and the Wall Street bombing in 1920. And we have had groups such as the Ku Klux Klan dedicated for decades to terrorizing an important segment of our population—black Americans.

The Efforts to Define Terrorism

Only relatively recently have there been attempts to define "terrorism" as clearly as we define murder, robbery, or rape. The effort has been less than successful. Germany's internal security agency, the Office for the Protection of the Constitution, says terrorism is the "enduringly conducted struggle for political goals, which are intended to be achieved by means of assaults on the life and property of other persons, especially by means of severe crimes [such as murder, kidnapping, arson]."[2] The British "Prevention of Terrorism Act" of 1974 described terrorism as "the use of violence for political ends, and includes any use of violence for the purpose of putting the public or any section of the public in fear." The U.S. State Department treats as terrorism any violence perpetrated for political reasons by subnational groups or secret state agents, often directed at noncombatant targets, and usually intended to influence an audience. Our federal statutes (18 U.S.C. 3077) define an "act of terrorism" as any activity that involves criminal violence that "appears to be intended (i) to intimidate or coerce a civilian population; (ii) to influence the policy of a government by intimidation or coercion; or (iii) to affect the conduct of a government by assassination or kidnapping." The group of European Interior Ministers working together to deal with terrorism made a point of excluding traditional warfare: "Terrorism is ... the use, or the threatened use, by a cohesive group of persons of violence (short of warfare) to affect political aims."

There is an appealing neutrality about state definitions of terrorism. That may not be surprising. States use violence themselves for political purposes—in wartime even against civilian populations. The state definitions suggest that terrorists are a hostile force pursuing political ends. But other definitions, often by academics, have far more of a moral or criminal flavor.

An extremely comprehensive review of possible definitions was conducted by Professor Alex P. Schmid of Leiden University in the Netherlands. After consulting 50 scholars, he came up with a definition far too lengthy to be useful but then found a far shorter definition that was almost as accurate and more useful. Noting that there is a strong degree of consensus about what actions count as war crimes—including attacks on persons taking no active part in hostilities and also hostage-taking—and that just such attacks on the undefended are "not an unsought side-effect but a deliberate strategy" of terrorists, Schmid proposes defining acts of terrorism as "peacetime equivalents of war crimes:" acts that would, if carried out by a government in war, violate the Geneva Conventions."[3]

The various definitions differ in two ways. First, "political" and "moral" definitions differ immensely in the amount of hatred they seek to arouse. Benjamin Netanyahu, prime minister of Israel, leader of its Likud party, and author of a 1995 book, *Fighting Terrorism*, emphasizes that "terrorism is the deliberate and systematic assault on civilians to inspire fear for political ends." As such, he argues, "*nothing* justifies terrorism ... it is evil *per se*." To his mind, "terrorism attacks the very foundations of civilization and threatens to erase it altogether by killing man's sense of sin. ... The unequivocal and unrelenting moral condemnation of terrorism must therefore constitute the first line of defense against its most insidious effect."[4] The cold and analytic definitions of the Western governments can not convey such fury.

Second, the variety of definitions reflects very different practical and administrative reasons for defining terrorism. Consider the variety of reasons. The term is the basis of U.S. statutes that allocate money and authority for dealing with certain problems. A finding of "terrorism" determines that the U.S. government (specifically, the Federal Bureau of Investigation and the Department of Justice) will take the lead in investigating and prosecuting certain crimes that might otherwise fall within the primary jurisdiction of state or local governments. If it is "terrorism," the intelligence agencies may be involved because the crime is also a matter of national security. In international settings, the need to define terrorism may arise because some crimes, such as assaulting or killing an American abroad, are only subject to U.S. prosecution if they occur for terrorist purposes. Western allies meet to discuss what is defined, for their purposes, as terrorism, and they grant and deny cooperation in intelligence and extradition on the basis of such definitions.

Two things are clear from this list of occasions where a definition of terrorism is needed. First, we cannot escape the task of defining terrorism for each of these purposes unless we are prepared to treat politically motivated and directed violence as no different from other crimes—a decision that would be risky business and strongly contrary to public reactions in almost every country. Second, the definitions are likely to differ, not only because of different judgments about the centrality of the moral issue, but also because definitions are meant to serve the particular purposes most relevant in the setting where they are being used.

Secret state violence against its own citizens is unlikely to be treated as state terrorism in meetings of allies. This is not because there is any great moral difference from secret state terrorism directed against citizens of another government, but because such violent repression of individuals in the home country is generally a far lesser concern to the governments of countries unaffected and unlikely to be affected by the practice. So in this setting, secret state violence against its own citizens is unlikely to be called "terrorism." Violence against civilians, particularly government officials, in the context of guerrilla warfare or during a war between states is not considered terrorism in many contexts simply because it is not subject to the same remedies (which are designed for times of peace). Many modern states have resorted to aerial bombing of civilian targets in order to induce fear in wartime. For similar reasons of practicality, violence that is carried out as a mere expression of anger without expectation of changing the conduct of any group or government, might or might not be included within the responsibilities of the agency that deals with "terrorist" crimes, depending on whether it posed a continuing danger and on whether it raised the same unusual public fears as more calculated political violence.

The definitions of terrorism thus differ markedly in what they include. In this book, I focus on the core of the problem by looking only at conduct that satisfies almost all the definitions. The violence I discuss involves in most instances politically motivated activity by groups, not individuals. It is more than a nonpolitical expression of rage, and it is meant to work by raising concerns and fears, and not just by the isolated assassination of a government leader such as Israeli Prime Minister Yitzhak Rabin or U.S. President John F. Kennedy. Borrowing from our State Department's definition, it is violence conducted as part of a political strategy by a subnational group or secret agents of a foreign state (although secret and violent repression of political opponents by an authoritarian government is just as bad).

The political violence I emphasize is plainly directed at noncombatant targets; I set aside the hard question of where to place off-duty soldiers or the industrial managers producing weapons of war. The violence is directed at people, not just property, and carried out for a political purpose, although that purpose may only be partially formed. Like the Committee of Interior Ministers of the European Union, I would exclude situations of warfare. And, to preserve moral fervor, I limit "terrorism" to political violence in or against true democracies.

Every state would consider activities fitting this core definition to be "terrorism." It overlaps very substantially with Alex Schmid's definition of terrorism as behavior that would amount to war crimes if it occurred during war. Like Netanyahu, I can think of very little excuse for an assault on civilians to advance political purposes. But an excessive moralism is likely to get in the way of clear thought about what the United States should do. I favor a more sophisticated strategy than Netanyahu's recommendation that we unleash "security services to take the vigorous action needed to uproot the terror in the midst of [our society]," and use our "operational capacity to eviscerate domestic terror."[5]

Not only Netanyahu's prescription, but also his moral judgements are simpler than many would adopt. Terrorism is inexcusable in a democracy, but would it have been "evil *per se*" for a German resistance group to adopt the same targets as Allied air forces chose in Hitler's Germany? The African National Congress, Provisional Irish Republican Army, and the radical organizations of the Jewish settlers before the creation of Israel all engaged in attacks on civilian targets, and yet their leaders have been treated as heroes.

The Difficulties of Categorizing Terrorism Sensibly

The fundamental difficulties of defining terrorism are compounded by the difficulties of shaping policy for a type of behavior that fits poorly into more familiar categories. Terrorist acts are both crimes and forms of warfare, and in both respects are unlike what we are used to. Terrorism involves unique psychological phenomena—no less real for being poorly understood—used as part of a totally unfamiliar type of political strategy based on violence. The likelihood and strength of a terrorist campaign depends upon sociological factors we are not accustomed to examining; the danger to the society in which the terrorism takes place depends upon the divisions within it before the terrorism occurs. Consider each of characteristics in turn.

As a crime, terrorism is different. Most crimes are the product of greed, anger, jealousy, or the desire for domination, respect, or position in a group, and not of any desire to "improve" the state of the world or of a particular nation. Most crimes do not involve—as part of the plan for accomplishing their objectives—trying to change the occupants of government positions, their actions, or the basic structures and ideology of a nation. Some would argue that violence carried out for political purposes is more altruistic; others would vigorously deny that. But all would agree that political violence is different from ordinary crime, in that it is planned to force changes in government actions, people, structure, or even ideology as a means to whatever ends the perpetrators are seeking with whatever motivations drive them towards those ends. It is in that sense that the U.S. State Department definition says that the violence is usually "perpetrated for political reasons."

As a form of combat, terrorism falls into the category of violent ways of pursuing political ends, a category that includes war between states, civil war, guerrilla warfare, and coup d'état. It differs from these other forms of violent combat for political ends in that it is carried out during peacetime in secret, without occupying or claiming to occupy any significant territory, and without organizing large groups to defy government authority openly. Indeed, for many, the same violent acts have a different status when they accompany a civil or guerrilla war. Nor are they considered "terrorism" when they accompany a war between nation states, for then they become a part of the normal craft of spies or bomber pilots rather than a form of politics or secret warfare that works primarily or exclusively through its own terrifying means.

Terrorism has traditionally used relatively unsophisticated weapons in a limited number of ways to inflict relatively little damage. Within these constraints terrorism can only hope to produce limited political results, since in almost every country the government controls vastly superior military and civilian security forces. Even such limited actions may occasionally force a change in particular occupants of office by carefully planned assassinations like those of Anwar Sadat and Yitzhak Rabin. They may even bring about a change in a particular policy by simply imposing sufficient costs upon a government that the government will choose to abandon a weakly held policy, as when the United States left Lebanon after the truck bombing of the U.S. Marine barracks in Beirut. But any broader objectives, such as pulling out of places of considerable strategic or political importance or abandoning important alliances or polices, are far more difficult and far less likely. And changing the government itself would require the politically violent group either to overpower the government's military force or to shift the loyalties of the government security forces or the public at large sufficiently that they would broadly deny their support to the state. Overthrow of a government may be the result of a civil war or a coup d'état, but it is a highly unlikely result of the relatively small-scale violence by those outside of government that we associate with terrorism.

Combining crime and armed combat, terrorism is an illegal form of clandestine warfare that is carried out by a sub-state group to change the policies, personnel, structure, or ideology of a government, or to influence the actions of another part of the population—one with enough self-identity to respond to selective violence. (The burning of African-American churches in the American South in 1996 would fall in the latter category.) Throwing domestic politics into this witches' brew, terrorism is also a form of violent domestic politics (directed at democratic regimes, if we are to retain for our definition of "terrorism" some moral clarity) carried out without organizing mass opposition.

The Politics of Violence

From the terrorists' perspective, the major force of terrorism comes not from its physical impact but from its psychological impact. Terrorism is rarely an effective form of insurgent violence in the sense of achieving its sponsors' ultimate goals, but it can cause enormous problems for democratic governments because of its impact on the psychology of great masses of citizens, the "audience" referred to in the U.S. State Department's definition. Terrorist bombings, assassinations, and hostage-taking have, in nations with a free press, the ability to hold the attention of vast populations. By generating a combination of fear and fascination, terrorists have been able to capture important parts of the agendas of great nations.

Realistic policymakers take this power of terrorism over the imagination of vast parts of the public, and the reaction to that power first by a free press and then by responsive elected officials, to be central facts of political life, whether or not the fascination and anxiety produced by terrorism can be adequately explained. The unusual power to generate mass concerns by relatively easily accomplished bombings, killings, or hostage-taking is useful to terrorists because it allows them to send extremely forceful messages to audiences who would otherwise be unaware even of their existence. That is the unusual politics of terrorism. To whom is the message sent and for what purpose? Despite what I have so far suggested, the answer is not always "the government."

The goals of terrorist groups are unrealistic in terms of the ordinary, mainstream politics of the country. To change this, terrorists sometimes address their frightening message to the center of a democratic political spectrum, to those who have been indifferent to the cause that is bringing forth violence. Part of the center's support of government policy flows from an assumption that the government can maintain order and security, and that it reaches fair results through an orderly process of decision. Terrorism can undermine this assumption. A sustained course of acts of political violence can show that safety does not necessarily flow from support of government policies.

The costs imposed by even small-scale political violence may cause people relatively indifferent to the merits of the cause to urge the government to pursue a policy of accommodation with the insurgent group in order to eliminate those costs. This objective seems to explain the long history of terrorism in Northern Ireland and Israel, which in both cases has had some measure of political success. Both the Provisional IRA and the Palestine Liberation Organization have achieved a legitimacy and encountered a spirit of accommodation that might not have been present without their campaigns.

Alternatively, the political violence may be addressed more directly to the government and its supporting elites. A campaign of assassinations may aim to cause resignations by bringing fear to those in particularly crucial positions, such as judges or prosecutors. The Italian mafia's killing in 1992 of the great anti-mafia magistrates Giovanni Falcone and Paolo

Boisellino had this purpose. Threats to kill mayoral candidates by guerrilla forces opposing the government in Colombia in 1997 had this intended effect. Terrorism may simply demand so much of the attention of government leaders that they find it necessary to compromise so that they can direct their energies elsewhere. For terrorists of the law-and-order Right, acts of random violence, disguised as acts perpetrated by insurgent radicals, can be "addressed" to the attention of security forces in the hope of provoking a coup and a military takeover. Such an effort occurred in Italy in the 1970s, most dramatically with bombings of crowded facilities.

A third potential audience for terrorist acts consists of those who are potential supporters of an insurgency. Acts of terrorism can show these people that the government is not as powerful as it portrays itself, but rather is weak and vulnerable. Or terrorist acts may generate a response by the government that is repressive enough to make allies of those who would otherwise be neutral. When the terrorist cause is to create a separate state, a particularly important subcategory within the audience of potential supporters consists of foreign governments that may be brought, by public accounts of repression, to support their separatist brothers. An act of terrorism—the assassination by a Serbian nationalist of Austrian Archduke Francis Ferdinand in 1914—was a major factor in precipitating World War I because it led Austria and Germany to declare war on Serbia and Russia.

Acts of small-scale political violence can deepen social divisions within a society by increasing anger, fear, and suspicion between groups, thereby furthering the cause of an insurgent group that wants to broaden demands for a separate state for its members. And once the society is severely divided along racial, religious, or ethnic lines, acts of terrorism may allow one group to claim leadership where there are many contestants for this post. After all, violent actions can show power and ruthlessness, two attributes generally sought in leaders in difficult times. This too was a part of the terrorist strategies in Northern Ireland and Israel.

A final audience of terrorist violence may be the active members of the terrorist group itself. Setting aside the ordinary crimes that may be committed to finance the violent organization, terrorist group members may engage in violence because dramatic actions are necessary to maintain the group's morale and self-esteem. In addition, the threat of punishment at the hands of the government for playing a role in violent acts of terrorism may lock in members who might otherwise quit. Violence is also frequently the means of punishing informers and even those who have merely left the group, and the means of sending a message to others who might contemplate the same actions.

However, it may be a mistake to classify audiences and messages too finely. Many acts of political violence are relatively uncalculated, and represent a desperate effort to be heard, i.e., to push a handful of people or their concerns onto the national stage, where attention is generally monopolized by presidents and senators, governors and mayors, cabinet officers and media stars. For many people there is no other way to get onto the stage of national attention for their policies, resentments, or personality. Most of us agree not to be on that stage and to be satisfied with the role of voters or contributors or persuaders. But a determination to be a far more central player can lead individuals to take the only readily available shortcut to world-wide prominence, and that may be to link a violent act to a deeply felt cause.

The Effectiveness of Terrorism

How can limited violence to convey a message hope to affect the policies of a modern democratic state? Often, it cannot. The terrorists are simply mistaken about their prospects or, perhaps like Timothy McVeigh, so angry that they are indifferent to them. But in two situations, terrorism can and does affect the policies of modern democratic states. First, it can be effective when it is operating in a country whose population is already severely divided into suspicious and hostile groups. That has been the situation, for example, in Northern Ireland, Israel, India, Sri Lanka, Spain, and a number of other states. Second, terrorism can work when a government deems acceptance of the terrorist demands, even considering the effect of acquiescence on the frequency of future demands, as far less onerous than the ongoing campaign of terror.

Nations Whose Populations are already Severely Divided Against Each Other

One factor is of greater importance than any other in predicting the consequences of political violence, the likely durability of a terrorist campaign, and the helpful or harmful effects of the steps the government may take. That factor is the extent to which the terrorists' cause is sympathetic to a sizeable, disaffected portion of the population in the place where they are operating. When a society is already dangerously divided, terrorism can do great damage and is likely to be resistant to government efforts—far more than in relatively healthy democracies that enjoy strong support across the broad spectrum of their populations. Fortunately, the United States is not a severely divided society with regard to any present domestic or foreign terrorist threat. Still, it is worth pausing to look at the risks faced by countries such as Israel, Northern Ireland, and Spain.

No extended explanation is necessary for the increased difficulties of capturing the members of a terrorist group or preventing their violent actions in a situation where sizeable numbers of a population sympathize with their cause. At a minimum, law enforcement will find it far harder to get information about what occurs among people and in areas sympathetic to the terrorists. Beyond this, the terrorists will find it far easier to secure communications channels, physical facilities, money, and recruits. This is particularly true when the societal divisions are not purely political but are also ethnic, religious, or racial, pulling on deep strands of group loyalty that rival national allegiance.

What is less obvious is how terrorist acts can affect the familiar dynamics of transition from a secure, multi-ethnic society into a dangerously divided society characterized by high levels of violence, hatred, and mistrust among ethnic groups. The steps of this process can be encouraged and accelerated by targeted political violence such as we have seen in Northern Ireland, Israel, Sri Lanka, and Bosnia. A dangerously divided society is thus, for many separatist groups, a promising stage on the way to a separate national government, and terrorism can force the pace of this dangerous transition.

How then does terrorism change the dynamics of social division? First, although ethnic tensions escalate into hatreds and then violence between members of opposing groups even without the encouragement of terrorists, the process can be speeded by terrorist attacks on an opposing group, inviting tit-for-tat responses and fanning the flames of hatred and fear. This was long common in Northern Ireland and in Israel. Indeed, retribution by members of the victim group against innocent members of the group from which the terrorists come—one of the most divisive of actions—is likely to be seen, mistakenly, as a deterrent to the terrorist attacks.

Second, a cycle of intergroup violence makes it difficult for members of either group to occupy a middle ground of tolerance and understanding. Even moderates may come to need an intense ethnic solidarity to remain secure, and the more violent members of each ethnic group are the natural leaders in providing that security. These processes can even be speeded by terrorists secretly attacking members of their own group. The process continues with increasing segregation of frightened ethnic communities. With this, prejudice grows and rumors are accepted as truth. Fewer members of either group find it comfortable to urge understanding of the other.

Third, each group will seek to bring the government to its side. The government may try to remain "neutral," but even the most natural steps—such as focusing investigation on the members of Group A if an attack was directed at a group they hate—are likely to solidify divisions, create deep distrust, and invite attacks on government security forces that can add a whole new dimension to the cycle of violence.

Accompanying all these forces are several others that sometimes produce still more threats. The group less favored by the government may turn to foreign enemies of the government for support. Others in the population may become less and less willing to consider ameliorative measures demanded by a besieged but combative portion of the population. Terrorist groups are likely to begin policing and enforcing their own demands on members of their ethnic group.

All of these paths towards hatred, fear, and division can be greased by the acts of even a few terrorists. The assassination of a leader of the opposition, an attack on one's own group falsely attributed to others, the killing of moderate rivals for leadership of a particular group, and attacks on law enforcement authorities—all of these can play major roles in speeding the dissolution of a multiethnic society. Thus, such societies are the most promising setting for important political "successes" for that form of violent politics accessible to even small groups—terrorism.

Where the Damage of Terrorism is Unusually Great Compared to the Costs and Risks of Giving in to the Terrorists' Demands

Understanding the relative costs to the government of giving in and of holding out is also critical to understanding the contest which terrorism is all about. The violent group's demands of the government determine in part how likely the government is to give in—only "in part" because giving in once will likely encourage further demands by this group or others using the same threat of violence. Moreover, looking at the contest from the terrorist side, the terrorist group is likely to hold together and pursue its course longer if it sees its prospects for success as substantial. It will see them as substantial if it believes that the cost of political violence to the government far exceeds the costs to the government of compliance with the terrorists' demands, even when the government takes into account the likelihood of encouraging future terrorist demands.

The simple fact is that a handful of people can use murder, arson, and kidnapping to create public concerns strong enough and widely enough held to affect the policies and politics of the United States in ways totally disproportionate to their numbers, but far less because of the damage they can actually impose than because of its psychological, political, and social effects.

Some explanations of the great psychological impact of the limited damage generally caused by terrorism are helpful. As a start, social scientists have noted that people give far more weight to events that are vivid.[6] We do not have to search far for what makes terrorist acts "vivid." They are particularly frightening because terrorists purposely kill or maim otherwise uninvolved citizens. They also deprive us of a safeguard, neutrality, which we normally consider sufficient for our safety: the protection obtained by avoiding active or prominent involvement on either side in situations of conflict. A further explanation for the great psychological impact of terrorism is that terrorist attacks *seem* to present an immediate as well as violent challenge to the existing governmental structure of order and authority and may herald the prospect of escalating disorder and a forcible change in government.

What costs can a terrorist group actually impose on a relatively healthy and stable democracy such as ours? For the United States, terrorism does not pose any great national security threat to our stability or well-being as a nation—unless the traditional reluctance of terrorists to use weapons of mass destruction changes. With a single bomb, the terrorists in

Oklahoma City killed as many people as die in homicides in three ordinary days in the entire United States. That is terrible, but even such an immense explosion represents far too small a percentage change in the annual violent death rate in the United States to be considered a threat to the nation as a whole.

Terrorism is, of course, a threat to public order that the national government must address. There is a real risk of the death of some citizens each year. If unpunished, terrorism can also encourage a spread of political violence by imitation as radical political groups compete for public attention or as others attempt to deal with the danger through forms of vigilantism. Psychologically, there is likely to be widespread fear, totally disproportionate to the actual danger, causing changes in economic and social behavior such as people avoiding air travel or downtown stores, or arming themselves unnecessarily.

National politics are also affected. Terrorism has an immense capacity to capture public attention, to cause otherwise ignored issues (such as the U.S. policy in the Middle East or at Waco) to displace others on a national agenda, and to make a few previously anonymous terrorists into relatively major participants in a political debate that would otherwise relegate them to very marginal roles. More fundamentally, terrorism threatens the domestic support for a government whose citizens consider their security its first obligation. Especially because politically motivated violence openly challenges the state's right to a monopoly of the use of force, a sense that the government is ineffective at keeping people safe from those who challenge the state's legitimacy can seriously undermine confidence, generating fear, disrespect, even ridicule. It is costly for a government to look impotent when being challenged so directly in its capacity to protect citizens.

All this is compounded by fears of international repercussions. An apparent inability to deal with an open challenge to the power and legitimacy of the government may make a nation look like a less strong and trustworthy ally.

What costs of giving in prevent a government from buying off the terrorist group? In some cases, the terrorist group is asking far too much, when the alternative is bearing the limited costs of terrorism until the group's members can be found, tried, and locked away. Israel would not, for example, comply with any demand that would significantly endanger its national security in order to end terrorist violence, which has never killed as many Israelis as traffic accidents do. Germany, Italy, and France had no adequate reason to change their forms of government to the satisfaction of the Red Army Faction, the Red Brigades, or Direct Action.

Terrorists can anticipate success only if what they are asking is of relatively minor importance to a strong and stable government. For example, the United States left Lebanon as a result of the bombing of the Marine barracks on October 23, 1983, and it secretly sold TOW anti-tank missiles to Iran in 1986 for use against Iraq in the hope of obtaining the release of a handful of American hostages, using the proceeds of the sale to support anti-Sandinista forces in Nicaragua. France promised, at about the same time, to obtain a very short sentence for a terrorist, Georges Ibrahim Abdallah, in order to end a bombing spree on his behalf. Even in such cases, governments must consider seriously the impact of giving in on future political demands and, to a lesser extent, on their relationships with other nations: allies may find them weak or untrustworthy in a shared battle against particular forms of political violence, or—in the case of the U.S. sale of missiles to Iran—hypocritical. So even making deals, as in these three cases, generally makes sense only if the capitulation can be sufficiently obscured. That hope and expectation lay behind the government action in each of these examples.

If the government concludes that the costs of giving in to terrorist demands are too high, compared to the expected cost of political violence until the group can be caught and dismantled, the terrorist group may try to raise these costs either by escalating the damage from individual attacks or by showing an ability and a willingness to continue a course of violence over months or years or even decades. Even with purely conventional terrorist weapons, the Provisional IRA in Northern Ireland and the Palestine Liberation Organization in the Middle East had the capacity and tenacity to continue a costly terrorist campaign, wearing down the willingness of both Britain and Israel to continue to bear the costs, and building the prospect that the violence would continue for a very long period. The negotiations that have resulted in Northern Ireland and the Middle East surely reflect some success of these strategies. But in both situations, the contest between the government and the violent groups took place in the only truly dangerous setting for resisting terrorism: a society already severely divided along racial, religious, or ethnic lines.

Notes

1. James Risen, "CIA Director Predicts Terrorism Rise," *Los Angeles Times*, December 20, 1995.
2. Alex P. Schmid and Ronald D. Crelinsten, *Western Responses to Terrorism* (London: Frank Cass, 1993), p. 11.
3. Ibid., pp. 7–13.
4. Benjamin Netanyahu, *Fighting Terrorism: How Democracies Can Defeat Domestic and International Terrorism* (New York: Farrar, Straus, and Giroux, 1995).
5. Ibid., p. 268.
6. Richard E. Nisbett and Lee Ross, *Human Inference: Strategies and Shortcomings of Social Judgement* (Englewood Cliffs, N.J.: Prentice-Hall, 1980), p. 62.

Reading 5.4

State and Local Fusion Centers: Emerging Trends and Issues

Kevin Eack

Introduction

The proliferation of state and local fusion centers and the efforts to partner them with the intelligence community have been compared to organizing a new little league baseball team. Just as each team in a league has different strengths and weaknesses each center has a different set of skills, abilities, and equipment.[1] This paper provides a brief overview of the present status of state and local fusion centers, as well as the current policy issues and obstacles these centers face.

Counter Terrorism: Not a New Mission for State and Local Law Enforcement

Combating terrorism in the United States is not a new concept for state and local law enforcement. There are a number of examples where state and local law enforcement have played a key role in detecting terrorist activity. A simple traffic stop of a subject on April 19, 1995, by an Oklahoma state trooper, for driving a vehicle without a license plate resulted in the arrest of Timothy McVeigh for the bombing of the Alfred P. Murrah Federal Building.[2] On May 31, 2003, a local patrolman arrested the notorious Eric Robert Rudolph, a domestic terrorist who was on the Federal Bureau of Investigation's (FBI) Ten Most Wanted List for a series of bombings including one at the 1996 Olympics. Rudolph was the subject of a tenacious manhunt in the Appalachian Mountains for several years before being arrested by a local police officer on routine patrol in the small town of Murphy, North Carolina. Rudolph specifically targeted police and other first responders with secondary devices in some of his bombings.[3] On April 4, 1980, the deadly Fuerzas Armadas de Liberacion Nacional (FALN), a small, heavily armed terrorist organization responsible for over 100 bombings in major cities including Chicago, New York, and Miami suffered its most serious setback when its members were arrested by patrolmen in Evanston, Illinois, as they assembled in a park with several stolen vehicles, thirteen weapons, disguises, and false identifications, preparing to heist an armored truck at the prestigious Northwestern University.[4]

Intelligence Not New to State and Local Law Enforcement

While the concept of "fusion centers" is certainly new, many states have had a centralized intelligence system of some sort for decades. Typically, these have been housed in state police agencies, as a central repository on intelligence related to violent gangs, drug trafficking, prostitution, child exploitation, weapons smuggling, theft rings, and other crimes. In those states with a major city or county police department (such as New York, Los Angeles and Chicago) those agencies have also operated intelligence units. For many states today's fusion center is simply an extension of these intelligence units, with a higher degree of vertical (federal intelligence community) and horizontal (state/local) collaboration. Some have compared today's fusion centers with "state police intelligence units on steroids."[5]

What is new is the mission of preventing international terrorist attacks on U.S. soil and law enforcement is adjusting to a new enemy with new methods. Law enforcement organizations are also adjusting to new operational issues that were previously not areas of concern. According to Congressional testimony these include:

1. The absence of a cohesive federal strategy regarding information sharing,
2. Too many federal information sharing networks, and
3. An inability or unwillingness on the part of the Department of Homeland Security (DHS) and the FBI to work effectively together.[6]

One example of an obstacle created by the lack of coordination between DHS and the FBI is security clearances. State and local fusion centers are required to have security clearances in order to receive, analyze, store, and disseminate classified material. Yet, in many cases it is reported the FBI is unwilling to accept those with DHS security clearances. In still other cases, DHS requires verification that someone from a state or major city possesses an FBI clearance through a process where the clearance is "passed" or certified to DHS from the FBI. Such problems can prove frustrating to state and local partners who are doing all they can to perform their role in homeland security.[7]

Another example is the apparent mission overlap between DHS and the FBI. A primary mission for many state and local fusion centers is collecting, analyzing, and disseminating critical infrastructure data to DHS. Since the creation of the department, DHS has conducted several data calls in order to populate the national critical infrastructure database. It also adopted the Automated Critical Asset Management Systems (ACAMS) system from the Los Angeles Police Department as a nationwide system to manage this data, urging state fusion centers to utilize this system.

Yet the FBI has continued to operate a critical infrastructure protection program of its own, called Infraguard, which is quite popular in some states among the private stakeholders. This presents a number of challenges for state and local fusion centers, which often find they are "caught in the middle," trying to show a cooperative spirit between both agencies while also trying to maintain credibility with their private stakeholders who own, operate, and have a vested interest in protection of critical infrastructure. Some in the private sector complain that the "federal government needs to get its act together" on this important issue soon, as its efforts appear to be disjointed and uncoordinated.[8]

State and local stakeholders who operate fusion centers are often frustrated with trying to provide the necessary information to both agencies. In order to be effective, fusion centers need to work with both the FBI and DHS; the FBI is a critical partner and DHS provides needed funding. According to one state fusion center commander, "we are anticipating this to be very challenging."[9]

As a recent Congressional report highlights, the evolution of state and local fusion centers leaves a number of looming issues.[10] One issue is that many state and local fusion centers are in some ways less familiar with civil liberties issues and the federal regulations regarding intelligence storage, handling, and dissemination. As a result, more privacy concerns are likely to develop due to unintentional violations of intelligence rules.

Fusion centers also face a number of long-term issues. Congress provided substantial resources to support the DHS grant program in the years following the 9/11 attacks. As time passes, such funding may taper off, leaving insufficient funding for fusion center operations.[11] As those who have opened and operated such centers know, while funding sources have varied widely from state to state the majority of states have leveraged homeland security funds for equipment and analysts, subject to certain limitations imposed by DHS.[12]

One of the most significant issues found in the Congressional research has been the absence of a well-defined long-term role for state and local fusion centers. According to testimony by Eileen Larence, Director of Homeland Security and Justice Issues

> The federal government has not clearly articulated the long term role it expects to play in sustaining fusion centers. It is critical for center management to know whether to expect continued federal resources, such as personnel and grant funding, since the federal government, through an information sharing environment, expects to rely on a nationwide network of centers to facilitate information sharing with state and local governments.[13]

According to Congressional findings, there are currently fifty-eight fusion centers at the state and local level. Forty-three are considered operational, while fifteen are in various stages of development. Nine centers opened shortly after the attacks of September 11, 2001. Thirty-four became operational after January, 2004. At least thirty-four fusion centers report employing federal personnel.[14]

While many efforts have been made by the federal government to support fusion centers, many fusion center officials report challenges accessing and managing multiple information systems. The FBI's Law Enforcement Online (LEO) system and the DHS Homeland Security Information Network (HSIN) are mentioned prominently in the Congressional reports. These multiple systems are reported to be causing "information overload" at many centers, often with redundant information.[15] To compound the problem, DHS continues to change the information-sharing platform, making it a challenge to establish stability among the fusion centers. Initially many fusion centers were operating on the Joint Regional Information Exchange System (JRIES), but then DHS directed they move to the HSIN system. Recent announcements suggest that platform will also soon be changing.[16]

For many fusion center officials at the state and local level, the single biggest concern is sustainability. Van Godsey, director of the Missouri Information and Analysis Center (MIAC) states it this way:

> With this tremendous focus on fusion centers, my concern is sustainability of these centers and the national effort. Currently, any federal funding for fusion centers is located within the federal allocation to the states. The use of these funds is subject to local demands, politics and views that may not always be supportive of the fusion center effort. If the federal government is going to look at the fusion centers and expect minimum capabilities, then I believe there are going to have to be controls to ensure a minimum level of funding.[17]

Godsey advocates specific line item funding for fusion centers instead of the present method of funding.[18]

As Congressional reports point out, ultimately the federal government needs to make a policy decision about the future of state and local fusion centers. As one report states, a number of questions need to be answered including the following:

1. Do fusion centers solve the pre-9/11 information sharing problems, and as such, make Americans safer?
2. Can fusion centers work if they aren't part of an integrated philosophy of intelligence and security?
3. Who benefits from fusion centers? Who should staff, fund, and oversee them? What role, if any, should fusion centers play in the Intelligence Community (IC)? What role should federal agencies play in fusion centers, to include funding?
4. Is some basic level of common standards necessary in order for fusion centers to offer a national benefit? Does the federal government have an integrated national fusion center strategy? How is their performance to be measured?

5. Is the current configuration of forty-plus fusion centers, with multiple centers in some states the most efficient way to structure them?[19]

2007 National Strategy for Information Sharing

The recent release of the *National Strategy for Information Sharing* in October, 2007, certainly supports earlier Congressional findings that more federal leadership with regard to fusion centers is needed.[20] Referencing Guideline 2 of the president's December 16, 2006 *Memorandum to Heads of Executive Departments and Agencies,* the strategy calls for a "common framework" to be developed governing the roles and responsibilities between the federal government, state, local, and tribal governments, and private sector entities.[21]

The strategy also acknowledges the important role of state and local fusion centers as follows: "State and major urban area fusion centers are vital assets critical to sharing information related to terrorism. They will serve as the primary focal points within the State and local environment for the receipt and sharing of terrorism-related information."[22]

The strategy also contemplates how state and local fusion centers may scrub and further disseminate classified terrorism-related intelligence to others in the region.

> Federal departments and agencies will provide terrorism-related information to State, local and tribal authorities primarily through these fusion centers. Unless specifically prohibited by law, or subject to security classification restrictions, these fusion centers may further customize such information for dissemination to satisfy intra- or inter State needs.[23]

Additionally, the *National Strategy* addresses the important issue of public and private collaboration to protect critical infrastructure. "This Strategy builds on these efforts to adopt an effective framework that ensures a two way flow of timely and actionable security information between public and private partners." It also acknowledges the sensitivity of critical infrastructure information provided by the private sector and the importance of maintaining the confidentiality of such data when it is provided to governmental units.[24]

Notes

1. Matthew M. Johnson, "Number of Databases Bogging Down Fusion Centers," *Congressional Quarterly,* October 9, 2007, www.cq.com. See also General Accounting Office, *Federal Efforts Are Helping to Alleviate Some Challenges Encountered by State and Local Information Fusion Centers, GAO-08-35,* October 2007, http://www.gao.gov/new.items/d0835.pdf.

2. Trial testimony, http://www.law.umkc.edu/faculty/projects/ftrials/mcveigharrest.html.

3. Maryanne Vollers, "Lone Wolf, Eric Rudolph: Murder, Myth and the Pursuit of an American Outlaw," (Harper Collins, 2006); see also www.cnn.com/2003/us/05/31/rudolph.main/.

4. CBS News, April 7, 1980, http://openweb.tvnews.vanderbilt.edu/1980-4/1980-04-07-CBS-22.html.

5. Todd Masse and John Rollins, *A Summary of Fusion Centers: Core Issues and Options for Congress* (Congressional Research Service, September 19, 2007).

6. Johnson, "Number of Databases Bogging Down Fusion Centers." See also GAO, *Federal Efforts Are Helping to Alleviate Some Challenges.*

7. Interview with Major Monte McKee, Indiana Intelligence Fusion Center, November 26, 2007.

8. Interview with Michael Crane, co-chair of the Illinois Terrorism Task Force Private Sector Committee, and Vice President and General Counsel for IPC International, a private security firm whose clients include most major malls in the U.S., and those in four other countries, November 26, 2007.

9. Interview with Major Monte McKee.

10. Masse and Rollins, "A Summary of Fusion Centers."

11. Ibid.

12. Electronic survey of Midwest fusion center commanders by author, July 2007.

13. Testimony of Eileen R. Larence, September 27, 2007 Before the Subcommittee on Intelligence, Information Sharing and Terrorism Risk Assessment, Committee on Homeland Security, House of Representatives, GAO-07-1241T.

14. Ibid.

15. Ibid, 8.

16. Federal Computer Week, *DHS to Modify Info-Sharing Network*, January 21, 2008, http://fcw.com/online/news/151380-1.html.

17. Interview with Director Van Godsey, Missouri Information and Analysis Center, November 26, 2007.

18. Ibid.

19. Masse and Rollins, "A Summary of Fusion Centers," 4.

20. *National Strategy for Information Sharing*, October 2007. http://www.whitehouse.gov/nsc/infosharing.

21. Ibid, 17.

22. Ibid, 20.

23. Ibid, 21.

24. Ibid, 21.

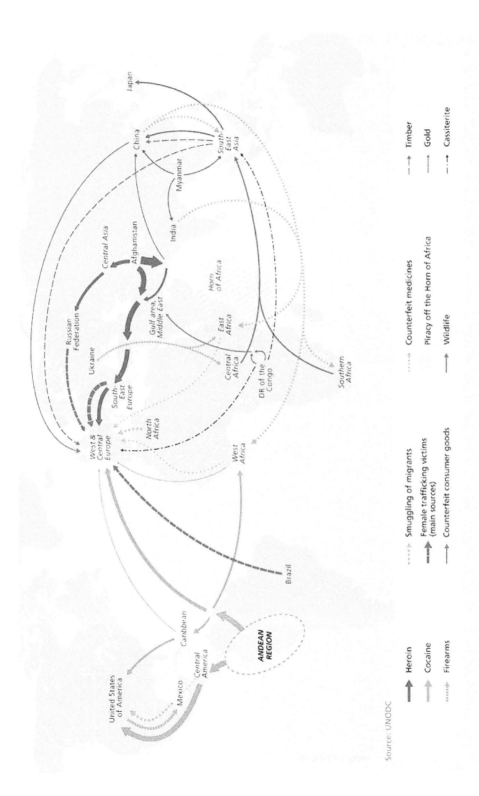

Source: UNODC

FIGURE 5.2   The Global Flows of Transnational Organized Crime. The figure displays a map with national boundaries and routes of contraband smuggling across the globe. It was developed by the United Nations Office on Drugs and Crime Organized Crime (UNODC), the major international law enforcement organization fighting TOC today. The legend at the bottom lists major contraband trafficked by TOC organizations: heroin, cocaine, firearms, smuggled immigrants, female trafficking victims, counterfeit consumer products, counterfeit medicines, piracy off the Horn of Africa, wildlife, timber, gold, and cassiterite. This map concisely shows the regions where contraband originates and how it is illegally transported to consumer nationals by TOC groups. As indicated, the United States, Western Europe, Japan and China are the primary consumers of international contraband. This figure clearly describes that TOC is a global issue for law enforcement through the use of several specific directional arrows superimposed on the world map. The tremendous number of surveillance and data collection techniques used in collecting the information required to draft this image are part of the new intelligence-lead policing technology we have been studying in this book. This one image is a product of over 100 national government law enforcement and intelligence agencies cooperating under the auspices of the UNODC. These techniques are important for two reasons: The technical ability to conduct global surveillance has only been available in the last few decades, and countries with different and even competing geopolitical agendas successfully cooperated through the UNODC to collect this information.

DISCUSSION QUESTIONS

Transnational crime is defined as "… crime that takes place across national borders and has had profound consequences for the ordering of the world system." Transnational crime is especially problematic in countries where the rule of law is weak and the government is unstable, as it can undermine the legitimacy of authority and economic growth. Criminal organizations are driven to TOC primarily for financial gain.

1. Identify the various factors that have vastly expanded transnational crime in recent years. What factors have contributed to the expansion of transnational crime?
2. List the various types of TOC groups in the world today.
3. Identify recommendations for improved law enforcement responses to TOC.
4. Describe how law enforcement at all levels can plan to address TOC in the future.

Figure Credit

Fig. 5.2: United Nations Office on Drugs and Crime, "Global Flows of Transnational Organized Crime (UNODC)," https://www.unodc.org/images/e4j/OrganizedCrime/figure_5.1.png. Copyright © 2010 by United Nations.

Chapter 6

Contemporary and Future Trends in Law Enforcement

INTRODUCTION

Law enforcement is a complex and difficult profession. The actions that a police officer takes can save a life or produce a string of catastrophic events with lasting negative effects. Although most police officers perform their duties honorably, ethically, and professionally, the actions of a single officer can tarnish the profession. In this chapter, we will discuss the necessary elements for police to conduct search and seizure under the Fourth Amendment and the implications for police procedure of the Fifth Amendment to the US Constitution. It is important to remember that the First through Tenth Amendments to the US Constitution are also known as the Bill of Rights. The due process addressed in the Bill of Rights, and its relation to policing and the Fourteenth Amendment to the US Constitution, are repeatedly cited in US Supreme Court cases that have an impact on contemporary policing. As we analyze some of the legal issues associated with the USA PATRIOT Act, homeland security, and terrorism, we will see that recent decisions have broadened police powers and authority in the United States. Is the broadening of police authority necessary in our world today? Is it possible that some new policies and procedures, such as the secret US Foreign Intelligence Surveillance Court (FISA Court) might undermine the very civil rights that they were intended to protect? It is sometimes difficult to determine what levels of freedom, privacy, and self determination we

FIGURE 6.1 A US Department of Justice graphic depicting the acronym for controversial legislation meant to enhance law enforcements abilities to fight terrorism, the USA PATRIOT Act (Uniting and Strengthening America by Providing Appropriate Tools Required to Intercept and Obstruct Terrorism Act). The image is meant to introduce students to this chapter on criminal statutes, court decisions and law enforcement.

FIGURE 6.2 The is the logo of the National Security Agency (NSA). It is meant to remind students of the importance of NSA information, sometimes obtained via controversial surveillance, in anti-terrorism law enforcement activities.

are willing to give up to achieve acceptable levels of community security in this changing and complex world. One of our Founding Fathers of the United States, Benjamin Franklin (1706–1790), said, "Those who would give up essential liberty, to purchase a little temporary safety, deserve neither liberty nor safety" (Labaree). In this chapter, we will discuss the veracity of Mr. Franklin's statement.

REFERENCE

Franklin, B., Pennsylvania Assembly. (1963). Reply to the Governor, November 11, 1755. In L. W. Labaree (Ed.). *The papers of Benjamin Franklin, vol. 6, April 1, 1755, through September 30, 1756* (pp. 238–243). Yale University Press.

Figure Credits

Fig. 6.1: Source: https://www.justice.gov/archive/ll/images/patriot-act.gif.

Fig. 6.2: Source: https://www.nsa.gov/portals/70/images/about/cryptologic-heritage/center-cryptologic-history/insignia/nsa-insignia-sm.png.

Reading 6.1

Policing by Numbers: Big Data and the Fourth Amendment

Elizabeth E. Joh

Introduction

The age of "big data" has come to policing. In Chicago, police officers are paying particular attention to members of a "heat list": those identified by a risk analysis as most likely to be involved in future violence.[1] In Charlotte, North Carolina, the police have compiled foreclosure data to generate a map of high-risk areas that are likely to be hit by crime.[2] In New York City, the N.Y.P.D. has partnered with Microsoft to employ a "Domain Awareness System" that collects and links information from sources like CCTVs, license plate readers, radiation sensors, and informational databases.[3] In Santa Cruz, California, the police have reported a dramatic reduction in burglaries after relying upon computer algorithms that predict where new burglaries are likely to occur.[4] The Department of Homeland Security has applied computer analytics to Twitter feeds to find words like "pipe bomb," "plume," and "listeria."[5]

Big data has begun to transform government in fields as diverse as public health, transportation management, and scientific research.[6] The analysis of what were once unimaginable quantities of digitized data is likely to introduce dramatic changes to a profession which, as

---

1   Jeremy Gorner, *Chicago Police Use 'Heat List' as Strategy to Prevent Violence*, CHI. TRIB. (Aug. 21, 2013), http://articles.chicagotribune.com/2013-08-21/news/ct-met-heat-list-20130821_1_chicago-police-commander-andrew-papachristos-heat-list.

2   Michael Bess, *Assessing the Impact of Home Foreclosures in Charlotte Neighborhoods*, GEOGRAPHY & PUB. SAFETY, Oct. 2008, at 2, 2.

3   Joe Coscarelli, *The NYPD's Domain Awareness System is Watching You*, N.Y. MAG. (Aug. 9, 2012, 5:50 AM), http://nymag.com/daily/intelligencer/2012/08/nypd-domain-awareness-system-microsoft-is-watching-you.html.

4   *See* Erica Goode, *Sending the Police Before There's a Crime*, N.Y. TIMES (Aug. 15, 2011), http://www.nytimes.com/2011/08/16/us/16police.html.

5   Somini Sengupta, *In Hot Pursuit of Numbers to Ward Off Crime*, N.Y. TIMES (June 19, 2013, 10:48 PM), http://bits.blogs.nytimes.com/2013/06/19/in-hot-pursuit-of-numbers-to-ward-off-crime/?_r=0.

6   *See, e.g.,* TECHAMERICA FOUND., DEMYSTIFYING BIG DATA: A PRACTICAL GUIDE TO TRANSFORMING THE BUSINESS OF GOVERNMENT 12–15 (2012) (describing potential uses of big data in healthcare, transportation, education, fraud detection, cyber security, and weather).

---

late as 1900, involved little more than an able-bodied man who was given a hickory club, a whistle, and a key to a call box.[7] Real-time access to and analysis of vast quantities of information found in criminal records, police databases, and surveillance data may alter policing[8] in the same way that big data has revolutionized areas as diverse as presidential elections,[9] internet commerce,[10] and language translation.[11] Some have even heralded big data's potential to change our assumptions about social relationships, government, scientific study, and even knowledge itself.[12]

In the private sector, retailers have harnessed big data to produce some seemingly trivial but surprising changes to their practices.[13] A much discussed example stems from Target's extensive use of data analytics to identify certain purchases, such as supplements commonly taken during pregnancy, to know whether a customer is pregnant, without the woman disclosing the pregnancy herself.[14] For a retailer, pregnancy is a prime opportunity to target a consumer when shopping habits change and expand. An irate father allegedly complained to Target that his daughter was unfairly targeted as a pregnant woman with coupons only to discover, to his chagrin, that Target was better informed than he was.[15] Similarly, Walmart, through its computerized retail tracking, has discovered that Strawberry Pop-Tarts and beer sell as briskly as flashlights when hurricanes are forecast. These products were quickly shipped to Florida Walmart stores in the path of Hurricane Frances in 2004.[16]

---

7   *See* Mark H. Haller, *Historical Roots of Police Behavior: Chicago, 1890–1925*, 10 L. & Soc'y Rev. 303, 303 (1976).

8   Beth Pearsall, *Predictive Policing: The Future of Law Enforcement?*, Nat'l Inst. Just. J., June 2010, at 16, 16, *available at* https://www.ncjrs.gov/pdffiles1/nij/230414.pdf (describing its development as having "the potential to transform law enforcement").

9   *See* Michael Scherer, *Inside the Secret World of the Data Crunchers Who Helped Obama Win*, Time (Nov. 7, 2012), http://swampland.time.com/2012/11/07/inside-the-secret-world-of-quants-and-data-crunchers-who-helped-obama-win/print/ (quoting one Obama campaign official as saying, "We ran the election 66,000 times every night" in computer simulations).

10   *See, e.g.,* Viktor Mayer-Schönberger & Kenneth Cukier, Big Data: A Revolution That Will Transform How We Live, Work, and Think 4–5 (2013) (describing development of Farecast, which analyzes data from billions of flight price records to predict airline ticket price variation).

11   *See id.* at 37–39 (describing language translation success of Google using trillion word data set).

12   *See, e.g.,* Adam Frank, *Big Data Is the Steam Engine of Our Time*, NPR (Mar. 12, 2013, 12:28 PM), http://www.npr.org/blogs/13.7/2013/03/12/174028759/big-data-is-the-steam-engine-of-our-time ("Big Data may be the steam engine of our time.").

13   Charles Duhigg, *How Companies Learn Your Secrets*, N.Y. Times (Feb. 16, 2012), http://www.nytimes.com/2012/02/19/magazine/shopping-habits.html?pagewanted=1 ("Almost every major retailer, from grocery chains to investment banks to the U.S. Postal Service, has a 'predictive analytics' department. ...").

14   *See id.*

15   *See id.*

16   Constance L. Hays, *What Wal-Mart Knows About Customers' Habits*, N.Y. Times (Nov. 14, 2004), http://www.nytimes.com/2004/11/14/business/yourmoney/14wal.html.

Yet unlike the data crunching performed by Target, Walmart, or Amazon, the introduction of big data to police work raises new and significant challenges to the regulatory framework that governs conventional policing. From one perspective, the Fourth Amendment has proven remarkably flexible over time. Constitutional law has governed ordinary policing whether the crimes involved bootlegging,[17] numbers running,[18] marijuana farming,[19] or cell phones.[20] As the sophistication of criminals has increased, so too have the tools of the police. In the twentieth century, perhaps no two tools have been as revolutionary to modern policing as the two way radio and the patrol car.[21]

In this century, big data—in a variety of forms—may bring the next dramatic change to police investigations. One researcher has concluded that it will soon be technologically possible and affordable for government to record *everything* anyone says or does.[22] How well will the Fourth Amendment's rules pertaining to unreasonable searches and seizures adapt to the uses of big data? Scholars have widely discussed the shortcomings of applying Fourth Amendment doctrines, once adequate for a world of electronic beepers, physical wiretaps, and binocular surveillance, to rapidly changing technologies.[23] But big data may magnify these concerns considerably.

---

17   *See, e.g.*, Olmstead v. United States, 277 U.S. 438, 455–58, 465–66 (1928); *see also Photo Gallery*, PBS, http://www.pbs.org/kenburns/prohibition/media_detail/2082733861-olmstead/ (last visited Feb. 17, 2014) (noting that Roy Olmstead was nicknamed the "King of Puget Sound Bootleggers").

18   *See, e.g.*, Katz v. United States, 389 U.S. 347, 348, 358–59 (1967) (illegal wagering).

19   *See, e.g.*, Kyllo v. United States, 533 U.S. 27, 29–33, 40 (2001).

20   In *United States v. Jones*, _U.S._, 132 S. Ct. 945 (2012), the Supreme Court held that the government's attachment of a GPS tracking device on the defendant's car required a warrant. *Id.* at 954. On remand, the government argued that cell site data could be relied upon without a warrant, which the district court permitted under the good faith exception to the exclusionary rule. *See* United States v. Jones, Crim. Action No. 05-0386 (ESH) (D.D.C. Dec. 14, 2012), *available at* https://ecf.dcd.uscourts.gov/cgi-bin/show_public_doc?2005cr0386-658.

21   *Cf.* Samuel Walker, *"Broken Windows" and Fractured History: The Use and Misuse of History in Recent Police Patrol Analysis*, 1 Just. Q. 75, 80 (1984) ("The mid-century revolution in American policing involved not just the patrol car but the car in conjunction with the telephone and the two-way radio.").

22   John Villasenor, Brookings Institute, Recording Everything: Digital Storage as an Enabler of Authoritarian Governments 1 (Dec. 14, 2011), *available at* http://www.brookings.edu/~/media/research/files/papers/2011/12/14%20digital%20storage%20villasenor/1214_digital_storage_villasenor.pdf.

23   A large literature has developed that critiques the limitations of modern search and seizure law as applied to computer software and hardware, the internet, new surveillance technologies, etc. *See, e.g.*, Orin S. Kerr, *The Fourth Amendment and New Technologies: Constitutional Myths and the Case for Caution*, 102 Mich. L. Rev. 801, 803 n.7 (2004) (collecting sources espousing this view); Dan Solove, *Digital Dossiers and the Dissipation of Fourth Amendment Privacy*, 75 S. Cal. L. Rev. 1083, 1086–87 (2002) (arguing that the current view on Fourth Amendment privacy "is not responsive to life in the modern Information Age").

This article identifies three uses of big data that hint at the future of policing and the questions these tools raise about conventional Fourth Amendment analysis. Two of these examples, predictive policing and mass surveillance systems, have already been adopted by a small number of police departments around the country. A third example—the potential use of DNA databank samples—presents an untapped source of big data analysis. Whether any of these three examples of big data policing attract more widespread adoption by the police is yet unknown, but it likely that the prospect of being able to analyze large amounts of information quickly and cheaply will prove to be attractive. While seemingly quite distinct, these three uses of big data suggest the need to draw new Fourth Amendment lines now that the government has the capability and desire to collect and manipulate large amounts of digitized information.

I. The Rise of Big Data

What is big data? While not everyone agrees on a single definition of big data, most agree that the term refers to: (1) the application of artificial intelligence (2) to the vast amount of digitized data now available.[24] From this basic definition, a few observations emerge about what is distinct and significant about big data.[25]

First, big data alerts us to the sheer *amount* of information that is being produced rapidly every year in *digital* form.[26] The turn towards digitized information has been rapid and dramatic. As recently as the year 2000, only a quarter of the world's stored information was digital; the majority of it was on film, paper, magnetic tapes, and other similar non-digital media.[27] Today, the opposite is true; nearly all of the world's stored information is digital: about 2.7 zettabytes in 2012.[28]

---

24 *See, e.g.*, Steve Lohr, *How Big Data Became So Big*, N.Y. Times (Aug. 11, 2012), http://www.nytimes.com/2012/08/12/business/how-big-data-became-so-big-unboxed.html?smid=pl-share ("Big Data is a shorthand label that typically means applying the tools of artificial intelligence, like machine learning, to vast new troves of data beyond that captured in standard databases.").

25 Here, too, there are some who dispute whether big data is a new phenomenon at all. *See, e.g.*, Samuel Arbesman, *Five Myths About Big Data*, Wash. Post (Aug. 16, 2013), http://www.washingtonpost.com/opinions/five-myths-about-big-data/2013/08/15/64a0dd0a-e044-11e2-963a-72d740e88c12_story.html (arguing that "big data has been around for a long time").

26 *See* Mayer-Schönberger & Cukier, *supra* note 10, at 8–11 (describing vast quantities of digitized data available today).

27 *See* Kenneth Neil Cukier & Viktor Mayer-Schöenberger, *The Rise of Big Data: How It's Changing the Way We Think About the World*, Foreign Aff., May–June 2013, at 28, 28.

28 Albert Pimental, *Big Data: The Hidden Opportunity*, Forbes (May 1, 2012), http://www.forbes.com/sites/ciocentral/2012/05/01/big-data-the-hidden-opportunity/. One zettabyte is 10 to the power of

Digital information continues to grow at a rapid pace. According to IBM, ninety percent of the world's data has been generated in the past two years.[29] The Executive Chairman of Google has claimed that we now create as much information in two days as we did from the beginning of human civilization to 2003.[30] Some have suggested that we may run out of ways to quantify numerically the amount of data generated.[31]

Nearly every piece of information today is capable of digitization and storage, including Internet searches, retail purchases, Facebook posts, cellphone calls, highway toll usage, and every last word in books.[32] Cheap, small, and sophisticated sensors and tracking devices have been built into every sort of product and object: smartphones, cars, toll transponders, library books, and internet use.[33] The city of Santander, Spain is a prototype of the coming "smart city," with 12,000 sensors buried underground that measure everything from air pollution to free parking spaces.[34] The resulting data doesn't disappear; it ends up in "data barns" that store the ever-growing amount of information.[35] Walmart handles more than a million customer transactions every hour, resulting in databases storing more than 2.5 petabytes

21 bytes. This is equivalent to the amount of data which could fill 250 billion DVDs. Melody Kramer, *The NSA Data: Where Does It Go?*, Nat'l Geographic (June 12, 2013), http://news.nationalgeographic.com/news/2013/06/130612-nsa-utah-data-center-storage-zettabyte-snowden/.

29   IBM, IBM Big Data Success Stories 1 (2011), *available at* http://public.dhe.ibm.com/software/data/sw-library/big-data/ibm-big-data-success.pdf.

30   Google, *Eric Schmidt at Technomy*, YouTube (Aug. 4, 2010), http://www.youtube.com/watch?v=UAcCIsrAq70.

31   The largest current recognized number is a yottabye: a digit with twenty-four zeros. *See* Charles Walford, *Information Overload: There Is So Much Data Stored in the World That We May Run Out of Ways to Quantify It*, Daily Mail (Dec. 12, 2012), http://www.dailymail.co.uk/sciencetech/article-2247081/There-soon-words-data-stored-world.html.

32   *See* Mayer-Schönberger & Cukier, *supra* note 10, at 83–97 (discussing the "datafication of everything").

33   UPS, for example uses telematics sensors in more than 46,000 vehicles; these tell the company about the speed, direction, braking, and drive train performance of their trucks. *See What is Big Data?*, SAS, http://www.sas.com/big-data/ (last visited Feb. 17, 2014).

34   Lauren Frayer, *High-Tech Sensors Help Old Port City Leap Into Smart Future*, NPR (June 4, 2013, 3:27 AM), http://www.npr.org/blogs/parallels/2013/06/04/188370672/Sensors-Transform-Old-Spanish-Port-Into-New-Smart-City.

35   Indeed, a series of investigative reports by the *New York Times* has revealed the relatively little-known environmental costs of huge data centers. *See, e.g.*, James Glanz, *Power, Pollution and the Internet*, N.Y. Times (Sept. 22, 2012), http://www.nytimes.com/2012/09/23/technology/data-centers-waste-vast-amounts-of-energy-belying-industry-image.html (quoting an industry executive as describing an "industry dirty secret"); James Glanz, *Data Barns in a Farm Town, Gobbling Power and Flexing Muscle*, N.Y. Times (Sept. 23, 2012), http://www.nytimes.com/2012/09/24/technology/data-centers-in-rural-washington-state-gobble-power.html?ref=us (reporting on "sprawling and ubiquitous" "data barns").

of information.[36] In 2008, Facebook boasted storage of 40 billion photos.[37] The Library of Congress decided in 2010 to archive every public "tweet" generated on Twitter: about 170 billion tweets (and counting) in January 2013.[38]

Second, because the term also refers to the artificial intelligence applied to these huge data sets, the big data phenomenon also suggests a change in the way we understand our world. If conventional scientific research begins with a hypothesis or question that then shapes the collection of the relevant data, the big data phenomenon turns such conventions upside down. Because data is being collected and stored all of the time, research questions do not have to shape or limit data collection at all.[39] Researchers need not limit themselves to data sampling, either. Big data permits the study of a phenomenon where the set is nearly everything that is possible to study (another way of stating that we are approaching n=all).[40] The existence of these massive data sets permits sifting and resifting of the information therein for multiple purposes.[41] Thus, the Library of Congress's continuous collection of "tweets" has interested researchers with questions as diverse as the role of public responses to smoking ads, changes in investor sentiments, and real-time hurricane analysis.[42]

Such massive quantities of information also suggest that the very kinds of questions posed by researchers will be different in the big data context. With so much data available, Viktor Mayer-Schönberger and Kenneth Cukier argue that two conventions of traditional research—a working hypothesis and the search for causality—are no longer necessary given the insights that can be derived from correlations found in big data.[43] The existence of huge

36 See SAS, BIG DATA MEETS BIG DATA ANALYTICS 1 (2012), available at http://www.sas.com/resources/white-paper/wp_46345.pdf.

37 See Doug Beaver, 10 Billion Photos, FACEBOOK (Oct. 14, 2008, 6:03 PM), http://www.facebook.com/note.php?note_id=30695603919.

38 Erin Allen, Update on the Twitter Archive at the Library of Congress, LIBRARY OF CONGRESS BLOG (Jan. 4, 2013), http://blogs.loc.gov/loc/2013/01/update-on-the-twitter-archive-at-the-library-of-congress/.

39 Mayer-Schönberger and Cukier discuss how the combination of cheap and easy data storage with powerful analytic technology makes it possible to constantly store data for purposes that may not be immediately apparent. See MAYER-SCHÖNBERGER & CUKIER, supra note 10, at 98–106.

40 See id. at 26 ("In many areas ... a shift is taking place from collecting some data to gathering as much as possible, and if feasible, getting everything: N = all.").

41 See id. at 122 ("The crux of data's worth is its seemingly unlimited potential for reuse: its option value.").

42 Victor Luckerson, What the Library of Congress Plans to Do with All Your Tweets, TIME (Feb. 25, 2013), http://business.time.com/2013/02/25/what-the-library-of-congress-plans-to-do-with-all-your-tweets/.

43 See MAYER-SCHÖNBERGER & CUKIER, supra note 10, at 61 ("In a small-data world, because so little data tended to be available, both causal investigations and correlation analysis began with a hypothesis, which was then tested to be either falsified or verified. ... Today, with so much data around and more to come, such hypotheses are no longer crucial for correlational analysis.").

amounts of data permits research into correlations that don't require an underlying hypothesis. For instance, Google's mathematical models have identified the forty-five search terms (e.g. "medicine for cough and fever") most strongly identified with historical flu data.[44] The resulting Google Flu Trends has proven to be remarkably accurate in matching the historical surveillance data collected by the Centers for Disease Control.[45] Thus, we can predict new outbreaks of the flu simply by identifying correlations between Google search terms and the spread of seasonal flu.[46] These predictions are useful in their predictive value even though they provide no causal explanation, much in the same way that Amazon's algorithms can predict that you might like a product based on its analysis without caring why.[47] A key contribution of big data is the ability to find useful correlations within data sets not capable of analysis by ordinary human assessment.

II. Use of Big Data in Policing

Across the country, some police departments have taken notice that they stand to benefit from big data. While the use of big data in the private sector has raised concerns about consumer privacy, its use by the police raises even bigger questions about the limits of using data to justify surveillance, investigation, and detention by the police. This section discusses three of the most important developments in use of big data by the police: crime prediction, mass surveillance, and DNA databanks.

---

44   *See id.* at 2.

45   *See id.*; *see also* Miguel Helft, *Google Uses Searches to Track Flu's Spread*, N.Y. TIMES (Nov. 11, 2008), http://www.nytimes.com/2008/11/12/technology/internet/12flu.html (reporting that Google found "a strong correlation" between five years of its data and the C.D.C.'s reports of flu).

46   *Explore Flu Trends—United States*, GOOGLE.ORG, http://www.google.org/flutrends/us/#US (last visited Feb. 17, 2014). Google has done the same with dengue trends around the world. *Dengue Trends Around the World*, GOOGLE.ORG, http://www.google.org/denguetrends/intl/en_us/ (last visited Feb. 17, 2014). The same approach has been taken with information generated by Twitter. *See* ADAM SADILEK ET AL., ASS'N FOR THE ADVANCEMENT OF ARTIFICIAL INTELLIGENCE, MODELING SPREAD OF DISEASE FROM SOCIAL INTERACTIONS (2012), *available at* http://www.cs.rochester.edu/~sadilek/publications/Sadilek-Kautz-Silenzio_Modeling-Spread-of-Disease-from-Social-Interactions_ICWSM-12.pdf (last visited Feb. 17, 2014). Such big data analysis is not perfect, however. Google's algorithms were grossly inaccurate in winter of 2012–13 and predicted far more cases than the CDC counted. Part of the problem may be that the flu gained widespread media attention in 2012, which then increased the use of the same search terms that had better predictive value before. *See* Nick Bilton, *Disruption, Data Without Context Tells a Misleading Story*, N.Y. TIMES (Feb. 23, 2013), http://bits.blogs.nytimes.com/2013/02/24/disruptions-google-flu-trends-shows-problems-of-big-data-without-context/; Declan Butler, *When Google Got Flu Wrong*, 494 NATURE 155, 155–56 (2013), *available at* http://www.nature.com/news/when-google-got-flu-wrong-1.12413.

47   *Cf.* MAYER-SCHÖNBERGER & CUKIER, *supra* note 10, at 59 ("The correlations show *what*, not *why*, but ... knowing *what* is often good enough.") (emphasis in original).

A. Crime Prediction: Predictive Policing

Perhaps the most visible use of big data by police departments thus far has been predictive policing: the application of computer modeling to historical crime data to predict future criminal activity.[48] While the police have long tried to find patterns of criminal activity on which to focus their resources,[49] predictive policing permits the police to harness thousands of data points to forecast where crime is likely to happen. The most basic models rely on past crimes, but data sources can include factors as variable as payday schedules, seasonal variation, liquor store locations, and potential escape routes.[50]

What is new about predictive policing is not the use of quantitative data.[51] In the 1990s, the N.Y.P.D. ushered in an era of intelligence-based policing.[52] Under Commissioner Bill Bratton, the N.Y.P.D. introduced the now famous CompStat system[53]: weekly meetings at the N.Y.P.D. headquarters at which a revolving group of commanding officers around the city gave accountings of themselves for the recent crime data collected in their precinct.[54] By evaluating performance by the rise or fall of crime data within their precincts, CompStat meetings forced accountability upon commanding officers. Such data-driven policing spread to other departments around the United States when crime rates began to fall dramatically within New York City,[55] a result the police attributed to its reliance upon CompStat, along

---

48   *See* JENNIFER BACHNER, PREDICTIVE POLICING: PREVENTING CRIME WITH DATA AND ANALYTICS 14 (2013), *available at* http://www.businessofgovernment.org/sites/default/files/Predictive%20Policing.pdf ("The fundamental notion underlying the theory and practice of predictive policing is that we can make probabilistic inferences about future criminal activity based on existing data.").

49   *See id.* at 7 (observing that "quantitative crime analysis spans centuries").

50   *See id.* at 16.

51   *See* WALTER L. PERRY ET AL., PREDICTIVE POLICING: THE ROLE OF CRIME FORECASTING IN LAW ENFORCEMENT OPERATIONS 2 (2013) ("The use of statistical and geospatial analyses to forecast crime levels has been around for decades."); Pearsall, *supra* note 8, at 18 (citing one police chief's skepticism that predictive policing is a break from older trends in intelligence based policing).

52   *See* BACHNER, *supra* note 48, at 6, 9 (noting that "predictive policing is viewed as one pillar of intelligence-led policing").

53   Bratton himself chronicled his tenure as Commissioner in his memoir *The Turnaround. See* WILLIAM BRATTON WITH PETER KNOBLER, THE TURNAROUND: HOW AMERICA'S TOP COP REVERSED THE CRIME EPIDEMIC (1998).

54   There are numerous accounts of the perceived innovation and success of the N.Y.P.D. during the 1990s. *See, e.g.*, VINCENT E. HENRY, THE COMPSTAT PARADIGM: MANAGEMENT ACCOUNTABILITY IN POLICING, BUSINESS AND THE PUBLIC SECTOR 17–18 (2003) (describing CompStat meetings as "intensive monthly performance evaluations for every commander of practically every operational unit in the agency"); ELI B. SILVERMAN, NYPD BATTLES CRIME: INNOVATIVE STRATEGIES IN POLICING 97–124 (1999) (describing development of CompStat meetings). In fact, some credit Bratton for thinking of a predictive policing model. *See* PERRY ET AL., *supra* note 51, at 4.

55   *See* BACHNER, *supra* note 48, at 9 (noting CompStat "has been adopted by nearly every law enforcement agency in the country").

with the adoption of "broken windows" policing[56] and aggressive stop and frisk tactics.[57] CompStat and similar programs inspired by it rely on the collection of crime statistics to inform police decision-making.[58]

The innovation of predictive policing is the application of artificial intelligence to such large data sets. CompStat relied heavily on the collection and display of past crime data; predictive policing applies computer analysis to similar information. The identification of future geographic *places* likely to be targeted by criminals has attracted the most attention. These predictive models all rely on well-established observations about the spatial distribution of criminal behavior. Crime is not found randomly across a city, but rather tends to fall within limited, and often very small, areas.[59] (Crime tends to be "lumpy.") For instance, researchers found that over a fourteen year period, about fifty percent of the crime in Seattle was limited to 4.5 percent of the city's street segments.[60] Based upon this connection between crime and place, computer models adopt different approaches towards the prediction of crime.

For instance, the Santa Cruz Police Department uses software that assumes that crime patterns follow a pattern similar to earthquake aftershocks.[61] The software applies a computer

---

56   "Broken windows" policing generally refers to a style of policing that focuses on minor offense enforcement on the assumption that such signs of disorder, if left unchecked, will lead to more serious crimes. *See* James Q. Wilson & George L. Kelling, *Broken Windows: The Police and Neighborhood Safety*, ATLANTIC MONTHLY, Mar. 1982, at 29, *available at* http://www.theatlantic.com/magazine/archive/1982/03/broken-windows/304465/.
57   More recently, however, the credit given to the use of CompStat by the N.Y.P.D. has been criticized. *See, e.g.*, David F. Greenberg, *Studying New York City's Crime Decline: Methodological Issues*, 31 JUST. Q. 154, 182 (2013) (concluding that there is an "absence of evidence pointing to large crime prevention effects in New York from [tactics including] CompStat. …"). And the stop and frisk policies of the N.Y.P.D. were eventually held to be unconstitutional. *See* Floyd v. City of New York, No. 08 Civ. 1034(SAS), 2013 WL 4046209 (S.D.N.Y. Aug. 12, 2013).
58   Of course, even knowing about these high crime areas might suggest future criminal activity taking place in the same place, but the identification of these areas does not involve prediction specifically. *See* Andrew Guthrie Ferguson, *Predictive Policing and Reasonable Suspicion*, 62 EMORY L.J. 259, 274 (2012).
59   *See, e.g.*, PERRY ET AL., *supra* note 51, at 2 ("[C]riminals tend to operate in their comfort zone. That is, they tend to commit the type of crimes that they have committed successfully in the past, generally close to the same time and location.").
60   Anthony A. Braga et al., *The Relevance of Micro Places to Citywide Robbery Trends: A Longitudinal Analysis of Robbery Incidents at Street Corners and Block Faces in Boston*, 48 J. RES. CRIME & DELINQ. 7, 10 (2011) (citing David L. Weisburd et al., *Trajectories of Crime at Places: A Longitudinal Study of Street Segments in the City of Seattle*, 42 CRIMINOLOGY 283 (2004)).
61   *See, e.g.*, Martin Kaste, *Can Software That Predicts Crime Pass Constitutional Muster?*, NPR (July 26, 2013, 4:55 PM), http://www.npr.org/2013/07/26/205835674/can-software-that-predicts-crime-pass-constitutional-muster (noting that the software creator "wanted to see if computers could model future crime the same way they model earthquake aftershocks. Turns out they can."). The software, designed by mathematicians and social scientists at UCLA, Santa Clara University, and U.C. Irvine, is called PredPol and is marketed to police departments. *See Policing Meets Big Data*, PREDPOL, http://www.predpol.com/about/ (last visited Feb. 17, 2014).

algorithm to a database representing five years' worth of crime data (including crime time, location, and type) to assess the likelihood of future crime occurring in the geographic areas within the city, narrowed to squares measured 500 by 500 feet (Figure 6.1.1).[62] Prior to each shift, Santa Cruz police officers receive information identifying 15 such squares with the highest probability of crime, and are encouraged—though not required—to provide greater attention to these areas.[63] After its experimental introduction in 2011, the Santa Cruz Police Department reported a significant drop in burglaries when compared to a period prior to the adoption of predictive policing.[64] Similar experiments relying upon this software are being conducted by the police in Los Angeles and Seattle.[65]

Other approaches may consider additional factors other than the timing and location of past crimes. Risk terrain theory, for example, looks at the social, physical, and behavioral factors that make it more likely certain areas will be targeted by crime.[67] The resulting risk terrain map, which gives each factor its own mapping "layer," is a composite map that assigns a risk assessment for all of the factors

FIGURE 6.1.1   Predictive Policing Map[66]

62   *See* Zach Friend, *Predictive Policing: Using Technology to Reduce Crime*, FBI LAW ENFORCEMENT BULL. (Apr. 9, 2013), http://www.fbi.gov/stats-services/publications/law-enforcement-bulletin/2013/April/predictive-policing-using-technology-to-reduce-crime.

63   *See* BACHNER, *supra* note 48, at 25.

64   *See id.* at 26. At least one investigative article has raised doubts, however, as to whether PredPol actually delivers on its claims about reducing crime. *See* Darwin Bond-Graham & Ali Winston, *All Tomorrow's Crimes: The Future of Policing Looks a Lot Like Good Branding*, S.F. WEEKLY (Oct. 30, 2013), http://www.sfweekly.com/2013-10-30/news/predpol-sfpd-predictive-policing-compstat-lapd/full/ (suggesting that PredPol's creators have been "most successful [with] its marketing algorithms").

65   *See, e.g.*, David Talbot, *L.A. Cops Embrace Crime-Predicting Algorithm*, MIT TECH. REV. (July 2, 2012), http://www.technologyreview.com/news/428354/la-cops-embrace-crime-predicting-algorithm/ (describing successful use of Predpol software in Foothill precinct of Los Angeles); Sengupta, *supra* note 5 (describing Seattle Police Department's use of PredPol software for property crimes).

66   *Looking Ahead, Not in the Rear View Mirror*, PREDPOL, http://www.predpol.com/technology/ (last visited Feb. 17, 2014).

67   67. *See, e.g.*, Leslie W. Kennedy et al., *Risk Clusters, Hotspots, and Spatial Intelligence: Risk Terrain Modeling as an Algorithm for Police Resource Allocations*, 27 J. QUANTITATIVE CRIMINOLOGY 339, 342–43 (2011).

associated with criminal activity.[68] For example, police in Morris County, New Jersey, use five factors for their risk terrain modeling: (1) past burglaries; (2) the residential location of individuals recently arrested for property crimes; (3) the proximity to major highways; (4) the geographic concentration of young men; and (5) the location of apartment complexes and hotels.[69]

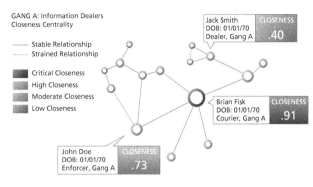

FIGURE 6.1.2   Hypothetical Social Network Analysis[76]

Morris County police attribute significant drops in violent and property crime to a reliance on risk terrain modeling.[70]

A second type of predictive technology focuses on the application of algorithms to social media in order to identify likely criminality based on the role an *individual* plays within a social network.[71] This social network analysis[72] begins with the assumption that social networks undergird many crimes: an illegal drug-dealing network may loosely follow the hierarchical structure of a legitimate business, with suppliers, distributors, buyers, and financiers.[73] (Indeed, this type of analysis has its roots in the military study of insurgent groups abroad.[74]) The algorithms used in social network software can help police visualize the density of connections an individual has within a social network. These connections might take the form of exchanges, communications, family ties, participation in crimes, or affiliations with an organization.[75]

---

68   *See id.* at 343.

69   Jeffrey S. Paul & Thomas M. Joiner, *Integration of Centralized Intelligence with Geographic Information Systems: A Countywide Initiative*, Geography & Pub. Safety, Oct. 2011, at 5, 7.

70   *See id.* at 7 (noting that since 2007, when the county created an intelligence crime task force, "the total crime index in the county has decreased by 11%, violent crime by 21%, and property crime by 7%").

71   IBM offers, for instance, a social media analytics tool that police departments can use to monitor Facebook and Twitter activity. *See* Somini Sengupta, *Privacy Fears Grow as Cities Increase Surveillance*, N.Y. Times (Oct. 13, 2013), http://www.nytimes.com/2013/10/14/technology/privacy-fears-as-surveillance-grows-in-cities.html.

72   Social network analysis should not be confused with police surveillance and infiltration of social media sites such as Facebook and Twitter, which have also proven to be valuable investigative tools.

73   *See* Bachner, *supra note* 48, at 22–23.

74   *See* Philip Ball, *Unmasking Organised Crime Networks with Data*, BBC (July 9, 2013), http://www.bbc.com/future/story/20130709-unmask-crime-networks-with-data/1.

75   *See* Bachner, *supra note* 48, at 23.

76   Aaron Lester, *Police Clicking into Crimes Using New Software*, Boston Globe (Mar. 18, 2013), http://www.bostonglobe.com/business/2013/03/17/police-intelligence-one-click-away/DzzDbrwdiNkjNMA1159ybM/"story.html (describing provisional use of new Nucleik software within Springfield, Massachusetts gang unit).

When used by a police department, social network analysis might be used to identify a "central node": a person with a high degree of "connectivity within the network" (Figure 6.1.2).[77] While traditional police work might easily identify leaders within a criminal organization, social network analysis can identify those with influence or those who transmit information within the group quickly and yet whose roles are not otherwise apparent.[78] The software can even reveal deliberately concealed affiliations. Even if an individual suspected of being part of a criminal organization does not admit his affiliation, social network software can calculate the probability of his membership.[79]

How does such software help police investigations? The identification of a highly "networked" individual could permit the police to infiltrate an organization in the most efficient way, or to identify a hidden source of influence within an organization for further investigation.[80] Also, by revealing hidden relationships among groups, police can disrupt subterfuges by rival criminal organizations. In a gang war, one group likely to retaliate may not do so directly, for fear of being targeted by the police, and instead may enlist an ally gang.[81] Social network analysis can help understand which alliances might require heightened surveillance.[82]

B. Mass Surveillance: Domain Awareness Systems

If predictive policing harnesses data to predict the future, computer surveillance systems help police create a software-enhanced picture of the present, using thousands of data points from multiple sources within a city. As with predictive policing, computer enhanced mass surveillance grows out of other policing techniques.[83] While surveillance has long been an essential tool of the police, what has changed is its supporting technology. Sophisticated yet inexpensive, the surveillance equipment used by the police today produces enormous amounts of information, often too much for the police to use in an efficient way without the help of technology. The N.Y.P.D., for instance, has a database of 16 million license plates

---

77   *See* BACHNER, *supra* note 48, at 23.

78   *See* Lester, *supra* note 76.

79   *See* Ball, *supra* note 74.

80   *See* BACHNER, *supra* note 48, at 22–24.

81   *See generally id.*

82   *See* Ball, *supra* note 74.

83   *Cf.* Jack M. Balkin, *The Constitution in the National Surveillance State*, 93 MINN. L. REV. 1, 3 (2008) ("Government's increasing use of surveillance and data mining is a predictable result of accelerating developments in information technology.").

captured from its license plate readers, along with the locations of where the plates were photographed.[84]

The N.Y.P.D. has responded to this big data problem by creating a software program with Microsoft. Dubbed a "domain awareness system" ("DAS"),[85] the software collects and analyzes information around the clock within New York City from sources as disparate as the city's 3,000 public surveillance cameras,[86] over 200 automatic license plate readers,[87] more than 2,000 radiation sensors,[88] and information from police databases.[89] The software's mapping features permit the police to see and understand the information in a way that was not possible before. Located within the N.Y.P.D.'s lower Manhattan Security Initiative Command Center, the Domain Awareness System's operators can quickly use the software to identify potential threats.[90]

This system gives the police real-time access to information that can reveal connections between persons, items, and places in ways that may not be obvious to individual crime analysts. The DAS employs video analytic software designed to detect threats, such as unattended bags.[91] The N.Y.P.D. claims that the DAS can track where a car associated with a suspect is located, and where it has been in the past days, weeks, or months.[92] The DAS can

---

84   Joseph Goldstein, *Weekly Police Briefing Offers Snapshot of Department and Its Leader*, N.Y. Times (Feb. 10, 2013), http://www.nytimes.com/2013/02/11/nyregion/weekly-briefing-provides-lengthy-snapshot-of-kelly-and-nypd.html.

85   Matt Sledge, *NYPD License Plate Readers Will Be Able to Track Every Car Entering Manhattan*, Huffington Post (Mar. 13, 2013, 5:08 PM), http://www.huffingtonpost.com/2013/03/13/nypd-license-plate-readers_n_2869627.html.

86   Cara Buckley, *New York Plans Surveillance Veil for Downtown*, N.Y. Times (July 9, 2007), http://www.nytimes.com/2007/07/09/nyregion/09ring.html; Mark Duell, *The Extraordinary 'Ring of Steel' Around Ground Zero: NYPD Steps Up Dirty Bomb Threat Protection with $200M Project*, Daily Mail (July 29, 2011), http://www.dailymail.co.uk/news/article-2020266/NYPD-steps-dirty-bomb-radiation-threat-protection-200m-Manhattan-project.html.

87   Al Baker, *Camera Scans of Car Plates Are Reshaping Police Inquiries*, N.Y. Times (Apr. 11, 2011), http://www.nytimes.com/2011/04/12/nyregion/12plates.html?pagewanted=all&_r=0 (observing that in 2011, the N.Y.P.D. had 238 license plate readers, 130 of them mobile). In March 2013, Police Commissioner Raymond Kelly announced plans to install license plate readers in every lane of traffic that serve as exists and entrances to Manhattan, all of which would be linked to the domain awareness system. *See* Sledge, *supra* note 85.

88   Two thousand belt-mounted mobile radiation detectors are carried by N.Y.P.D. officers. *See* Duell, *supra* note 86. The N.Y.P.D. also plans to use very sensitive radiation scanners to detect the presence of concealed weapons on individuals in high crime areas. *See* Slate V Staff, *NYPD Plans Public Radiation Scanners to Detect Guns*, Slate (Jan. 24, 2013), http://www.slate.com/blogs/trending/2013/01/24/nypd_radiation_scanners_gun_detectors_to_be_set_up_in_public_spaces.html.

89   *See* Sledge, *supra* note 85.

90   Duell, *supra* note 86.

91   *Id.*

92   *See, e.g.*, Press Release, Mayor Bloomberg, Police Commissioner Kelly and Microsoft Unveil New, State-of-the-Art Law Enforcement Technology That Aggregates and Analyzes Existing Public Safety Data in

also check license plate numbers, compare them to watch lists, and provide the police with immediate access to any criminal history associated with the car owner.[93] In November 2013, the N.Y.P.D. relied on its DAS to watch nearly every portion of the New York City Marathon route, a potential terrorist target after the Boston Marathon bombings in April 2013.[94]

While New York City has received the most attention for its high-tech approach to surveillance, other cities have shown interest in these mass surveillance systems. Oakland, California, a much smaller city in comparison but plagued with a high crime rate,[95] has decided to launch a Domain Awareness Center[96] poised to collect and analyze surveillance data "from gunshot-detection sensors in the barrios of East Oakland to license plate readers mounted on police cars patrolling the city's upscale hills."[97] The resulting analysis will be displayed on a bank of giant monitors providing Oakland police with a unified visual representation of the very different sources: police and fire dispatch systems, gunshot detectors, license plate readers, private alarm detection programs, and social media feeds.[98]

Real Time to Provide a Comprehensive View of Potential Threats and Criminal Activity (Aug. 8, 2012), *available at* http://www.nyc.gov/portal/site/nycgov/menuitem.c0935b9a57bb4ef3daf2f1c701c789a0/index.jsp?pageID=mayor_press_release&catID=1194&doc_name=http%3A%2F%2Fwww.nyc.gov%2Fhtml%2Fom%2Fhtml%2F2012b%2Fpr291-12.html&cc=unused1978&rc=1194&ndi=1.

93   Rocco Paranscandola & Tina Moore, *NYPD Unveils New $40 Million Super Computer System that Uses Data from Network of Cameras, License Plate Readers and Crime Reports*, N.Y. Daily News (Aug. 8, 2012, 8:50 PM), http://www.nydailynews.com/new-york/nypd-unveils-new-40-million-super-computer-system-data-network-cameras-license-plate-readers-crime-reports-article-1.1132135.

94   *See* Michael Schwirtz, *After Boston Bombings, New York Police Plan Tight Security at Marathon*, N.Y. Times (Nov. 1, 2013), http://www.nytimes.com/2013/11/02/sports/video-surveillance-to-be-a-key-component-of-marathon-security.html?_r=0.

95   Forbes named Oakland the third most dangerous city in America in 2012 with a population between 100,000 and 499,000. *See The 10 Most Dangerous U.S. Cities*, Forbes, http://www.forbes.com/pictures/mlj45jgg-j/3-oakland/ (last visited Feb. 17, 2014) (stating that Oakland's violent crime rate is "1,683 per 100,000 residents").
96   The project was initially sought by the Port of Oakland, but expanded to include the city of Oakland itself. *See* Steven Tavares, *Big Brother in Oakland? There Might Be an App Coming For That*, EBCitizen (July 10, 2013), http://www.ebcitizen.com/2013/07/big-brother-in-oakland-there-might-be.html?utm_source=feedburner&utm_medium=email&utm_campaign=Feed%3A+EastbaycitizenBreakingNewsPoliticsLife+%28EastBayCitizen+%7C+Breaking+News+Politics+ Life%29.

97   Sengupta, *supra* note 71.

98   Ali Winston, *Oakland Surveillance Center Raises Concerns*, SFGate (July 17, 2013, 9:46 PM), http://www.sfgate.com/crime/article/Oakland-surveillance-center-raises-concerns-4671708.php. In February 2014, however, Oakland officials delayed voting on a contract to build its DAS after local residents raised concerns about privacy. *See* Associated Press, *Oakland Delays Vote on Surveillance System*, Wash. Times (Feb. 19, 2014), http://www.washingtontimes.com/news/2014/feb/19/oakland-delays-vote-on-surveillance-system/.

C. Genetic Big Data: DNA Databanks

Perhaps less obvious but no less important a big data matter is the collection of DNA for criminal justice databases, which as of June 2013 contained DNA profiles for 10.7 million offenders and 1.7 million arrestees.[99] The United States has used this information to amass the largest DNA database in the world.[100] Police agencies around the country rely on CODIS—the shorthand for the system that links information among the different DNA databases around the country[101]—to match crime scene samples with offender or arrestee DNA profiles.[102] The millions of DNA samples now accessible by the police present another potential use of big data.

The rapid growth of American DNA databases can be attributed to the ever-expanding categories of those deemed eligible for compulsory DNA collection. While the first state DNA databases collected samples only from violent felons or felony sex offenders, today every state collects DNA from all convicted felons.[103] A majority of states collect DNA from those convicted of misdemeanor sex offenses.[104] In 2012, New York became the first "all crimes

---

99 *See CODIS—NDIS Statistics*, FBI, http://www.fbi.gov/about-us/lab/biometric-analysis/codis/ndis-statistics (last visited Feb. 17, 2014).

100 *See* Solomon Moore, *F.B.I. and States Vastly Expand DNA Databases*, N.Y. TIMES (Apr. 18, 2009), http://www.nytimes.com/2009/04/19/us/19DNA.html (noting that CODIS is "the largest [database] in the world"). The U.K., however, has the distinction of having the largest portion of its population—about ten percent—in its DNA database. *See, e.g.*, Jill Lawless, *Spread of DNA Databases Sparks Ethical Concerns*, ASSOCIATED PRESS (July 12, 2013, 8:50 AM), http://bigstory.ap.org/article/spread-dna-databases-sparks-ethical-concerns.

101 Although CODIS specifically refers to the software that links DNA databases around the country for information sharing purposes, it is also used generically as a term to describe the American DNA database system more generally. *See Frequently Asked Questions (FAQs) on the CODIS Program and the National DNA Index System*, FBI, http://www.fbi.gov/about-us/lab/biometric-analysis/codis/codis-and-ndis-fact-sheet (last visited Feb. 17, 2014).

102 *See, e.g., id.* (describing how CODIS would be used in a hypothetical sexual assault case). CODIS permits states and the federal government to upload and compare DNA profiles on the National DNA Index System (NDIS). *See id.* While state laws specify the types of profiles that can be included in state databases, federal law determines which DNA profiles can be stored and shared at the national level. *See* 42 U.S.C. § 14132(a) (2006). Many resources provide helpful explanatory information on DNA and how it is used in criminal investigations. *E.g.*, SHELDON KRIMSKY & TANIA SIMONCELLI, GENETIC JUSTICE: DNA DATA BANKS, CRIMINAL INVESTIGATIONS, AND CIVIL LIBERTIES 3–27 (2010); *DNA Evidence Basics*, NAT'L INST. JUST. (Aug. 9, 2012), http://www.nij.gov/topics/forensics/evidence/dna/basics/pages/welcome.aspx.

103 *See* NATHAN JAMES, CONG. RESEARCH SERV., R41800, DNA TESTING IN CRIMINAL JUSTICE: BACKGROUND, CURRENT LAW, GRANTS, AND ISSUES 7 (2012).

104 *See id.*

state."[105] Nearly every person convicted of a crime in New York, regardless of its gravity, will be required to submit a DNA sample for inclusion in the state's DNA database.[106]

The reliance of states upon arrestee DNA collection appears to be following a similar path. In 1997, Louisiana became the first state to authorize the collection of DNA from some categories of arrestees.[107] Today, twenty-eight more states and the federal government have followed Louisiana's lead in requiring some categories of arrestees to provide DNA samples.[108] The Supreme Court's 2013 decision in *Maryland v. King*[109] upholding compulsory arrestee DNA collection[110] will likely mean that the practice will expand to many other states.[111]

How do DNA databases raise big data questions? First, the emerging and controversial use of familial matches is in fact a big data issue. Based on the assumption that close relatives share more genetic information than unrelated individuals, familial searches are searches of DNA databases that look for profiles that only partially match the thirteen STR markers[112] on a DNA profile.[113] (Such a search might take place, for instance, if a CODIS search yields no identical match.[114]) Familial searches take advantage of the big data set that is CODIS: the

---

105   *New York DNA Database: Governor Cuomo Signs 'All Crimes' DNA Testing Into Law*, HUFFINGTON POST (Mar. 3, 2012, 10:22 AM), http://www.huffingtonpost.com/2012/03/20/new-york-dna-database-governor-cuomo-all-crimes-dna-testing_n_1366624.html.

106   *See id.* (noting minor exemption "for those convicted of possession of a small amount of marijuana as long as they have no prior convictions").

107   *See* Julie Samuels et al., *Collecting DNA From Arrestees: Implementation Lessons*, NAT'L INST. JUST. J., June 2012, at 18, 19, *available at* https://www.ncjrs.gov/pdffiles1/nij/238484.pdf.

108   *See DNA Arrestee Laws*, NAT'L CONFERENCE OF ST. LEGISLATURES, http://www.ncsl.org/research/civil-and-criminal-justice/dna-arrestee-laws.aspx (last visited Feb. 17, 2014) (reporting that in May 2013, Nevada became the most recent state to require DNA samples from all felony arrestees).

109   _U.S._, 133 S. Ct. 1958 (2013).

110   *Id.* at 1980.

111   The Katie Sepich Enhanced DNA Collection Act provides federal funding for those states that wish to establish arrestee DNA collection programs. *See* Katie Sepich Enhanced DNA Collection Act of 2012, Pub. L. No. 112-253, § 3, 126 Stat. 2407 (2013). For further commentary on the decision, see Elizabeth E. Joh, Maryland v. King: *Policing and Genetic Privacy*, 11 OHIO ST. J. CRIM. L. 281 (2013).

112   The thirteen STR markers refer to the thirteen places on the human chromosome where there is high variability. These identification markers provide law enforcement with a unique identifier for everyone who provides a DNA sample. *See The FBI and DNA*, FBI (Nov. 28, 2011), http://www.fbi.gov/news/stories/2011/november/dna_112811.

113   *See, e.g.*, Erin Murphy, *Relative Doubt: Familial Searches of DNA Databases*, 109 MICH. L. REV. 291, 297–300 (2010) (describing mechanics of familial searches). How those genetically related to the sought after offender turn up depends on a number of factors, including whether a jurisdiction intentionally searches the database for partial matches or whether such matches turn up as the result of a search because the parameters of the search permitted less than an identical match between the sample and the DNA profile. *See id.* at 299.

114   *Id.* at 297–98.

capability to search millions of individual DNA profiles.[115]Additional testing on DNA samples may be necessary to confirm potential matches.[116]

Similar to other uses of big data, a familial search repurposes (genetic) data collected for another reason (identical matches).[117] Critics of familial searches have focused on issues of privacy and equity, including the concern that familial searches will draw disproportionate attention to racial and ethnic minorities who may be unfairly targeted for genetic surveillance.[118] Yet if we think of familial searches as big data problems, we might also make some useful connections to other areas in which data is being amassed in large quantities for one purpose and later used for another. For instance, policies on familial searches might follow principles of informational privacy used in other database contexts, including limited later analysis to the specific original purpose for which the information was collected.[119]

This potential for repurposing is not limited to familial searches of CODIS, either. A profile in the national DNA database is a string of numbers referring to the thirteen STR locations.[120] Most courts analyzing Fourth Amendment challenges to the compulsory collection of DNA have focused only on the DNA *profile* to deny that their collection and storage by the government raises serious privacy concerns.[121] What is often ignored, however, is that

---

115   *See id.* at 296. In 2008, California became the first state to formally authorize intentional partial matches, or "familial" searches. *Id.* at 293.

116   Matching STRs on the Y chromosomes, in addition to a partial match on the CODIS loci, can show how closely related two men are through their male ancestors. This Y-STR typing can show whether two men share the same genetic father or paternal grandfather. *See, e.g.,* Michael Chamberlain, *Familial DNA Searching: A Proponent's Perspective,* CRIM. JUST., Spring 2012, at 18, *available at* http://www.americanbar.org/content/dam/ aba/publications/criminal_justice_magazine/sp12_dna_search_proponents.authcheckdam.pdf (explaining basics of California familial match policy).

117   *See supra* Part I.

118   *See, e.g.,* Murphy, *supra* note 113, at 304 ("Familial searches should be forbidden because they embody the very presumptions that our constitutional and evidentiary rules have long endeavored to counteract: guilt by association, racial discrimination, propensity, and even biological determinism. They are akin to adopting a policy to collect and store the DNA of otherwise database-ineligible persons, solely because they share a blood relation with a convicted person. ..."); Sonia M. Suter, *All in the Family: Privacy and DNA Familial Searching,* 23 HARV. J.L. & TECH. 309, 368–70 (2010).

119   *See, e.g.,* David Lazer & Viktor Mayer-Schönberger, *Statutory Frameworks for Regulating Information Flows: Drawing Lessons for the DNA Data Banks from Other Government Data Systems,* 34 J.L. MED. & ETHICS 366, 372 (2006).

120   *See, e.g.,* Moore, *supra* note 100 (describing CODIS profile as "numerical sequence").

121   *See, e.g.,* Maryland v. King, U.S., 133 S. Ct. 1958, 1979 (2013) (observing that "the CODIS loci come from noncoding parts of the DNA that do not reveal the genetic traits of the arrestee").

these numbers are generated from biological samples.[122] These samples pose rich data possibilities; information that could be analyzed in different ways for a variety of purposes.[123] Indeed, David Lazer and Viktor Mayer-Schönberger argue that the very existence of these DNA samples "*invites* re-purposing at a later stage."[124]

At the moment, however, practical and legal barriers bar this possibility.[125] Although state laws vary with regard to storage, retention, and disclosure requirements,[126] federal law imposes conditions on those samples used to generate profiles for CODIS. For instance, federal law requires that all samples used for CODIS profiles are subject to disclosure only to "criminal justice agencies for law enforcement identification purposes," "in judicial proceedings," "for criminal defense purposes," and for a "population statistics database, identification research and protocol development purposes, or for quality control purposes."[127] At the same time,

---

122   *See, e.g.*, Suter, *supra* note 118, at 331 ("Courts often minimize or fail to address the fact that the collection of DNA samples involves two privacy intrusions: the actual collection of biological samples and the retention of samples that contain one's genetic information.").

123   Scholars and judges have expressed a wide range of opinions on whether privacy interests are truly threatened by DNA samples held by the government. *Compare* N. Van Camp & K. Dierickx, *The Retention of Forensic DNA Samples: A Socio-Ethical Evaluation of Current Practices in the EU*, 34 J. Med. Ethics 606, 606 (2008), *and* Tania Simoncelli & Barry Steinhardt, *California's Proposition 69: A Dangerous Precedent for Criminal DNA Databases*, 33 J.L. Med. & Ethics 279, 284 (2005) ("While law enforcement authorities would like us to believe that the samples will never be used for anything besides catching criminals, an unlimited span of improper uses remain plausible so long as those samples are retained."), *and* Suter, *supra* note 118, at 335 ("[W]e should be wary of [sample retention] given its substantial threat to privacy and civil liberties."), *with* David H. Kaye, *A Fourth Amendment Theory for Arrestee DNA and Other Biometric Databases*, 15 U. Pa. J. Const. L. 1095, 1155–58 (2013) (expressing extreme skepticism that DNA samples will ever be used beyond biometric identification).

124   Lazer & Mayer-Schönberger, *supra* note 119, at 372 (emphasis added); *see also* Lawless, *supra* note 100 (quoting one supporter of genetic databases as acknowledging "[t]here is an argument to be made that because that biological sample exists, the government could go back and do other things with it that are not authorized by the law").

125   These legal barriers, however, do not apply to the emerging issue of "offline" or "rogue" DNA databases that are being established by local law enforcement agencies that have no intention of sharing the information with CODIS. *See, e.g.*, Joseph Goldstein, *Police Agencies Are Assembling Records of DNA*, N.Y. Times, June 13, 2013, at A1 ("These local databases operate under their own rules, providing the police much more leeway than state and federal regulations.").

126   *See, e.g.*, Sarah B. Berson, *Debating DNA Collection*, Nat'l Inst. Just. J., Nov. 2009, at 9, 11, *available at* https://www.ncjrs.gov/pdffiles1/nij/228383.pdf ("State laws … vary with regard to how samples may be used beyond law enforcement and quality control purposes.").

127   *See* 42 U.S.C. § 14132(b)(3) (2006). Some have suggested, however, that a "criminal justice purpose" could be broadly construed to permit law enforcement agencies to analyze samples for a variety of purposes beyond simple matches to crime scene evidence. *See, e.g.*, Suter, *supra* note 118, at 336.

most state laws contemplate indefinite retention of most DNA samples.[128] Justifications for indefinite DNA sample retention include the need to identify potential sample contamination or mix-ups, to implement changes in the technology used to analyze samples, and to provide lab quality assurance.[129]

For the now, practical barriers also bar comprehensive analysis of the millions of samples collected for criminal justice purposes. While human genome sequencing is vastly cheaper today than it was a few years ago, it likely remains prohibitively costly for states to undertake on a massive scale.[130] These practical and legal impediments may, however, change one day. As technological capabilities change, costs decrease, and a greater understanding of genetic information emerges, the use of DNA databases will raise serious questions for lawmakers about the appropriate balance of big data analysis and privacy protections.[131]

III. How Big Data Challenges Fourth Amendment Analysis

These evolving areas raise new questions about how best to regulate the use of big data by the police. In particular, they arise from three characteristics of big data: the use of artificial intelligence, the scale of data storage, and the repurposing of collected data. This section considers some of the difficult questions that judges and lawmakers will face.

---

128   *See, e.g.*, JAMES, *supra* note 103, at 5; Mark A. Rothstein & Meghan K. Talbott, *The Expanding Use of DNA in Law Enforcement: What Role for Privacy?*, 34 J.L. MED. & ETHICS 153, 158 (2006) ("There is no national policy on sample retention, but in almost every state the samples are retained indefinitely."). Many of these observations have relied upon a 2005 study by the American Society of Law, Medicine and Ethics. *See* SETH AXELRAD, AM. SOC'Y OF L., MED. & ETHICS, SURVEY OF STATE DNA DATABASE STATUTES, http://www.aslme.org/dna_04/grid/guide.pdf (last visited Feb. 17, 2014).

129   M. Dawn Herkenham, *Retention of Offender DNA Samples Necessary to Ensure and Monitor Quality of Forensic DNA Efforts: Appropriate Safeguards Exist to Protect the DNA Samples from Misuse*, 34 J.L. MED. & ETHICS 380, 381–82 (2006) (Herkenham was the chief of the FBI unit responsible for implementing the NDIS); *see also* JOHN M. BUTLER, FUNDAMENTALS OF FORENSIC DNA TYPING 280–81 (2009) (noting that samples should be preserved for quality control and for "technology advancements in the future" regarding new genetic markers or assays).

130   In the years since the human genome was first sequenced, the cost of sequencing has fallen dramatically, from nearly $100 million in 2001 to less than $6,000 in 2013. The National Human Genome Research Institute tracks the costs of genome sequencing. *See* K.A. Wetterstrand, *DNA Sequencing Costs: Data from the NHGRI Genome Sequencing Program (GSP)*, NAT'L HUMAN GENOME RES. INST., http://www.genome.gov/sequencing-costs/ (last visited Feb. 17, 2014).

131   *See, e.g.*, Phil Reilly, *Legal and Public Policy Issues in DNA Forensics*, 2 NATURE REVIEWS GENETICS 313, 317 (2001) (suggesting establishment of "a permanent commission to oversee [DNA databanks], which could review and monitor all requests to use samples for purposes other than forensic identification").

A. Human Judgment and Police Suspicion

While popular accounts misleadingly suggest that predictive policing involves police decision-making *controlled* by computers,[132] even partial reliance on artificial intelligence does raise important Fourth Amendment questions. Police are using predictive policing software to direct them to places where they believe there is a high likelihood of criminal activity. Having been directed there by computer analysis, the police must then determine whether any persons located there warrant further investigation. What role should artificial intelligence and human judgment play in Fourth Amendment individualized suspicion?

At a minimum, ordinary investigative detentions by the police require reasonable suspicion[133] based on a totality of the circumstances.[134] The Supreme Court's decisions have permitted the police to formulate reasonable suspicion based not only on their own personal observations, but also on other information, including fellow officers,[135] tips (even anonymous ones),[136] and sometimes even on determinations that particular geographic locations may be labeled as "high crime areas."[137] In particular, tips relied upon by the police must be sufficiently particularized to an individual, in some part predictive of future activity, and corroborated by the observation of the police themselves.[138]

The question here is whether predictive software based on historical crime data is similar to other uses of third party information that have already been held to support a reasonable suspicion determination.[139] Imagine that such software directs the police to a city block to

---

132   *See, e.g.*, Perry et al., *supra* note 51, at 115–16 ("Although much of news coverage promotes the meme that predictive policing is a crystal ball, these algorithms simply predict risks.").

133   Terry v. Ohio, 392 U.S. 1, 20–21 (1968).

134   Alabama v. White, 496 U.S. 325, 330 (1990) ("Reasonable suspicion … is dependent upon both the content of information possessed by police and its degree of reliability. Both factors—quantity and quality—are considered in the 'totality of the circumstances—the whole picture' that must be taken into account when evaluating whether there is reasonable suspicion." (citation omitted)).

135   *Cf.* United States v. Ventresca, 380 U.S. 102, 111 (1965) ("Observations of fellow officers of the Government engaged in a common investigation are plainly a reliable basis for a warrant applied for by one of their number.").

136   Illinois v. Gates, 462 U.S. 213, 244–46 (1983).

137   Illinois v. Wardlow, 528 U.S. 119, 124 (2000).

138   *See, e.g.*, *Gates*, 462 U.S. at 245–46 (noting that anonymous tip "contained a range of details relating … to future actions of third parties ordinarily not easily predicted"); Florida v. J.L., 529 U.S. 266, 271 (2000) (noting that the tip in the case "provided no predictive information and therefore left the police without means to test the informant's knowledge or credibility"); 2 Wayne R. LaFave, Search & Seizure § 3.3f (5th ed. 2012) ("[I]t seems wise in light of subsequent events to read *Gates* to mean that corroboration of part of an anonymous informant's information will constitute a sufficient substitute for directly-established veracity and basis of knowledge *only* if the corroborated events are in and of themselves quite suspicious.").

139   Professor Andrew Ferguson was among the first to recognize the Fourth Amendment challenges raised by the adoption of predictive policing programs. *See* Ferguson, *supra* note 58, at 305–12 (discussing these analogies).

look for property crime, and they observe activity that by itself may not appear obviously suspicious, such as carrying a duffel bag, or peering in windows.[140] A probabilistic determination is not exactly like an informant's tip, particularly since predictive software provides assessments about geographic *areas* and not persons.[141] Nevertheless, a court might analogize computerized predictions to informant-based predictions about specific places—such as drug houses and hourly motels—to add to the reasonable suspicion assessment.[142] While likely not sufficient on its own to provide justification for a stop (because of its lack of specificity with regard to persons), such predictions could form the basis of police observation and corroboration.[143]

So long as predictive software is not the sole justification used by police, courts are likely to accept its place within the reasonable suspicion analysis. If, for instance, courts were to borrow assessments of credibility and veracity from the informant context,[144] predictive software may provide more justification than an anonymous informant. The assumptions and inputs of such software, after all, are capable of verification.[145] Indeed, to the extent that the Supreme Court has emphasized that the reasonable suspicion determination is to be objective,[146] reliance on a computer analysis of crime data is arguably more objective than an inference made by an officer or a tip provided by a third party. Software with a demonstrated history of successfully predicting high crime areas based on verifiable crime data is likely to be a highly persuasive factor in the reasonable suspicion formulation.

---

140   *See id.* at 309 (citing example).

141   Because such programs only make predictions about areas where crime is likely to happen, it would seem more difficult to justify probable cause in the predictive policing analysis, although certainly many stops can ripen into full blown arrests once more information about the suspect is made known to the police during the course of a stop.

142   *See* Ferguson, *supra* note 58, at 306–07.

143   *See id.* at 310 (observing that "a common theme in the Fourth Amendment" analysis of reasonable suspicion is "[c]orroboration of individual actions").

144   While the Court in *Illinois v. Gates* adopted a totality of the circumstances tests for probable cause, it nevertheless reaffirmed that these factors continued to be "all highly relevant" and "should be understood [to] illuminate the commonsense, practical question" of probable cause. *See* 462 U.S. 213, 230 (1983). The same can be said of the reasonable suspicion standard as well. *See* Alabama v. White, 496 U.S. 325, 330 (1990) ("Reasonable suspicion is a less demanding standard than probable cause not only in the sense that reasonable suspicion can be established with information that is different in quantity or content than that required to establish probable cause, but also in the sense that reasonable suspicion can arise from information that is less reliable than that required to show probable cause.").

145   *Cf.* Ferguson, *supra* note 58, at 307 (noting that "an objective, well-functioning computer program seems more reliable than your typical police informant").

146   *See, e.g.,* United States v. Cortez, 449 U.S. 411, 417–18 (1981) ("[In an investigative detention] officers must have a particularized and objective basis for suspecting the particular person stopped of criminal activity.").

Indeed, predictive software may remove some of the problems raised by the types of information used. Informants, particularly anonymous ones, can have questionable motivations in aiding the police.[147] In addition, most courts are highly deferential to generalized police judgments of what constitutes a "high-crime area."[148] Software that eliminates undesirable biases and requires quantitative precision can introduce more fairness into the police decision-making process.[149]

Some caveats remain, however. First, no predictive policing program is entirely objective. The basic building blocks of a predictive software program necessarily involve human discretion.[150] The assumptions underlying any method of crime prediction rely upon the decision to choose one model of risk prediction over another. The data used to build the models will depend on discretionary judgments about the types of crimes used for prediction, and the type of information used to predict those crimes. Should a police department focus on burglaries; and if so, how are burglaries to be measured? For example, reliance on arrest rates is surely problematic[151] because arrests themselves are discretionary decisions that, if used as the basis to justify more attention, may simply reinforce unjustified police stereotypes that certain neighborhoods need heavier police attention.[152]

---

147   The tip that led to the investigation of Lance and Sue Gates was allegedly given by Sue Gates's hairdresser, annoyed with Sue's boasting. Thomas Y. Davies, *The Supreme Court Giveth and the Supreme Court Taketh Away: The Century of Fourth Amendment 'Search and Seizure' Doctrine*, 100 J. Crim. L. & Criminology 933, 1005 n.383 (2010). On the problems raised by the "informant institution," see generally Alexandra Natapoff, *Snitching: The Institutional and Communal Consequences*, 73 U. Cin. L. Rev. 645 (2004).

148   *See, e.g.*, Andrew Guthrie Ferguson & Damien Bernache, *The "High-Crime Area" Question: Requiring Verifiable and Quantifiable Evidence for Fourth Amendment Reasonable Suspicion Analysis*, 57 Am. U. L. Rev. 1587, 1607 (2008) ("[T]he majority of jurisdictions ... have relied on an officer's testimony that an area is a 'high-crime area' without much analysis as to the basis of that conclusion.").

149   I have argued elsewhere that an automated traffic enforcement system made possible by a federal intelligent highway initiative could improve fairness and reduce or eliminate racial profiling in traffic stops. *See* Elizabeth E. Joh, *Discretionless Policing: Technology and the Fourth Amendment*, 95 Calif. L. Rev. 199 (2007).

150   Not only are there decisions about which model to use, each model itself involves discretionary judgments about the type and amount of data to use, as well as how to display it. *See, e.g.*, Bachner, *supra* note 48, at 21 ("Just as with the other clustering methods, the final map is sensitive to analyst judgment.").

151   Measures of crime based on arrest rates—and particularly arrests in minor offenses—are problematic because they represent the greatest exercise of police discretion. *See* Wayne A. Logan, *Policing Identity*, 92 B.U. L. Rev. 1561, 1590 (2012). As a result, the resulting data may often reflect racial biases in policing. *See, e.g.*, Simon A. Cole, *Fingerprint Identification and the Criminal Justice System: Historical Lessons for the DNA Debate, in* DNA and the Criminal Justice System: The Technology of Justice 63, 82 (David Lazer ed., 2004) (observing that criminal histories "appear to be pure, objective information, when in fact they may reflect the prejudices of police or judicial practitioners").

152   *See, e.g.*, *Predictive Policing: Don't Even Think About It*, Economist (July 20, 2013), http://www.economist.com/news/briefing/21582042-it-getting-easier-foresee-wrongdoing-and-spot-likely-wrongdoers-dont-even-

Second, prediction models might nudge police judgments in favor of investigative detention in borderline cases because the police rely too heavily on probabilistic information.[153] If, for example, a predictive model directs the police to look at a particular block for burglaries, then it may encourage the police to "see" suspicious behavior when there may be none.[154] The danger here is that an overreliance on the objectivity of prediction—which is in fact an informed probabilistic guess—will be determinative, rather than a supplement to independent assessments by the police.

B. Privacy and Surveillance Big Data

What we do in public can be seen by anyone and therefore we generally cannot claim those activities are private. That intuition is embodied in the *Katz* reasonable expectation of privacy test to determine whether the Fourth Amendment applies to police activity at all.[155] But does assuming the risk of police surveillance mean something different when the police have mass surveillance capabilities?

Computer enhanced mass surveillance systems would seem to be the latest example of the increasing sophistication of police technologies to monitor public activity. Decades of police reliance upon CCTV cameras, electronic beepers, listening devices, surveillance aircraft, and other similar sense enhancements have prompted concerns that these measures have significantly eroded any social sense of privacy individuals have in public.[156] Indeed, the Supreme Court has emphasized in a number of cases that our public activities, movements,

---

think-about-it ("It matters … whether software crunches reports of crimes or arrests; if the latter, police activity risks creating a vicious circle.").

153   The predictive software may drive the officer to use personal observation to *confirm* the potentially suspicious behavior rather than independently assess whether it is truly suspicious. *Cf.* Andrew E. Taslitz, *Police Are People Too: Cognitive Obstacles to, and Opportunities for, Police Getting the Individualized Suspicion Judgment Right*, 8 Ohio St. J. Crim. L. 7, 29–30 (2010) (discussing "continuum model" in which observer uses further assessment to confirm initial judgments rather than challenging them).

154   A court may see the issue characterized as a kind of reliable tip—albeit from a computer—that requires less police corroboration precisely because of its reliability. *See, e.g.*, Ferguson, *supra* note 58, at 308 (making this observation).

155   Katz v. United States, 389 U.S. 347, 361 (1967) (Harlan, J., concurring).

156   In fact, the problems of a mass surveillance system like the total domain awareness program were anticipated years before such programs actually existed. *See, e.g.*, Robert H. Thornburg, Comment, *Face Recognition Technology: The Potential Orwellian Implications and Constitutionality of Current Uses Under the Fourth Amendment*, 20 J. Marshall J. Computer & Info. L. 321, 343 (2002) (noting in 2002 that "a networked system could identify an individual in one location on a specific date, and identify that same person at a different location afterwards").

and even our literal physical characteristics visible to the public lack Fourth Amendment protection.[157]

Moreover, a line of Supreme Court cases suggests that any "scientific enhancement" of the senses used by the police to watch activity falls outside of the Fourth Amendment's protections if the activity takes place in public.[158] Thus, the Supreme Court concluded in *United States v. Knotts* that police use of an electronic beeper to follow a suspect surreptitiously did not constitute a Fourth Amendment search.[159] The premise underlying such a conclusion is that if the police could themselves pursue a suspect over the same public roads, then so too could an electronic beeper concealed within a container given to the unwitting suspect.[160]

The surveillance capacities of the police today, however, far exceed even what armies of police officers could accomplish without access to big data.[161] That difference should alter the absence of Fourth Amendment protections. Indeed, several Justices have recently indicated concerns about the big data surveillance capacities of the police.[162] For example, in *United States v. Jones*[163] (regarding the twenty-eight day GPS tracking of a single suspect[164]), five Justices expressed concerns that long-term police surveillance, even of a person's public movements, might constitute a Fourth Amendment search.[165] The premise here, sometimes referred to as the "mosaic theory," is that the danger to Fourth Amendment privacy lies in the aggregation of discrete bits of data, even if each piece standing alone would not

---

157   *See, e.g.*, United States v. Dionisio, 410 U.S. 1, 14 (1973) ("The physical characteristics of a person's voice, its tone and manner, as opposed to the content of a specific conversation, are constantly exposed to the public. ... No person can have a reasonable expectation that others will not know the sound of his voice, any more than he can reasonably expect that his face will be a mystery to the world."); Davis v. Mississippi, 394 U.S. 721, 727 (1969) ("Fingerprinting involves none of the probing into an individual's private life and thoughts that marks an interrogation or search."). Christopher Slobogin has convincingly argued, however, that a right to anonymity—even in public—should be protected by the Fourth Amendment. *See* Christopher Slobogin, *Public Privacy: Camera Surveillance of Public Places and the Right to Anonymity*, 72 Miss. L.J. 213 (2002).

158   *E.g.*, United States v. Knotts, 460 U.S. 276, 285 (1983).

159   *Id.*

160   *Id.* ("A police car following [the defendant] at a distance throughout his journey could have observed him leaving the public highway and arriving at the cabin owned by respondent, with the drum of chloroform still in the car.").

161   *See, e.g.*, People v. Weaver, 909 N.E.2d 1195, 1199 (N.Y. 2009) ("The potential for a similar capture [to GPS technology] of information or 'seeing' by law enforcement would require, at a minimum, millions of additional police officers and cameras on every street lamp.").

162   Certainly a number of lower court judges have expressed these concerns as well.

163   _U.S._, 132 S. Ct. 945 (2012).

164   *Id.* at 948.

165   *See id.* at 955 (Sotomayor, J., concurring); *id.* at 964 (Alito, J., concurring in judgment).

be subjected to constitutional protections.[166] Indeed, the majority in *Knotts* acknowledged that "dragnet-type law enforcement practices," such as "twenty-four hour surveillance of any citizen of this country," might raise a Fourth Amendment problem while the use of a beeper did not.[167]

Not only is the quantity of information collected in the big data context far greater, the very nature of surveillance itself is different. If conventional surveillance involves the intentional tracking of one or a few suspects by actual police officers, what happens when a person "emerges" as a surveillance target as a result of a computer analysis? In the traditional surveillance context, the police have not been constrained by the Fourth Amendment so long as their investigations neither interfered with an individual's movements, nor ranged beyond public spaces.[168] As the Supreme Court has observed, there is no constitutional right to be free from police investigation.[169]

But this *surveillance discretion* may mean something different in the big data context. The intentional surveillance of targeted individuals is not equivalent to the perpetual "indiscriminate data collection"[170] of entire populations. While both approaches involve watching by the government, a program like the N.Y.P.D.'s "total domain awareness" system differs from traditional surveillance enough to warrant a different approach.[171] The very quality of public life may be different when government watches everyone—surreptitiously—and stores all of the resulting information.[172]

---

166   The "mosaic theory" is generally attributed to the decision in *United States v. Maynard*, 615 F.3d 544, 562 (D.C. Cir. 2010) ("Prolonged surveillance reveals types of information not revealed by short-term surveillance, such as what a person does repeatedly, what he does not do, and what he does ensemble. These types of information can each reveal more about a person than does any individual trip viewed in isolation."). *See, e.g.*, Orin S. Kerr, *The Mosaic Theory of the Fourth Amendment*, 111 Mich. L. Rev. 311, 326 (2012) ("[F]ive justices wrote or joined opinions that … suggest that a majority of the Court is ready to embrace some form of the D.C. Circuit's mosaic theory.").

167   United States v. Knotts, 460 U.S. 276, 283–85 (1983).

168   *See, e.g.*, Terry v. Ohio, 392 U.S. 1, 19 n.16 (1968) ("Obviously, not all personal intercourse between policemen and citizens involves 'seizures' of persons. Only when the officer, by means of physical force or show of authority, has in some way restrained the liberty of a citizen may we conclude that a 'seizure' has occurred.").

169   Michigan v. Chesternut, 486 U.S. 567, 576 (1988) ("The police [are] not required to have 'a particularized and objective basis for suspecting [respondent] of criminal activity,' in order to pursue him." (quoting United States v. Cortez, 449 U.S. 411, 417–18 (1981))); *cf.* Oyler v. Boles, 368 U.S. 448, 456 (1962) ("[T]he conscious exercise of some selectivity in [law] enforcement is not in itself a federal constitutional violation.").

170   Stephen Rushin, *The Judicial Response to Mass Police Surveillance*, 2011 U. Ill. J.L. Tech. & Pol'y 281, 286.

171   *See* 1 LaFave, *supra* note 138, § 2.7(g) (raising similar concerns).

172   *See* United States v. Jones, U.S., 132 S. Ct. 945, 956 (2012) (Sotomayor, J., concurring) ("Awareness that the Government may be watching chills associational and expressive freedoms.").

Practical barriers have long served to protect individual privacy by forcing the police to selectively apply their resources and interests,[173] but those barriers have now largely eroded.[174] The ability of government to record, store, and analyze nearly everything we do is now becoming technologically possible and affordable.[175] By 2015, it will cost just two cents to store all of the audio data generated by the average person in one year; storing a year's worth of a person's movements generated by their cellphone will cost next to nothing.[176] These expanded capabilities raise the possibility of a "surveillance time machine": the capacity of the government to identify a person of interest and then search retrospectively through all of the data that has been stored and collected about that person.[177] While some people have already changed their personal habits to avoid this mass surveillance, many likely have not.[178]

The longstanding doctrines declaring that we lack any Fourth Amendment protections in the public sphere should not hold its traditional force once the police deploy the tools of big data.[179] "Knowing exposure" suggests a degree of control over one's information that is lacking when the government is capable of recording and storing every small detail in perpetuity.[180] Thus the traditional assumptions about Fourth Amendment protections in

---

173   *See, e.g., id.* at 963 (Alito, J., concurring in judgment) ("In the pre-computer age, the greatest protections of privacy were neither constitutional nor statutory, but practical. Traditional surveillance for any extended period of time was difficult and costly and therefore rarely undertaken.").

174   *See* Scott Shane, *Data Storage Could Expand Reach of Surveillance*, N.Y. Times (Aug. 14, 2012), http://thecaucus. blogs.nytimes.com/2012/08/14/advances-in-data-storage-have-implications-for-government-surveillance/?_php=true&_type=blogs&_r=0.

175   *See id.*

176   *See id.*

177   *See* Villasenor, *supra* note 22, at 1. Wayne Logan has persuasively argued that such a capacity has exposed the need to distinguish between identity evidence used strictly for identity verification and that used for forensic investigation. *See* Logan, *supra* note 151, at 1581–93.

178   On the various ways in which people might protest the growing surveillance capacities of the government, see Elizabeth E. Joh, *Privacy Protests: Surveillance Evasion and Fourth Amendment Suspicion*, 55 Ariz. L. Rev. 997 (2013); *see also* Villasenor, *supra* note 22, at 7 (observing that the use of encryption, for instance, might attract *greater* government attention).

179   Kevin Bankston and Ashkan Soltani have demonstrated the enormous differences in cost between traditional and new surveillance methods. They estimate that the cost of a using a traditional covert five police car surveillance operation over 28 days—the days the government followed Antoine Jones—is "nearly *775 times more expensive* than the cost of using GPS." Kevin S. Bankston & Ashkan Soltani, *Tiny Constables and the Cost of Surveillance: Making Cents out of* United States v. Jones, 123 Yale L.J. Online 334, 335 (2014), http://yalelawjournal.org/2014/1/9/bankston-soltani.html.

180   Katz v. United States, 389 U.S. 347, 351 (1967) ("What a person knowingly exposes to the public, even in his own home or office, is not a subject of Fourth Amendment protection.").

public spaces, absent statutory protections from Congress, call out for reexamination and doctrinal adaptation.

C. Repurposing Information

Google's reuse of search terms to identify flu outbreaks represents an upending of a core research convention: formulate a hypothesis first, and then collect the appropriate data.[181] With big data, we can collect (nearly all) the data first, and apply the questions later.[182] Indeed, the data can be analyzed in multiple ways at multiple times.[183] It is this repurposing or resifting of data that has led to some of big data's unexpected insights, like Google's flu analysis.

When it is the police who sift through the data, however, the Fourth Amendment is ill-suited to this particular relationship of data collection and analysis. The Fourth Amendment is primarily interested in the legitimacy of *how* information is acquired.[184] If the acquisition is permissible, how the police use that information thereafter is generally not subject to an additional Fourth Amendment challenge.[185] This suggests that once legitimately within the government's possession, information can be repurposed and reanalyzed without any additional Fourth Amendment justification.[186] In the case of genetic information, courts have been generally dismissive of claims that individuals have any Fourth Amendment claims

---

181 *See supra* text accompanying notes 43–47.

182 *See supra* text accompanying notes 43–47.

183 *See* Mayer-Schönberger & Cukier, *supra* note 10, at 104 ("In the big-data age, data is like a magical diamond mine that keeps on giving long after its principal value has been tapped.").

184 *See, e.g.,* Russell D. Covey, *Pervasive Surveillance and the Future of the Fourth Amendment*, 80 Miss. L.J. 1289, 1294–95 (2011) ("Fourth Amendment law ... has proved singularly inept at dealing with the technological revolution. ... [This is because it] has purported to regulate and control the non-consensual governmental acquisition of information from individuals in the name of privacy protection.").

185 *See* Erin Murphy, *Back to the Future: The Curious Case of* United States v. Jones, 10 Ohio St. J. Crim. L. 325, 330–31 (2012) ("Current Fourth Amendment law emphasizes acquisition: how did the police acquire the DNA sample or financial record or biometric image? It cares little for what happens next—to what use that information is put.").

186 Thus in a case from the 1990s, the New York Court of Appeals rejected a Fourth Amendment challenge to the use of a DNA analysis to connect a defendant to a rape, although the warrant for the blood sample was approved with regard to a different case. People v. King, 663 N.Y.S.2d 610, 614 (N.Y. App. Div. 1997) ("It is also clear that once a person's blood sample has been obtained lawfully, he can no longer assert either privacy claims or unreasonable search and seizure arguments with respect to the use of that sample. Privacy concerns are no longer relevant once the sample has already lawfully been removed from the body, and the scientific analysis of a sample does not involve any further search and seizure of a defendant's person.").

to DNA samples once lawfully acquired by the police, but used for investigative purposes unrelated to the original justification for the sample's collection.[187]

Is a secondary analysis of an individual's DNA sample to find a familial match sufficiently similar to an analysis to find whether that same individual is responsible for another crime? Are there other sorts of information to be derived from DNA samples that ought to require distinct Fourth Amendment justifications? Repurposing a DNA sample to look for information regarding *someone other than the source of the sample* raises sufficient privacy concerns that some further government justifications may be necessary.[188] Such a search does more than "identify" again the source of the DNA sample in a subsequent police investigation.[189]

The government's ability to reanalyze information—of any sort—in the age of big data calls out for a new approach. What courts could do is shift the focus of the Fourth Amendment from data collection to a more rigorous scrutiny of its intended uses by the government.[190] Indeed, Harold Krent proposed nearly twenty years ago that the repurposing of information by the government obtained at an earlier time could be deemed unreasonable for Fourth Amendment purposes.[191] Professor Krent suggested, for instance, that courts might consider whether the seizure of a person's information would have been reasonable had the government articulated the later use initially.[192] The closer the government's secondary purpose is

---

187   *See, e.g.*, State v. Hauge, 79 P.3d 131, 144 (Haw. 2003) ("[T]he appellate courts of several states have ruled that expectations of privacy in lawfully obtained blood samples ... are not objectively reasonable by 'society's' standards. Specifically, a number of jurisdictions have held on analogous facts that once a blood sample and DNA profile is lawfully procured from a defendant, no privacy interest persists in either the sample or the profile."); State v. Emerson, 981 N.E.2d 787, 792–93 (Ohio 2012) (rejecting defendant's claims of privacy in subsequent uses of DNA *profile*); Smith v. State, 734 N.E.2d 706, 710 (Ind. Ct. App. 2000) ("[L]aw enforcement agencies may retain validly obtained DNA samples for use in subsequent unrelated criminal investigations. ..."), *aff'd*, 744 N.E.2d 437 (Ind. 2001).

188   Kelly Lowenberg argues that subsequent searches of DNA samples that yield new information should require further government justification and a consideration of the reasonableness of that additional search. In the familial search context, Lowenberg suggests that Y-STR typing of a DNA sample of a convicted offender would be permissible without a warrant, while the same analysis conducted on another type of sample (e.g. a volunteer sample) would not. *See* Kelly Lowenberg, *Applying the Fourth Amendment When DNA Collected for One Purpose is Tested for Another*, 79 U. Cin. L. Rev. 1289, 1319–23 (2011).

189   *Cf.* Logan, *supra* note 151, at 1586 (distinguishing evidence showing "one's identity (*who* one is), [from the] entirely different question ... presented by identifying information (revealing *what* one might have done or perhaps will do") (emphasis in original) (footnote omitted)).

190   *See* Covey, *supra* note 184, at 1302.

191   Harold J. Krent, *Of Diaries and Data Banks: Use Restrictions Under the Fourth Amendment*, 74 Tex. L. Rev. 49, 60–63 (1995).

192   *See id.* at 80–81.

to its original purpose at the time of acquisition, the more likely it should be that the government could use the data without further justification.

The case for Fourth Amendment protections regarding repurposed information is stronger still should the government one day be interested in gleaning information from DNA samples other than matching profiles to crime scene samples. Here, the Supreme Court has hinted at a willingness to reassess the balance of privacy and government utility at some future date. In *Maryland v. King*,[193] in which the Court upheld the compulsory collection of DNA from arrestees,[194] Justice Kennedy suggested that "[i]f in the future police analyze [DNA] samples to determine [other information], that case would present additional privacy concerns not present here."[195] The resolution by the Court regarding such a dispute may well turn, however, on the purposes claimed by the government to mine that information. In *King*, the Court was willing to permit defendant's cheek swab, and the subsequently generated DNA profile, without individualized suspicion because the police were permitted to find out King's "identity": a term broad enough to encompass any other crimes King had committed.[196]

For now, however, the Court has left open the possibility that it may give greater scrutiny to some sorts of repurposing. That, plus the existing statutory protections on access and disclosure, may allay the concerns of many.[197] Yet it would be overly optimistic to ignore two developments in the other direction: the trend of Fourth Amendment law away from protection in these secondary searches, and the Court's recent expansion of what the government may do for purposes of "identification" when it comes to genetic information.[198]

---

193   _U.S._, 133 S. Ct. 1958 (2013).

194   *Id.* at 1980.

195   *Id.* at 1979.

196   *Id.* at 1980. Justice Scalia's dissent in *King* was much less sanguine about the threats to privacy in the case, and strongly disputed that the government's interest in the case could be justified as one of "identification." *See id.* at 1988 (Scalia, J., dissenting) (noting "it may one day be possible to design a program that uses DNA for a purpose other than crime-solving").

197   *Cf.* United States v. Jones, U.S., 132 S. Ct. 945, 964 (2012) (Alito, J., concurring in judgment) ("A legislative body is well situated to gauge changing public attitudes, to draw detailed lines, and to balance privacy and public safety in a comprehensive way.").

198   In the *King* case, the majority comfortably found that arrestee DNA profiles could be used to link the defendant to a crime unrelated to the crime of arrest, *King*, 133 S. Ct. at 1965, 1970–80, a definition of "identification" to which Justice Scalia dissented, dramatically. *See id.* at 1982–90 (Scalia, J., dissenting). For further discussion of this issue, see Joh, *supra* note 111.

D. Beyond the Fourth Amendment

Apart from the Fourth Amendment challenges raised by big data policing, an uncritical embrace of these new technologies raises other concerns beyond regulating the police. Whether practical or abstract, these concerns will be easily swept aside by departments eager to be part of the next technological wave in policing.

First, many of these new technologies have been developed by private companies whose motivations and concerns may not always be consonant with those of a public police department. For instance, IBM has spent billions acquiring data analytics companies in order to develop and market predictive tools to the police.[199] Although PredPol was initially developed by academics, it is now a for-profit company.[200] Similarly, Microsoft—and the N.Y.P.D.—will profit from every new police department that adopts a total domain awareness system.[201] Future interest in the further analysis of DNA samples will also benefit some private laboratories.

Second, the introduction of new big data technologies requires attention not only to appropriate regulation, but also to questions about how well these privately developed tools actually help to reduce crime. New technologies possess understandable appeal for departments seeking innovative crime fighting strategies. New strategies lend themselves toward positive media attention in a way that "a poorly attended community meeting in a church basement" does not.[202] Yet, for-profit purveyors of big data products may not provide the best objective assessment of their products. The desirability of these new technologies should not steer attention away from questions about how well they reduce crime and conserve limited public resources compared to traditional methods.

A final concern is much more fundamental. The reliance on big data by the police also poses the risk that the very definition of policing may be changing. The promise of big data is a vision of policing that is driven and assessed by quantitative measurements. Indeed,

---

199   *See* Sengupta, *supra* note 5. Indeed, to the extent that these companies may market both to public police departments and private corporations interested in reducing crime privately, special attention must be paid to claims of public benefit. For further discussion on how private interests can distort public police goals, see Elizabeth E. Joh, *The Forgotten Threat: Private Policing and the State*, 13 IND. J. GLOBAL LEGAL STUD. 357, 384–88 (2006).

200   *See, e.g.,* Bond-Graham & Winston, *supra* note 64 (noting that PredPol incorporated in January 2012 and "has emerged early to dominate the [predictive policing] market").

201   The N.Y.P.D. is said to receive thirty percent of gross revenues from sales of the system to other departments. Sam Roberts, *Police Surveillance May Earn Money for City*, N.Y. TIMES, Apr. 4, 2013, at A23.

202   David Alan Sklansky, *The Persistent Pull of Police Professionalism*, NEW PERSPECTIVES IN POLICING (Harvard Kennedy Sch., Cambridge, Mass. & Nat'l Inst. of Just.), Mar. 2011, at 9, *available at* https://www.ncjrs.gov/pdf-files1/nij/232676.pdf.

those police chiefs that have already embraced big data tout the potential to rely on numbers when budgets for police departments are shrinking.[203] The problem, however, is that a technocratic solution to crime is not the only objective of democratic policing.[204]

Reducing crime is not the only job of the police. Policing as an institution has never been amenable to a single objective,[205] and indeed over time its aims have shifted.[206] What is clear, however, is that democratic policing aims at more than mere crime control and, at its core, relies on skills that do not always lend themselves to statistical analysis. No amount of data-driven policing is likely to assuage communities soured by long histories of tension with the police. Nor will demonstrations of little red boxes on a smartphone necessarily justify to a community the need for a heavy-handed police presence.

Conclusion

The use of big data is likely to become an ordinary aspect of policing. The application of artificial intelligence to crime data promises immediate and tangible benefits. We can gain some real insights about how to direct police resources efficiently and effectively in ways that intuition, tradition, and limited information have been unavailing. At the same time, the reliance upon artificial intelligence and the collection of vast amounts of information poses some special challenges in the policing context. Courts and legislatures will need to think of Fourth Amendment issues in new ways to adequately protect notions of individual privacy.

---

203 *See, e.g.*, Charlie Beck & Colleen McCue, *Predictive Policing: What Can We Learn from Wal-Mart and Amazon about Fighting Crime in a Recession?*, POLICE CHIEF (Nov. 2009), http://www.policechiefmagazine.org/magazine/index.cfm?fuseaction=display_arch&article_id=1942&issue_id=112009 (arguing that "predictive policing represents an opportunity to prevent crime and respond more effectively, while optimizing increasingly scarce or limited resources, including personnel") (Charlie Beck is the Chief of Detectives for the L.A.P.D.).

204 *Cf.* Sklansky, *supra* note 202, at 9–10 ("A fixation on technology can distract attention from the harder and more important parts of [policing], the parts that rely on imagination and judgment.").

205 Perhaps the ambiguities of policing was best stated by sociologist Egon Bittner, who described the job of policing as: "a mechanism for the distribution of non-negotiably coercive force employed in accordance with the dictates of an intuitive grasp of situational exigencies." *See* EGON BITTNER, THE FUNCTIONS OF THE POLICE IN MODERN SOCIETY: A REVIEW OF BACKGROUND FACTORS, CURRENT PRACTICES, AND POSSIBLE ROLE MODELS 46 (1970).

206 *See, e.g.*, Eric H. Monkkonen, *History of Urban Police*, 15 CRIME & JUST. 547, 555 (1992) (observing that early in American policing history the police were expected to dole out social services to the city's needy).

Reading 6.2

Selections from "Ending the Zero-Sum Game: How to Increase the Productivity of the Fourth Amendment" from *Harvard Journal of Law and Public Policy*, vol. 36, no. 2

Ric Simmons

Introduction

Every criminal procedure student learns on the first day of class that Fourth Amendment policy represents a zero-sum game: a constant struggle between the individual privacy of citizens and the needs of law enforcement.[1] The job of the courts is to mediate that struggle, to be referees in the "game" of cat-and-mouse between the police officer and the criminal. Before the Fourth Amendment was ever written, the parameters of the "game" were well-established when Benjamin Franklin declared, "[t]hey who can give up essential liberty to obtain a little temporary safety, deserve neither liberty nor safety."[2] The implication is clear: there is, and always will be, a trade-off between liberty and security, and the only way to get more security is to forfeit some liberty.

Judges frequently refer to criminal investigations as a competitive enterprise, in which the job of the courts is to maintain the status quo between both sides. The Supreme Court has repeatedly stated that the purpose of the Fourth Amendment is to act as a safeguard against the law enforcement officer "engaged in the often competitive enterprise of ferreting out crime."[3] Most recently, the concept of ensuring a fair competition between opposing sides

---

1   In game theory, a "zero-sum game" is a situation in which a participant's gain (or loss) of utility is exactly balanced by the losses (or gains) of the utility of the other participant.

2   1 Benjamin Franklin, Memoirs of the Life and the Writings of Benjamin Franklin 270 (London, Henry Colburn 1818).

3   Lo-Ji Sales, Inc. v. New York, 442 U.S. 319, 326 (1979) (quoting Johnson v. United States, 333 U.S. 10, 14 (1948)); United States v. Chadwick, 433 U.S. 1, 9 (1977) (quoting *Johnson*, 333 U.S. at 14).

has been on display in the cases involving the government's use of Global Position System (GPS) tracking devices. Judges opposed to these devices argue that their use unfairly tips the balance in favor of the government because the devices are so inexpensive that surveillance becomes too easy[4] and because the usual countermeasures one employs against government surveillance become worthless.[5] In a recent article in the *Harvard Law Review*,[6] Professor Orin Kerr claimed that "the basic dynamic of Fourth Amendment law resembles a zero-sum game,"[7] arguing that the fundamental principle driving Fourth Amendment jurisprudence over the past hundred years has been the courts' desire to maintain an "equilibrium" between police power and civil liberties.[8]

In reality, however, the "competition" between law enforcement and criminals is not zero-sum. In order to see why, we need to see the criminal justice system not as a *competition*, but instead as an *industry*. In the decades since the beginning of the law and economics movement,[9] there has been surprisingly little application of economic principles to criminal procedure.[10] Richard Posner's foundational textbook *Economic Analysis of the Law*, for

---

4   *See, e.g.*, United States v. Jones, 132 S. Ct. 945, 963–64 (2012) (Alito, J., concurring in the judgment).

5   *See* United States v. Pineda-Moreno, 617 F.3d 1120, 1126 (9th Cir. 2010) (Kozinski, J., dissenting) ("You can preserve your anonymity from prying eyes, even in public, by traveling at night, through heavy traffic, in crowds, by using a circuitous route, disguising your appearance, passing in and out of buildings and being careful not to be followed. But there's no hiding from the all-seeing network of GPS satellites that hover overhead, which never sleep, never blink, never get confused and never lose attention."); *see also* United States v. Garcia, 474 F.3d, 994, 998 (7th Cir. 2007) ("There is a tradeoff between security and privacy, and often it favors security.").

6   Orin S. Kerr, *An Equilibrium-Adjustment Theory of the Fourth Amendment*, 125 HARV. L. REV. 476 (2011).

7   *Id.* at 543.

8   *Id.*

9   The Law and Economics movement is generally thought to have begun with the publication of two groundbreaking articles in the early 1960's: Ronald Coase, *The Problem of Social Cost*, 3 J.L. & ECON. 1 (1960) and Guido Calabresi, *Some Thoughts on Risk Distribution and the Law of Torts*, 70 YALE L.J. 499 (1961).

10   *Cf.* Craig S. Lerner, *The Reasonableness of Probable Cause*, 81 TEX. L. REV. 951 (2003); Steven Penney, *Reasonable Expectations of Privacy and Novel Search Technologies: An Economic Approach*, 97 J. CRIM. L. & CRIMINOLOGY 477 (2007); Hugo M. Mialon & Sue H. Mialon, *The Effects of the Fourth Amendment: An Economic Analysis*, (Emory Law Sch. Pub. Law & Legal Theory Research Paper Series, Paper No. 06-3, 2006), *available at* http://papers. ssrn.com/abstract=755035; Andrew Song, *Technology, Terrorism, and the Fishbowl Effect: An Economic Analysis of Surveillance and Searches*, (Berkman Ctr. For Internet & Soc'y, Working Paper No. 73, 2003), *available at* http:// papers.ssrn.com/abstract=422220. *See generally* Frank H. Easterbrook, *Criminal Procedure as a Market System*, 12 J. LEGAL STUD. 289 (1983) (discussing law and economics with regard to the trial aspects of criminal procedure, such as prosecutorial discretion, plea bargaining, and sentencing). There have also been a number of articles using economic principles to determine the effect of the exclusionary rule. For an example, see Myron W. Orfield, Jr., *The Exclusionary Rule and Deterrence: An Empirical Study of Chicago Narcotics Officers*, 54 U. CHI. L. REV. 1016 (1987).

example, devotes only five of its 716 pages to criminal procedure.[11] Perhaps this is because criminal procedure, unlike tort law or contract law, deals with fundamental rights, which are less amenable to cost-benefit analysis.[12] But the mere fact that the Fourth Amendment protects fundamental rights does not mean that we cannot apply economic principles to evaluate it. Fourth Amendment law is about balancing privacy rights with the needs of law enforcement, and economic principles can inform that analysis.

Our goal in applying these economic principles to Fourth Amendment law is to increase the efficiency of the criminal justice system—that is, to maximize output while minimizing costs. This focus on efficiency does not mean that we are indifferent to the constitutional rights of our citizens. To the contrary, the potential infringement of these rights is one of the costs that we are seeking to minimize. Another cost, more easily measured, is the tangible monetary cost incurred by law enforcement organizations (and thus ultimately by society as a whole) to undertake a given type of surveillance.[13] The output that we are seeking is crime control, or more specifically in the Fourth Amendment context, the identification of those who are guilty of a crime and collection of evidence that can be used to demonstrate their guilt.[14] Roughly speaking, the more money we spend, or the more willing we are to infringe on our own freedoms, the more output we receive in terms of identifying the guilty and recovering incriminating evidence.

Once we apply economic analysis to this question, however, we can see that there are two reasons why Fourth Amendment doctrine could in fact be a positive-sum game. First, advances in technology can increase the effectiveness of surveillance in catching criminals without reducing the privacy rights of ordinary citizens—that is, it is possible to increase the output without increasing the cost.[15] Second, changing norms and attitudes may decrease

---

11   Richard A. Posner, Economic Analysis of Law (6th ed. 2003). Posner briefly discusses plea bargaining, *Terry* stops, the exclusionary rule, and coerced confessions. *Id.* at 577–80, 712–16.

12   Penney, *supra* note 10, at 478–79.

13   Throughout this Article I will use the word "surveillance" to cover any method of investigation carried out by law enforcement officials, from accessing a Department of Motor Vehicles database to wiretapping a telephone to strip-searching a suspect. This rather awkward terminology is required because the term "search" has a very particular meaning in Fourth Amendment jurisprudence as a method of surveillance that implicates the Fourth Amendment to the degree that it requires probable cause or a warrant. *See* Katz v. United States, 389 U.S. 347, 350–53 (1967).

14   Of course, more efficient crime control is not just about identifying the guilty; it also entails collecting evidence that can exonerate the innocent.

15   *See* United States v. Knotts, 460 U.S. 276, 284 (1983) ("Insofar as respondent's complaint appears to be simply that scientific devices such as the beeper enabled the police to be more effective in detecting crime, it simply has no constitutional foundation. We have never equated police efficiency with unconstitutionality, and we decline to do so now.").

the value of certain kinds of privacy to individuals, causing the cost of certain types of surveillance to decrease. This can work in the other direction as well: When criminals, rather than police, take advantage of technological advances, the output of the system will decrease even if costs are held constant. Likewise, societal norms could change to make certain types of privacy more valuable, thus increasing the cost to the system. In these situations, the criminal justice system becomes a negative-sum game.

Another advantage of applying economic tools is that the application helps identify potential trade-offs in the system between different costs. For example, more money spent on training police could result in less infringement on constitutional rights while maintaining the same level of output (that is, the same level of gathering evidence and apprehension of criminals). More controversially, we may be able to maintain the same level of output by adopting newer types of surveillance that are less expensive but result in greater infringement on our privacy rights. It may well be that this latter trade-off is one that many people will never want to undertake, as even a savings of millions of dollars is not worth even a slight loss of privacy rights. But an economic analysis of the question at least makes that choice more transparent.

Once we have identified the productivity of different forms of surveillance, we can take steps to encourage more productive types of surveillance and discourage the less productive ones. This can be accomplished by adjusting the legal standard of suspicion that law enforcement is required to demonstrate before engaging in different methods of surveillance, from no suspicion at all, to reasonable suspicion, to probable cause, or to something even higher. If a certain surveillance method is very productive—that is, if it produces a high level of success with a low cost in terms of resources and infringements on our privacy—then we should encourage law enforcement agents to conduct the surveillance by removing any constitutional or statutory restrictions on the activity. And if a certain method of surveillance is particularly unproductive, we should require law enforcement agents to demonstrate a high level of suspicion—probable cause or greater—before being allowed to engage in that activity.

Part I of this article will sketch out a basic formula for analyzing the productivity of different surveillance methods by measuring the cost of the inputs and the benefits of the outputs. Part II will apply this formula to different methods of surveillance to see how certain methods of surveillance are more productive than others, and will look for ways to increase the productivity of surveillance generally. The article concludes by offering some suggestions for changing the way we regulate surveillance techniques to maximize the efficiency of the process.

I. Applying Economic Analysis to Fourth Amendment Doctrine

Until quite recently, scholars had done very little to apply economic principles to questions of criminal procedure.[16] Those that did tended to focus on the post-arrest aspects of criminal procedure—for example, how to regulate plea bargaining or prosecutorial discretion to produce an optimal result.[17] In 2003, Professor Craig Lerner provided the first serious attempt to apply economic principles to the Fourth Amendment when he proposed a formula for determining whether probable cause exists in a certain case.[18] Professor Lerner chose as his starting point the famous Learned Hand formula from tort law, which is used to calculate whether a party has been negligent. Under Hand's formula, a party is negligent if the burden, or cost, of taking precautions to prevent an accident (B) is less than the probability of the accident occurring (P) times the social loss of the accident (L). In mathematical terms, if $B < P * L$, then the defendant was negligent.[19]

Professor Lerner adapts the formula and applies it to the probable cause context by proposing that a search would be reasonable if the social cost of the search in terms of the intrusion on privacy (C) is less than the social benefit (B) of the search multiplied by the probability of the search being successful (P).[20] In mathematical terms: If $C < P * B$, then the search is reasonable and probable cause exists.[21] Professor Lerner finetunes his formula with a few more variables,[22] but this basic principle remains the foundation of his argument.

---

16   There has been a substantial amount of law and economics work in the substantive criminal law area—for example, using economic tools to determine the proper sanction for certain crimes. *See, e.g.,* Gary S. Becker, *Crime and Punishment: An Economic Approach,* 76 J. POL. ECON. 169 (1968); Richard A. Posner, *Optimal Sentences for White-Collar Criminals,* 17 AM. CRIM. L. REV. 409 (1980). Other scholars have argued for privatization of the criminal justice system. *See, e.g.,* BRUCE L. BENSON, TO SERVE AND PROTECT: PRIVATIZATION AND COMMUNITY IN CRIMINAL JUSTICE (1998). Some scholars have applied econometric principles to determine the effects of certain criminal law doctrines such as the exclusionary rule. *See, e.g.,* Raymond A. Atkins & Paul H. Rubin, *Effects of Criminal Procedure on Crime Rates: Mapping Out the Consequences of the Exclusionary Rule,* 46 J.L. & ECON. 157 (2003).

17   *See, e.g.,* Easterbrook, *supra* note 10.

18   Lerner, *supra* note 10, at 1019–22.

19   *See* United States v. Carroll Towing Co., 159 F.2d 169, 173 (2d Cir. 1947).

20   Lerner, *supra* note 10, at 1019–20.

21   *Id.*

22   Professor Lerner would reduce the social cost (C) by the factor "(1-P)," because he argues that the Supreme Court has determined there is no constitutionally recognized privacy intrusion if the search is successful. *Id.* at 1020. This factor, however, seems to misinterpret the Supreme Court doctrine in this area. The Supreme Court has held that if the surveillance can detect *only* information about illegal activity, then the surveillance does not infringe on any constitutionally protected rights—for example, a drug sniffing dog that tells the police nothing about the object of the search other than the fact that contraband is or is not present. *See, e.g.,* Illinois

Professor Lerner intentionally deviates from established Fourth Amendment doctrine in one very significant way: He considers both the likelihood of success of the surveillance and the severity of the crime being investigated as factors in determining whether probable cause exists.[23] In other words, the social benefit "B" in his formula is not a constant, but a variable—it will be higher if the police are investigating a rape or a murder, and lower if they are investigating a petty larceny or a simple assault. It will also be higher if the search is very likely to uncover evidence of a crime, and lower if it is a mere fishing expedition that has a small likelihood of producing useful information. Consequently, under Professor Lerner's standard, a court may find probable cause to support an intrusive search (with a high "C") if the police are investigating a particularly severe crime or had a good chance of uncovering evidence. On the other hand, under this formula, a court would conclude that there was no probable cause to support the same search if the alleged crime were less severe or the likelihood of success was low.[24] This approach is consistent with Professor Lerner's economic analysis methodology: To weigh the costs and benefits of a particular course of action, it is important to have a realistic—as opposed to a formalistic—evaluation of the likely "benefits." Professor Lerner also argues that this approach is supported both by common sense and by the "reasonableness" language of the Fourth Amendment.[25] Indeed, a number of other scholars have proposed that courts take into account the severity of the crime at hand in assessing Fourth Amendment "reasonability,"[26] though this approach has gained very little traction with the courts.[27]

---

v. Caballes, 543 U.S. 405, 408–09 (2005). But this doctrine does not mean that a certain type of surveillance does not infringe on any constitutionally protected rights in every case in which the police find contraband. If the police search a suspect's house and find narcotics, the search still infringed on the suspect's rights—and definitely impacted the Fourth Amendment—because the police saw a lot of other private information while looking for the narcotics. Under Professor Lerner's revised formula, there would be no privacy intrusion and the social cost of this search would be zero.

Professor Lerner would also increase the social cost (C) by the factor "m," which he calls a "privacy multiplier," in order to "reflect the fact that not all seemingly identical searches are in fact identical, at least in the subjectively experienced intrusion on one's privacy." Lerner, *supra* note 10, at 1021. For example, Professor Lerner argues that an African-American person who is pulled over for the tenth time that year may subjectively feel a greater infringement than a white person who is pulled over for the first time. *Id.* As I note below, I am in favor of a using a more generalized "cost to society" rather than trying to calculate a specific subjective cost for each individual. *See infra* notes 32–42 and accompanying text.

23   Lerner, *supra* note 10, at 1015.

24   *Id.* at 1020 ("[t]he expected social benefit of a successful search increases if the crime under investigation is, say, aircraft privacy rather than tax fraud.").

25   *Id.* at 1019–20.

26   *See, e.g.*, Akhil Amar, *Fourth Amendment First Principles*, 107 Harv. L. Rev. 757, 801–02 (1994).

27   *See, e.g.*, Dunaway v. New York, 442 U.S. 200, 207–12 (1979).

We will use Professor Lerner's formula as the starting point for our analysis. The principle is simple: Every type of surveillance has a cost and an expected benefit. Professor Lerner uses this formula in order to determine whether probable cause exists in a particular case. If the expected benefit exceeds the expected cost, there is probable cause, and a search should be permitted.[28] Our focus, however, is somewhat different. We are not attempting to create a minimum standard for when a type of surveillance should be permitted; instead, we are attempting to maximize the efficiency of searches that do occur. Once we determine which type of searches are the most efficient, we can devise legal rules that encourage more efficient searches and discourage the less efficient ones.[29]

Therefore, our formula should take the form of an equation in which the resources and costs (C) are the inputs to the system and the benefits (B) are the output.[30] To make the equation balance, we will add a variable X to the left side of the equation to act as the conversion rate between the costs and the benefit. In economic terms, X is the "productivity" of the system—if X is high, we receive a large amount of output in exchange for a small amount of input. If X is low, we receive a small amount of output in exchange for a large amount of input.[31] Our equation thus begins rather simply:

$$(C * X) = B$$

---

28 Lerner, *supra* note 10, at 1019–20.

29 Essentially Professor Lerner is engaged in the process of calculating productivity as well, although his ultimate goal is to determine a minimum level of productivity at which a surveillance method will be permitted. This minimum level will be termed "probable cause." Under Professor Lerner's theory, the minimum level is a productivity of "1" which occurs when the costs of the search equal the expected benefits of the search. Thus, this is the level at which he argues that judges should find probable cause.

30 The output of a system is defined as "[t]he various useful goods or services that are either consumed or used in further production." PAUL A. SAMUELSON & WILLIAM D. NORDHAUS, ECONOMICS 747 (18th ed. 2004). In our case, the output of the system is the identification of criminals and the collection of evidence.

31 I am using the term "productivity" in the most basic sense: as a simple ratio of output to input. For example, assume a factory produces $10,000 worth of widgets in an hour, using one hundred workers being paid $20 per hour, raw supplies at the rate of $2,000 per hour, and equipment and capital which depreciates at $1,000 per hour. Thus, the factory spends $5,000 each hour and produces $10,000 worth of products, and has a productivity ratio of 10/5, or 2. There are a number of ways to increase the productivity of the factory: If the workers can be trained at negligible cost to produce $15,000 worth of widgets per hour using the same equipment, the productivity would increase to a ratio of 15/5 or 3. Or, if cheaper raw materials were used, salaries could be cut (without sacrificing output), or new, cheaper equipment could be installed, the same $10,000 of output could be produced at a cost of $4,000, for a productivity ratio of 10/4, or 2.5.

The productivity, X, will vary depending on the type of surveillance that is being conducted. But in order to determine the productivity for each type of surveillance, we must first define the costs and benefits of the equation.

A. Costs of Surveillance

The cost of a given type of surveillance can be divided into two categories: (1) the amount of resources (money, time, and equipment) that are used in conducting the surveillance; and (2) the degree to which the surveillance violates privacy interests. The expenses of the first category, known as "administrative costs," are borne directly by law enforcement.[32] The costs in the second category are external—that is, they are borne not by the actor conducting the surveillance, but by those who are the subjects of the surveillance.[33] The degree to which the surveillance violates privacy rights encompasses many different factors: the level of physical intrusion onto the suspect, the number of people affected by the search, the amount of time the search takes, the intimacy of the intrusion, and whether the search was conducted in public or in private.

Quantifying the value of an invasion of privacy is a challenging exercise. Lack of privacy creates at least two types of tangible economic costs: avoidance costs and defensive costs.[34] Avoidance costs are the losses that occur when a lack of privacy causes individuals to refrain from some socially useful (but perhaps embarrassing) activities, such as buying condoms or visiting a therapist.[35] Defensive costs denote the money people spend to protect their privacy when they feel their privacy is at risk—such as encoding e-mails, building high fences over their yards, or driving to meet someone in person rather than speaking to him over the telephone.[36]

In addition to these tangible costs, surveillance has an intangible cost because privacy has value as an intrinsic good. Privacy allows us to engage in many activities which may not have economic value but which create utility for those who engage in them, whether it is sunbathing naked in one's backyard or saying intimate things to a spouse over the telephone. Privacy is also critical to our political system, as an increase in privacy fosters communication and interaction among those who hold political views which may be unpopular in a given place or time.

---

32 Song, *supra* note 10, at 16–17.

33 In a strict economic sense, it is the presence of these externalities that requires government regulation of surveillance in the first place.

34 Penney, *supra* note 10, at 492–94; Song, *supra* note 10, at 11–16.

35 Penney, *supra* note 10, at 492–93; Song, *supra* note 10, at 11–14.

36 Penney, *supra* note 10, at 493–94; Song, *supra* note 10, at 14–16.

Calculating the value of a privacy interest is further complicated by the fact that our conception of privacy is a moving target that evolves over time. Two hundred years ago, citizens had a very different conception of privacy than we do today.[37] In certain aspects, modern citizens experience—and therefore expect—greater privacy than citizens did in the past. Two hundred years ago, most Americans worked in the open fields, travelled from one place to another by walking or riding on horseback while exposed to the world, and engaged in private conversations only when visiting each other in their homes. Today, many Americans have a private workspace, most travel insulated in a private car, and almost everyone expects to be able to have a private conversation with anyone else in the country at any time or place that they choose. In other ways, however, our expectation of privacy is lower today than in the past. For example, given the ubiquitous nature of electric light, we no longer expect the darkness of nighttime to hide our activities.[38] We also know that, at any time, planes and satellites (whether used by the government or a private company like Google) can see and record the exterior of our homes and private land, and perhaps even our own movements. We expect to see surveillance cameras in private businesses and even in public spaces.[39] We are also in a privacy revolution of sorts with regard to data, as we struggle to understand how the Internet, YouTube, Facebook, and other social media sources are changing our perceptions about what information should be kept private and what information is fair game for public exposure.

The Supreme Court has acknowledged that our standard of privacy can change as technology and society change.[40] Most notably, in *United States v. Kyllo*, the Court held that using a thermal imager to detect heat coming out of a home violated the homeowner's reasonable expectation of privacy, in part because the thermal imager was "not in general public use."[41] This holding implies that as a piece of technology becomes increasingly prevalent, society will adjust its expectations of privacy regarding government use of that technology. This principle was at work long before *Kyllo*. Fifteen years earlier, the Court held in *California v. Ciraolo* that an individual does not have a reasonable expectation of privacy in any part of his curtilage that was visible from the air—even though the individual had erected a ten-foot fence to hide it from anyone on ground level—because "[a]ny member of the public flying in

---

37   *See generally* Ric Simmons, *Why 2007 Is Not Like 1984: A Broader Perspective on Technology's Effect on Privacy and Fourth Amendment Jurisprudence*, 97 J. Crim. L. & Criminology 531, 537–40 (2007).

38   *See, e.g.*, Kerr, *supra* note 6, at 486–87.

39   For a more detailed discussion of how technology has increased our privacy, see Simmons, *supra* note 37, at 536–40.

40   *See infra* Part II.B.2.

41   533 U.S. 27, 40 (2001).

this airspace who glanced down could have seen everything that these officers observed."[42] This certainly would not have been the outcome one hundred years before *Ciraolo*.

Different forms of surveillance will cost different amounts in terms of resources spent and privacy lost. Thus, another challenge in comparing the costs of different types of searches is the difficulty of making the conversion between administrative costs and privacy costs. For example, wiretapping a telephone for thirty days is relatively inexpensive in terms of administrative costs, but it carries a high cost in terms of infringing on the suspect's privacy. Staking out a suspect's home for thirty days has a high administrative cost, but a relatively lower cost in terms of privacy intrusion. We therefore need to update our formula to separate these types of costs:

$$(C_A + C_P) * X = B$$

In other words, any given type of surveillance will have an administrative cost (C_A) and a privacy cost (C_P), as well as a level of productivity that makes the search more or less effective. Thus, there could be a trade-off between administrative costs and privacy costs, and in deciding which type of search is preferable, we should consider all of the costs of the search. Sometimes more money could be spent to carry out a search that is less intrusive, and in those cases, we should decide whether the trade-off is worth it. But before we can make those decisions, we must first consider the other side of the equation: the expected benefits of the search.

B. Benefits of Surveillance

The benefit of a search is a function of two factors: the chance that the surveillance will be successful multiplied by the societal value of a successful surveillance. Both of these factors require a bit more explanation. First, there are two different ways that a search can be "successful": gathering evidence that helps police identify the perpetrator of a crime, and gathering evidence that can be used to help convict the perpetrator in court. A given type of surveillance might provide either or both of these results, and may be successful in either category to a different degree. For example, confidential informants may help law enforcement agents learn the identity of the perpetrator, and may provide probable cause to arrest him, but would not be used to help convict the perpetrator in court.[43] Conversely, once a

---

42   476 U.S. 207, 213–14 (1986).
43   *See* McCray v. Illinois, 386 U.S. 300 (1967) (stating that the government may rely on confidential information to support probable cause for a warrant, but need not produce the confidential informant at the suppression hearing).

suspect is in custody, law enforcement may conduct a number of searches of the defendant's home, car, computer, or office in order to gain more evidence to use against him.

For the purposes of our analysis, there is no reason to distinguish between the two different types of "successful" surveillance. Rather, what we care about is the probability that the surveillance will be useful in convicting the correct person in court, however that might happen. Thus, we can gauge the "successfulness" of a surveillance on a scale of zero to one—"zero" meaning that the surveillance has absolutely no chance of providing any useful information leading to the conviction of the perpetrator, and "one" meaning that the search will, with absolute certainty, reveal information that will be sure to convict the correct perpetrator. Although in the real world there will be no method of surveillance that can reach this ideal probability level, there are some that come close. Dashboard cameras on police cruisers that are activated during drunk-driving arrests, for example, have a very strong chance of providing nearly incontrovertible evidence that a particular defendant committed the crime: There will be video evidence of erratic driving, video evidence of the defendant emerging from the driver's seat, and video evidence of his performance on the field sobriety tests.[44] On a more Orwellian level, covert video cameras in every home would be almost certain to succeed in identifying and gathering incontrovertible evidence of many crimes, from domestic violence to illicit drug use. Of course, the extraordinary cost of such surveillance—both in terms of the administrative costs and the infringement on privacy— makes this method of surveillance extremely low in productivity.

In evaluating the "success rate" of different types of surveillance, we should also consider another type of success: Certain types of surveillance—what we could call proactive surveillance—can prevent a potential crime entirely or halt a crime in progress. In contrast, reactive surveillance, even when successful, will serve only to apprehend or convict a criminal who has already committed a crime. For example, wiretaps on telephones and *Terry* stops are proactive surveillance techniques, which are more likely to identify potential criminals before they have committed a more severe crime.[45] Plainly visible video cameras in public parks or in private stores can deter potential criminals from committing the crime in the first place, because the potential criminals realize their chances of apprehension and conviction are

---

44 *See Dash-cam video: Maitland Vice Mayor Phil Bonus wobbling after DUI stop*, Orlando Sentinel, Oct. 11, 2012, http://www.orlandosentinel.com/videogallery/72789605/News/Dash-cam-video-Maitland-Vice-Mayor-Phil-Bonus-wobbling-after-DUI-stop.

45 They are still caught committing a lesser crime—conspiracy instead of murder, or possession of a firearm instead of armed robbery.

prohibitively high.[46] On the other hand, reactive surveillance techniques do not provide this benefit: Searches of a home after an arrest are likely to only find evidence of a crime that has already been committed—that is, the crime for which the suspect was originally arrested. For that matter, surveillance for most low-level drug crimes does nothing to prevent more serious crimes from occurring[47]—the drugs have already been sold or possessed, and the successful surveillance after the crime has been committed can lead only to an arrest of the perpetrators after the crime has already occurred. From these few examples, however, it is already obvious that although proactive surveillance provides an extra benefit, it frequently comes at a greater cost—the surveillance may affect larger numbers of innocent people (as with *Terry* stops) or the surveillance may be more intrusive (as with video surveillance).

As for the second category of benefits, the societal value of any successful surveillance is dependent upon the severity of the crime being investigated. Professor Lerner adopts this method in his original formula.[48] Other scholars, such as Akhil Amar, have argued that the "reasonableness" standard in the Fourth Amendment ought to take the severity of crime into account.[49] Although courts have not incorporated this factor into the definition of reasonableness, it is sensible to include the severity of the crime when conducting a cost-benefit analysis of any surveillance: The more severe the crime that is being investigated, the greater the societal benefit of the surveillance. For example, we would be more willing to bear a high-cost surveillance to gather evidence in a terrorism investigation than we would to gather evidence in a shoplifting investigation.

Determining the severity of the crime being investigated is actually one of the easiest aspects of our project, because the criminal justice system already provides us with an unambiguous ranking of each crime on the books. Thus, we can use the expected sentence after conviction as a proxy for the severity of the crime: The higher the expected sentence, the greater the societal benefit in a successful search.

Given this definition of "benefits," we can now rewrite our formula as follows:

$$(C_A + C_P) * X = E(S_1) + P(S_2)$$

---

46   *See* Steve Chapman, *Do cameras stop crime? What has been learned in Chicago*, CHI. TRIBUNE, Feb. 20, 2011, http://articles.chicagotribune.com/2011-02-20/news/ct-oped-0220-chapman-20110220_1_cameras-crime-justice-policy-center.

47   Of course, basic deterrence doctrine leads us to expect that any successful surveillance that leads to the conviction of a criminal will deter that criminal and others from committing the crime in the future, but that type of indirect crime prevention is true for every type of surveillance. Proactive crime surveillance is a more direct method of deterring crime altogether or preventing a more serious crime from occurring.

48   *See supra* notes 10, 23–25 and accompanying text.

49   *See supra* note 26 and accompanying text.

In this formula, "E" is the percentage chance that the surveillance results in successfully providing information that will lead to the conviction of the perpetrator (whether by correctly identifying him or by gathering admissible evidence against him), "P" is the percentage chance that the surveillance will proactively prevent a crime, "S1" is the multiplier based on the seriousness of the crime for which the evidence is being gathered, and "S2" is the multiplier based on the crime which is being prevented. In the case of a reactive search, P will be zero. In the case of many proactive surveillance techniques, S1 and S2 will be identical—for example, video cameras on street corners known for drug dealing both will gather evidence against drug dealers and help to prevent the crime of narcotics trafficking. In such cases, P and E will be inversely related—that is, the greater the chance is that the surveillance technique will prevent the crime altogether, the lesser the chance is that the surveillance technique will successfully gather evidence about the crime, because the crime is much less likely to occur. In other cases, S2 will be a more severe crime than S1, and the success in gathering information leading to arrest and conviction will directly affect the success of preventing the more serious crime. For example, a *Terry* stop might reveal a firearm carried by a suspect who was intending to rob a jewelry store later in the day. In those cases, P and E will be nearly identical.

[...]

Conclusion

The stated goal of this article was to determine the productivity of different methods of government surveillance by taking into account all the relevant costs and benefits of the surveillance. Once we have determined the most productive methods, however, we need a way to encourage law enforcement officers to use the more productive methods and avoid using the less productive methods. Left to their own devices, law enforcement officers cannot be counted on to use the most productive methods of surveillance because they are relatively insensitive to privacy costs. At any rate, they are ill-equipped to determine what those privacy costs actually are. Thus, we need to adjust the law governing surveillance to provide law enforcement officers with the proper incentive.[50]

The simplest way of accomplishing this goal is by aligning the legal standard required to conduct a given surveillance method with the productivity of that method. Today we live in a

---

50   *See, e.g.,* United States v. Alvarado, 495 F.2d 799, 806 (2d Cir. 1974); United States v. Cyzewski, 484 F.2d 509, 512 (5th Cir. 1973).

legal regime in which there are numerous different legal standards for different surveillance methods, some set by courts and some set by statutes. Many types of surveillance require no showing of suspicion at all on the part of law enforcement.[51] Some require a showing of "certified relevance"—little more than a ministerial approval by the courts.[52] Some require reasonable suspicion[53] or probable cause,[54] but allow the police officer to make that judgment on the spot, to be reviewed later by a neutral magistrate. Others require law enforcement to prove probable cause to a neutral magistrate before conducting the surveillance.[55] Still others require an even greater showing: probable cause in addition to proving that the surveillance is the only feasible means of conducting the investigation and that minimization protocols will be followed.[56]

Once we have calculated the productivity of each type of search, we should attach the lowest standards to the most productive searches and the highest standard to the least productive searches. As of now, the severity of the standard roughly tracks only one of the factors of productivity—the intrusiveness of the search—and ignores the others, such as the administrative cost, the likelihood of success, and the severity of the crime being investigated. Sometimes the standard is untethered from even the intrusiveness factor—for example, if the search is carried out in order to accomplish a "special need" distinct from criminal law enforcement.[57] A more sensible method of setting legal standards for surveillance methods would be to align the standard to the overall productivity of the search and then to adjust the standard regularly as the productivity changes. New technologies can make the surveillance more successful, less intrusive, or less expensive; evolving standards of privacy can make the surveillance more or less intrusive; shifting legislative priorities can change the importance of certain types of crime. All of these factors can affect the productivity of a surveillance method.

---

51   If the surveillance is not a "search" under the Fourth Amendment and is not covered by any statutory restrictions, the government is free to conduct the surveillance with no showing of individualized suspicion. *See, e.g.*, United States v. Place, 463 U.S. 696 (1983).

52   This is the standard under the ECPA for gathering "non-content information" (such as address information) from real-time surveillance. *See* 18 U.S.C. § 3122(b) (2006).

53   This is the standard for a *Terry* stop. Terry v. Ohio, 392 U.S. 1, 30 (1968).

54   In some contexts police still must show probable cause, but they are allowed to conduct the search without first getting a warrant—for example, searches of automobiles. Chambers v. Maroney, 399 U.S. 42, 48 (1970).

55   Kyllo v. United States, 533 U.S. 27, 40 (2001).

56   This is the statutory standard for real-time interception of telephone or electronic transmissions. *See* 18 U.S.C. § 2518 (2006).

57   For example, roadblocks are meant to check for drunk drivers to protect the safety of motorists on the road. *See* Michigan v. Sitz, 496 U.S. 444 (1990).

Who should calculate the productivity for different methods of surveillance and set these standards? We have already seen that law enforcement, being relatively indifferent to the externality of the privacy costs, cannot be counted on to make the correct decision. For a number of reasons, however, the courts—which we generally rely upon to set the proper boundaries for government surveillance—are also an imperfect institution to make these determinations. First, their job is not to determine what is the *best* kind of search, but rather to set the outer limits as to what searches are permissible or impermissible. Second, just as law enforcement officers are insensitive to the privacy costs of their surveillance techniques, courts have devised tests that ignore a number of important factors in determining whether surveillance is permissible. For the most part, courts ignore the severity of the crime being investigated when evaluating a surveillance technique,[58] as well as the financial outlay required to conduct the surveillance.[59] But most importantly, we have seen that courts, like law enforcement officers, are unable to gauge accurately the level of intrusiveness of various types of technologies. They lack the investigative infrastructure required to understand how technologies function in practice and how often certain investigative techniques result in the successful apprehension of a suspect or the uncovering of evidence. Even in measuring intrusiveness—the one factor which they have been focusing on for decades—they lack the ability to learn how a majority of society views certain different uses of surveillance technologies. This task is particularly challenging as society's views on privacy are evolving as quickly as new technologies are being invented. Thus, courts tend to refer merely to their own idea of what should or should not be private in lieu of examining any data as to what degree of privacy society is prepared to accept as reasonable.[60] When courts do attempt to tell us what "society" thinks is reasonable, they occasionally are spectacularly wrong—such

---

58   This is not true for every type of Fourth Amendment analysis. *See supra* notes 24–27 and accompanying text; Max Minzner, *Putting Probability Back into Probable Cause*, 87 Tex. L. Rev. 913, 940 (2009) ("Currently, the Fourth Amendment is blind to the type of crime underlying the search.").

59   Had the caselaw evolved in a different way, courts may have considered these factors in determining whether a surveillance was "reasonable" under the Fourth Amendment. Instead, however, courts have chosen to essentially ignore these factors.

60   *See* Minnesota v. Carter, 525 U.S. 83, 97–98 (1998) (Scalia, J., concurring) ("In my view, the only thing the past three decades have established about the *Katz* test ... is that, unsurprisingly, those 'actual (subjective) expectation[s] of privacy' 'that society is prepared to recognize as "reasonable,"' bear an uncanny resemblance to those expectations of privacy that this Court considers reasonable. ... [The Fourth Amendment] did not guarantee some generalized 'right of privacy' and leave it to this Court to determine which particular manifestations of the value of privacy 'society is prepared to recognize as "reasonable."' Rather, it enumerated ('persons, houses, papers, and effects') the objects of privacy protection to which the *Constitution* would extend, leaving further expansion to the good judgment, not of this Court, but of the people through their representatives in the legislature.") (citations omitted).

as when the Supreme Court told us in *Olmstead* that a person who uses a telephone "intends to project his voice to those quite outside" and therefore does not deserve the protection of the Fourth Amendment.[61] Luckily, Congress stepped in to correct this mistake a few years later.[62] Later, the Court told us that we should not reasonably expect any amount of privacy in information that we turn over to third parties—even if the third party is a bank[63] or a telephone company,[64] and that disclosing the information the third party is a necessary element of modern commerce. This miscalculation regarding what society actually expects to be kept private could have disastrous results in the Internet age. Once again, Congress stepped in a few years later to realign the law with what a majority of Americans believed should be kept private.[65]

Even when courts are not spectacularly wrong, many of their judgments do not seem to line up well with what a majority of society *actually* reasonably believes ought to be kept private. Surveys have shown a significant amount of disconnect between the conduct that the Supreme Court believes violates a reasonable expectation of privacy and what individual citizens believe violates a reasonable expectation of privacy.[66] And as some scholars have noted, the Court does not seem very interested in empirical evidence on this issue.[67]

Luckily, neither law enforcement nor the courts are the primary source of surveillance regulation today. Over the past few decades, legislatures have taken a much more aggressive role in regulating surveillance. Today there are dozens of federal provisions that limit the use of technology by law enforcement, such as Title III of the Omnibus Crime Control and Safe Streets Act of 1968 (Title III),[68] which regulates oral and wire communications; the 1986 Electronic Communications Privacy Act (ECPA),[69] which extends Title III to electronic communications; the Stored Communications Act (SCA),[70] which was part of ECPA and

---

61 Olmstead v. United States, 277 U.S. 438, 466 (1928).

62 *See* Communications Act of 1934, Pub. L. No. 416-73D, § 605, (codified as amended at 47 U.S.C. § 605 (2006)).

63 United States v. Miller, 425 U.S. 435, 442–43 (1976).

64 Smith v. Maryland, 442 U.S. 735, 743–44 (1979).

65 *See* Electronic Communications and Privacy Act, 18 U.S.C. §§ 3121–3127 (2006) (regulating, among other things, surveillance information provided to third parties).

66 *See* Slobogin & Schumacher, *supra* note 141, at 738–41. Professors Slobogin and Schumacher's article lists the "average intrusiveness" level for dozens of different types of surveillance based on a survey and then notes "frequent contrasts" between the survey results and the Supreme Court rulings on what constitutes a search. In areas ranging from the use of undercover officers to reviewing of bank records to seizures of luggage on buses, the Court has apparently misjudged the actual level of privacy that society considers to be reasonable.

67 *Id.* at 743.

68 *See* 18 U.S.C. §§ 2516–2518 (2006).

69 *See* Pub. L. No. 99-508, 100 Stat. 1848 (1986).

70 *See* 18 U.S.C. §§ 2701–2712 (2006).

regulates government access to stored wire and electronic communications held by third-party ISPs; the Foreign Intelligence Surveillance Act of 1978 (FISA),[71] which sets out rules for electronic surveillance of agents of foreign powers; and the Uniting and Strengthening America by Providing Appropriate Tools Required to Intercept and Obstruct Terrorism Act of 2001 (USA PATRIOT Act), which, among other effects, broadens the type of surveillance allowed under FISA and the ECPA.[72] All of these statues create a complex regime of surveillance regulation, so that when courts are evaluating the legality of a surveillance method—particularly if the surveillance method involves a relatively new technology—the court will frequently apply statutory rules rather than the Fourth Amendment.[73] Many scholars view the increasing involvement by Congress as a positive development, because the legislature is better equipped to determine the proper balance between the needs of law enforcement and the privacy rights of individuals.[74] Legislative bodies can act more quickly in response to changes in technologies and law enforcement needs, and they have the resources to learn what these changes are and how they affect surveillance methods.[75] In addition, measuring the productivity of surveillance requires a number of similarly important judgment calls that only legislatures are able to make. A legislature is uniquely qualified to calculate how intrusive a search is perceived to be by the general population. A legislature has the ability to hear from experts and gather information about the administrative costs of different methods of surveillance, as well as their likelihood of achieving success. Furthermore, a legislature is the very body that decides the severity of each crime, which is another factor in determining the benefit of any kind of surveillance.

Obviously, Congress is constrained by the courts' interpretation of the Fourth Amendment: If the Supreme Court decides that a particularly productive surveillance method requires law enforcement officers to obtain a warrant or demonstrate a similarly high standard of suspicion, Congress's ability to encourage that surveillance method is somewhat limited. But the Supreme Court has shown some willingness to defer to Congress on standards for surveillance methods, especially where Congress has been willing to step in and take the

---

71   *See* Pub. L. No. 95-511, 92 Stat. 1783 (1978).

72   *See* Pub. L. No. 107-56, 115 Stat. 272 (2001).

73   Part of the problem with legislation in this area is that there are many different statutes covering many different situations. A broader, more comprehensive piece of privacy legislation would be easier to follow law enforcement to follow and easier for courts to implement.

74   *See* Orin Kerr, *The Fourth Amendment and New Technologies: Constitutional Myths and the Case for Caution*, 102 MICH. L. REV. 801, 853, 864–77 (2004). *But see* LAWRENCE LESSIG, CODE AND OTHER LAWS OF CYBERSPACE 216 (1999) (arguing that courts must be counted on to apply consistent constitutional values to all types of surveillance).

75   Kerr, *supra* note 175, at 864–77.

lead.[76] This deference gives Congress the room it needs to redefine the way we think about surveillance regulation. It is time to move away from an intrusion-only based analysis and begin to consider all of the relevant factors of productivity when evaluating the desirability of surveillance methods.

---

76   For example, in a recent case, the Fourth Circuit warned against "wield[ing] the amorphous 'reasonable expectation of privacy' standard in a manner that nullifies the balance … struck by Congress in Title III," and affirmed that the "primary job of evaluating [new technologies'] impact on privacy rights and of updating the law must remain with … the legislature." United States v. McNulty (*In re* Askin), 47 F.3d 100, 105–06 (4th Cir. 1995). When the courts began looking for rules to regulate covert video surveillance, they showed even greater deference to Congress by adopting the exact standards that Congress set up to regulate wiretapping and holding that those same standards were mandated under the Fourth Amendment—essentially allowing the legislature to define the scope of Fourth Amendment protection in this area. *See, e.g.,* United States v. Torres, 751 F.2d 875, 885 (7th Cir. 1984) (explaining its intent to "borrow the warrant procedure of Title III, a careful legislative attempt to solve a very similar problem, and hold that it provides the measure of the government's constitutional obligation of particular description in using television to investigate crime").

Reading 6.3

Secrecy, Subpoenas and Surveillance

Katie Townsend

Access to information is vital for reporters. Through confidential sources or Freedom of Information Act requests, the ability to obtain information about the government is necessary for reporters to do their jobs and keep the public informed. Yet almost any reporter or editor will tell you that gathering information is more difficult than ever. Increased government secrecy, subpoenas, search warrants targeting journalists and the ongoing threat of government surveillance have made sources harder to come by and have obstructed the flow of information to reporters and, in turn, to the public. Reporters and news organizations are fighting back and taking steps to minimize the harm to journalists' ability to gather the news and report on the issues that matter most to the public. Although obtaining information about the government is likely to remain one of the biggest challenges facing reporters in the years to come, the Reporters Committee for Freedom of the Press and others are working tirelessly to help journalists confront and overcome those obstacles.

Since it was revealed in the summer of 2013 that the U.S. government had seized Associated Press phone records and emails of Fox News reporter James Rosen, warrants and subpoenas aimed at journalists, particularly in national security leak cases, have been cause for alarm. Journalists routinely rely on promises of confidentiality to sources in order to report the news. And with the U.S. Supreme Court in June declining to hear the appeal of James Risen, a Pulitzer Prize-winning reporter for *The New York Times* who has refused to testify about the identity of his sources, the government's relentless pursuit of leakers is jeopardizing journalists' ability to maintain confidential relationships with sources.

Risen's legal saga began in 2010, when the United States Department of Justice indicted former CIA agent Jeffrey Sterling on Espionage Act charges. The government suspected that Sterling had leaked classified information to Risen for his 2006 book "State of War: The History of the CIA and the Bush Administration." Risen was subpoenaed to testify, and he fought the subpoena. In July of 2013, a federal appeals court concluded that Risen had no First Amendment or common law right to refuse to testify about the identity of his sources and, since the Supreme Court's denial of review, Risen has been in legal limbo. At a hearing in December, the Justice Department indicated that Risen would be subpoenaed to answer questions in advance of Sterling's trial, but that prosecutors would not specifically ask the reporter whether Sterling was his anonymous source. And there is additional confusion regarding what Sterling's attorneys will ask Risen, if anything. It is unclear whether Risen will be willing to answer any of the questions posed to him and, if he refuses to, he will be faced with fines and potential jail time. So, although Attorney General Eric Holder had indicated that the government will not seek to jail Risen for refusing to identify a source, as of now, the future for Risen remains uncertain."

Policy Changes

It is unclear whether the President's appointment of U.S. Attorney Loretta Lynch to replace Holder will impact the Justice Department's approach to the press. But Risen's case is a striking example to which the government has been willing to go to pursue suspected leakers, and it demonstrates the need for greater federal protection for reporters who promise confidentiality to sources.

Forty-nine states and the District of Columbia have statutes or court precedents that offer such protection. (Wyoming hasn't addressed the shield law issue.) Yet, despite growing national support for federal legislation aimed at providing journalists a privilege against being forced to testify as to the identities of their sources in federal court cases, a reporter shield bill has stalled in Congress. After the Supreme Court declined to hear Risen's appeal in June, more than 70 media organizations, including the Reporters Committee, sent a letter to Senate leaders urging them to schedule a vote on a bipartisan shield bill, The Free Flow of Information Act (S.987). Congress, however, has yet to act, and further progress on the legislative front appears unlikely.

Justice Department policy is one area where journalists and news organizations have begun to see some improvement when it comes to limiting warrants and subpoenas targeting journalists. The department issued new internal media guidelines in February of 2014. The Reporters Committee and a coalition of more than 50 news organizations had recommended revisions to the guidelines, which were originally written in 1970, to address situations like the department's subpoena for the AP's telephone records and the warrant targeting Rosen's email. Among other things, the current Holder guidelines now cover warrants, not just subpoenas, and make it more difficult for the department to withhold notice from a journalist or media organization when it seeks journalists' records from a third party telephone or email provider. Yet, while an improvement from the prior guidelines in certain respects, the Holder guidelines are far from a panacea. For example, while the guidelines now expressly apply to search warrants, they make no mention of national security letters or warrants issued under the Foreign Intelligence Surveillance Act (FISA), other legal mechanisms that the Department may use to obtain the records of journalists and news organizations.

FIGURE 6.3.1   The U.S. Supreme Court in June declined to hear the appeal of James Risen, a reporter for *The New York Times* who has refused to testify about the identity of his sources. In 2013, a federal appeals court concluded that Risen had no right to refuse to testify.

Data provided to the Reporters Committee by the Justice Department in response to a request made under the Freedom of Information Act suggests that after 2010, when Risen was subpoenaed, the number of source-related subpoenas approved by the Attorney General fell. The Reporters Committee is in the process of seeking clarification from the Justice Department concerning this data, which does not appear, for example, to account for search warrants. But, according to the data provided by the Justice Department, at least one source-related subpoena was approved by the Attorney General just last year, making subpoenas and warrants targeting reporters a continued threat to the confidentiality of their relationships with sources.

Justice Department policy is one area where journalists and news organizations have begun to see some improvement when it comes to limiting warrants and subpoenas targeting journalists.

Warrants and subpoenas are not, however, the only threat to reporters' ability to obtain information from government sources. The revelations by former National Security Agency contractor

Edward Snowden concerning broad government surveillance programs, coupled with new policies forbidding government employees from having any unauthorized contact with reporters, have also made sources reluctant to talk, even about routine, unclassified matters.

The Surveillance Age

In October of 2011, after Army Private First Class Chelsea Manning provided thousands of documents from a classified database to WikiLeaks, the government launched the Insider Threat Program to encourage government employees to report one another for suspicious behavior that might suggest an intention to leak classified information. And in March, Director of National Intelligence James Clapper issued a directive forbidding intelligence agency employees from talking with members of the media about any matter related to intelligence, even if it is unclassified. Only public affairs representatives and other government employees who are expressly authorized to speak to reporters may do so, and employees are required to report any "unplanned or unintentional contact with the media on covered matters," which are broadly defined to include "intelligence sources, methods, activities, and judgments." Government employees who violate this policy may be fired or lose their security clearances, a punishment that can effectively end a career in intelligence.

The Insider Threat Program and the Clapper directive have made many government sources unwilling to speak to reporters for fear of losing their jobs or damaging their careers. And the fear felt by many sources that any communication with a reporter, even about unclassified matters, could have life-altering consequences has been amplified by revelations of mass government surveillance of electronic communications in the United States and abroad.

It has been more than a year since Snowden made public the extent of the National Security Agency's collection and surveillance of telephone and email communications, and the issue remains at the forefront of reporters' concerns about maintaining the confidentiality of their communications with sources. A recent 120-page joint report by the American Civil Liberties Union and Human Rights Watch, "With Liberty to Monitor All:

FIGURE 6.3.2 *New York Times* reporter James Risen speaks this summer at a National Press Club briefing held in his support.

How Large-Scale U.S. Surveillance is Harming Journalism, Law, and American Democracy," documents how sources' fear of surveillance has made it increasingly difficult for reporters to gather news and keep the public informed. Numerous journalists have reported that an awareness of the NSA's surveillance practices has changed the way they contact and communicate with sources, and in some cases it has even prevented them from pursuing stories.

Reporters and news organizations are increasingly turning to encryption and other technological solutions in an effort to keep their communications with sources secure. A growing number of news organizations, for example, are signing on to use SecureDrop, an open-source system managed by the Freedom of the Press Foundation that allows organizations to securely accept documents and communications from anonymous sources. But journalists and sources are largely operating in an area of uncertainty, particularly given the lack of public information about the way in which the government utilizes the data it collects on a mass scale. That uncertainty will continue to interfere with reporters' ability to communicate with confidential sources or even establish relationships with sources in the first place.

Reporters and news organizations are increasingly turning to encryption and other technological solutions in an effort to keep their communications with sources secure.

There are signs that courts are becoming more skeptical of warrantless mass data collection by the government. In June, the U.S. Supreme Court held unanimously that the Fourth Amendment requires the government to obtain a warrant before searching a cell phone seized after an arrest. The Court's decision in Riley v. California has implications not only for cases involving digital records searches but also for those challenging the NSA's bulk record collection as well. But whether courts will set meaningful limits on the ability of the government to monitor electronic communications between reporters and their sources remains to be seen. In the meantime, reporters and news organizations will be forced to continue to look for new ways to safeguard communications with confidential sources.

FIGURE 6.3   Special Agents with US Immigration and Customs Enforcement's (ICE) Homeland Security Investigations (HSI).

DISCUSSION QUESTIONS

The USA FREEDOM Act (Uniting and Strengthening America by Fulfilling Rights and Ensuring Effective Discipline Over Monitoring Act) of 2015 technically replaced the USA PATRIOT Act that was passed in the wake of the massive terrorist attacks on the United States in 2001. The USA FREEDOM Act changed some of the components of the previous laws, but also maintained many of the intrusive powers that were authorized in previous legislation. These included an expansion of the FISA Court by law enforcement officers. The FISA Court is quite literally a secret court that can and does authorize the secret surveillance of both US citizens and foreigners in the United States.

1. Discuss the relationship that the FISA Act and the USA FREEDOM Act have to the Fourth and Fifth Amendments to the US Constitution.
2. Do you believe that this relatively contemporary legislation is required to keep America safe? Has the recent evolution and use of these police powers been a violation of civil rights protected by the US Constitution and the Bill of Rights? Why or why not?
3. The USA PATRIOT Act, the USA FREEDOM Act and the FISA Act grant law enforcement vast authority and power today. This legislation was passed by the US Congress and signed into law by US presidents. As a current or future law enforcement

practitioner, what is one example of how you might utilize these powerful investigative tools that are granted to you in these laws?

Figure Credit

Fig. 6.3: Source: https://www.ice.gov/news/releases/hsi-arrests-7-members-international-drug-trafficking-organization.